D1593452

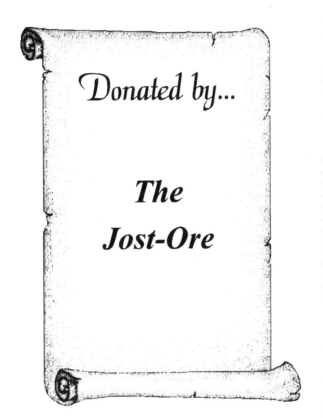

Donated by...

**The
Jost-Ore**

EDMUND BURKE

The Library of Conservative Thought

Victor A. Kravchenko, *I Chose Freedom* with a new introduction by Rett R. Ludwikowski 1988. ISBN: 0-88738-754-3

Victor A. Kravchenko, *I Chose Justice* with a new introduction by Ludmilla Thorne. 1988. ISBN: 0-88738-756-X

William Hurrell Mallock, *A Critical Examination of Socialism* with a new introduction by Russell Kirk. 1988. ISBN: 0-88738-264-9

Kenneth Shorey, ed., *John Randolph and John Brockenbrough: Their Correspondence* with a new foreword by Russell Kirk. 1988. ISBN: 0-88738-194-4

George Scott-Moncrieff, *Burke Street* with a new introduction by Russell Kirk. 1989. ISBN: 0-88738-250-9

John J. Stanlis, *Edmund Burke: The Enlightenment and Revolution* with a new introduction by Russell Kirk. 1990. ISBN: 0-88738-359-9

Orestes Brownson, *Selected Political Essays* with a new introduction by Russell Kirk. 1990. ISBN: 0-88738-825-6

Dan E. Ritchie, *Edmund Burke: Appraisals and Applications.* 1990. ISBN: 0-88738-328-9

Francis Graham Wilson, *The Case For Conservatism* with a new introduction by Russell Kirk. 1990. ISBN: 0-88738-322-X

EDMUND BURKE

Appraisals and Applications

Edited by

Daniel E. Ritchie

Transaction Publishers

New Brunswick (U.S.A.) and London (U.K.)

Library of Congress Catalog Number: 89-28010
ISBN: 0-88738-328-9
Printed in the United States of America

Library of Congress Cataloging-in-Publication Data

Edmund Burke: Appraisals and Applications/edited by Daniel E. Ritchie.
    p. cm.
  Includes bibliographical references.
  ISBN 0-88738-328-9
  1. Burke, Edmund, 1729–1797—Contributions in political science.
2. Burke, Edmund, 1729–1797—Language. I. Ritchie, Daniel E..
JC176.B83C75 1990   89-28010
320.5′2′092—dc20   CIP

*Dedicated to the generation of Burke scholars
who revived and redirected our knowledge
of Edmund Burke after World War II*

Grateful acknowledgement is made to the following copyright holders for permission to use their work:

Matthew Arnold: Lectures and Essays in Criticism. Vol. 3 of *The Complete Prose Works of Matthew Arnold,* edited by R. H. Super. Copyright © 1962 by the University of Michigan Press.

"Burke and the Moral Imagination," by Irving Babbitt. Copyright © 1924 by Irving Babbitt. Copyright © 1952 by Esther Babbitt Howe. Reprinted from *Democracy and Leadership* by permission of the National Humanities Institute, Washington, D.C.

The Collected Works of Walter Bagehot, edited by Norman St. John-Stevas. Vol. 1, *Literary Essays.* Copyright © 1965 by The Economist, London.

Walter Jackson Bate, "Introduction" to *Edmund Burke: Selected Works.* Copyright © 1960 by Random House, Inc.

"Reconsideration: Edmund Burke," by Alexander Bickel. Reprinted by permission of *The New Republic.* Copyright © 1973 by The New Republic, Inc.

"Burke and the Fall of Language," by Steven Blakemore. Reprinted by permission of the American Society for Eighteenth-Century Studies.

Edmund Burke: Prescription and Providence by Francis Canavan. Copyright © 1987 by Francis Canavan. Published by Carolina Academic Press, Durham, N.C.

Edmund Burke: The Practical Imagination, by Gerald W. Chapman. Published by Harvard University Press. Copyright © 1967 by the President and Fellows of Harvard College. Reprinted by permission.

The Collected Works of Samuel Taylor Coleridge, edited by Kathleen Coburn and Bart Winer, Bollingen Series 75. Vol. 4: *The Friend,* edited by Barbara E. Rooke, Copyright © 1969 by Routledge and Kegan Paul, Ltd. Excerpts reprinted with permission of Princeton University Press. Vol. 7: *Biographia Literaria,* parts I and II, Copyright © 1983 by Princeton University Press and Routledge & Kegan Paul. Reprinted by permission.

Conor Cruise O'Brien, "Introduction" to *Reflections on the Revolution in France.* Introduction Copyright © 1968 Penguin Books Ltd.

Collected Writings of Thomas De Quincey, edited by David Masson, published by A. & C. Black.

The Complete Works of William Hazlitt, edited by P. P. Howe. Copyright © 1934 by J. M. Dent—Everyman's Library.

"A Revolution Not Made, But Prevented," by Russell Kirk. Copyright © 1985 by the Intercollegiate Studies Institute. Reprinted from *Modern Age* by permission of the publisher.

Statesmanship and Party Government: A Study of Burke and Bolingbroke, by Harvey Mansfield. Copyright © 1965 by The University of Chicago. All rights reserved.

Conservatism by Robert Nisbet. Copyright © 1986 by Open University Press.

Edmund Burke and the Practice of Political Writing by Christopher Reid. Copyright © 1985 by St. Martin's Press, and Gill and Macmillan Ltd. Reprinted by permission.

Edmund Burke and the Natural Law by Peter Stanlis. Copyright © 1958 by The University of Michigan Press. Copyright © 1985 by Peter Stanlis. Reprinted by permission of Peter Stanlis.

"Burke's Conservative Revolution," by George Watson. Copyright © 1984. Reprinted by permission of George Watson and *Critical Quarterly.*

Culture and Society, by Raymond Williams. Copyright © 1980 by Columbia University Press and Chatto & Windus. Reprinted by permission of the Estate of Raymond Williams.

Contents

Foreword

Two centuries ago, Edmund Burke found his fortune at a stay. Deprived of office, with the younger Pitt entrenched as prime minister, Burke then seemed ineffectual to many. His Whig party, the first geniune political party of the English-speaking world, had suffered defeat and eclipse; his private affairs were troubled. He was immersed in the prosecution of Warren Hastings, which trial would drag on to the spring of 1795. This was no cheerful prospect. Burke feared from the first that the House of Lords would not find Hastings guilty as charged. "We know that we bring before a bribed tribunal a prejudged cause," he had written to Philip Francis on December 10, 1785.

In 1790, nevertheless, Burke (almost alone) commenced the undoing of the French Revolution: he published the most brilliant piece of political writing in the English language, began to alter the whole drift of British foreign policy, won back the clergy to the national cause, and achieved in political isolation a reputation and an influence exceeding that he had enjoyed while still a manager of party. It is especially this later Burke who attracts the interest of reflective people in the year 1990.

Dr. Daniel Ritchie, in this most commendable anthology of essays about Burke, does not confine us to Burke the political thinker, nevertheless, nor to Burke the British statesman. For, apprehending the enduring power of Burke's imagination, he commences this book with a valuable group of essays on Burke's place in the realm of humane letters. When all the political and ideological battles of our era are done and forgotten, Burke's speeches and writings may endure as models of imaginative rhetoric. Precisely as such, indeed, Burke's speeches on American affairs were taught in nearly every American high school, even into the early years of the twentieth century.

Yet in the year of the bicentenary of the publication of *Reflections on the Revolution in France*, which year is also the bicentenary of increasing ferocity in the French Revolution, naturally enough most readers of this volume turn first to Edmund Burke as a social philosopher. (If they hope to extract from him an ideology, they will be disappointed; Burke detested ideology, calling it "an armed doctrine.") In his sections on "Burke and Revolution," "Burke and Constitutional, Party Government," "Burke and the Radical Mind," and "Burke and the Conservative Mind," Dr. Ritchie gives us a judicious diversity of judgments on the political Burke.

Is Burke's thought relevant to our present discontents? Some part of the institutions and the social order which Burke knew has passed away, quite as the America of our time is markedly different from the seaboard republic of Adams and Jefferson. Because we cannot restore—even if we would—either Georgian England or Jeffersonian America, the test of the pertinence of political writings to the challenges of our own age is not merely the question of whether a political thinker was "European" or "American."

Because Burke addressed himself to matters that transcended nationality and generation, he endures as a man of genius whom men of our time oppose to Karl Marx. With his prophetic gifts, Burke perceived the shape of things to come in this bent world of ours. His passionate refutation of leveling ideology and totalist politics has lost little of its force with the passing of two centuries. What he said of the Jacobins is yet more true of the Marxist ideologues in our rough era. "I have laid the terrible spirit of innovation which was striding over all the world." Those are the words of Napoleon, whose coming Burke predicted. Yet it was Burke, rather than Napoleon, who in truth exorcised the fierce spectre of revolutionary fanaticism.

As some of the essays in this anthology point out, no other statesman or writer of the past two centuries has been more prescient than Burke. Perhaps it is as well that a proper understanding of Burke has been reserved for these years of the closing decade of the twentieth century. Once more we find ourselves in what Matthew Arnold called "an epoch of concentration," during which thinking men and women endeavor to restore order and justice to a bewildered society. "I attest the rising generation!" Burke cried, at the end of the prosecution of Hastings. Indeed Burke did win over the rising generation of Britain about the year of his death. And as the twentieth century draws to a close, in America Burke's moral imagination begins to defeat Jean-Jacques Rousseau's idyllic imagination—which commanded a huge popular following among young people a quarter of a century ago.

To suggest the relevance of Burke's ideas to our present troubles, I quote a passage from a letter of Burke, written on June 1, 1791, to the Chevalier Claude-François de Rivarol. Burke is discussing the illusions of poets and philosophers.

I have observed that the Philosophers in order to insinuate their polluted Atheism into young minds, systematically flatter all their passions natural and unnatural. They explode or render odious or contemptible that class of virtues which restrain the appetite. These are at least nine out of ten of the virtues. In place of all these they subsititute a virtue which they call humanity or benevolence. By these means, their morality has no idea in it of restraint, or indeed of a distinct settled principle of any kind. When their disciples are thus left free and guided by present feeling, they are no longer to be depended on for good or evil. The men who today snatch the worst criminals from justice, will murder the most innocent persons tomorrow."

An so it came to pass. When Burke wrote those lines, the Terror of 1793 lay in wait two years distant.

Burke's "Parisian philosophers" of two centuries gone live on as today's "intellectuals" of Manhattan, with incessant talk of "compassion" and advocacy of new rights—among them the inalienable right to expand the empire of unnatural vices. From age to age we human beings fight the same battles over and over again, under banners bearing diverse devices. To resist the idyllic imagination and the diabolical imagination, we need to know the moral imagination of Edmund Burke. For Burke is one of those dead who give us energy.

Russell Kirk
Piety Hill
Mecosta, Michigan

Acknowledgements

Many people have helped in the production of this book with their advice and encouragement. I especially wish to thank Russell Kirk, the general editor of the "Library of Conservative Thought," who approved the project and offered timely, useful suggestions. I owe thanks as well to Regina Jaynes and Steve Blake for help with eighteenth-century Indian affairs, and to Michael McConnell for suggestions regarding the Introduction. The inter-library loan staffs at Bethel College, the College of St. Thomas, and Marquette University generously and efficiently provided the volumes I needed. I owe a special debt to the Computer Science staff at Bethel College, particularly Dave Holter and Glen Wiebe, who enabled me to produce a camera-ready, laser-printed text. I wish to express appreciation also to the Marguerite Eyer Wilbur Foundation, which provided the funds needed to undertake this project. To Paul Fussell I give particular thanks for introducing me to the irony, richness, and ethical subtlety of eighteenth-century literature.

Introduction

One of Edmund Burke's misfortunes is that he never uttered his most famous saying—and even what he didn't say is taken out of context: "All that is necessary for the forces of evil to triumph is for enough good men to do nothing." It's a stirring aphorism, usually delivered to urge high moral purpose on individuals. It has the Burkean sense of the fragility of civilization, the organized power of evil, and the threat of imminent apocalypse, but it is not Burke. The closest Burke comes to this statement is found in his *Thoughts on the...Present Discontents* [1770]: "When bad men combine, the good must associate; else they will fall, one by one, an unpitied sacrifice in a contemptible struggle." The context is Burke's defense of party government, which is in some degree a *critique* of those who urge that national salvation will come from morally passionate individuals. Yet for some reason, Burke often remains little more than a bundle of excellent aphorisms:

> War never leaves where it found a nation.
> Good men do not suspect that their destruction is attempted through
> their virtues.
> To innovate is not to reform.
> Nobody will be argued into slavery.

But however brilliant, Burke's aphorisms do not account for his significance, nor would they justify reading his works. Still, as soon as most readers open up Burke's writings and speeches, they find them difficult to grasp. What is their context? What questions is Burke discussing? And what do the concerns of an eighteenth-century British parliamentarian have to do with current affairs? The difficulty is compounded, in the long works especially, by the lack of obvious organization.

The purpose of this book is to provide an introduction for the general reader by reproducing essays on the most important issues in Burke's works. The essays have been chosen to help the reader discern the large contours and significant details.

By taking Burke's thought and language in context, and by treating his entire extant *œuvre*, the essays in this book go far beyond Burke's aphoristic quality. They attempt to discover and analyze the permanently valuable elements of Burke's political thought and language. Harvey Mansfield's essay on Burke's theory of party government, for instance, shows that Burke's theory was a revolutionary development, essential to modern, constitutional democracy. As a Whig politician, Burke naturally looked up to the remarkable men of 1688-89 who were responsible for the Glorious Revolution, which deposed James II and asserted the primacy of constitutional, parliamentary rule. But Burke wanted to develop a way for merely honest, unremarkable men to form political associations and pursue political activities that would preclude the necessity of further revolutions. His solution was party government, which was considered disloyal to the crown at the time. That is the context for Burke's statement that "the good must associate," which has been turned into the famous, if apocryphal, aphorism. We take party government so much for granted today that we are apt, without Burke's help, to miss its continuing relevance. Consider this: as politics becomes more ideological, it gets increasingly easier to justify bypassing traditional and unwieldy party structures for the achievement of necessary ends. For instance, if the president of the United States cannot depend upon party loyalty to carry out his objectives in foreign policy, a remarkable man within his administration is likely to attempt extra-constitutional means to carry them out.

While this entire book is an introduction to Burke, the essays by Nisbet, Chapman, and Bickel stand out as excellent introductions in their own right. For those new to Burke, these are good places to begin.

Burke's writings remain alive because of their imaginative depth in treating the moral foundations of government, constitutionality, revolution, tradition, and the international responsibilities of great powers. The book attempts to introduce the reader to Burke with respect to the range of these issues and of interpretations by insightful commentators over the two centuries since his death.

The earliest as well as many of the most recent works included here speak primarily about Burke's imagination. A recent essay by James Boyd White (which is regrettably absent from this book) illustrates how a modern reader perceives Burke's "Constitution" as simultaneously a legal, literary, social, and political idea: "The center of Burke's achievement is to see that culture and the self exist in a reciprocal relation, subject to perpetual reconstitution; that the processes by which such reconstitution occurs are both personal and social...; that the language in which they occur must be what I have called literary—merging fact, value, and reason, fusing the particular and the general, uniting thought and emotion, logic and image—rather than theoretical and conceptual....For Burke, civilization is a kind of art, for it involves, as he repeatedly says, the 'composition' or 'constitution' of a world out of preexisting 'materials'; but it is an art of a remarkable kind, for the composition affects...both the human and the physical materials of which it is made. The culture shapes the man, who shapes the culture; love of family and respect for nature convert England into a landscape at once prosperous and beautiful, while the French 'gardener' reduces 'everything to an exact level' and produces poverty" (*When Words Lose Their Meaning*, p. 229).

Throughout the nineteenth century, many of England's best writers tried to explain the workings of Burke's prose. Coleridge, De Quincey, Hazlitt, Arnold, and Macaulay each found in Burke's language a quality of imagination that illuminated his own efforts. Coleridge and De Quincey saw that Burke's imagination fused his content (or "meaning") with imagery and with passion. Burke does not "create his own reality," as an extreme, solipsistic romantic might try to do. Nor does he attempt a purely and exclusively empirical argument, as a positivist or utilitarian might try to do. It would be anachronistic to call his approach a synthesis of the two approaches, because they hadn't yet split apart.

Burke's imagination must be understood first in its own terms; and we are fortunate that Burke himself wrote an early, extended treatise on that subject, *A Philosophical Enquiry into...the Sublime and Beautiful* (1757). Christopher Reid's essay is the best of many recent attempts to interpret Burke's later, political language in the light of his earlier aesthetic treatise. The sublime and beautiful, for Burke, were two psychological laws that described the workings of the imagination. Far from being a mere receptacle and re-arranger of sense impressions, like the imagination as conceived by some other eighteenth-century psychologists, Burke's imagination has a "creative" role. The imagination does not simply imitate reality, according to Burke. Rather, imaginative language must affect the passions, in particular the passions of self-preservation (which set in motion "the sublime") or society (which set in motion "the beautiful"). Reid notes that Burke's aesthetic categories are "based on the relationship between the individual and society." Burke did not see the full political implications of this early in his career. But his late, anti-Jacobin rhetoric becomes extraordinarily rich—Macaulay calls it "ungracefully gorgeous"—because of his exploitation of the powerful and paradoxical categories of sublime and beautiful.

William Hazlitt emphasizes the author's need to identify, sympathetically, with his object in order to affect the reader powerfully and imaginatively. Burke, with whom Hazlitt disagreed violently in politics, demonstrated this ability better than any other prose writer: "He was completely carried away by his subject. He had no other object but to produce the strongest impression on his reader, by giving the truest, the most characteristic, the fullest, and most forcible description of things, trusting to his own mind to mold them into grace and beauty." Like Hazlitt, T. B. Macaulay and Matthew Arnold found in Burke a language that made them reflect on their deepest intellectual and artistic enterprises. For Macaulay, Burke's historical imagination was a model for his own; for Arnold, Burke's ability to "live by ideas" served as a vantage point to scout out the weaknesses of Philistine culture. This section of the book includes, as well, Steven Blakemore's analysis of Burke's language in light of modern literary theory. Since the rise of structuralism, in the beginning of this century, theorists have asserted the power of language to construct—and, lately, deconstruct—reality. Burke saw the same power, Blakemore argues, in the deconstructive language of the French revolutionaries. Once they had assaulted "the cosmic ording of the Logos," says Blakemore, "the sanctity and authority of the Word [was] also assaulted." The leading decon-structionist, Jacques Derrida, has said much the same—in relation, appropriately enough, to Rousseau (*Of Grammatology*, pp. 97-100). Burke's battle, in his anti-Jacobin writings, is then both a linguistic and political one, a logomachy, a struggle against the "uncreating Word" of Pope's *Dunciad*, a struggle for language, morality, constitutionality, and civility.

This book is anchored by long sections on "Burke and the Literary Imagination" and "Burke and the Conservative Mind," for there his significance has been the deepest and most abiding. But Burke has attracted interpreters on many other issues as well. Russell Kirk and George Watson take up the difficult and pressing question of revolution. Burke was a defender of the English Revolution of 1688, and he believed that the Americans in 1776 stood in relation to the English crown exactly as Englishmen had stood in relation to James II in 1688. Yet he was the first Englishman of note to oppose the Revolution of 1789, the French Revolution. This has struck many people as paradoxical at best, venal at worst, for in 1794 Burke received a pension from the very King he had attacked for most of his career. (See time line, immediately following this introduction.) Yet Watson sees that the true paradox is that revolution should be thought of as necessarily radical, rather than conservative. Burke praised revolutions that restored and broadened political liberties in accordance with ancient traditions. The French, Bolshevik, and many other twentieth-century revolutions began by turning their back on the past and destroying contemporary political institutions. We are still living with the effects of those revolutions, even as some of the communist nations attempt to extricate themselves from their own revolutionary experience.

In 1988, before the communist government in Poland lost so many legislative seats to the Polish labor movement Solidarity, Polish historian Adam Michnik invoked Burke with reference to the political problems of eastern Europe: "Burke was a counter-reformer," Michnik told the *Times Literary Supplement.* "Following in the footsteps of Montesquieu, he recognized clearly the complex problems posed by the Revolution. He argues that the values of the Revolution should be assimilated by working for change by means of compromise....Unfortunately [Burke's *Reflections*] is today banned in Poland. If I were proficient in English I would translate this book and present [Mikhail] Gorbachev and others with a complimentary copy—to teach them the philosophy of compromise" (19-25 Feb. 1988). Burke's theory and practice of political compromise and reform placed a premium on continuity with ancient practices, the very opposite of smashing the state machinery, to invoke Lenin's reading of Marx. In fact, Burke looked with favor on the Polish constitution of May 1791, in explicit contrast to the French Revolution (*Appeal* in *Works* (Bohn) 3:101, 103). Today he would no doubt be searching the same "rotten parchments and musty records" of the past to find a passable road out the other side of revolution. Russell Kirk's essay applies Burke's theory of revolution to the particular circumstances of America. The truly revolutionary actions of the 1760s and 1770s, Kirk argues, were the the King's reassertions of royal prerogatives, which had been more honored in the breach than the observance for several centuries. The Americans' action was therefore preventive, deterring the King's attempt to destroy traditional constitutional rights.

In the third section of this book, Alexander Bickel and Harvey Mansfield discuss Burke's views of constitutionality and party government—aspects of modern democracy that we take too much for granted at present. Mansfield's reading of Burke's writings on party government is a model of close textual analysis. Bickel's essay, which appeared in March 1973, also picks up the theme of party government, applying it briefly to Watergate: President Richard Nixon's White House staff parallels "the King's men," in Burke's *Thoughts on the...Present Discontents*, whose political activities threaten to undermine the constitution. Also in the background is the *Roe v. Wade* decision of the U.S. Supreme Court to remove abortion restrictions eight weeks before Bickel's essay appeared: Bickel considers—with an eloquent silence—Burke's probable opinion of "[d]octrinaire theories of the rights of man" as they are expressed in "some luxuriant outburst of theory in the Supreme Court, whether the theory is of an absolute right to contract, or to stand mute, or to be private."

One mark of a living text is that its meaning is disputed and interpreted by people of different outlooks. Raymond Williams and Conor Cruise O'Brien offer readings that claim Burke for the radical sensibility. Williams discerns in Burke a critic of the emerging bourgeois democracy of the nineteenth century. The individualism of that era is vulnerable to attack from a Burkean strategy, for the political goals of Burke were social and cooperative: "The embodiment and guarantee of the proper humanity of man," says Williams, "is the historical community." The essay by Williams illustrates, in addition, a general strength of the essays in the book as a whole by choosing substantial, occasionally surprising quotations from Burke to illustrate his points.

Conor Cruise O'Brien emphasizes Burke's Irish upbringing and his sensitivity to oppression by the "Protestant ascendancy" foisted upon Ireland by Britain. Burke felt a tension between his upbringing and his acceptance of British ways, which was released, O'Brien feels, by the French Revolution. Burke's anti-Jacobin writings attempt to exorcise this tension. O'Brien's essay is remarkable as well for analyzing the language of Burke as the first exercise in self-conscious propaganda, and for his attempt to distance Burke from anticommunist thought since World War II.

The Irish writings of Burke, paradoxically, have also been crucial to the conservative interpretation of Burke. Peter Stanlis's essay is the most thorough attempt to argue that natural law is at the heart of Burke's politics—not expediency, the "state of nature," mere common sense, compromise, or utilitarianism. Influential scholars, writing between 1860 and 1920 held that utilitarianism and expediency were the sole principles that guided Burke; and consequently, they overlooked his fundamental criticism of "natural right" (as explained by Hobbes, Locke, and Rousseau) and his adherence to an older tradition of natural law. Burke's early, fragmentary *Tract on the Popery Laws* criticizes Hobbes's belief that the will of the state, drawn solely from consensus can—by itself, and without regard to transcendent truths—provide true justice and political authority. As Werner Dannhauser has said, "Conservatism's fundamental assertion has always been that human order is part of a cosmic order" (*Commentary*, December 1985). In the Irish (and Indian) writings, as Stanlis maintains, Burke describes the relationship between the two kinds of order.

Nevertheless, another major theme in Burke, especially in his well-known writings against the French Revolution, is his argument against the politicians who attempt to put transcendent ideals, like those of the French *Declaration of the Rights of Man* (1789), directly into practice. Burke argues from prescription, note many critics of the conservative interpreters, and to allow natural law to trump prescriptive law would merely repeat the strategy of Burke's Jacobin opponents. This is probably the most significant problem in the conservative interpretation of Burke, repeated in a variety of permutations: since current democracies have all institutionalized the welfare state (in their actual, "prescriptive" laws), conservatives should defend it; America has a revolutionary "tradition," and therefore American conservatives should defend revolutionary movements. Francis Canavan's essay in this book is the most forthright, thorough attempt to reconcile Burke's dual emphasis on prescriptive and natural law. An established, prescriptive law—or even a constitution—is not authoritative *merely* because it has lasted long. That was, in fact, the defense of Warren Hastings, the Governor-General of India, whom Burke labored to impeach and convict of gross injustices. Canavan argues that prescriptive law is a part of natural law, not opposed to it. Established, ancient laws and constitutions are the most likely to win over the opinion of the people, says Burke, and their opinion is necessary for government to maintain its authority. But prescriptive laws and constitutions must have the natural purpose of furthering the good of the people. "Constitutions," Canavan quotes Burke as saying, "furnish the civil means of getting at the natural."

Burke's rediscovery by modern conservatives is attributable in some degree to the essay by Irving Babbitt, "Burke and the Moral Imagination." Babbitt distinguishes Burke's thought from that of Rousseau and Locke, locating Burke's foundations ultimately in Christianity and Platonism. The result, Babbitt explains, is a freedom connected with order, common sense connected with imagination, reform connected with tradition, humanism connected with religion. Connecting these apparent opposites holds the promise of achieving a kind of unity, sometimes called "organic unity," in society. That unity is the subject of Gerald Chapman's fine chapter; that is, the truth of the whole is embodied in the sometimes paradoxical particulars.

The difficulties of maintaining the connections between apparent opposites, particularly the connection descried by Dannhauser between the human and the cosmic order, has been especially acute since the advent of modernity. The Enlightenment saw the final destruction of the medieval continuity between God and His Great Chain of Being, with its ramifications throughout the categories of politics and religion as well as those of science. When John Dalberg-Acton, later Lord Acton, wrote that "there was much that was essentially Catholic in Burke's mind," I believe he was thinking of more than contemporary history and politics (*Rambler* 9 (1858), p. 272). Burke's mind attempted a new synthesis of the centrifugal tendencies in modernity. What appeals to many conservatives, I believe, is Burke's sympathy for the medieval project of uniting human and divine truths, and his skepticism of the Enlightenment's self-congratulatory presupposition of intellectual superiority.

John MacCunn's chapter in this book analyzes the religious foundations of Burke's thought. It clearly distances Burke from contemporary Enlightenment thought, which attempted to found the state on a purely secular basis. Such a foundation pretends to be "natural" because it is not supernatural. But if, as Burke believes, nature itself has a supernatural origin, a purely secular government is *unnatural*. "[I]f civil society…be not vitalised through and through by the spirit of God, it must be evident…that Burke's political teaching is false," MacCunn states.

Robert Nisbet's essay shows how a distinguished modern conservative introduces his subject to the general reader. As his opening paragraph states: "Rarely in the history of thought has a body of ideas been as closely dependent upon a single man and a single event as modern conservatism is upon Edmund Burke and his fiery reaction to the French Revolution." For Nisbet, the central issues distinguishing the mind of Burke (and his intellectual heir, Alexis de Tocqueville) from his opponents' are those of tradition, property, and the limits to knowledge.

Whenever possible, I have tried to achieve continuity by including entire essays or chapters in this anthology, or to eliminate discrete portions of the essays that required cutting. The source and publication date of each essay is given at the beginning of the Notes with which each chapter ends. Brackets indicate that the title is my own, not the original author's. In general, I have provided footnotes for the essays published before 1900 only. The spelling and punctuation have occasionally been modernized and put into American conventions when I felt the older or British conventions would be distracting. Typographical errors and minor errors of fact have been silently corrected. Within each section of the book, essays are arranged chronologically.

One problem for the student of Burke is the lack of a standard edition of Burke's writings and the proliferation of editions of his *Reflections on the Revolution in France*. Oxford University Press is in the process of publishing the standard edition of Burke's *Writings and Speeches*, under the general editorship of Paul Langford, but to date only two volumes have appeared. To make this book as useful as possible, I have adopted a convention similar to one found in the prose works of Matthew Arnold, published by the University of Michigan. References to Burke's works are (in general) given as the author of each essay originally gave them; but then I have estimated the location of each reference in Burke's text in terms of percentage. That way, regardless what edition one has, one can estimate the approximate location of each reference. The only exception to this practice is Peter Stanlis's essay. Stanlis uses material from the four-volume, 1816 edition of Burke's *Speeches*, some of which has never been republished in any edition of Burke's *Works*. In that case, I have given the date and subject of the speech, in hopes that they will all be published, ultimately, in the new Oxford edition.

Burke is hard reading because nearly all of his writings and speeches are occasional. His eighteenth-century audience knew the occasions and the relevant questions at issue; we require footnotes. Yet this is what we would expect of a man like Burke, who imagined the general through the particular, the eternal in the temporal. We would expect lots of particulars, lots of contemporary people and events whose currency would depreciate with the years. But we might also expect Burke's thought to live throughout history, if indeed he successfully unites the part with the whole, image with content, prescriptive with natural, human with cosmic order. These essays are testimony to that achievement and to Burke's continuing relevance to the problems of political thought and language.

Daniel E. Ritchie   *Bethel College*
St. Paul, Minnesota

Important Dates in the Life of Edmund Burke

1729   Born in Dublin, January 12; his father was a middle-class solicitor, his mother Roman Catholic.

1736-43   Attends Catholic school until 1741, when he enters a boarding school at Ballitore, 30 miles from Dublin, run by a Quaker, Abraham Shackleton.

1743-48   Educated at Trinity College, Dublin.

1750   Comes to London, at father's insistence, to study law at Middle Temple. Unhappy, Burke abandons the law for literature.

1757   Marries Jane Nugent. They have two children, Richard (1758-94) and Christopher, also born in 1758, who died in infancy.

1756   *A Vindication of Natural Society,* a satire and impersonation of Bolingbroke's views of society.

1757   *A Philosophical Enquiry Into the Origin of Our Ideas of the Sublime and Beautiful.*

1758   The publishers of Burke's *Enquiry* engage him to edit and write for the *Annual Register,* which he continues until 1765-66.

1761-65   Although his reputation is rising, Burke is short on money and decides to become private secretary to William Gerard Hamilton. Spends two years in Ireland—Hamilton was secretary to the Lord Lieutenant of Ireland—during which he gathers material for the "Tract on Popery Laws."

1764   Charter member of "The Club," with Johnson, Reynolds, et al.

1765   Becomes private secretary to Marquis of Rockingham, who was just beginning his one-year administration as Prime Minister. Elected Member of Parliament for the pocket borough of Wendover.

1766   Participates in Rockingham's repeal of the Stamp Act and passage of the Declaratory Act, temporarily settling the American question. Rockingham ministry falls, June 7.

1768   Burke is now the guiding spirit of the Rockingham Whigs;

purchases an estate at Beaconsfield.

1769   *Observations on a Late Publication Intituled "The Present State of the Nation,"* an attack on Grenville.

1770   *Thoughts on the Cause of the Present Discontents,* Burke's defense of party government.

1771-75   Parliamentary agent for the colony of New York; opposes petition of clergy to be relieved from subscription to the 39 Articles (1772); visits France (1773); supports bill for relief of Protestant Dissenters from the provisions of the Test Act.

1774   *Speech on American Taxation.* Burke becomes M.P. for Bristol, the second largest city in England.

1775   *Speech on Conciliation with America.* Battles of Lexington and Concord.

1777   *Letter to the Sheriffs of Bristol,* explains his views on America and colonial rule.

1780   Loses Bristol seat, largely due to his views on America and support for free trade and religious tolerance for Ireland. Elected M.P. for Malton. Opposes anti-Catholic sentiment in the Gordon Riots; *Speech on Economical Reform.*

1781   Begins studying colonial abuses in India as member of Select Committee of the House.

1782   American War ends; becomes Paymaster-General in the second Rockingham ministry (March-June); Rockingham dies (July 1) and Burke resigns his post. "Speech on the Reform of Representation in Commons."

1783   Fox and North form coalition government; Burke again Paymaster-General for eight months, his last public office; *Speech on Fox's East India Bill;* the bill fails, and the ministry falls (December). The younger Pitt forms a ministry, and Burke's influence begins to decline.

1784   Samuel Johnson dies.

1785   *Speech on the Nabob of Arcot's Debts.*

1786-95   The impeachment of Warren Hastings is moved (by Burke) in 1786, and the prosecution begins in 1788. Burke is deeply involved in the trial until Hastings's acquittal.

1788   Supports abolition of slave trade.

1789   Outbreak of the French Revolution.

1790   *Reflections on the Revolution in France.* Whig Party begins to split over the Revolution. (Its leader, Charles James Fox, is still sympathetic to the Revolution.)

1791 *Letter to a Member of the National Assembly* (January); formal, public break with Fox, Sheridan (May 6); *Appeal from the New to the Old Whigs; Thoughts on French Affairs.*

1792 "Letter to Sir Hercules Langrishe" on Catholic disabilities; France declares war on Austria, overthrows monarchy.

1793 Louis XVI executed; France declares war on England, institutes the Committee of Public Safety and the Terror; *Remarks on the Policy of the Allies; Observation on the Conduct of the Minority; Letter to Richard Burke.*

1794 Ends his parliamentary career with the "Speeches in Reply," in the trial of Warren Hastings; Portland Whigs join Pitt ministry; Burke retires to Beaconsfield with a pension from the Crown, but is overcome with grief at the unexpected death of his son.

1795 *Thoughts and Details on Scarcity. Letter to a Noble Lord; Letter to William Smith; Second Letter to Sir Hercules Langrishe.*

1796 Two of the *Letters on a Regicide Peace* published; the others are published posthumously.

1797 July 9, dies at Beaconsfield, where he was buried.

Short Titles

Clarendon Press, 1981– .

Works (Rivington) *The Works of the Right Honourable Edmund Burke.*
16 vols. London: C. and J. Rivington, 1826–1827.

Part One

Burke and the Literary Imagination

1
Coleridge's Fragments on Burke

I. The Friend, No. 9. Oct. 12, 1809

...I wished to give every advantage to the Opinions [of Rousseau and the French revolutionaries], which I deemed it of importance to confute. It is bad policy to represent a political System as having no charm but for Robbers and Assassins, and no natural origin but in the brains of Fools or Madmen, when Experience has proved, that the great danger of the System consists in the peculiar fascination, it is calculated to exert on noble and imaginative Spirits; on all those, who in the amiable intoxication of youthful Benevolence, are apt to mistake their own best Virtues and choicest Powers for the average qualities and Attributes of the human Character. The very Minds, which a good man would most wish to preserve or disentangle from the Snare, are by these angry misrepresentations rather lured into it. Is it wonderful, that a Man should reject the arguments unheard, when his own Heart proves the falsehood of the Assumptions by which they are prefaced? or that he should retaliate on the Aggressors their own evil Thoughts? I am well aware, that the provocation was great, the temptation almost inevitable; yet still I cannot repel the conviction from my mind, that in part to this Error and in part to a certain inconsistency in his fundamental Principles, we are to attribute the small number of Converts made by BURKE during his life time. Let me not be misunderstood. I do not mean, that this great Man supported different Principles at different æras of his political Life. On the contrary, no Man was ever more like himself! From his first published Speech on the American Colonies to his last posthumous Tracts, we see the same Man, the same Doctrines, the same uniform Wisdom of *practical* Councils, the same Reasoning and the same Prejudices against all abstract grounds, against all deduction of Practice from Theory. The inconsistency to which I allude, is of a different kind: it is the want of congruity in the Principles appealed to in different parts of the same Work, it is an apparent versatility of the Principle with the Occasion. If his Opponents are Theorists, *then* every thing is to be founded on PRUDENCE, on mere calculations of EXPEDIENCY: and every Man is represented as acting according to the state of his own immediate self interest. Are his Opponents Calculators? *Then* Calculation itself is represented as a sort of crime. God has given us FEELINGS, and we are to obey them! and the most absurd Prejudices become venerable, to which these FEELINGS have given Consecration. I have not forgotten, that Burke himself defended these half contradictions, on the pretext of balancing the too much on the one side by a too much on the other. But never can I believe, but that the straight line must needs be the nearest; and that where there is the most, and the most unalloyed Truth, there will be the greatest and most permanent power of persuasion. But the fact was, that Burke in his most public Character found himself, as it were, in a Noah's Ark, with a very few Men and a great many Beasts! he felt how much his immediate Power was lessened by the very circumstance of his measureless Superiority to those about him: he acted, therefore, under a perpetual System of Compromise—a Compromise of Greatness with Meanness; a Compromise of Comprehension with Narrowness; a Compromise of the Philosopher (who armed with the twofold knowledge of History and the Laws of Spirit, as with a Telescope, looked far around and into the far Distance) with the mere Men of Business, or with yet coarser Intellects, who handled a Truth, which they were required to receive, as they would handle an Ox, which they were desired to purchase. But why need I repeat what has been already said in so happy a manner by Goldsmith, of this great Man:

> "Who, born for the universe narrow'd his mind,
> And to party gave up what was meant for mankind.
> Tho' fraught with all learning, yet straining his throat,
> To persuade Tommy Townshend to give him a vote;
> Who too deep for his hearers, still went on refining,
> And thought of convincing, while they thought of dining."[1]

And if in consequence it was his fate to "*cut blocks with a razor*," I may be permitted to add, that in respect of *Truth*, though not of *Genius*, the Weapon was injured by the misapplication.

II. The Friend [1818]

What is that which first strikes us, and strikes us at once, in a man of education? And which, among educated men, so instantly distinguishes the man of superior mind, that (as was observed with eminent propriety of the late Edmund Burke) "we cannot stand under the same arch-way during a shower of rain, *without finding him out?"* [2]...It is the unpremeditated and evidently habitual *arrangement* of his words, grounded on the habit of foreseeing, in each integral part, or (more plainly) in every sentence, the whole that he intends to communicate. However irregular and desultory his talk, there is *method* in the fragments.

III. Biographia Literaria [1817]

...Edmund Burke possessed and had sedulously sharpened that eye, which sees all things, actions, and events, in relation to the *laws* that determine their existence and circumscribe their possibility. He referred habitually to *principles*. He was a *scientific* statesman; and therefore a *seer*. For every *principle* contains in itself the germs of a prophecy; and as the prophetic power is the essential privilege of science, so the fulfilment of its oracles supplies the outward and (to men in general) the *only* test of its claim to the title. [3] ...In Mr. Burke's writings indeed the germs of almost all political truths may be found.

IV. Table Talk

The very greatest writers write best when calm, and exerting themselves upon subjects unconnected with party. Burke rarely shows all his powers, unless where he is in a passion. The French Revolution was alone a subject fit for him. *(January 4, 1823)*

Burke was, indeed, a great man. No one ever read history so philosophically as he seems to have. Yet, until he could associate his general principles with some sordid interest, panic of property, Jacobinism, &c., he was a mere dinner-bell. Hence you will find so many half-truths in his speeches and writings. Nevertheless, let us heartily acknowledge his transcendent greatness. He would have been more influential if he had less surpassed his contemporaries, as Fox and Pitt, men of much inferior minds, in all respects. *(April 8, 1833)*

Notes

The sources for selections I-III of Coleridge's works are:
The Collected Works of Samuel Taylor Coleridge. Edited by Kathleen Coburn, and Bart Winer. 16 vols. Bollingen Series, no. 75. Princeton: Princeton University Press; London: Routledge & Kegan Paul, 1969-

I. *The Friend*. Edited by Barbara E. Rooke, 1969. vol. 4, part 2, pp. 123-124.
II. *The Friend*, Edited by Barbara E. Rooke, 1969. vol. 4, part 1, pp. 448, 449.
III. *Biographia Literaria*, Edited by James Engell and W. Jackson Bate, 1983, vol. 7, part 1, pp. 191-92, 217.

The source for selection IV, from Coleridge's *Table Talk* is:
Specimens of the Table Talk of Samuel Taylor Coleridge. Edited by Henry Nelson Coleridge
(London, 1858), pp. 10-11, 227.
The notes below are by the present editor, except as indicated.

1. Here and in the next phrase, Coleridge is remembering Oliver Goldsmith's poem *The Retaliation* [1774], ll. 31-36, 42. Goldsmith's original of line 34 reads: "To persuade Tommy Townshend to lend him a vote." Goldsmith's assertion that Burke "to party gave up what was made for mankind" has been vigorously debated ever since the poem appeared.
2. As observed by Samuel Johnson. See *Boswell's Life of Johnson*, ed. G. Birbeck Hill, rev. L. F. Powell (Oxford 1934-1950) 5:34, 465; 4:275. —BER
3. *Principle* and *prophecy* in this passage are technical terms in the vocabulary of Coleridge. They are linked with other, related terms, such as *reason, idea, image, metaphor, symbol,* and, ultimately, *imagination.* Coleridge criticized many eighteenth-century theories of the imagination, especially as exemplified in Hume, for their reliance on "the universal law of passive fancy and mechanical memory" (*Biographia Literaria* 1:104). In Burke, by contrast, Coleridge found a truly imaginative (as opposed to a merely "mechanical") mind, one that habitually "reason[ed] in metaphor" (*Watchman*, Vol. 2, pp. 30-31 in *The Collected Works of Samuel Taylor Coleridge*). In his fragmentary *Notebooks* he compared Burke's quality of imagination with that of Jeremy Taylor and Shakespeare: "English by its...marvelously metaphorical Spirit (...What language can exhibit a style that resembles that of Shakespere, Jeremy Taylor, or Burke?) can express more meaning, image, and passion *tri-unely* in a given number of articulate sounds than any other in the world, not excepting even the ancient Greek" (*The Notebooks of Samuel Taylor Coleridge*, ed. Kathleen Coburn. 3 vols. Bollingen Series no. 50. New York: Pantheon, 1957, 3:2431f4).
   The *Watchman* essay [March 1, 1796], a review of Burke's *Letter to a Noble Lord* [February 24, 1796], is worth consulting in its own right.

WILLIAM HAZLITT

2
Hazlitt's Criticism of Burke

Character of Mr. Burke [1807]

...[T]he only specimen of Burke is, *all that he wrote.* With respect to most other speakers, a specimen is generally enough, or more than enough. When you are acquainted with their manner, and see what proficiency they have made in the mechanical exercise of their profession, with what facility they can borrow a simile, or round a period, how dextrously they can argue, and object, and rejoin, you are satisfied; there is no other difference in their speeches than what arises from the difference of the subjects. But this was not the case with Burke. He brought his subjects along with him; he drew his materials from himself. The only limits which circumscribed his variety were the stores of his own mind. His stock of ideas did not consist of a few meagre facts, meagrely stated, of half a dozen common-places tortured in a thousand different ways: but his mine of wealth was a profound understanding, inexhaustible as the human heart, and various as the sources of nature. He therefore enriched every subject to which he applied himself, and new subjects were only the occasions of calling forth fresh powers of mind which had not been before exerted. It would therefore be in in vain to look for the proof of his powers in any one of his speeches or writings: they all contain some additional proof of power. In speaking of Burke, then, I shall speak of the whole compass and circuit of his mind—not of that small part or section of him which I have been able to give:[1] to do otherwise would be like the story of the man who put the brick in his pocket, thinking to show it as the model of a house. I have been able to manage pretty well with respect to all my other speakers, and curtailed them down without remorse. It was easy to reduce them within certain limits, to fix their spirit, and condense their variety; by having a certain quantity given, you might infer all the rest; it was only the same thing over again. But who can bind Proteus, or confine the roving flight of genius?...

...The only public man that in my opinion can be put in any competition with [Burke] is Lord Chatham:[2] and he moved in a sphere so very remote, that it is almost impossible to compare them. But though it would perhaps be difficult to determine which of them excelled most in his particular way, there is nothing in the world more easy to point out in what their peculiar excellences consisted. They were in every respect the reverse of each other. Chatham's eloquence was popular: his wisdom was altogether plain and practical. Burke's eloquence was that of the poet; of the man of high and unbounded fancy: his wisdom was profound and contemplative. Chatham's eloquence was calculated to make men *act*. Burke's was calculated to make them *think*. Chatham could have roused the fury of a multitude, and wielded their physical energy as he pleased: Burke's eloquence carried conviction into the mind of the retired and lonely student, opened the recesses of the human breast, and lighted up the face of nature around him. Chatham supplied his hearers with motives to immediate action: Burke furnished them with *reasons* for action which might have little effect upon them at the time, but for which they would be the wiser and better all their lives after. In research, in originality, in variety of knowledge, in richness of invention, in depth and comprehension of mind, Burke had as much the advantage of Lord Chatham as he was excelled by him in plain common sense, in strong feeling, in steadiness of purpose, in vehemence, in warmth, in enthusiasm, and energy of mind. Burke was the man of genius, of fine sense, and subtle reasoning; Chatham was a man of clear understanding, of strong sense, and violent passions. Burke's mind was satisfied with speculation: Chatham's was essentially *active*: it could not rest without an object. The power which governed Burke's mind was his Imagination; that which gave its *impetus* to Chatham's was Will. The one was almost the creature of pure intellect, the other of physical temperament.

There are two very different ends which a man of genius may propose to himself either in writing or speaking, and which will accordingly give birth to very different styles. He can have but one of these two objects; either to enrich or to strengthen the mind; either to furnish us with new ideas, to lead the mind into new trains of thought, to which it was before unused, and which it was incapable of striking out for itself; or else to collect and embody what we already knew, to rivet our old impressions more deeply; to make what was before plain still plainer, and to give to that which was familiar all the effect of novelty. In the one case we receive an accession to the stock of our ideas; in the other, an additional degree of life and energy is infused into them: our thoughts continue to flow in the same channels, but their pulse is quickened and invigorated.... In my opinion, [Burke] united the two extremes of refinement and strength in a higher degree than any other writer whatever....

...I do not say that his [political] arguments are conclusive; but they are profound and *true*, as far as they go. There may be disadvantages and abuses necessarily interwoven with his scheme, or opposite advantages of infinitely greater value, to be derived from another order of things and state of society. This however does not invalidate either the truth or importance of Burke's reasoning; since the advantages he points out as connected with the mixed form of government are really and necessarily inherent in it: since they are compatible in the same degree with no other; since the principle itself on which he rests his argument (whatever we may think of the application) is of the utmost weight and moment; and since on whichever side the truth lies, it is impossible to make a fair decision without having the opposite side of the question clearly and fully stated to us. This Burke has done in a masterly manner. He presents to you one view or face of society. Let him, who thinks he can, give the reverse side with equal force, beauty, and clearness. It is said, I know, that truth is *one*; but to this I cannot subscribe, for it appears to me that truth is *many*.[3] There are as many truths as there are things and causes of action and contradictory principles at work in society. In making up the account of good and evil, indeed, the final result must be one way or the other; but the particulars on which that result depends are infinite and various....

Burke was so far from being a gaudy or flowery writer, that he was one of the severest writers we have. His words are the most like things; his style is the most strictly suited to the subject. He unites every extreme and every variety of composition; the lowest and the meanest words and descriptions with the highest. He exults in the display of power, in showing the extent, the force, and intensity of his ideas; he is led on by the mere impulse and vehemence of his fancy, not by the affectation of dazzling his readers by gaudy conceits or pompous images. He was completely carried away by his subject. He had no other object but to produce the strongest impression on his reader, by giving the truest, the most characteristic, the fullest, and most forcible descriptions of things, trusting to the power of his own mind to mould them into grace and beauty. He did not produce a splendid effect by setting fire to the light vapours that float in the regions of fancy, as the chemists make fine colours with phosphorus, but by the eagerness of his blows struck fire from the flint, and melted the hardest substances in the furnace of his imagination. The wheels of his imagination did not catch fire from the rottenness of the materials, but from the rapidity of their motion. One would suppose, to hear people talk of Burke, that his style was such as would have suited the *Lady's Magazine*; soft, smooth, showy, tender, insipid, full of fine words, without any meaning. The essence of the gaudy or glittering style consists in producing a momentary effect by fine words and images brought together, without order or connection. Burke most frequently produced an effect by the remoteness and novelty of his combinations, by the force of contrast, by the striking manner in which the most opposite and unpromising materials were harmoniously blended together; not by laying his hands on all the fine things he could think of, but by bringing together those things which he knew would blaze out into glorious light by their collision. The florid style is a mixture of affectation and common-place. Burke's was an union of untameable vigour and originality.…

Burke has been compared to Cicero—I do not know for what reason. Their excellences are as different, and indeed as opposite, as they well can be. Burke had not the polished elegance; the glossy neatness, the artful regularity, the exquisite modulation of Cicero: he had a thousand times more richness and originality of mind, more strength and pomp of diction.

It has been well observed, that the ancients had no word that properly expresses what we mean by the word *genius*. They perhaps had not the thing. Their minds appear to have been too exact, too retentive, too minute and subtle, too sensible to the external differences of things, too passive under their impressions, to admit of those bold and rapid combinations, those lofty flights of fancy, which, glancing from heaven to earth, unite the most opposite extremes, and draw the happiest illustrations from things the most remote. Their ideas were kept too confined and distinct by the material form or vehicle in which they were conveyed, to unite cordially together, or be melted down in the imagination. Their metaphors are taken from things of the same class, not from things of different classes; the general analogy, not the individual feeling, directs them in their choice. Hence, as Dr. Johnson observed, their similes are either repetitions of the same idea, or so obvious and general as not to lend any additional force to it; as when a huntress is compared to Diana, or a warrior rushing into battle to a lion rushing on his prey. Their *forte* was exquisite art and perfect imitation. Witness their statues and other things of the same kind. But they had not that high and enthusiastic fancy which some of our own writers have shown. For the proof of this, let any one compare Milton and Shakespeare with Homer and Sophocles, or Burke with Cicero.

It may be asked whether Burke was a poet. He was so only in the general vividness of his fancy, and in richness of invention. There may be poetical passages in his works, but I certainly think that his writings in general are quite distinct from poetry; and that for the reason before given, namely, that the subject-matter of them is not poetical. The finest parts of them are illustrations or personifications of dry abstract ideas;[4] and the union between the idea and the illustration is not of that perfect and pleasing kind as to constitute poetry, or indeed to be admissible, but for the effect intended to be produced by it; that is, by every means in our power to give animation and attraction to subjects in themselves barren of ornament, but which at the same time are pregnant with the most important consequences, and in which the understanding and passions are equally interested.

I have heard it remarked by a person, to whose opinion I would sooner submit than to a general council of critics, that the sound of Burke's prose is not musical;[5] that it wants cadence; and that instead of being so lavish of his imagery as is generally supposed, he seemed to him to be rather parsimonious in the use of it, always expanding and making the most of his ideas. This may be true if we compare him with some of our poets, or perhaps with some of our early prose writers, but not if we compare him with any of our political writers or parliamentary speakers. There are some very fine things of Lord Bolingbroke's on the same subjects, but not equal to Burke's. As for Junius, he is at the head of his class; but that class is not the highest.[6] He has been said to have more dignity than Burke. Yes—if the stalk of a giant is less dignified than the strut of a *petit-maître*. I do not mean to speak disrespectfully of Junius, but grandeur is not the character of his composition; and if it is not to be found in Burke, it is to be found nowhere.

On the Prose-Style of the Poets [1822]

...It has always appeared to me that the most perfect prose-style, the most powerful, the most dazzling, the most daring, that which went the nearest to the verge of poetry, and yet never fell over, was Burke's. It has the solidity, and sparkling effect of the diamond:[7] all other *fine writing* is like French paste or Bristol-stones in the comparison. Burke's style is airy, flighty, adventurous, but it never loses sight of the subject; nay, is always in contact with, and derives its increased or varying impulse from it. It may be said to pass yawning gulfs "on the unstedfast footing of a spear:"[8] still it has an actual resting-place and tangible support under it—it is not suspended on nothing. It differs from poetry, as I conceive, like the chamois from the eagle: it clings to an almost equal height, touches upon a cloud, overlooks a precipice, is picturesque, sublime—but all the while, instead of soaring through the air, it stands upon a rocky cliff, clambers up by abrupt and intricate ways, and browzes on the roughest bark, or crops the tender flower. The principle which guides his pen is truth, not beauty—not pleasure, but power. He has no choice, no selection of subject to flatter the reader's idle taste, or assist his own fancy: he must take what comes, and make the most of it. He works the most striking effects out of the most unpromising materials, by the mere activity of his mind. He rises with the lofty, descends with the mean, luxuriates in beauty, gloats over deformity. It is all the same to him, so that he loses no particle of the exact, characteristic, extreme impression of the thing he writes about, and that he communicates this to the reader, after exhausting every possible mode of illustration, plain or abstracted, figurative or real. Whatever stamps the original image more distinctly on the mind, is welcome. The nature of this task precludes continual beauty; but it does not preclude ingenuity, force, originality. He had to treat of political questions, mixed modes, abstract ideas, and his fancy (or poetry, if you will) was ingrafted on these artificially, and as it might sometimes be thought, violently, instead of growing naturally out of them, as it would spring of its own accord from individual objects and feelings. There is a resistance in the *matter* to the illustration applied to it—the concrete and abstract are hardly co-ordinate; and therefore it is that, when the first difficulty is overcome, they must agree more closely in the essential qualities, in order that the coincidence may be complete. Otherwise, it is good for nothing; and you justly charge the author's style with being loose, vague, flaccid and imbecil. The poet has been said

> To make us heirs
> Of truth and pure delight in endless lays.
> (Wordsworth, "Personal Talk," altered)

Not so the prose-writer, who always mingles clay with his gold, and often separates truth from mere pleasure. He can only arrive at the last through the first. In poetry, one pleasing or striking image obviously suggests another: the increasing the sense of beauty or grandeur is the principle of composition: in prose, the professed object is to impart conviction, and nothing can be admitted by way of ornament or relief, that does not add new force or clearness to the original conception. The two classes of ideas brought together by the orator or impassioned prose-writer, to wit, the general subject and the particular image, are so far incompatible, and the identity must be more strict, more marked, more determinate, to make them coalesce to any practical purpose. Every word should be a blow: every thought should instantly grapple with its fellow. There must be a weight, a precision, a conformity from association in the tropes and figures of animated prose to fit them to their place in the argument, and make them *tell,* which may be dispensed with in poetry, where there is something much more congenial between the subject-matter and the illustration—

Like beauty making beautiful old rime!
(Shakespeare, *Sonnet 106*)

What can be more remote, for instance, and at the same time more apposite, more *the same*, than the following comparison of the English Constitution to "the proud Keep of Windsor," in the celebrated *Letter to a Noble Lord?*

Such are *their* ideas; such *their* religion, and such *their* law. But as to *our* country and *our* race, as long as the well-compacted structure of our church and state, the sanctuary, the holy of holies of that ancient law, defended by reverence, defended by power—a fortress at once and a temple—shall stand inviolate on the brow of the British Sion; as long as the British Monarchy—not more limited than fenced by the orders of the State—shall, like the proud Keep of Windsor, rising in the majesty of proportion, and girt with the double belt of its kindred and coeval towers; as long as this awful structure shall oversee and guard the subjected land, so long the mounds and dykes of the low, fat, Bedford level will have nothing to fear from all the pickaxes of all the levellers of France. As long as our Sovereign Lord the King, and his faithful subjects, the Lords and Commons of this realm—the triple cord which no man can break; the solemn, sworn, constitutional frank-pledge of this nation; the firm guarantees of each other's being, and each other's rights; the joint and several securities, each in its place and order, for every kind and every quality of property and of dignity—As long as these endure, so long the Duke of Bedford is safe: and we are all safe together—the high from the blights of envy and the spoliations of rapacity; the low from the iron hand of oppression and the insolent spurn of contempt. Amen! and so be it: and so it will be,

> *Dum domus Æneæ Capitoli immobile saxum*
> *Accolet; imperiumque pater Romanus habebit.*[9]

Nothing can well be more impracticable to a simile than the vague and complicated idea which is here embodied in one; yet how finely, how nobly it stands out, in natural grandeur, in royal state, with double barriers round it to answer for its identity, with "buttress, frieze, and coigne of 'vantage'" for the imagination to "make its pendant bed and procreant cradle," till the idea is confounded with the object representing it—the wonder of a kingdom; and then how striking, how determined the descent, "at one fell swoop," to the "low, fat, Bedford level!" Poetry would have been bound to maintain a certain decorum, a regular balance between these two ideas; sterling prose throws aside all such idle respect to appearances, and with its pen, like a sword, "sharp and sweet," lays open the naked truth![10] The poet's Muse is like a mistress, whom we keep only while she is young and beautiful, *durante bene placito*; the Muse of prose is like a wife, whom we take during life, *for better for worse.* Burke's execution, like that of all good prose, savours of the texture of what he describes, and his pen slides or drags over the ground of his subject, like the painter's pencil. The most rigid fidelity and the most fanciful extravagance meet, and are reconciled in his pages. I never pass Windsor but I think of this passage in Burke, and hardly know to which I am indebted most for enriching my moral sense, that or the fine picturesque stanza, in Gray,

> From Windsor's heights the expanse below
> Of mead, of lawn, of wood survey, &c.
>   ("Ode on a Distant Prospect of Eton College," altered)

I might mention that the so much admired description in one of the India speeches, of Hyder Ali's army (I think it is) which "now hung like a cloud upon the mountain, and now burst upon the plain like a thunder bolt," would do equally well for poetry or prose.[11] It is a bold and striking illustration of a naturally impressive object. This is not the case with the Abbe Sieyes's far famed "pigeon-holes," nor with the comparison of the Duke of Bedford to "the Leviathan, tumbling about his unwieldy bulk in the ocean of royal bounty."[12] Nothing here saves the description but the force of the invective; the startling truth, the vehemence, the remoteness, the aptitude, the perfect peculiarity and coincidence of the allusion. No writer would ever have thought of it but himself; no reader can ever forget it. What is there in common, one might say, between a Peer of the Realm, and "that sea-beast," of those

> Created hugest that swim the ocean-stream?
>   (Milton, *Paradise Lost* 1:202)

Yet Burke has knit the two ideas together, and no man can put them asunder. No matter how slight and precarious the connection, the length of line it is necessary for the fancy to give out in keeping hold of the object on which it has fastened, he seems to have "put his hook in the nostrils" of this enormous creature of the crown, that empurples all its track through the glittering expanse of a profound and restless imagination.[13]

Notes

The selections from Hazlitt come from
The Complete Works of William Hazlitt. 21 vols. Edited by P. P. Howe.
London and Toronto: Dent, 1930-34.
Character of Mr. Burke is found in Vol. 7, *The Plain Speaker*, pp. 301-313.
On the Prose-Style of the Poets is found in Vol. 12, *Political Essays*, pp. 5-17.
The notes below are by the present editor, except as indicated.

1. Hazlitt is writing this "character" as a preface to Burke's speech "On Economical Reform," (February 11, 1780), which Hazlitt printed as part of his work, *The Eloquence of the British Senate* (1807). He is apologizing for giving so small a "part" of Burke.
2. William Pitt, "the elder," (1708-1778), first earl of Chatham.
3. Hazlitt's belief in the many-sided quality of truth is a consequence of his theory of the imagination. When a writer conveyed a strong impression of nature, Hazlitt considered his writing "true," for the writer had successfully identified with the "power" latent in nature. The language of poetry, he wrote, "is not the less true to nature, because it is false in point of fact; but so much the more true and natural, if it conveys the impression which the object under the influence of passion makes on the mind" (Hazlitt, *Complete Works*, 5:4). Hazlitt never agreed with Burke's politics, but as early as a 1798 conversation with Coleridge, he maintained that "the speaking of [Burke] with contempt might be made the test of a vulgar democratical mind. This was the first observation I ever made to Coleridge, and he said it was a very just and striking one" (*Complete Works*, 17:111).

4. Hazlitt here points to Burke's comparison of the British Constitution to the "proud Keep of Windsor" in the *Letter to a Noble Lord*, quoted below.   In an omitted section of this "Character," Hazlitt singled out Burke's *Thoughts on the Cause of the Present Discontents* for praise—a work that did not often appeal to the nineteenth century—along with the *Reflections, Letters on a Regicide Peace,* and *Letter to a Noble Lord.*

5. Howe speculates that Hazlitt is referring to his early friend Joseph Fawcett.

6. Henry Saint-John, Viscount Bolingbroke (1678-1751).   The "Junius" letters, a series of harsh, personal attacks on Chatham, Bedford, Grafton, North, and the King, appeared in 1769-1771.   Burke's friend and close associate, Sir Philip Francis (1740-1818) is widely held to be the author.

7. Howe notes that "[b]rilliant crystals of colourless quartz, found on St. Vincent's Rocks near Bristol, go by the name of Bristol Diamonds."

8. Shakespeare, *I Henry IV*, 1.3.193. —PPH

9. The quotation from *LNL* is found in *Works* (Bohn) 5:137, appr. 66% into the work. Burke himself notes that he is comparing the British Constitution (the "fortress and temple") to the temple of Jerusalem, described by Tacitus as "a temple in the form of a fortress." Burke's Latin quotation is from *Aeneid* 9.448-49: "As long as the house of Aeneas dwells on the immovable rock of the Capitol, and the father of Rome maintains authority."   Hazlitt's description of Burke's prose, both before and after this quotation, relates directly to his theory of the imagination. For Hazlitt, the imagination begins to work as the writer's passions or power heighten his sense impressions—here, Burke's impression of the British Constitution. As the writer identifies sympathetically with the "power" in the object (again, the Constitution in this case), he is able to write with "gusto" and produce "poetry."   Hazlitt's praise for Burke's writing is all the more remarkable for his utter disagreement with Burke on the political issues of the French Revolution.

10. *Buttress, frieze...procreant cradle. Macbeth* 1.6.7.
At one fell swoop. Macbeth 4.3.219.
Sharp and sweet. Cf. "As sweet as sharp," *All's Well that Ends Well* 4.4.33. —PPH

11. *Speech on the Nabob of Arcot's Debts* in Burke, *Works* (Oxford) 5:519, appr. 52% into the work. Hazlitt is quoting from memory.

12. *LNL* in *Works* (Bohn) 5:142, 129 respectively; appr. 78% and 47% into the work. Burke's comparison of the Duke of Bedford to the Leviathan is drawn from Milton's image for Satan in *Paradise Lost* 1:193-201, as Hazlitt's next lines indicate.

13. *Put his hook in the nostrils. Job* 41:1-2. —PPH

3
Rhetoric

...All hail to Edmund Burke, the supreme writer of his century, the man of the largest and finest understanding! Upon that word, *understanding*, we lay a stress: for, oh! ye immortal donkeys who have written "about him and about him," with what an obstinate stupidity have ye brayed away for one third of a century about that which ye are pleased to call his "fancy."[1] Fancy in your throats, ye miserable twaddlers! As if Edmund Burke were the man to play with his fancy for the purpose of separable ornament! He was a man of fancy in no other sense than as Lord Bacon was so, and Jeremy Taylor, and as all large and discursive thinkers are and must be: that is to say, the fancy which he had in common with all mankind, and very probably in no eminent degree, in him was urged into unusual activity under the necessities of his capacious understanding. His great and peculiar distinction was that he viewed all objects of the understanding under more relations than other men, and under more complex relations. According to the multiplicity of these relations, a man is said to have a *large* understanding; according to their subtlety, a *fine* one; and in an angelic understanding all things would appear to be related to all. Now, to apprehend and detect more relations, or to pursue them steadily, is a process absolutely impossible without the intervention of physical analogies. To say, therefore, that a man is a great thinker, or a fine thinker, is but another expression for saying that he has a *schematizing* (or, to use a plainer but less accurate expression, a figurative) understanding. In that sense, and for that purpose, Burke is figurative: but, understood, as he *has* been understood[2] by the long-eared race of his critics, not as thinking in and by his figures, but as deliberately laying them on by way of enamel or after-ornament,—not as *incarnating,* but simply as *dressing* his thoughts in imagery,—so understood, he is not the Burke of reality, but a poor fictitious Burke, modelled after the poverty of conception which belongs to his critics.

It is true, however, that in some rare cases Burke *did* indulge himself in a pure rhetorician's use of fancy; consciously and profusely lavishing his ornaments for mere purposes of effect. Such a case occurs, for instance, in that admirable picture of the degradation of Europe where he represents the different crowned heads as bidding against each other at Basel for the favour and countenance of Regicide.[3] Others of the same kind there are in his ever-memorable letter on the Duke of Bedford's attack upon him in the House of Lords; and one of these we shall here cite, disregarding its greater chance for being already familiar to the reader, upon two considerations: first, that it has all the appearance of being finished with the most studied regard to effect; and, secondly, for an interesting anecdote connected with it which we have never seen in print, but for which we have better authority than could be produced perhaps for most of those which are. The anecdote is that Burke, conversing with Dr. Laurence and another gentleman on the *literary* value of his own writings,[4] declared that the particular passage in the entire range of his works which had cost him the most labour, and upon which, as tried by a certain canon of his own, his labour seemed to himself to have been the most successful, was the following:—

[De Quincey here reproduces the same passage that Hazlitt quoted above (pp. 13-14) from *A Letter to a Noble Lord.*]

This was the sounding passage which Burke alleged as the *chef-d'œuvre* of his rhetoric; and the argument upon which he justified his choice is specious, if not convincing. He laid it down as a maxim of composition that every passage in a rhetorical performance which was brought forward prominently, and relied upon as a *key* (to use the language of war)[5] in sustaining the main position of the writer, ought to involve a thought, an image, and a sentiment; and such a synthesis he found in the passage which we have quoted. This criticism, over and above the pleasure which it always gives to hear a great man's opinion of himself, is valuable as showing that Burke, because negligent of trivial inaccuracies, was not at all the less anxious about the larger proprieties and decorums (for this passage, confessedly so laboured, has several instances of slovenliness in trifles), and that in the midst of his apparent hurry he carried out a jealous vigilance upon what he wrote [with] the eye of a person practised in artificial effects....

...The rhetorical manner is supported in the French [theological] writers chiefly by an abundances of *ohs* and *ahs*; by interrogatories, apostrophes, and startling exclamations; all which are mere mechanical devices for raising the style; but in the substance of the composition, apart from its dress, there is nothing properly rhetorical. The leading thoughts in all pulpit eloquence, being derived from religion, and in fact the common inheritance of human nature, if they cannot be novel, for that very reason cannot be undignified; but for the same reason they are apt to become unaffecting and trite unless varied and individualized by new infusions of thought and feeling. The smooth monotony of the leading religious topics, as managed by the French orators, receives under the treatment of Jeremy Taylor at each turn of the sentence a new flexure, or what may be called a separate *articulation.*[6]

We may take the opportunity of noticing what it is that constitutes the peculiar and characterizing circumstances in Burke's manner of composition. It is this: that under his treatment every truth, be it what is may, every thesis of a sentence, *grows* in the very act of unfolding it. Take any sentence you please from Dr. Johnson, suppose, and it will be found to contain a thought, good or bad, fully preconceived. Whereas in Burke, whatever may have been the preconception, it receives a new determination or inflexion at every clause of the sentence. Some collateral adjunct of the main proposition, some temperament or restraint, some oblique glance at its remote affinities, will invariably be found to attend the progress of his sentences, like the spray from a waterfall, or the scintillations from the iron under the blacksmith's hammer. Hence, whilst a writer of Dr. Johnson's class seems only to look back upon his thoughts, Burke looks forward, and does in fact advance and change his own station concurrently with the advance of the sentences. This peculiarity is no doubt in some degree due to the habit of extempore speaking, but not to that only....

Notes

Thomas De Quincey's essay "Rhetoric," [1828] comes from
Literary Theory and Criticism, vol. 10, of
Collected Writings of Thomas De Quincey, 14 vols. Edited by David Masson.
London: A.&C. Black, 1896-97.
The notes are by the present editor.

1. The phrase *about him and about him* alludes to the failed intellectuals and hack writers—the "long-eared race of critics"—that populate Pope's *Dunciad,* esp. at 4:252. Earlier in the essay,

De Quincey had argued for a union of the thought and imagery of "rhetoric" with the sentiment (or feeling) of "eloquence." At this point, however, he shifts his terms and argues that Burke's language united "fancy" and "understanding." I believe the union of "fancy and understanding" is parallel (in De Quincey's vocabulary) to both (a) the union of rhetoric and eloquence and (b) the "synthesis" of thought, image, and sentiment that De Quincey sees (below) in Burke.

2. I.e., incorrectly understood. De Quincey's point is that one *cannot* separate the products of Burke's fancy (such as his "ornaments" or figurative language) from the products of his understanding. The attempt to do so is the mistake of Burke's critics.

3. Burke *Works* (Bohn) 5:171, appr. 25% into the first of the *Letters on a Regicide Peace*.

4. Dr. French Laurence (1757-1809), contributor to the *Rolliad* and an M.P. noted for his expertise in international law, was an intimate friend of Edmund Burke. He served, along with Dr. Walker King, as Burke's literary executor after Burke's death.

5. *Key:* "A place which from the stategic advantages of its position gives its possessor control over the passage into or from a certain district, territory, inland sea, etc." —OED.

6. De Quincey puts the following paragraph ("We may take the opportunity....") in a footnote. Like Coleridge, he proceeds to compare Burke to Jeremy Taylor, concluding that the imagery of both writers will usually "extend and amplify the thought," rather than simply echo or repeat it: "[w]e are thus reconciled to the proposition by the same image which illustrates it."

4
Macaulay's Comments on Burke

Lord Bacon [1837]

...[Bacon's] later writings are far superior to those of his youth. In this respect the history of his mind bears some resemblance to the history of the mind of Burke. The treatise on the *Sublime and Beautiful*, though written on a subject which the coldest metaphysician could hardly treat without being occasionally betrayed into florid writing, is the most unadorned of all Burke's works. It appeared when he was twenty-five or twenty six.[1] When, at forty, he wrote the *Thoughts on the Causes of the Existing Discontents* [sic], his reason and his judgment had reached their full maturity; but his eloquence was still in its splendid dawn. At fifty, his rhetoric was quite as rich as good taste would permit; and when he died, at almost seventy, it had become ungracefully gorgeous. In his youth, he wrote on the emotions produced by mountains and cascades, by the master-pieces of painting and sculpture, by the faces and necks of beautiful women, in the style of a parliamentary report. In his old age, he discussed treaties and tariffs in the most fervid and brilliant language of romance. It is strange that the *Essay on the Sublime and Beautiful*, and the *Letter to a Noble Lord*, should be the productions of one man. But it is far more strange that the *Essay* should have been a production of his youth, and the *Letter* of his old age....

Warren Hastings [1841]

[Burke's] knowledge of India was such as few, even of those Europeans who have passed many years in that country, have attained, and such as certainly was never attained by any public man who had not quitted Europe.[2] He had studied the history, the laws, and the usages of the East with an industry such as is seldom found united to so much genius and so much sensibility. Others have perhaps been equally laborious, and have collected an equal mass of materials. But the manner in which Burke brought his higher powers of intellect to work on statements of facts and on tables of figures was peculiar to himself. In every part of those huge bales of Indian information, which repelled almost all other readers, his mind, at once philosophical and poetical, found something to instruct or to delight. His reason analyzed and digested those vast and shapeless masses; his imagination animated and colored them. Out of darkness and dulness and confusion he formed a multitude of ingenious theories and vivid pictures. He had, in the highest degree, that noble faculty whereby man is able to live in the past and in the future, in the distant and in the unreal.[3] India and its inhabitants were not to him, as to most Englishmen, mere names and abstractions, but a real country and a real people. The burning sun; the strange vegetation of the palm and the cocoa tree; the rice-field; the tank; the huge trees, older than the Mogul empire, under which the village crowds assemble; the thatched roof of the peasant's hut; the rich tracery of the mosque where the imaum prays with his face to Mecca; the drums and banners and gaudy idols; the devotee swinging in the air; the graceful maiden, with the pitcher on her head, descending the steps to the river-side; the black faces; the long beards; the yellow streaks of sect; the turbans and the flowing robes; the spears and the silver maces; the elephants with their canopies of state; the gorgeous palanquin of the prince and the close litter of the noble lady—all these things were to him as the objects amidst which his own life had been passed, as the objects which lay on the road between Beaconsfield and St. James's Street. All India was present to the eye of his mind—from the halls where suitors laid gold and perfumes at the feet of sovereigns, to the wild moor where the gypsy camp was pitched; from the bazaar, humming like a beehive with the crowd of buyers and sellers, to the jungle where the lonely courier shakes his bunch of iron rings to scare away the hyenas. He had just as lively an idea of the insurrection of Benares as of Lord George Gordon's riots,[4] and of the execution of Nuncomar as of the execution of Dr. Dodd. Oppression in Bengal was to him the same thing as oppression in the streets of London.

He saw that Hastings had been guilty of some most unjustifiable acts. All that followed was natural and necessary in a mind like Burke's. His imagination and his passions, once excited, hurried him beyond the bounds of justice and good sense. His reason, powerful as it was, became the slave of feelings which it should have controlled. His indignation, virtuous in its origin, acquired too much of the character of personal aversion. He could see no mitigating circumstance, no redeeming merit.[5] His temper, which though generous and affectionate, had always been irritable, had now been made almost savage by bodily infirmities and mental vexations. Conscious of great powers and great virtues, he found himself, in age and poverty, a mark for the hatred of a perfidious court and a deluded people.   In Parliament his eloquence was out of date. A young generation, which knew him not, had filled the House. Whenever he rose to speak, his voice was drowned by the unseemly interruption of lads who were in their cradles when his orations on the Stamp Act called forth the applause of the great Earl of Chatham.[6] These things had produced on his proud and sensitive spirit an effect at which we cannot wonder. He could no longer discuss any question with calmness, or make allowance for honest differences of opinion. Those who think that he was more violent and acrimonious in debates about India than on other occasions are ill informed respecting the last years of his life. In the discussions on the Commercial Treaty with the Court of Versailles, on the Regency, on the French Revolution, he showed even more virulence than in conducting the impeachment. Indeed, it may be remarked that the very persons who called him a mischievous maniac for condemning in burning words the Rohilla war and the spoliation of the Begums exalted him into a prophet as soon as he began to declaim, with greater vehemence, and not with greater reason, against the taking of the Bastille and the insults offered to Marie Antoinette.[7] To us he appears to have been neither a maniac in the former case nor a prophet in the latter, but in both cases a great and good man, led into extravagance by a sensibility which domineered over all his faculties.

Notes

The selections from Macaulay are found in
The Essays of Thomas Babington Macaulay. Whitehall edition. New York: Putnam, 1898.
Lord Bacon is found at vol. 4:1-165. The selection above comes from pp. 159-160.
Warren Hastings is found at vol. 5:188-337. The selection above comes from pp. 301-304.
The notes are by the present editor.

1.   When the *Philosophical Enquiry into...the Sublime and Beautiful* was published, in April 1757, Burke was 28. Macaulay calls the work Burke's *Essay*.

2. Macaulay served in India from 1834-37 as a member of the supreme council. In that capacity he led the effort to write the criminal code and the code of criminal procedure for India.

3. In these sentences, Macaulay has suggested the goal that he held for himself as a historian. The "India" he proceeds to describe is his own, not Burke's. Unlike De Quincey and Coleridge, who admired the *fusion* of the various faculties of the mind, Macaulay wanted to keep them separate, though in tension. He thought the historian should at some times be "under the sole and absolute dominion" of "reason," at others, under the dominion of "imagination" (*History* in *Essays* 1:180-81). The scene that Macaulay is about to paint, of the opening of the trial of Warren Hastings, appealed to both faculties: "there was never a spectacle so well calculated to strike a highly cultivated, a *reflecting,* an *imaginative* mind" (*Essays* 5:314, emphasis mine). For Macaulay, the imagination is an "associative" faculty, rather than a Coleridgean (and, I would say, Burkean) faculty of re-creation. Macaulay said that Burke's speeches contributed substantially to his own understanding of India. In the lines 'hat follow, Macaulay demonstrates the ability to use his reading of Burke to reassociate his many ideas and experiences of India in striking and almost preternaturally vivid ways. See *The Letters of Thomas Babington Macaulay*, ed. Thomas Pinney. Cambridge University Press, 1974-81, 3:41; John Clive, *Macaulay: The Shaping; of the Historian*, Knopf, 1973, p. 231; G.O. Trevelyan, *The Life and Letters of Lord Macaulay*, Oxford University Press, 1978, 1:235-36.

4. The Maharajah *Nuncomar*, a Hindu ruler and bitter enemy to Warren Hastings (Governor-General of India), charged Hastings with peculation. While the case was pending, he was indicted for forgery and executed in 1775. Burke and Macaulay considered the actions of Hasings and Sir Elijah Impey (the chief justice of India) in this case to be judicial murder. *Benares* (mod: Varanasi) is both a city and the name of the Hindu kingdom. Pursuing the money and troops he needed for the Mahratta War, Hastings arrested the raja of Benares (Cheyt Sing, mod: Chait Singh), sparking a rebellion in that region (1781). The *Gordon riots* (June 1780) were sparked by Protestants seeking to repeal the Catholic Relief Act of 1778. Burke in particular was threatened for having sought to protect and extend the civil rights of Catholics. William *Dodd* was the unfortunate clergyman whose mind was wonderfully concentrated, said Dr. Johnson, by the prospect of being hanged in a fortnight.

5. Despite his realization of Hastings's faults, Macaulay had a generally high estimate of him.

6. *Stamp Act*. Passed by Parliament in March 1765, and immediately opposed by the American colonists. The Grenville ministry fell in July, and the Rockingham ministry (of which Burke was a part) repealed the Act (February 1766). By that time the *Earl of Chatham* (William Pitt the elder, 1708-1778) had had a long, distinguished career in government. His conduct of the Seven Years' War in the previous decade had brought England to its point of greatest power in the eighteenth century.

7. The *Regency* debates, over declaring the dissolute Prince of Wales (Later George IV) regent, occurred because of the King's bouts of insanity. In the fall of 1788 the debates were particularly violent. See Carl B. Cone, *Burke and the Nature of Politics*, 2 vols. (Lexington, KY: University of Kentucky Press, 1964), 2:257-282. The *Rohillas* were a tribe of Afghan warriors who lived in northwest India. In the early eighteenth century they came to the area around Benares, and by the latter part of the century they had established a modest kingdom. Burke considered their defeat by the British in 1774 the destruction of a great nation. *Begum* (mod: Begam) is a title of respect for a Muslim woman. In Burke's writings, the term usually refers to the mother and grandmother of the Wazir of Oudh. See Burke's *Speech on Fox's India Bill* [1783] in *Writings* (Oxford) 5:392, 410, 411, (appr. 18% and 43% into the speech) and the accompanying footnotes.

5

Mr. Macaulay

...This peculiarity of character gives to Macaulay's writing one of its most curious characteristics.[1] He throws over matters which are in their nature dry and dull,—transactions—budgets—bills,—the charm of fancy which a poetical mind employs to enhance and set forth the charm of what is beautiful....

Only a buoyant fancy and an impassive temperament could produce a book so combining weight with levity.

Something similar may be remarked of the writings of a still greater man—of Edmund Burke. The contrast of the manner of his characteristic writings to their matter is very remarkable. He, too, threw over the detail of business and of politics those graces and attractions of manner which seem in some sort inconsistent with them; which are adapted for topics more intrinsically sublime and beautiful. It was for this reason that Hazlitt asserted that "no woman ever cared for Burke's writings." The matter, he said, was "hard and dry," and no superficial glitter or eloquence could make it agreeable to those who liked what is, in its very nature, fine and delicate. The charm of exquisite narration has, in a great degree, in Mr. Macaulay's case, supplied the deficiency; but it may be *perhaps* remarked, that some trace of the same phenomenon has occurred again, from similar causes, and that his popularity, though great among both sexes, is in some sense more masculine than feminine. The absence of this charm of narration, to which accomplished women are, it would seem, peculiarly sensitive, is very characteristic of Burke. His mind was the reverse of historical. Although he had rather a coarse, incondite temperament, not finely susceptible to the best influences, to the most exquisite beauties of the world in which he lived, he yet lived in that world thoroughly and completely. He did not take an interest, as a poet does, in the sublime because it is sublime, in the beautiful because it is beautiful; but he had the passions of more ordinary men in a degree, and of an intensity, which ordinary men may be most thankful that they have not. In no one has the intense faculty of intellectual hatred—the hatred which the absolute dogmatist has for those in whom he incarnates and personifies the opposing dogma—been fiercer or stronger; in no one has the intense ambition to rule and govern,—in scarcely any one has the daily ambition of the daily politician, been fiercer and stronger: he, if any man, cast himself upon his time. After one of his speeches peruse one of Macaulay's: you seem transported to another sphere. The fierce living interest of the one contrasts with the cold rhetorical interest of the other; you are in a different part of the animal kingdom; you have left the viviparous intellect; you have left products warm and struggling with hasty life; you have reached the oviparous, and products smooth and polished, cold and stately.

Notes

Walter Bagehot's essay "Mr. Macualay" [1856] appears in *Literary Studies,* vol. 1 of *The Collected Works of Walter Bagehot,* Edited by Norman St. John-Stevas London: The Economist; and Cambridge, MA: Harvard University Press, 1965- , pp. 397-428.

1. The "peculiarity of character" is Macaulay's union of the "poetic" and the historical mind. Bagehot is reviewing Macaulay's *History of England.* For Bagehot, Macaulay is the embodiment of the man whose imagination is divorced from his everyday life, producing a "cold rhetorical interest" in his writing. Burke, by contrast, brings a "fierce living interest" to everything he does, both speaking and acting. While Bagehot clearly admires Burke more than Macaulay, he is suspicious of the brilliance, single-mindedness, and imagination of men like Burke and Disraeli, preferring instead the "stupidity" of men like Sir Robert Peel, Disraeli's predecessor, in the House of Commons, as leader of the Conservative Party. [—DR]

MATTHEW ARNOLD

6

The Function of Criticism
at the Present Time

...[B]y quitting the intellectual sphere and rushing furiously into the political sphere, [the French Revolution] ran, indeed, a prodigious and memorable course, but produced no such intellectual fruit as the movement of ideas of the Renascence, and created, in opposition to itself, what I may call an *epoch of concentration.*[1] The great force of that epoch of concentration was England; and the great voice of that epoch of concentration was Burke. It is the fashion to treat Burke's writings on the French Revolution as superannuated and conquered by the event; as the eloquent but unphilosophical tirades of bigotry and prejudice. I will not deny that they are often disfigured by the violence and passion of the moment, and that in some directions Burke's view was bounded, and his observation therefore at fault. But on the whole, and for those who can make the needful corrections, what distinguishes these writings is their profound, permanent, fruitful, philosophical truth. They contain the true philosophy of an epoch of concentration, dissipate the heavy atmosphere which its own nature is apt to engender round it, and make its resistance rational instead of mechanical.

But Burke is so great because, almost alone in England, he brings thought to bear upon politics, he saturates politics with thought.[2] It is his accident that his ideas were at the service of an epoch of concentration, not of an epoch of expansion; it is his characteristic that he so lived by ideas, and had such a source of them welling up within him, that he could float even an epoch of concentration and English Tory politics with them. It does not hurt him that Dr. Price and the Liberals were enraged with him;[3] it does not even hurt him that George the Third and the Tories were enchanted with him. His greatness is that he lived in a world which neither English Liberalism nor

-27-

English Toryism is apt to enter;—the world of ideas, not the world of catchwords and party habits. So far is it from being really true of him that he "to party gave up what was meant for mankind,"[4] that at the very end of his fierce struggle with the French Revolution, after all his invectives against its false pretensions, hollowness, and madness, with his sincere conviction of its mischievousness, he can close a memorandum on the best means of combating it, some of the last pages he ever wrote,—the *Thoughts on French Affairs,* in December 1791,—with these striking words:—

> The evil is stated, in my opinion, as it exists. The remedy must be where power, wisdom, and information, I hope, are more united with good intentions than they can be with me. I have done with this subject, I believe, for ever. It has given me many anxious moments for the last two years. *If a great change is to be made in human affairs, the minds of men will be fitted to it; the general opinions and feelings will draw that way. Every fear, every hope will forward it; and then they who persist in opposing this mighty current in human affairs, will appear rather to resist the decrees of Providence itself, than the mere designs of men. They will not be resolute and firm, but perverse and obstinate.*[5]

That return of Burke upon himself has always seemed to me one of the finest things in English literature, or indeed in any literature. That is what I call living by ideas: when one side of a question has long had your earnest support, when all your feelings are engaged, when you hear all round you no language but one, when your party talks this language like a steam-engine and can imagine no other,—still to be able to think, still to be irresistibly carried, if so it be, by the current of thought to the opposite side of the question, and, like Balaam, to be unable to speak anything "but what the Lord has put in your mouth."[6] I know nothing more striking, and I must add that I know nothing more un-English.

Notes

"The Function of Criticism at the Present Time" [1865] comes from
Lectures and Essays in Criticism, vol. 3:266-68 of
The Complete Prose Works of Matthew Arnold, Edited by R. H. Super.
Ann Arbor, MI: University of Michigan Press, 1960-1977.
The notes below are by the present editor.

1. Although Arnold's terms are not always consistent, an "epoch of concentration" is defined in opposition to an "epoch of expansion." The latter is defined by "a movement of ideas," which presumably suggests the absence of such movement in an "epoch of concentration." Nevertheless, Arnold admired the eighteenth century, which he considered an epoch of concentration, for the dignity and lofty spirit of its aristocracy. The presence of Burke, a man who lived by ideas (says Arnold), in such an era strikes Arnold as an "accident." The term "idea" is itself an important one for Arnold's entire critical practice. While the term has many ramifications, its most important one is implied in this selection: ideas enable the person who lives by them to question his own judgments, to see both sides of a question, to believe in the development of culture more than the clap-trap of one's own party. Burke and Lord Falkland were two such men, in Arnold's view.

   For a more detailed analysis of Burke's importance to Arnold's critical practice see Dan Ritchie, "The Literary Significance of Edmund Burke for Matthew Arnold," *Victorian Newsletter* 75 (Spring 1989): 28-35.

2. Arnold's editor notes that this sentence echoes a letter of January 1864, written by Arnold to his sister, Mrs. W. E. Forster: "What makes Burke stand out so splendidly among politicians is that he treats politics with his thought and imagination; therefore, whether one agrees with him or not, he always interests you, stimulates you, and does you good. I have been attentively reading lately his *Reflections on the French Revolution,* and have felt this most strongly, much as there is in his view of France and her destinies which is narrow and erroneous. But I advise...you...indeed to read something of Burke's every year."

3. The sermon of nonconformist minister Richard Price (1723-91), "A Discourse on the Love of Our Country" (Nov. 4, 1789), praised the French Revolution, moving Burke to write his *Reflections on the Revolution in France.*

4. Goldsmith, "The Retaliation" l. 32.

5. *Thoughts on French Affairs* in Burke *Works* (Bohns) 3:393, the final lines of the work. The italics are supplied by Arnold. Arnold makes many biographical mistakes in the sentences surrounding this quotation. These were by no means "some of the last pages" Burke ever wrote on French or other affairs. There was no "party talking Burke's language" in December of 1791. Burke had already been repudiated by his own Whig party, and in November of 1791 he wrote his patron, the Whig leader Fitzwilliam, to decline any further financial support. The Portland Whigs did not finally break from their party leader, Charles James Fox, to join the Tory ministry of William Pitt until July 1794. Arnold also overlooks Burke's active support of the very "party habits" he condemns (see Mansfield, below).

6. *Numbers* 22:38.

7
Burke and the Sense of Process

Burke's long study and plea on behalf of India show him (at least in two respects) at his very greatest. And this is completely aside from the obvious historical importance—aside from the fact that this spectacular, thorough airing of the whole matter was slowly, over generations, to leave its effect. It is also despite the two facts that Hastings himself, to begin with, was being made a scapegoat, and also that this huge mass of material is inevitably dated and is far too detailed to arouse much interest. No collected body of writing so highly praised has been so little read.

But the appeal is still hypnotic. For, first, simply as a sheer feat of mind, this *tour de force* of Burke is unrivalled in its own way, and compels unqualified admiration. He studied and digested every available work on the history, religions, geography, and economy of India. Moreover, "[b]ales of official correspondence, of pamphlets, folio volumes of reports," as [Bertram] Newman said, "so far from choking his assimilative powers, served to exercise his mind, to fire his imagination, and, most important, to widen his sympathies." Secondly, this assimilative power is constantly fed by a moral and imaginative vision that is richly meshed with fact and freighted with concreteness (not yet cut loose from this strong purchase, as some of the writings on the French Revolution were to be). Above all, there is the appeal of Burke's sense of process and time. In the trial of Warren Hastings, as Macaulay perceptively wrote, everything calculated to strike an imaginative and reflecting mind was present: interests that belonged to the near and distant were collected. "Every step in the proceedings carried the mind backward, through many troubled centuries, to the days when the foundations of our constitution were laid; or...over boundless seas and deserts," to a vast, distant land. In the hall of William Rufus, with its associations that reached back to Richard the Lionhearted, and in forms handed down since the Plantagenets, Burke, with his own vivid knowledge of England's long past, tried to present to this audience what he had learned of a remote subcontinent of so many millions.[1] To the medieval and Far Eastern associations is also added the glance backward to the great orations of classical antiquity. Finally there is added (as in all of Burke's greater writing) a prophetic anticipation of the modern world's haunting sense of time.

For in one special, very important way, Burke is closer to the modern educated sensibility than any other writer between Shakespeare and Wordsworth. He is closer because of his constant sense of process, and the almost tender protectiveness of his imagination when it turns to the tragic past. If the phrase, "the tragic past," is used here, it is partly with the thought of Whitehead's distinction: that the essence of "tragedy" is not unhappiness, but rather the solemn, remorseless working out of events. The past is tragic partly because it is finished. There is the sheer fact that all life is over, as our own will only too quickly be. What that vast diversity of life did, suffered or hoped, can never be changed. As in Proust's great book, with its remarkable title (*À la Recherche du Temps perdu*), or Eliot's *Four Quartets*, the greater writing of the twentieth century—and perhaps of the nineteenth century—is saturated with the vivid sense of the way in which the past is forever locked in an unalterable pattern. Hence the tenderness to the past since the onset of the romantic era. It touches every aspect of our lives. Even Henry Ford, who could mutter that "History is bunk," devoted a good deal of worried and even sentimental effort to salvaging the relics of a vanished America he himself had helped to usher from the scene. The point is the modernity of Burke in his sense of process and change: the fact that there is always the sense of a large finished past which can be rescued only by the interpretative imagination that meditates on it, as music can come alive only when the printed pattern of notes is scanned and repeated, for a little time, by some later intelligence. And the past is tragic not only because it is irrevocable, without any second chance, so to speak, but also because so much of it was blind (as we ourselves are now): blind because of the enormous waste, the conflicts, frustrations, defeats; because of the freight it carries of the diversity of each life, and of the ways in which the cramped, primitive minds of all of us, poisoned by fear and self-defense, torture each other in our bewildered stupidity. The sense of all this stirs in Burke the desire to shelter this huge accumulation of past life, and to give it, so to speak, at least the shadow of a second chance, if only in the meditative imagination that tries to learn from it. "Their imagination" (he said later of the systematic theorists of the French Revolution) "is not *fatigued* with the contemplation of human suffering through the wild waste of centuries added to centuries of misery and desolation. *Their humanity is at their horizon,*—and, like the horizon, it always flies before them."[2]

But the earth, of course, belongs to the living. And this almost obsessive desire to shelter, which extends to the present and future as well as the past, especially focuses on continuities in which the interplay of all three is sensed dynamically. Those only, said Coleridge, gave the true "philosophical imagination" who can "interpret and understand the symbol that the wings of the air-sylph are forming within the skin of the caterpillar." The vision of process that increasingly absorbed Burke is that suggested by Yeats, a century and a half later—

And haughtier-headed Burke, that proved the State a tree,
That this unconquerable labyrinth of birds, century after century,
Cast but dead leaves to mathematical equality.
["Blood and the Moon," ll. 22-24]

Yeats catches the situation exactly. For in Burke's ideal of unity through slow, organic growth is the capacious sense of variety—of the "unconquerable labyrinth" of actual life ("dead leaves" being all that can be garnered by the "mathematical" or systematic hunt for simple, clean-cut shape). And the essence of the image lies in the fact that the tree, grown so slowly ("century after century"), offers shelter simply through the labyrinthine interlacing of its boughs. "Unconquerable" in its rooted strength, it provides an infinitely varied protection for the "birds"—the innumerable flickers of vivid life—that are ourselves.

Notes

The selection from W.J. Bate comes from pp. 22-25 of his introduction to *Selected Writings of Edmund Burke*. New York: Random House—Modern Library, 1960.

1. Bate is quoting and paraphrasing from Macaulay's essay, *Warren Hastings.* See *The Essays of Thomas Babington Macaulay* (Whitehall edition, New York: Putnam, 1898), 5:315 ff.
2. *LNL* in Burke *Works* (Bohn) 5:142, appr. 79% into the work.

STEVEN BLAKEMORE

8

Burke and the Fall of Language:
The French Revolution as Linguistic Event

Readers of Burke are familiar with the sense of desperation and despair which emanates from his writing on the French Revolution, a revolution which he characterizes as a "total revolution," a "great revolution in all human affairs"—the most astonishing thing that has hitherto happened in the world."[1] Indeed, we are aware that the French Revolution threatens Burke's precarious eighteenth-century world, but Burke also sees his "world" threatened by a new linguistic revolution in which old words·are torn from their historical context and emptied of their historical meaning. These words are then "filled" with the "new" revolutionary meaning; in Burke's writings there is a correspondent connection between the new revolution in France and the new revolution in language. Suddenly the accumulated cultural treasures of the European world are ransacked along with the very language which had brought and held that world in "presence." In his *Preface to the Address of M. Brissot to his Constituents*, Burke specifically connects this revolution in language with the revolution in France, and in his *Appeal from the New to the Old Whigs* he links the new linguistic revolution with the revolution which has abolished the French monarchy and threatened the principles of the English Revolution of 1688. He contrasts the "danger" of the "new theoretic language" with the "form of sound words" the English Parliament "religiously adheres to"—the "principles upon which the English Revolution was justified."[2] Burke believed in a kind of Gresham's law of language in which "bad" meaning drove out "good" meaning, and he was preoccupied with the power of words to affect men's psychic and social lives. In *A Philosophical Enquiry*, he had discussed the power of words to move the "passions" and in his *Letter to Richard Burke, Esq.*,[3] he warned that "a very great part of the mischiefs that vex the world arises from words." Burke believed that words could create a linguistic world of illusion and fantasy, and he often alluded to the error of confusing word with thing, and language with reality.[4]

But in his thinking about the French Revolution his thinking about language became more dialectical. For instance, while he warns about the dangerous powers of the "new" language, he also insists that the traditional vocabulary of Europe, the semantic vocabulary shared by the European community despite the differences in respective "languages," profoundly expresses the permanent values and truths of European civilization. He contrasts this traditional vocabulary with the new cant and "gipsy jargon" of the Revolution.[5] Burke felt that the French Revolution violently fragmented the coherent linguistic community of Europe. Consequently, there was no shared language, there was no way to "talk" to the new government of France.[6] Two critics have crystallized this thematic and linguistic contrast between the two dialectic "languages" in Burke's writings. David Cameron has suggested that the image of polity and politics which emerges in Burke's writings is the traditional language man inherits from his ancestors in which linguistic change occurs only in a slow, accumulated, and circumscribed order.[7] In regard to the new revolutionary "language," Chris Reid has argued that the changing language of chemistry, especially in the works of Joseph Priestley, became for Burke a metaphor for the semantic revolution which was convulsing Europe:

> The chemical revolution of the late eighteenth century was matched by a revolution in its language. This is precisely the kind of pressure Burke felt it necessary to resist, fearing that language, like money, like chemical processes, could hopelessly proliferate, get out of control. Burke's dislike of political innovation has a parallel in his aversion to radical departures in the language.[8]

Burke's allusions to chemical and economical changes became a sustained metaphor for the radical semantic changes which he saw subverting the linguistic "order" of Europe.

In this context Burke's reflections are a logomachy; they are a battle of words and books in which documents of what Burke considers the ontological order of civilization, ranging from quotations from the Bible and other "classical" sources to extracts from various legal charters and laws, are thematically positioned against quotations from various modern pamphlets and books which Burke regards with apprehension and alarm. The result is a battle of "texts" in which Burke's own words and works are reflexively at war with oppositional texts (for instance, Price's sermon in the *Reflections*). In this new Battle of the Books there is a linguistic battle over "meaning" in which Burke represents the "ancients" in his defense of tradition and classical sources while the supporters of the Revolution represent the "moderns" in their celebration of the new revolutionary literature issuing from England and France. Burke sees these modern books and pamphlets in terms of a radical, new language, a language of corruption and subversion. His controlling metaphor for this sinister new language is that of Babel, and Babel becomes the symbol and metaphor for all the insane chaos and confusion which threatens to darken and destroy the established "written" monuments of civilization. Burke considers the propagation of this new babel as an assault on the very fabric and structure of civilization. This is to say that he sees civilization ordered by the language which expresses and supports it, but he also sees how language can be used to assault civilization while altering the perceived meaning and "facts" of human reality. In short, Burke sees the French Revolution as a radical linguistic event; he sees it as a new Babel, as a new Fall of language, and he presents a theory of language which explains both the old world and the Revolution which causes it to fall.[9]

I

In the *Reflections* the "language" of the English and French revolutions is Burke's immediate concern. Burke is concerned with distinguishing the English Revolution of 1688 from the French Revolution of 1789, both of which were being confounded by certain political parties in England. Burke felt that if the French Revolution could be justified by comparing it favorably with the English Revolution, then the very legitimacy, the very principles of the English Revolution could be called into question. To Burke the principles of the English Revolution were sacredly spelled out in a series of unalterable documents, ranging from the Magna Charta to the *ratio scripta* of English legal tradition. Burke, therefore, suggests that the English Revolution was "natural," that it embodied the organic rhythms of English history, that its fundamental principles had been incarnated and written into various documents, documents which constitute a mystical and corporate contract of the English people. He meticulously traces the fundamental principles from the Magna Charta to the *Declaration of Right,* all of which he suggests are organic expressions of the English constitution. There was and is, of course, no English constitution in the sense of the written Constitution of the United States. The English constitution consists of a series of historical documents and legal precedents, but Burke often refers to it as if it were a single, coherent document because he sees and feels a whole tradition of language, a language which expresses the coherent order of the English world he wishes to defend.

In this regard, J. G. A. Pocock has shown that Burke was defending the idea of the "Ancient Constitution": the idea that "the laws and liberties of England are rooted in the Magna Charta, and that the Charta of 1215 [is rooted] in a body of law very much more ancient than itself."[10] This idea was a "myth" (in its positive sense) which celebrated the Ancient Constitution as the formalization of laws and liberties which had existed in an "oral" and hence "unwritten" past, subsequently reaffirmed by the custom and experience of each generation. The creation of this "myth" was the result of insular seventeenth-century common-law thought, especially as it was shaped by lawyers ignorant of European contributions to English law.[11] In the seventeenth century the "Ancient Constitution" became a political ideology which envisioned English laws and liberties descending in an unbroken line, uncorrupted by foreign influences. It was inevitable that comparative studies of European law would discredit a myth which appealed to the authority of tradition, but was antihistorical. However, by 1790 the myth had been reaffirmed in a series of documents which allowed Burke to locate its presence in a vocabulary which had its roots in seventeenth-century thought. If Burke's understanding of tradition and history is grounded in seventeenth-century legal semantics, then this would, in part, explain why Burke and his adversaries could both claim that the other was speaking an "unintelligible" language. Burke confronted a revolutionary world ignorant and hostile to his semantic foundations.[12]

In the *Reflections* Burke insists that his English adversires have fallen from the language of the Ancient Constituion, through which Burke sees the past and present world. Moreover, Burke sees history and tradition embodied in and passed through the "traditionary language" of the Constitution, and he locates the real meaning of England in the language of its documents. In his discussion of the *Declaration of Right,* he stresses its "traditionary language" and traces "as from a rubric the language of the preceding acts of Elizabeth and James…the orderly Succession [on] which the 'unity, peace, and tranquility of this nation doth, under God, wholly depend.'"[13] Burke locates this orderly process of circumscribed change *in* the "traditionary language" which crystallizes and orders the English polity.

Alluding to Jeremiah 31:33, he declares that the clarity of this language "...engraved in our ordinances, and in our hearts, the words and spirit of that immortal law."[14] As Burke reviews what to him is the natural order, the natural succession of English principles expressed in various historical documents, he envisions a coherent and consistent order of English history, incarnated and expressed in the language of these documents. Burke attempts to repossess English history through these legal documents; he attempts to repossess the palpable presence of the English mind which he sees through a series of inviolable "contracts" between the past, present, and future; between the dead, the living, and the unborn.

Although there had been a sustained attack on the idea of written law by seventeenth-century lawyers in their defense of a *jus non scriptum* which existed "time out of mind,"[15] Burke could, by 1790, celebrate the Ancient Constitution in terms of its written language as well as a *jus non scriptum* existing in a prewritten past. Burke would not see any contradiction as the reaffirming documents of the Constitution continually echo and articulate the oral past. The significant difference between seventeenth-century defenders of the Ancient Constitution and Burke resides in Burke's great insight that history, tradition, and reality are essentially linguistic and that the recovery of their presence resides in the recovery of their meaning through the inherited documents of the "written past" recreated and reaffirmed in present and future documents. From this follows his effort to crystallize and conserve the "real" authority and meaning of words.[16]

Burke insists that these documents compose a concrete link with the real and, hence, lived experience of the English people. He contrasts these "human" documents with various proclamations and statements issued by the French assembly, proclamations which have no inherent link with the historical and lived experience of the French people. In this sense, Burke's *Reflections*, like other eighteenth-century works such as *The Dunciad* and *Gulliver's Travels*, is a sustained attack against the abstractions of language; it is an attack against a language which no longer expresses human reality. Burke is concerned with the radical split between word and thing, a split in which language no longer brings the real world into presence. Burke sees the new, written "world" as a falsification of man's experience in time, a falsification which constitutes a kind of radical antihistory. But even as he sees a semantic split between the new written word and the thing it expresses, Burke is conscious of the power of the written word, the power of human language to change and affect human lives. For instance, the French revolutionaries dismiss ecclesiastics and "fictitious persions," as abstract creatures of the state who may be concretely robbed and destroyed, and this culminates in the "intolerance of the tongue and pen" which strikes at "property, liberty, and life."[17] Here language is used to reduce concrete people to "nonpersons" by a bogus linguistic fiction which insists that these people are only linguistic abstractions—fictitious creations of the old European language. In his *Appeal from the New to the Old Whigs,* Burke specifically rejects the new linguistic fictions of revolutionaries who speak a "jargon" that is "unintelligible," and he vehemently denies that they can rob people of their land and money by merely proclaiming that it is theirs.[18]

Burke also notes that the removal of men's liberty and property is connnected to the removal of their "real" names. Thus the "old aristocratic landlords" are unrecognizably "displumed, degraded, and metamorphosed," and the sign of their transmogrification is the onomastic robbery of their names and hence their identities:

> ...we no longer know them. They are stangers to us. They do not even go by the names of our ancient lords. Physically they may be the same men; though we are not quite sure of that, on your new philosophic doctrine of personal identity.[19]

In addition, just as Burke no longer recognizes the old aristocratic landlords, so he no longer recognizes old familiar words suddenly changed by subversive meanings acquired from "new dictionaries." Later, in the first letter on a *Regicide Peace*, Burke exclaims:

> God forbid, that if you were expelled from your house by ruffians and assassins, that I should call the material walls, doors and windows of [—], the ancient and honorable family of [—]. Am I to transfer to the intruders, who, not content to turn you out naked to the world, would rob you of your very name, all the esteem and respect I owe to you?[20]

Burke sees that the power of the human name also gives material walls, doors, and windows their corresponding "identity," and he refuses to countenance a corresponding onomastic robbery which would reduce the concrete person to an abstract blank—the violence of the dash empties and crosses out the name which brings the house and the person into presence. It denies the frustrated genitive its identity. There is a thematic parallel between the expropriation of property and the absence of the name. Burke repeatedly sees the Revolution as a new form of linguistic terror; he sees the language which embodies it as a radical new violence which tears man from his word and world.

In fact, the murderous powers of the new language become a kind of linguistic alchemy, a Black Mass where the "ink" of language is turned into blood, where the spilling of ink on pamphlets and proclamations causes real blood to be spilled and shed. For instance, Burke notes that the victims of the Revolution were "delivered over to lawyers; who wrote in their blood the statutes of the land, as harshly, and in the same kind of ink, as they and their teachers had written the rights of man."[21]   Likewise, the revolutionaries (with "malice" in "their tongues and hearts") tore the "reputation of the clergy to pieces by their infuriated declamations and invectives, before they lacerated their bodies by their massacres."[22]

This connection between linguistic and revolutionary violence is emphasized again in the process of leveling "all conditions of men" and fragmenting the inherited social order with a plan which would abolish all "hereditary name and office."[23]   The attacks on the social fabric of the nation are connected to attacks on the social language of the nation, and Burke suggests that when the inherited language of society is altered the order and "meaning" of that society is also altered. He implies that the old names and titles express the social and psychic identities of concrete men. Indeed, he implies that the old names and words are ontologically connected to the persons, places, and things which they bring into presence. Therefore, for Burke, the attempt to abolish and erase human names and peoples, the attempt to write away or erase kings, queens, and states is the result of a subversive linguistic ideology. To Burke the revolutionaries' attitude toward language is expressed in their attitude toward concrete societies and peoples. Their belief that human language is arbitrary and transient is reflected in their belief that kings, queens, societies, and laws are arbitrary and transient. Thus their effort to destroy old meanings and old societies by creating new meanings and new societies involved a language theory masking an ideology which justified radical change or any change at all. In the *Reflections* Burke underscores this when he quotes a leading member of the French assembly:

Tous les établissemens en France couronnent le malheur du peuple: pour le rendre heureux il faut le rénouveler; changer ses idées; changer ses loix; changer ses mœurs; ...changer les hommes; changer les choses; changer les mots...tout détruire; oiu, tout détruire; puisque tout est à recréer.

[All the establishments in France crown the unhappiness of the people: to make them happy they must be renewed, their ideas, their laws, their customs must be changed; ...men changed, things changed, words changed...destroy everything; yes, destroy everything; then everything is to be recreated.][24]

Burke deconstructs the ideology behind the revolutionaries' language theory, but he is too close to his own precarious languaged world to see that this theory presupposes the eventual destruction of the new society and language; it makes the French Revolution simply another transient event in the flux of time. He does, however, glimpse how the writers of revolutionary history are blind to their own social and linguistic presuppositions, and that the effort to abolish names, titles, and kings necessarily requires the rewriting of history in the "name" of a new linguistic ideology.

II

This connection between people and names leads to one of Burke's more provocative thematic equations—the equation of regicide with logocide. In the *Reflections* Burke's famous lament for the death of chivalry is as much about the degradation and death of the old language as it is about the degradation and death of kings and queens. When the "decent drapery of life" (the language and ideas of chivalry) is "rudely torn off," a king is reduced to "but a man; a queen is but a woman; a woman is but an animal, and an animal not of the highest order."[25] Burke connects the degrading physical reduction to the corresponding semantic reduction of kings and queens. This reduction is traced to a linguistic violence which tears the palpable idea of kings and queens from the hearts and minds of men, tearing them from a cultural and connotative space, the linguistic "wardrobe" which had covered and surrounded them. This violent removal of the "wardrobe of...moral imagination" is a second Fall in which man is also left exposed, like Adam and Eve, with no "covering" for the "defects of our naked shivering nature."[26] Burke's subsequent lament that "all homage paid to the [female] sex in general is forgotten" then conjures up the "plight" of the French queen in terms of the physical and linguistic violation which he has just suggested: the reader remembers his description of Marie Antoinette fleeing *en déshabillé* from her frenzied pursuers.[27] The suggested "stripping" of the queen is associated with the stripping of language, the stripping of the connotative wardrobe with which she was properly draped in the hearts and minds of the people The linguistic violence which reduces the queen to an animal is associated with the potential sexual violation which Burke imagines the queen to have suffered.[28]   To Burke this semantic reduction looms as a monstrous affront—a linguistic *lèse majesté* which exposes the queen to the lewd eyes of the new masses, correspondently stripped of any "decent drapery."

Moreover, Burke connects the murder of kings and queens to a perverted vocabulary which glosses over "regicide...parricide...and sacrilege" as "fictions of supersition...The murder of a king, or a queen, or a bishop, or a father, are only common homicide."[29] When he refers to "the French King, or king of the French," he sarcastically adds "or by whatever name he is known in the new vocabulary of your constitution."[30] In *A Letter to a Member of the National Assembly* the linkage between regicide and logocide becomes even clearer. Burke predicts that the revolutionaries will look for any pretext to "throw off the very name of a king," as they now use it solely to "catch those Frenchmen to whom the name of king is still venerable."[31] When these sentiments are "expiring," they will "not trouble themselves with excuses for extinguishing the name, as they have the thing"; when the connotations of the name expire in the minds of men, the king will be killed. As the imprisoned king has already been reduced to a "thing," the revolutionaries use the name "as a sort of navel-string to nourish their unnatural offspring from the bowels of royalty itself." The allusion to *Paradise Lost* connects the revolutionaries with Satan, Sin, and Death, and as the king's name is suggestively eaten in a grotesque inversion of the Eucharist, the "word" is devoured by their "unnatural" children (read their "incestuous" followers). The anticipated murder of the king means that "his name will no longer be necessary to their designs." In *Appeal from the New to the Old Whigs*, the culmination of this method of killing the king through his name is traced by Burke to the two contending revolutionary parties: "the one contending to preserve for awhile his name and his person, the more easily to destroy the royal authority—the other clamoring to cut off the name, the person, and the monarchy together, by one sacrilegious execution."[32]

In his war against a logocide peace, Burke believed that to tamper with language was to tamper with all human endeavor. He insisted that language which is fragmented from the facts of human existence, language which is used to artificially rewrite human nature and reality, inevitably leads with a kind of insane logic to assassinations and death by fiat. In analyzing the peculiar human mentality which dislocates language from its human context,

Burke also found its correspondent expression in the economic destruction of France, in which reams of worthless *assignats* were issued by a bankrupt government.

In fact, the economical bankruptcy of France is a microcosm of the correspondent moral, spiritual, and intellectual bankruptcy that Burke sees. He focuses on these connections by focusing on the language of *assignats* which France's new economists speak, "as no other language would be understood."[33] If the old *assignats* are depreciated, these economists merely issue more of the same, like the doctor in Molière's *Le Malade Imaginaire*:

> *Mais si maladia, opiniatria, non vult se garire, quid illi facere?*
> *assignare—postea assignare; ensuita assignare.* The word is a
> trifle altered. The Latin of your present doctors may be better than
> that of your old comedy; their wisdom, and the variety of their
> resources, are the same.

In Molière's satire of pompous doctors and pompous Latin, the doctors are examining a medical candidate. They ask him what he would do to the patient if the "stubborn sickness will not be cured?" The unqualified candidate answers as he does every question, "Give him a clyster, then bleed, then purge."[34] Burke changes the "word" to the "remedy" of the new quackery—issue more *assignats*. The allusion to Molière's play connects medical quackery with economical quackery, and it provides a moral context in which the economic placebo is connected to the pointless degradation of gratuitous enemas and purgings.

Moreover, I suggest that the allusion to the Latin in the old comedy is an insider's joke. It depends on an audience who would recognize the allusion and understand the Latin—thus Burke's ironic reference to the "better" Latin of the new "doctors" actually exposes them as bogus doctors who would neither understand the Latin nor the allusion, albeit their "wisdom" is the same. Burke correctly identified the French Revolution as a bourgeois revolution, a revolution, as he saw it, of parvenus who lacked the culture and language of the past. In the past Latin had been used to separate people linguistically. For example, Walter Ong[35] has shown that Latin (A.D. 500-700) briefly became a "sex-linked language, a kind of badge of masculine identity," which was used to exclude women from the "difficult" linguistic terrain of the masculine world. I am similarly suggesting that Latin and its association with "classical" literature was used by Burke and his ideological supporters to separate the "gentlemen" from the new middle class.[36] Burke, of course, used Latin throughout his life; it was the natural linguistic environment in which he moved and lived.   But with the threatening revolution of the new middle class, Latin became a class-linked language which set off and separated the "gentlemen" from the parvenus. Burke was writing for an audience which shared his education and his antirevolutionary values, so when he ironically alludes to the nonexistent Latin of the bourgeois "doctors," he skewers them with the literature and language of the past, writing in a language (reversing his complaint in the *Reflections*) which they cannot understand or "enter."   Latin becomes a class weapon, it becomes an insider's joke and passport because only the insider can enter into the meaning of the language and the allusions. This is to suggest that as Burke sees all order and distinctions arbitrarily abolished or removed by the revolutionary middle class, he reestablishes linguistic and hence social boundaries through the language and allusions of his classical sources. Consciously or unconsciously, he attempts to reestablish, at least in his linguistic "world" that sense of circumscribed order which he sees either threatened or destroyed in the external world.

III

Burke's world, however, is threatened on two linguistic fronts. Besides the parvenus and the mediocre writers of England and France, Burke traces the "revolution in sentiments, manners, and moral opinions" to the writings of established men of literature.[37] He notes that the Revolution was assisted and defended by them.   In fact, Burke traces the roots of the French Revolution to the subversive seeds planted in the French mind by prominent writers. Suddenly those who had traditionally sustained and defended the organic order of civilization are the source of its corruption and subversion, in Burke's version of the betrayal of the intellectuals. It is the power of this new class of intellectuals, it is the power of their words that Burke fears. Specifically, it is the convincing but corrupting power of their words which he fears will subvert both the Christian religion and the legal forms of civil government, erasing all distinctions and "rewriting" the majestic communal contracts which have traditionally given man his expressed sense of place. More precisely, it is old words with new meanings which threaten Burke's world. What Burke documents is the transvaluation of specific words which are torn from their historical context and then emptied of their accumulated cultural meaning by a linguistic violence which then stamps these words with the revolutionary signet of its artificially imposed meaning. Thus, such words as *nature, liberty, freedom, property; the People, natural law,* and *natural rights* were "changed" in a semantic revolution which coincided with the revolution which was convulsing Europe.

Burkean scholarship has elucidated Burke's own understanding of these words.[38] With notable exceptions there is a general consensus that Burke was reacting against the semantic pillage of rich, traditional words which were stripped and then filled with new antithetical meanings. Various critics maintain that this revolution in meaning actually started with Hobbes and then Locke; the traditional vocabulary of "natural law," for instance, was still used but emptied of its old meaning. Consequently, there was a semantic shift from the traditional emphasis on man's "duty" to man's "rights." This semantic shift radically altered the "meaning" of the European world. In this context it is crucial to observe that Burke's lament for the *ancien régime* is a lament, among other things, for the fall of a coherent European linguistic community once united in its celebration of what words and world meant. Burke does not fear French or English words per se, but he is alarmed about the new pseudomeanings which separate man from his history, his society, and his self. He fears the subversive semantics of words which distort and hide the "real" semantic relationship between man and the world which is created and sustained through his language.

For even when Burke does not refer specifically to the French Revolution, the corrupt state of language corresponds to the corruptness of that time. For instance, in his *Letter to Richard Burke, Esq.* he associates his son's efforts in behalf of the "oppressed people" of Ireland with his own on behalf of the oppressed people of France.[39] He notes that the old word *ascendancy,* meaning "an influence obtained over the mind of some other person by love and reverence, or by superior management and dexterity," has been perverted into a new meaning—'*honestum nomen imponitur vitio.*'" [40] An honest name is placed over vice; the old word is used to gloss over the vicious new meaning. "New ascendancy is the old mastership... In plain old English it signifies *pride* and *dominion* on...one part...and on the other *subserviency* and *contempt*—and it signifies nothing else." This semantic transformation leads to his warning about the "untuning" of old words:

> The poor word *ascendancy,* so soft and melodious in its sound, so lenitive and emollient in its first usage, is now employed to cover to the world the most rigid, and perhaps not the most wise, of all plans of policy.... The old words are as fit to be set to music as the new; but use has long since affixed to them their true signification, and

they sound as the other will, harshly and odiously to the moral and intelligent ears of mankind.

The allusion to the music of the spheres suggests that words once set in an orderly orbit now clash with discordant sounds, and as they fall out of their semantic orbit the "sound" sense of the old words clashes with the new imposed sense, violating and breaking the semantic harmony of the linguistic universe. Likewise, Burke observes that the word *protestant* has ceased to have an essentially religious meaning. As it is unnaturally yoked to the new meaning of *ascendancy* and the "policy which is engrafted on it, the name protestant becomes nothing more or better than the name of a persecuting faction."[41] Indeed, this word is "the charm that locks up in the dungeon of servitude three millions of your people." It is a "spell of potency," an "abracadabra that is hung about the necks of the unhappy, not to heal, but to communicate disease." Burke suggests that to tamper with the established meaning of words is to simultaneously tamper with the social and psychic meaning of society, unleashing oppressive new powers in *old* forms: the word *protestant* is changed into its semantic opposite; it becomes a new kind of persecuting superstition, a new kind of contagious disease. Burke's own language evokes the semantic and hence, in his terms, the moral corruption of the word's meaning, associating it with a new kind of old witchcraft, supersitition, and black magic—a new dungeon of meaning which locks up an already enslaved people, wounding and contaminating them with the authority of its dark power. To Burke a radical breach of language which is diseased and contaminated reflects a society which is diseased and contaminated. In this sense, the new semantic disease he saw contaminating the world was also a semantic Black Mass—an inversion of all established meaning, the decarnation of word and world.[42]

Burke's war against this new semantic disease, his war against a logocide peace, was an effort to prevent a perversion of meaning which would keep man from a "true" understanding of his "real" history, society, and self. His lament for the passing of chivalry, for the fall of kings and queens is simultaneously a lament for the fall of language; for the fall of a linguistic community and the semantic vocabulary which had ordered and sustained it. The new words blowing through England and France suddenly threaten all that Burke holds dear: tradition, place, property, and religion; in short, the civil and transcendent order of eighteenth-century man. But Burke simultaneously tries to repossess and see, again, his world through language, especially the written language of the traditional and classical works of religion, government, and literature—all of which give him a palpable sense of human time which is immediate, concrete, and meaningful. At several points we have the strong suggestion that Burke sees this body of literature as part of that mystical contract which binds all generations (past, present, and future) in a communal understanding of each person's place in that "civilization." Concurrently, there are intimations that any tampering with these "contracts" is tantamount to violating the Great Chain of Being. While reading Burke one has the accumulated sense that all of his quotations from the Bible, from tracts of government, and literature are correspondent links in a Great Chain of Words which are meant to remind eighteenth-century man of his history and place within the timeless space of his "tradition."[43] These documents form a semantic chain, and as Burke moves the reader back into "history" through the language of the documents, each document exists as a link which establishes and expresses man's place in his "tradition." The reader is then taken from the past to the present through an inherited language Burke believes is consistent and unchanging. His analysis of these documents provides a linguistic perspective in which past, present, and future are enfolded into a common language which expresses the cosmic ordering of the eighteenth-century world. In a profound sense these words, for Burke, reflect and mime the cosmic ordering of the Logos.

Conversely, the language of these documents threatens a revolutionary like Paine, and this contrast allows us to compare the dialectical language theories which emerge as opposing linguistic ideologies in Burke's and Paine's writings. In this context, Ronald Paulson has noted how Paine's attack on Burke, in *The Rights of Man*, is significantly in terms of "the old topos of life versus (and being constricted by) the written or printed word of the past, with its power of binding and controlling posterity to the end of time....The past are the 'dead,' embodied in 'musty records and mouldy parchments' and now in Burke's writings and in his sources."[44] Likewise, Chris Reid observes that "through Priestley, Thomas Paine's arguments against Burke's notion of an 'hereditary wisdom' are voiced in terms of a theory of language." In his twelfth lecture on the *Theory of Language* (1762), "Priestley argues that *authority* in language cannot simply be invested in an idea of traditional practice: 'In modern and living language, it is absurd to pretend to set up the compositions of any person...as the standard of writing....With respect to customs, laws, and everything that is changeable, the body of a people...will certainly assert their liberty in making what innovations they judge to be expedient and useful.'" As Reid notes: "Though written almost thirty years before the Revolution, it is easy...to see how such a linguistic theory might relate to the political struggle; for Priestley poses the problem of the development of a language in...political terms, in terms of 'liberty' and 'innovation' (whereas the linguistic formulations of a late-Augustan such as Johnson are generally made in terms of authority, prescription and constraint)."[45] Paine thus recognizes the conservative language theory which emerges in all of Burke's citations from historical "sources," and Paine's own attacks on these written documents also express a theory of language, a linguistic ideology which stresses the transient and mutable nature of kings, states, and words. This is to suggest that as Burke sees the Revolution as a radical event of language, the revolutionaries also see it as a radical break from the traditional "language" of the European world: a language which confines man in an artificial linguistic dungeon. Thus both supporters and opponents of the Revolution have an implied theory of language, a covert language ideology which colors all their writing and "talk" about tradition and change.

In Burke's writings, then, there is a dialectical war of words in which the established and traditional literature of Burke's "world" confronts the new and disturbing literature of English hacks and French *philosophes*. This war of words turns into a battle of books and pamphlets, a battle between two contending kingdoms of force, in which the texts are ostensibly stacked as Burke, in the text and footnotes, thematically quotes and exposes the absurdity and madness of oppositional "texts" which he contrasts to the lucidity and integrity of ancient and modern texts: texts in which words are supposedly tied to the ontological "facts" of human reality. Indeed, Burke delights in exposing a kind of Cartesian split between the words and "facts" of his enemies, conjuring up a chaotic world of falsification and fantasy in which France is envisioned as a kind of library for the insane. This new insanity is part of the new and pernicious power of the written word to pervert human nature: "These writings and sermons have filled the populace with a black and savage atrocity of mind, which supersedes in them the common feelings of nature, as well as all sentiments of morality and religion."[46]

IV

The central metaphor Burke uses for this new corrupting power of language is Babel.[47] In the *Reflections*, for instance, Babel is the metaphor and symbol for all that Burke feels is radically wrong with a world in which language deforms and distorts the essential facts of human reality. In the beginning, Burke contrasts the English people, in contact with the reality of their "law" and figuratively speaking a kind of prelapsarian language, with the fallen French and English men who speak the new language of Babel: "…we, on our parts, have learned to speak only the primitive language of the law, and not the confused jargon of their Babylonian pulpits."[48] Likewise, the French constitution is contrasted to the English constitution; the former is written in a "new vocabulary." Throughout the *Reflections* Burke suggests that the French Revolution radically altered the delicate correspondence between language and reality, and he continues to insist that, even in England, the effects of this new language are manifest. There was still, however, the traditional, prelapsarian language of the British constitution which Burke contrasts, again, with the fallen language of Dr. Price's sermons "and the after-dinner toasts of the revolution society."[49] In the British constitution, Burke tells us, "you will find other ideas and another language." Burke seriously maintains, both figuratively and literally, that the language of the Revolution is part of a new Fall, part of a new fallen world which he describes as an "antagonistic world of madness, discord, vice, confusion, and unavailing sorrow."[50] In contrast, those who have kept the original purity of their laws, their contracts, and their language remain in the "world of reason, and order, and peace, and virtue, and fruitful penitence."

But the new Fall is a fall into a world of madness where men "are obliged to adopt all the crude and desperate measures suggested by clubs composed of a monstrous medley of all conditions, tongues, and nations."[51] Babel remains the controlling metaphor for all this chaos and confusion. Indeed, as Burke sees the lights going out all over Europe, the chaos and confusion, the allusions to babel, jargon, and cant; the references to new dictionaries and new meanings become an objective correlative for the new Babel, the new linguistic disorder which Burke finds in the fallen European world. But despite his dark pessimism there is a corresponding countermessage in which he reaffirms the power of language to make sense of the world—a world in which the English people still recognize the deceptive language of the new Babel. Thus, they are "distinguishing"; they recognize the language of lies and babel when they hear it: "They hear these men speak broad. Their tongue betrays them. Their language is in the *patois* of fraud; in the cant and gibberish of hypocrisy."[52] These fallen Englishmen "speak broad" in two senses: their words miss the mark, and Burke's pun suggests that they are appropriately addressed to a revolutionary audience "abroad." In addition, his clever use of the word *patois* suggestively makes the speakers of this gibberish the speakers of an alien dialect (again stressing the corrupting

"French" influence) and insinuates the provincial narrowness, the illiteracy—in short, the *lowness* of these new speakers of babel.

Burke's renunciation and exorcism of this new Babel is thematically announced in the language of the old world Latin. Thus he refuses to listen to the new babel; in his declining age, he refuses "to squall in their new accents, or to stammer, in my second cradle, the elemental sounds of their barbarous metaphysics. *Si isti mihi largiantur ut repueriscam, et in eorum cunis vagiam, valde recusem!"*[53] The quotation is from Cicero's essay on old age (*Cato Maior De Senectute* 23.83), and it illustrates how Burke uses the established language of the old world to banish his opponents. The context is appropriate because the speaker is supposedly Cato the Elder, the conservative censor who expressed the traditional values of the Roman Republic. Thus, Burke metaphorically becomes Cato of England, the eloquent defender of traditional values and language. In Cicero's version, which Burke has modified, Cato exclaims: "Nay, if some god should give me leave to return to infancy from my old age, to weep once more in my cradle, I should vehemently protest."[54] Burke changes "some god" to the (in this context) pejorative pronoun *isti* (similar to "those guys") and "my cradle" to "their cradle": "But if those guys should give me leave to return to infancy from my old age, to weep once more in their cradle, I should vehemently protest." The two changes emphasize the encroaching presumption which is checked by the language and the authority of Burke's classical source. The recasting of his vigorous refusal into Cicero's Latin is strongly insistent, as Burke uses the Latin line to exorcise the imagined squall of the new babel—eloquently underscoring his defiance in the old language of classical world order.

V

In retrospect, we can see that Burke's reflections on language are important for many reasons, not the least being that Burke is one of the first of our historical "contemporaries" to consciously recognize that language alters and shapes our perception of reality. He was among the first to see how language makes or deconstructs our "world," how it shapes our perception of what our world "is," and he realized that any perspective or "talk" about great human interests is bounded by the very language which expresses it. His hostility to the French Revolution can be traced, in part, to his feeling that the new semantic vocabulary dealing with the rights of man was, in effect, a new and dangerous language which tore man from his history and his heritage, both of which were linguistic in nature. He cannily saw how history is often not what happened but what is written; he saw how written history is part of the linguistic horizon of the writer, and he offered what can be characterized as one of the first modern critiques of totalitarian language. He documented the emergence of Ideology as a national force which would chain history and language to its procrustean bed. The additional relevance of totalitarian distortions of language in the twentieth century provides another context for Burke's concerns, as he decried the radical transvaluation of language by which "the most meaningful of words (*the people, reason, liberty, philosophy, humanity,* etc.) are debased into omnibus abstractions and used to justify crimes."[55] Burke revealed how language is used to hide and distort "reality," he showed how words are perverted into their semantic opposites, how "the whole compass of language is tried to find synonymes and circumlocutions for massacre and murder. Things are never called by their common names. Massacre is sometimes *agitation*, sometimes *effervescence*, sometimes *excess*; sometimes too continued an exercise of *revolutionary power*."[56] He recognized that language shapes our perception of world and reality, and he anticipated the beginning of a nightmare world of language in which words, as he saw them, deracinated from certain existential and moral facts would become an awesome force of distortion and oppression.

As he writes about the death of words and kings, as he laments the linguistic and physical assaults on families, societies, and Christianity, Burke depicts the French Revolution as a second Fall, a second Babel, a second Golgotha in which the cosmic ordering of the Logos, the sanctity and authority of the Word is also assaulted. In the dark interstices of Burke's texts, the new murder of language, the new experiment in logocide, swells into a vicious and presumptuous parody of the old Logocide. Burke was convinced that the health and sanity of a society are intimately intertwined with its language, and he used his own magnificent words to battle against homicide, regicide, and logocide, to war against the murder of men, kings, fathers, and "mother" tongues. In his references to the old meanings of words, he focuses on their new meanings and insists that the violent removal of their historical contexts and circumstances "robs" them of their special meaning and life: the very thing that was happening to people in France was happening to language. We see now that his probing semantic analysis was a linguistic strategy to reestablish the context, the circumstances, the history, and the meaning of the old world. It was a linguistic effort to reestablish the semantic links between the old world and its language. For as Burke attempts to focus on the meaning of words and world, he attempts to recover that world through the language which made it flesh.

To read Burke, then, is to read about a battle, a logomachy of good and evil in which the real presence of the human world reflected through the Logos struggles against the dark chaos of the new pseudoword, or what Pope, at the end of *The Dunciad*, called the "uncreating word." In this battle, Burke dialectically sets off documents, books, and pamphlets in a war of words, a battle of books and languages in which the dominant biblical and classical quotations eventually establish a semantic space where Burke's world and vision are brought into presence. But it is the enduring presence of Burke's own language which semantically sustains this linguistic world of order and grace, banishing briefly the conflicting chaos and confusion of the antagonistic Revolutionary world. It is the majestic presence of Burke's language which brings this world into our presence and "presents" his reflections on the French Revolution as the last, great flowering statement of the old eighteenth century.

Notes

Steven Blakemore published "Burke and the Fall of Language" in
Eighteenth-Century Studies 17 (Spring 1984):284-307.
It also appears, in an updated form, as the final chapter of his book,
Burke and the Fall of Language. Hanover and London: University Press of New England, 1988.

1. In *Works* (LB-9) 5:79, appr. 75% into the fourth of the *Letters on a Regicide Peace*. See also *Remarks on the Policy of the Allies*, 4:104, appr. 50% into the work; and *Reflections* at 3:28, appr. 3% into the work.
2. *Appeal* in *Works* (LB-9) 3:375, appr. 34% into the work. Blakemore's reference to the *Preface to the Address of M. Brissot* comes from 4:217, the final sentences of that work.
3. *Works* (LB-9) 5:312, appr. 41% into the *Letter to Richard Burke, Esq.*
4. See, for instance, *Letter to a Member of the National Assembly*, in *Works* (LB-9) 3:321, appr. 79% into the work, and Gerald W. Chapman's comments in *Edmund Burke: The Practical Imagination* (Cambridge, MA: Harvard University Press, 1967), pp. 53-54.
5. *Works* (LB-9) 4:350, appr. 22% into the first of the *Letters on a Regicide Peace*.
6. *Works* (LB-9) 4:501, appr. 48% into the third of the *Letters on a Regicide Peace*.
7. David R. Cameron, *The Social Thought of Rousseau and Burke* (London: Weidenfeld and Nicolson, 1973), pp. 154-55.
8. Chris Reid, "Language and Practice in Burke's Political Writing," *Literature and History* 6 (1977), p. 211. As an example of Burke's linguistic conservatism, Reid quotes his remark in the *Philosophical Enquiry* about the word 'delight': "'I thought it better to take up a word already known...than to introduce a new one which would not perhaps incorporate with the language. I

should never have presumed the least alteration in our words, if the nature of the language…did not in a manner necessitate me to it. I shall make use of this liberty with all possible caution.' Cf. Burke's *Conciliation with the Colonies"* (Reid, p. 212).

9. This is not to suggest that Burke assigns priority to linguistic issues when discussing the French Revolution, but language is a major thematic preoccupation for him because he realizes that it is intimately bound with the very things the Revolution was attacking: institutions, tradition, history, and law.

10. J. G. A. Pocock, "Burke and the Ancient Constitution," in *Politics, Language and Time: Essays on Political Thought and History* (New York: Atheneum, 1971), p. 207. See also Pocock's *The Ancient Constitution and the Feudal Law* (Cambridge: Cambridge University Press, 1957), which I have also relied on.

11. David Cameron notes that "a political vocabulary of highly generalized concepts was very much in vogue on the Continent, while the idiom of common law was still embedded in the political structure and was still informing political thinking in England" (*The Social Thought of Rousseau and Burke*, p. 39).

12. Pocock has begun an exploration of these semantic foundations in his discussion of *property* and *inheritance* in "Burke and the Ancient Constitution," pp. 210-13. Later, he contends that the "concept of immemorial custom, founded on the interpretation of the common law" had been in "decay" since the end of the seventeenth century, although it still permeated the "political language" of the eighteenth century (see *The Ancient Constitution*, pp. 239 ff., and "Burke and the Ancient Constitution," pp. 229-30). This is undoubtedly true of Burke and his ideological supporters, but it needs to be established which, if any, of the Revolution's supporters, other than Paine, were familiar with this "political language." Burke's adversaries were tacitly aware that a philosophy of language is central to the *Reflections*, and this governs their response to Burke's own language. In this context it is instructive that Sir Henry Spelman, whose posthumous works contributed to the discrediting of the Ancient Constitution, anticipated Paine in viewing the old language as a dead language. Spelman saw the history of law, in the words of Pocock, "as a question of words no longer used and of meanings that words have now lost" (*The Ancient Constitution*, p. 94)

13. *Works* (LB-9) 3:37, apr. 6% into the *Reflections*.

14. *Reflections*, 3:38, appr. 6% into the work.

15. See Pocock, *The Ancient Constitution*, ch. 2.

16. Burke is the quintessential Whig when he is appealing to the authority of English documents. As Garry Wills reminds us, "Freedom, for whigs of the eighteenth century, always had a pedigree. It was a child of paper, a *chartered* liberty" *(Inventing America* [New York: Vintage], 1979), p. 38.

17. *Works* (LB-9) 3:130, 136, appr. 42% and 44%, respectively, into the *Reflections*.

18. *Works* (LB-9) 3:423, appr. 72% into the *Appeal*.

19. *Works* (LB-9) 3:257, appr. 90% into the *Reflections*.

20. *Works* (LB-9) 4:405, appr. 86% into the first Letter. The reference to a "new dictionary" comes at 3:222, appr. 76% into the *Reflections*.

21. *Appeal* in *Works* (LB-9) 3:431, appr. 79% into the work.

22. *Works* (LB-9) 4:435, appr. 50% into the second of the *Letters on a Regicide Peace*.

23. *Works* (LB-9) 4:13, appr. 50% into *Thoughts on French Affairs*.

24. *Works* (LB-9) 3:196, appr. 70% into the *Reflections*.

25. *Works* (LB-9) 3:99, appr. 30% into the *Reflections*.

26. *Works* (LB-9) 3:99, appr. 30% into the *Reflections*.

27. See *Works* (LB-9) 3:93, appr. 28% into the *Reflections*. [This is the famous "purple patch" for which Burke was criticized by his friend Philip Francis. —DR]

28. See Isaac Kramnick's psychobiography, *The Rage of Edmund Burke: Portrait of an Ambivalent Conservative* (New York: Basic Books, 1977), pp. 152-54, for a discussion of Burke's preoccupation with the "violation" of the queen.

29. *Works* (LB-9) 3:99, appr. 30% into the *Reflections*.

30. *Works* (LB-9) 3:105-106, appr. 32% into the *Reflections*.

31. *Works* (LB-9) 3:300-301. The next several quotations are from this location, appr. 33% into the *Letter to a Member of the National Assembly*.

32. *Works* (LB-9) 3:456, three paragraphs from the end of the *Appeal*.

33. *Works* (LB-9) 3:268, appr. 94% into the *Reflections*. The following quotation, where Burke comments on Molière, is from the same location.

34. *Le Malade Imaginaire*, Troisième Intermède, 2.9-15. (My translation—SB)

35. Walter J. Ong, *The Presence of the Word: Some Prolegomena for Cultural and Religious History* (New Haven: Yale University Press, 1967), p. 250. See also Ong's "Latin and the Social Fabric," in *The Barbarian Within* (New York: Macmillan, 1962), pp. 206-19, and "Latin Language Study as a Renaissance Puberty Rite," *Studies in Philology* 56 (1959): 103-24.

36. It never occurred to Burke whether or not the revolutionaries and their supporters were actually competently learned in Latin and the classics. Burke assumes they are not, just as he assumes they have middle- and lower-class origins. Cf. James T. Boulton on how Burke's "learned" language was made an issue by his opponents: *The Language of Politics in the Age of Wilkes and Burke* (London: Routledge and Kegan Paul, 1963), pp. 139 ff.

37. *Works* (LB-9) 3:102, appr. 31% into the *Reflections*.

38. For a discussion of what these specific words meant for Burke and the revolutionaries, see the following works, passim: Jeffrey Hart, "Burke and Radical Freedom," *Review of Politics* 29 (April 1967): 221-38; Burleigh Taylor Wilkins, *The Problem of Burke's Political Philosophy* (Oxford: Clarendon, 1967); Peter J. Stanlis, *Edmund Burke and the Natural Law* (Ann Arbor: University of Michigan Press, 1958); Gerald W. Chapman, *Edmund Burke: The Practical Imagination*; Boulton, *The Language of Politics*.

39. *Works* (LB-9) 5:304, near the opening.

40. *Works* (LB-9) 5:307, appr. 18% into the *Letter to Richard Burke*. The next two quotations ("New ascendancy..." and "The poor word...") are also from the *Letter* (5:308, 309), appr. 23% into it.

41. *Works* (LB-9) 5:309, appr. 27% into the *Letter to Richard Burke, Esq.* The next two sentences also quote from the *Letter* (5:312), appr. 40% into that work.

42. Cf. *Works* (LB-9) 4:97, appr. 36% into the *Policy of the Allies*, for "the contagion of the horrid practices, sentiments, and language of the Jacobins"; and 3:168, appr. 56% into the *Reflections*, for a discussion of how the revolutionaries use old words as pretexts to oppress while fondly imagining that new words and meanings can alter or change reality. As Burke points out, these distortions of meaning "speak nothing very new. The same thing has been said in all times and all languages. The language of tyranny has been invariable: the general good is inconsistent with my personal safety" (*Letter to Richard Burke*, 5:319, appr. 72% into that work). Thus, Burke seems to waver between seeing the revolutionary world in terms of a new semantic revolution or as a revolution which hypocritically disguises and dignifies old and pejorative meanings in the form of old, positive words. He sees, however, that the result is the same radical transformation of meaning.

43. For allusions or references to the Chain of Being, see *Reflections* at 3:66, 101, 103, 117, 253. [To Blakemore's list, I would add 3:53, the famous lines appr. 12% into the *Reflections* which begin: "Our political system is placed in a just correspondence and symmetry with the order of the world...." -DR] Donald Greene has suggested that the concept of the Chain of Being was used to rationalize the *theodicy* by which the "haves" could keep the "have nots" in

their "place" (see "Augustianism and Empiricism," *Eighteenth-Century Studies* 1 (Fall 1967), p. 64, and *The Age of Exuberance* (New York, Random House, 1970), pp. 114-16. In the *Reflections*, I suggest, the Chain of Being becomes a symbol of man's "place" crystallized in and through the traditional links of his written history (in its fullest sense) and the language which informs it.

44. Ronald Paulson, "Burke's Sublime and the Representation of Revolution," in *Culture and Politics: From Puritanism to the Enlightenment*, ed. Perez Zagorin (Berkeley and Los Angeles: University of California Press, 1980), p. 244. (Paine also takes Burke's criticism of the revolutionaries' "jargon" and cant and turns it against him: as Burke complains that the new babel is unfit for "rational ears," Paine correspondingly complains of Burke's "learned jargon" which he then translates for the common reader. See Boulton, *The Language of Politics*, p. 140.)

45. Reid, "Language and Practice in Burke's Political Writing," *Literature and History* 6 (1977), pp. 212-13.

46. *Works* (LB-9) 3:181, appr. 61% into the *Reflections*.

47. Babel was, by Burke's time, an established symbol of linguistic chaos and cant. Samuel Butler in *Hudibras*, for instance, accused the Presbyterians and Independents of trying to "outcant the Babylonian Labourers,/ at all their Dialects and Jabberers" (3.2.151-52). For an illuminating study of the idea of Babel, see George Steiner, *After Babel: Aspects of Language and Translation* (New York: Oxford University Press, 1975).

48. *Works* (LB-9) 3:48, appr. 11% into the *Reflections*. The reference to the "new vocabulary" in the next sentence comes from 3:105, appr. 32% into the *Reflections*.

49. *Works* (LB-9) 3:50, appr. 11% into the *Reflections*. The next sentence quotes the same page of the *Reflections*.

50. *Works* (LB-9) 3:121, appr. 38% into the *Reflections*. The next sentence quotes the same location in the *Reflections*.

51. *Works* (LB-9) 3:89, appr. 26% into the *Reflections*.

52. *Works* (LB-9) 3:128, appr. 41% into the *Reflections*.

53. *Works* (LB-9) 3:249, appr. 87% into the *Reflections*.

54. I follow William Falconer's translation in the Loeb Classical Library edition of *De Senectute* (New York, 1923), p. 95.

55. Chapman, *Edmund Burke: The Practical Imagination*, p. 223.

56. *Works* (LB-9) 4:208, appr. 60% into the *Preface to M. Brissot....*

CHRISTOPHER REID

9
The Politics of Taste

Your admiration of Shakespeare would be ill sorted indeed, if your Taste (to talk of nothing else) did not lead you to a perfect abhorrence of the French Revolution, and all its Works.

Burke to Edmond Malone, 5 April 1796

Until recently Burke's *Philosophical Enquiry into the Origin of Our Ideas of the Sublime and Beautiful* [1st ed., 1757] could be expected to receive at the most a bare mention in discussions of his political thought. It was seen as an exception among his writings, the sole product of his early and unfulfilled literary ambition. It was thought of as more relevant to the history of British aesthetics than to the development of Burke's own outlook. More recently, however, the *Philosophical Enquiry* has been identified as the primary source of ideas and attitudes which were to shape Burke's political thinking throughout his life. His aesthetics and politics, it is now often said, are intimately allied.[1] The new emphasis reflects a more general readiness to extend the range of meanings and applications available to politics. The boundaries of the "political" have been revised so as to take in areas of experience which lie well beyond the traditional political spheres of statecraft and public affairs. If authority were needed for this change, it is provided by Burke himself, in his response to the French Revolution. The extreme urgency of that response was prompted by his perception that more was at stake than an alteration in a system of government. In order to counter the threat of revolution, Burke touches on a wide range of feelings and attachments, drawing his readers' experience of a whole way of life into the arena of political struggle.

Such appeals were based upon Burke's understanding of the principles of human nature, principles which he had first laid down systematically in the *Philosophical Enquiry*. The aim of that work was not only to formulate aesthetic categories but also to put them on a "natural" basis, to trace back our ideas of the sublime and beautiful to their origins in the mechanisms of sensation, perception, and response.   The *Philosophical Enquiry* can therefore be related to the political works which followed it both at the general level of category and concept and at the level of Burke's own perception, apprehension, and presentation of particular political events. In a discussion of the first kind of relation Neal Wood has argued that "Burke's two basic aesthetic categories, the sublime and the beautiful, inform and shape several of his fundamental political ideas." He suggests that "these aesthetic categories are a unifying element of Burke's social and political outlook."[2]   Thus the pattern of authority I described in the preceding chapter finds a counterpart in Burke's aesthetics.[3]   In the well-tempered state the principles of justice and mercy will act in unison, but their modes of operation will remain quite distinct.   In the realm of aesthetics the *Philosophical Enquiry* presents a similar set of oppositions. Elements of aesthetic experience are classified in two categories, according to the ideas of the sublime and beautiful.   This division in aesthetics is not simply analogous to the one which governs social and political life. For the sublime and beautiful are, by virtue of their definition, based on the relationship between the individual and society.   The sublime, Burke tells us, is associated with those "passions which belong to SELF-PRESERVATION"; it is the expression in aesthetics of our fears for our own safety.   The beautiful, on the other hand, is associated with "the passions which belong to SOCIETY"; it is the expression of our sociality and sympathy.[4]

Most of the *Philosophical Enquiry* is devoted to the detailed illustration of the various physical and psychological sources of the sublime and beautiful—terror, obscurity, vastness, smoothness, delicacy, sweetness, and so on. These qualities, as we shall see, find a place in the language and imagery of Burke's political writing.   But even in the course of the *Philosophical Enquiry* itself Burke will occasionally afford them a political significance. Perhaps the most striking instance occurs in the section entitled "Power."[5] Admitting that he knows "of nothing sublime which is not some modification of power," Burke proceeds to examine power in both its natural and political manifestations. In the former, as found in the lion, the tiger, and the wolf, it is awe-inspiring and terrible. Likewise, "The power which arises from institution in kings and commanders, has the same connection with terror.   Sovereigns are frequently addressed with the title of *dread majesty*." A few years earlier William Hogarth had remarked in his own aesthetic treatise, *The Analysis of Beauty*, that "The robes of state are always made large and full, because they give a grandeur of appearance, suitable to the offices of the greatest distinction. The judge's robes have an awful dignity given them by the quantity of their contents...."[6] In the *Philosophical Enquiry* Burke systematises this occasional semiotics of power. The range of qualities he associates with the sublime—terror, astonishment, reverence, admiration, and awe—seems to anticipate the coercive style of authority he invokes in his counter-revolutionary tracts.

In this way the *Philosophical Enquiry*, projected as a treatise on the mechanisms of the sensibility, sometimes shifts its ground to take up moral, social, and political issues. In section X of the third part these issues are brought together in a disquisition on the nature of virtue. Burke decides that, in effect, the virtues are of two kinds. Those which belong to authority and the power to command are described as "sublime." Those which operate in personal life, and consort with the means of charity, compassion, and love, are defined as "beautiful." Although Burke's discussion of these virtues is organised on aesthetic principles, their relation to a legal and political structure of authority could hardly be more explicit:

> Those virtues which cause admiration, and are of the sublimer kind, produce terror rather than love. Such as fortitude, justice, wisdom, and the like. Never was any man amiable by force of these qualities. Those which engage our hearts, which impress us with a sense of loveliness, are the softer virtues; easiness of temper, compassion, kindness and liberality; though certainly those latter are of less immediate and momentous concern to society, and of less dignity. But it is for that reason that they are so amiable. The great virtues turn principally on dangers, punishments, and troubles, and are exercised rather in preventing the worst mischiefs, than in dispensing favours; and are therefore not lovely, though inferior in dignity. Those persons who creep into the hearts of most people, who are chosen as the companions of their softer hours, and their reliefs from care and anxiety, are never persons of shining qualities, nor strong virtues. It is rather the soft green of the soul on which we rest our eyes, that are fatigued with beholding more glaring objects.[7]

Here Burke not only affords his aesthetic categories a moral and social meaning, but also establishes a hierarchy among them in which the "sublime" virtues take precedence over the "beautiful." The latter, however, are by no means useless in social life. As Wood argues, the "beautiful" qualities (sympathy, affection, friendship, and the like) are the modes in which society, in most circumstances, is able to cohere. They appear to establish a series of "lateral" alliances, while the political relations of the sublime are essentially those of subordination.

In a well-ordered society these virtues will be combined, for, as Burke tells us in his political tracts, justice and mercy have the same interests. It is in the aesthetics of the *Philosophical Enquiry* that Burke seems to develop this pattern of authority for the first time. In the second edition of the work (1759) he was at pains to point out that the sublime and beautiful are categorically distinct, and related in most cases only by way of opposition:

> If the qualities of the sublime and beautiful are sometimes found united, does this prove, that they are the same, does it prove, that they are any way allied, does it prove even that they are not opposite and contradictory? Black and white may soften, may blend, but they are not therefore the same.[8]

The final part of this remark is important. It is true that the conjunction of the two categories may culminate in the destruction of the weaker one, but it may also lead to modification and restraint:

> There is something so over-ruling in whatever inspires us with awe, in all things which belong ever so remotely to terror, that nothing else can stand in their presence. There lie the qualities of beauty either dead and unoperative; or at most exerted to mollify the rigour and sternness of the terror, which is the natural concomitant of greatness.[9]

In general Burke's aesthetic categories are rigidly, even mechanistically applied. It is his aim in the *Philosophical Enquiry* to determine what he calls "the logic of Taste." The passage I have just quoted does not in itself contradict this, but Burke leaves himself a little room for manoeuvre. Although in natural objects (and presumably in works of art) he dislikes the combination of sublime and beautiful qualities, he at least allows for the possibility of interaction. In an abstract concept such as society or the state, as opposed to physical objects of the kinds discussed in the *Philosophical Enquiry*, the functions of the sublime and beautiful virtues may even be complementary. In periods of stability the beautiful may act "to mollify the rigour and sternness" of the magisterial sublime.   But in extreme circumstances, when the state is faced by war and revolution abroad and by the threat of subversion at home, it must be allowed to exercise its powers unqualified and undiminished.

In this respect Burke's counter-revolutionary tracts (indeed, his political writings in general) might be read as an attempt to work out the respective roles of the sublime and the beautiful in politics. It is not, I think, too much to claim that Burke perceives the French Revolution in aesthetic terms. When it is experienced in its magnitude and its terror as a sublime event, the only effective response on the part of its opponents must itself be a politics and rhetoric in the grand style. In the *Letters on a Regicide Peace*, to which I shall refer throughout this chapter, a foremost concern is the stress on the national sensibility caused by the war against a Jacobinised France. Terror, in the *Philosophical Enquiry,* had been the quintessentially sublime emotion, one which "robs the mind of all its powers of acting and reasoning."[10] Following the disasters which had dogged the campaign against France, Burke is anxious lest this fear should become the ruling passion in government and the nation at large:

> There is a courageous wisdom: there is also a false reptile prudence, the result not of caution but of fear. Under misfortunes it often happens that the nerves of the understanding are so relaxed, the pressing peril of the hour so completely confounds all the faculties, that no future danger can be properly provided for, can be justly estimated, can be so much as fully seen.[11]

Burke images this state of moral inertia as a paralysis of the organs of sensation. Such is the power and military might of the Revolution that "the eye of the mind is dazzled and vanquished," a remark which again seems to have a basis in the aesthetics of the *Philosophical Enquiry*. For in the section entitled "Light" (II.xiv) Burke observes that while brightness is generally less productive of the sublime than darkness is, "such a light as that of the sun, immediately exerted on the eye, as it overpowers the sense, is a very great idea."[12]

The French Revolution is one of those "glaring objects" which subdue the organs of sight, an event capable of exciting sublime sensations—fear, astonishment, and awe. But Burke does not wish us to respond to it as we would to an awe-inspiring work of art. The connection between the political and the aesthetic does not always run along a line of simple analogy. In the

Philosophical Enquiry he describes a group of emotions (terror, astonishment, awe, and so forth) associated with self-preservation and excited by the immediate prospect of pain. He also devises a category of aesthetic experience called the sublime which implies a distancing from the source of those emotions: "terror is a passion which always produces delight when it does not press too close."[13] As Paulson reminds us, it was not Burke's purpose in his counter-revolutionary writings to distance his readers from the revolutionary threat or to instil in them that sense of security upon which the true sublime depends. On the contrary, he mobilises a kind of rhetoric of terror in order to alert them to the perils of the situation.

Yet there are times, in his presentation of revolutionary events, when Burke falls back (perhaps without realising it) upon the effects of distancing he had described in the *Philosophical Enquiry*. Paulson may be thinking of this when he remarks that "Burke could come to terms with the Revolution by distancing it as a sublime experience, even while denying its sublimity and realizing that it might not keep its 'distance.'"[14] Burke is inclined to frame his response to the Revolution in dramatic terms.[15] It is when he presents the Revolution as tragedy, as he does in one of the best-known passages in the *Reflections*, that the aesthetic distancing of the sublime comes into its own:

> when kings are hurled from their thrones by the Supreme Director of this great drama, and become the objects of insult to the base, and of pity to the good, we behold such disasters in the moral, as we should behold a miracle in the physical order of things. We are alarmed into reflection; our minds (as it has long since been observed) are purified by terrour and pity; our weak unthinking pride is humbled, under the dispensations of a mysterious wisdom. Some tears might be drawn from me, if such a spectacle were exhibited on the stage. I should be truly ashamed of finding in myself that superficial, theatrick sense of painted distress, whilst I could exult over it in real life.[16]

Pity of this kind, genuine enough in itself, is unlikely to issue in immediate political action, since it confirms Burke and his reader in their role as spectators. The aesthetic model—tragedy—brings with it a sense of the inevitability of revolution, fused with a Christian acceptance of its place in a divine plan beyond human comprehension.

More often, however, Burke exposes us directly to the source of the terror and fuels those passions he considers most likely to quell it. He insists that the Revolution has declared war on the beautiful and social virtues. This is the symbolic significance of the celebrated portrait of Marie Antoinette in the *Reflections on the Revolution in France*. The desecration of the queen's person signals the end of an era in which the exercise of power had been tempered by a respect for the softer passions. Thus the Revolution is charged with precipitating the demise of

> all the pleasing illusions, which made power gentle, and obedience liberal, which harmonized the different shades of life, and which, by a bland assimilation, incorporated into politicks the sentiments which beautify and soften private society....[17]

Burke's task in the *Reflections* and other pamphlets of the 1790s is to devise a course of political action, and a style of political writing, capable of countering this threat. He gives us an intimation of what this style might comprise in a letter he wrote to Lady Elliot in december 1787, praising her husband's recent speech in the impeachment of Sir Elijah Impey. In this letter, one of the few examples of detailed rhetorical criticism in Burke, Elliot's speech is particularly commended for its range of emotional effects:

> This well combined piece was so very affecting, that it drew Tears from some of his auditory, and those not the most favourable to his Cause. In Truth the whole came from the heart, and went to the heart. At the same time, in some parts, and towards the End particularly, it was something awful and even terrible. It was humanity, compelled, even by the gentleness and mildness of its Character, to pass a stern Sentence upon Cruelty and oppression. It was Abdiel rebuking Satan. Look at the passage in your Milton, and you will conceive something of the Effect.[18]

In this analysis Burke draws upon the psychological and aesthetic vocabulary of the *Philosophical Enquiry*. He describes a composition in which the beautiful passions give way, of necessity, to a rhetoric of the sublime, but which provide the emotional impulse behind the entire oration. Elliot's manner and tone move from pity (in the realm of the beautiful) to a sublime attitude of command ("something awful and even terrible"). Pity, an emotion which Elliot's speech would appear to have inspired in its audience, finds its most powerful expression in Burke in the portrait of Marie Antoinette. Indeed, it is arguable that in that passage sympathy spills over into the sentimental, where the object of pity is valued for its ability to raise that passion. Defending himself against Philip Francis's charge that the description of the queen was "pure foppery," Burke refused to apologise for the sentimentality of the portrait. Instead he insisted that

> the recollection of the manner in which I saw the Queen of France in the year 1774 and the contrast between that brilliancy, Splendour, and beauty, with the prostrate Homage of a Nation to her, compared with the abominable Scene of 1789 which I was describing did draw Tears from me and wetted my Paper. These Tears came again into my Eyes almost as often as I lookd at the description. They may again[19]

Yet however sincere this may have been as an initial response, in the long run it is scarcely an adequate riposte to the challenge of the Revolution. In spite of—perhaps because of—Francis's charge of "foppery" and Thomas Paine's derisive dismissal of the "weeping effect" of his "tragic paintings," Burke's stance in his pamphlets of the 1790s is more often "awful" and "terrible" than gentle and mild.[20] His writings are characterised less by sympathy, conciliation, and love than by the more rigorous virtues of the sublime. He feels compelled to cast himself as a defiant and heroic Abdicl, engaged in an epic war against Jacobinism. If we follow the advice Burke had offered to Lady Elliot, and turn to the passage in Milton, we find Abdiel warning Satan to expect a similar shift in the exercise of power:

> That golden sceptre which thou didst reject
> Is now an iron rod to bruise and break
> Thy disobedience.
>   (*Paradise Lost* 5:886-88.)

In his anti-Jacobin writings Burke, like Elliot, cases aside the golden sceptre, an emblem of mercy, and picks up the iron rod of justice.

The qualities and passions required to sustain this stance are those which distinguish Burke's fine (and neglected) *Letter to William Elliot* (1795). Burke calls there for a return to the principles of the sublime in government. Before 1789, he recalls, society could be both sublime ("august") and lovely. He claims that "never was so beautiful and so august a spectacle presented to the moral eye, as Europe afforded the day before the revolution in France" (a comment in which, as so often, Burke presents a concept—the culture and polity of the *ancien régime*—as a scene, object of sight, or work of art). But in the subsequent crisis "it was necessary that in the sanctuary of government something should be disclosed not only venerable, but dreadful. Government was at once to shew itself full of virtue and full of force."[21] Burke resolves to add his voice "to draw down justice, and wisdom and fortitude from heaven," just those virtues which, in the *Philosophical Enquiry*, he had declared to be most characteristic of the sublime: "Those virtues which cause admiration, and are of the sublimer kind, produce terror rather than love. Such as fortitude, justice, wisdom, and the like."[22]

So far I have argued that Burke response to the French Revolution is shaped by, if not precisely modelled on, the aesthetics and psychology of the *Philosophical Enquiry*. The term which links the social and aesthetic spheres, and on which many of Burke's judgments turn, is *taste*. For taste is the social ratification of the individual aesthetic response; it carries with it a set of moral, social, and even political standards. In the second edition of the *Philosophical Enqury* Burke included an introductory chapter "On Taste" in which he sought to demonstrate that the potential for a uniform standard of taste exists in all human beings. In the 1790s, moving into the realm of aesthetic judgment, he accuses the Jacobins of having violated this standard. Their "barbarous philosophy," he declares in the *Reflections*, "is destitute of all taste and elegance."[23] Later, in a more detailed piece of analysis, it is on aesthetic grounds that Burke attacks Rousseau, whom he regards as the preceptor of the Revolution. He objects not only to the alleged naivety of Rousseau's social theory and the immorality of his personal conduct, but also to his disorderly and incorrect mode of writing. Thus, in the *Letter to a Member of the National Assembly* (1791), we are told that

> Taste and elegance, though they are reckoned only among the smaller and secondary morals, yet are of no mean importance in the regulation of life. A moral taste is not of force to turn vice into virtue; but it recommends virtue with something like the blandishments of pleasure; and it infinitely abates the evils of vice. Rousseau, a writer of great force and vivacity, is totally destitute of taste in any sense of the word.... We certainly perceive, and to a degree we feel, in this writer, a style glowing, animated, enthusiastick; at the same time that we find it lax, diffuse, and not in the best taste of composition; all the members of the piece being

pretty equally laboured and expanded, without any due selection or subordination of parts.[24]

Burke's literary criticism confirms the opinion he had already reached of Rousseau's morals and politics. The Genevan's style is "glowing, animated enthusiastick" (terms which are not in themselves positively complimentary); but it is also, like his sexual conduct and moral outlook, "lax" and "diffuse." Moreover, this apostle of equality lacks any sense of literary decorum. His literary works, like his vision of society, are composed "without any due selection or subordination of parts."

In this way Burke's standard of taste and criterion of the "correct" in writing contribute to a broader political argument. In the *Letters on a Regicide Peace* this occasional critique is developed into a thoroughgoing rhetorical analysis of political texts. Burke quotes extensively from various official notes and royal declarations, compares their differences in style and address, and considers the relationship between literary form and political function. The royal declaration of 29 October 1793 is for Burke a model text. It states, with clarity and panache, the objectives of the war against France. There can be no question for Burke of a contradiction between form and content, between the correct political position and the proper form of address. Belligerent in its sentiments, the declaration is also, Burke notes with approval,

> the most eloquent and highly finished in the style, the most judicious in the choice of topics, the most orderly in the arrangement, and the most rich in the colouring, without employing the smallest degree of exaggeration, of any state paper that has ever yet appeared.[25]

As such it is worthy of comparison with the declarations of the great Whigs of the reign of William III. It shares, for instance, the "manly, spirited and truly animating style" of an address to the Crown; delivered in 1697 by a House of Commons which remained resolute after eight years of war with Louis XIV.

It is upon similarly stylistic grounds that Burke approves of the Downing Street "note" of 10 April 1796, but in subsequent ministerial pronouncements he can discern nothing but disorder and passivity, a degeneration not only in the practice of diplomacy but in the language of politics itself. In the third of the *Letters on a Regicide Peace* Burke subjects two specimens of this decline—the "declaration" of 27 December 1796 and the ministerial speech which followed it—to a sustained and critical analysis. The declaration, Burke insists, transgresses both the principles of rhetoric and the elementary rules of politics. His reading of the paper reveals a flaw in its structure, a disparity between the exordium and the peroration. The declaration opens with a stark but accurate history of the humiliations suffered by Lord Malmesbury and other English diplomats during the recent negotiations with France. According to Burke, rhetorical practice and conventional expectations demand that such an introduction should be followed by a resolution to prosecute the war with renewed vigour. He even goes so far as to suggest the form that such an exhortation might take. Casting Pitt in a sublime and heroic role, he provides him with a selection of patriotic lines from *Henry V*, a play often plundered for its store of bellicose, anti-Gallic sentiments. The minister, Burke proclaims,

> is place on a stage, than which no muse of fire that had ascended the highest heaven of invention, could imagine any thing more awful and august. It was hoped, that in this swelling scene...he would have stood forth in the form, and in the attitude of a hero. On that day, it was thought he would have assumed the port of Mars....[26]

But the declaration itself, devoid of the true language of statecraft, is unable to rise to the occasion. It cannot sustain the sublime style. It concludes with a tame pledge to resume negotiations at the earliest opportunity, notwithstanding the humiliating rebuffs Britain had already received. "This exordium," laments Burke, reviewing the entire declaration in its formal aspect, "as contrary to all the rules of rhetorick, as to those more essential rules of policy which our situation would dictate, is intended as a prelude to a deadening and disheartening proposition."[27] The communications of the state are marred by a formal collapse which Burke regards as a symptom of the enfeebled and as he would have it, "effeminate" spirit of Pitt's administration.

While Burke often resorts to aesthetic judgments in his political tracts, this attention to the language of diplomacy and political debate is particularly marked. In a sense the principles of rhetorical criticism provide the terms in which that debate is conducted. We have seen how, in the third of the *Letters on a Regicide Peace*, Burke examines various notes, declarations, and speeches, the products of "official" discourse. In the *Letter to the Earl Fitzwilliam* (the so-called "fourth" of the *Letters on a Regicide Peace*) he casts his critical eye on the writings of one of his political opponents. In this case the victim is Lord Auckland, the author of a pamphlet entitled *Some Remarks on the Apparent Circumstances of the War in the Fourth Week of October 1795*. In his reply to Auckland, whose pamphlet recommended the merits of peace with France, Burke again introduces aesthetic criteria into the conduct of political argument. Auckland's work is ridiculed for the unnecessary pedantry of its title, and for a political passivity which scars its very sentence structure. Like the later "declaration" of 1796, which Burke discusses in the third of the *Letters*, it is unable to emulate the grand style, declining, within the space of a sentence, from the heroic to the banal:

> In the very womb of this last sentence, pregnant, as it should seem, with a Hercules, there is formed a little bantling of the mortal race, a degenerate, puny parenthesis, that totally frustrates our most sanguine views and expectations, and disgraces the whole gestation.[28]

There is a powerful fusion here of detailed textual criticism, classical allusion, and passionate political conviction. Burke is evidently as much concerned with the style as with the substance of Auckland's argument. Indeed, he regards them as inseparable. It is at such moments that he makes his most explicit statements about the relationship between politics and language. Denouncing Auckland's tract as a travesty of a once dignified form of address, he exclaims despairingly:

> Would that when all our manly sentiments are thus changed, our manly language were changed along with them; and, that the English tongue were not employed to utter what our Ancestors never dreamed could enter into an English heart![29]

Burke believed that the French tongue had alread undergone that kind of catastrophic change. In a letter to his "kinsman," William Burke, who was working on a translation of an address by the Girondist, Jacques-Pierre Brissot, he remarked that "the very Language of France has sufferd considerable alteration since you were conversant in French books, the way of thinking of the nation and the correspondent Official and publick Style is no longer the same."[30] Developing this point in a preface he contributed to the translation, Burke observed of Brissot's work that "There are some passages...in which his language requires to be first translated into French, at

least into such French as the academy would in former times have tolerated."
Like his predecessor Rousseau, Brissot "writes with great force and vivacity;
but the language, like every thing else in his country, has undergone a
revolution."[31]

   This was not an altogether extravagant claim. As Higgonet has
described, the revolutionary upheaval brought with it proposals for the
transformation of the French language, both in its relationship with the
numerous dialects of France and in its standards of orthography and
grammar.[32] Burke was peculiarly sensitive to such changes in language and
forms of address. As an aesthetician and man of letters (as well as a
statesman) he was quick to spot the currents of a cultural revolution. The
French Revolution is perceived in his writings not only as a social and
political upheaval but also as a revolution in taste. At the same time he
detects a deterioration in the official style of the British state. Implicit in
Burke's detailed and critical remarks on the various state papers and political
pamphlets is a conception of the correct mode of public address. In the
recurrent crises of the 1790s, we gather, political writing and action should
above all possess grandeur, inspire reverence, and command authority. What
is required, as Burke tells us in the third of the *Letters on a Regicide Peace,*
is "the true, unsuborned, unsophisticated language of genuine natural
feeling." In order to illustrate the qualities of this language, so conspicuously
missing from the "declaration" of 1796, Burke alludes to various classes of
artistic production and the relation they bear on the passions:

> Never was there a jar or discord, between genuine sentiment and
> sound policy. Never, no, never did nature say one thing and
> wisdom say another. Nor are sentiments of elevation in themselves
> turgid and unnatural. Nature is never more truly herself, than in her
> grandest forms. The Apollo of Belvedere (if the universal robber
> has yet left him at Belvedere) is as much in nature, as any figure
> from the pencil of Rembrandt, or any clown in the rustic revels of
> Teniers.[33]

In this passage the Apollo Belvedere is seen to project the grandeur and
dignity (if not the terror) which Burke had earlier associated with the
sublime. It is a figure capable of inspiring those "sentiments of elevation"
which he considers to be requisite at this juncture for purposes of public
address. In his *Discourses on Art*[34] Sir Joshua Reynolds seems to agree with
Burke that the Apollo is an example of the "grand style" of sculpture.

Rembrandt, on the other hand, is criticised for his "narrow conception of nature," for his adherence to a mode of portraiture based on particularities rather than on the "universal," "central" forms of the Grand Style. Teniers, though praised for his "elegance and precision," is a representative of a lesser school of painting, one which chooses to confine its energies to "low and confined subjects." The aesthetic categories of Reynolds and Burke do not always coincide, but in this case their judgments seem compatible.

Reynolds was himself fond of portraying his subjects in grand and epic attitudes. In what has been described as his "noblest portrait" he depicts a shipwrecked Admiral Keppel, the great naval commander, friend of Burke, and prominent Rockingham Whig, in a pose which "is roughly that of the Apollo Belvedere, reversed and very slightly modified."[35] It is to another of Reynolds's heroic portraits of Keppel that Burke alludes in the closing pages of the *Letter to a Noble Lord*. Concluding his invective against the Duke of Bedford, Burke reflects upon his own retirement from public life and his withdrawal to his estate in Beaconsfield:

> It was but the other day, that on putting in order some things which had been brought here on my taking leave of London for ever, I looked over a number of fine portraits, most of them of persons now dead, but whose society, in my better days, made this a proud and happy place. Amongst these was the picture of Lord Keppel. It was painted by an artist worthy of the subject, the excellent friend of that excellent man from their earliest youth, and a common friend of us both, with whom we lived for many years without a moment of coldness, of peevishness, of jealousy, or of jar, to the day of our final separation.[36]

Burke introduces the portrait of Keppel almost casually, as he describes the melancholy though not entirely unpleasant task of unpacking his gallery. The passage is written in a style of resigned and reflective intimacy, one to which Burke often resorts in his final works. And yet, in spite of the apparent artlessness of its mode, the passage is as rhetorical as any in Burke. His choice of the portrait of Keppel is purposeful. It was painted in 1779, in celebration of Keppel's acquittal at a famous court martial. On receiving the portrait from the admiral, Burke declared that his son,[37] "whenever he sees that picture...will remember what Englishmen, and what English seamen were, in the days when name of nation, and when eminence and superiority in that profession were one and the same thing." Depicting this military and political hero in his moment of triumph, the portrait is a political symbol rather than a mere item in the inventory of Burke's possessions. The allusion to Reynolds's picture prepares the way for the sustained panegyric on Keppel which will bring the *Letter to a Noble Lord* to a close. The grandson of a Dutchman who had accompanied William of Orange to England in 1688, Keppel is for Burke the perfect representative of a Whig aristocracy based on the Revolution settlement. He is the very embodiment of heroic, Old Whig values. Painted by Sir Joshua Reynolds (an artist with close Whig associations), and owned by Burke, this portrait of the Rockinghamite lord discloses the connections at the heart of political society. In the portrait of Keppel, politics and aesthetics come together in the concrete form of a political work of art.

Notes

"The Politics of Taste" appears as chapter three in
Christopher Reid, *Edmund Burke and the Practice of Political Writing*
Dublin: Gill and Macmillan; New York: St. Martin's Press, 1985, pp. 34-50.

1. For differing approaches to this question see Neal Wood, "The Aesthetic Dimension of Burke's Political Thought," *Journal of British Studies* 4 (1964): 41-64; Burleigh Taylor Wilkins, *The Problem of Burke's Political Philosophy* (Oxford: Clarendon, 1967), pp. 119-51; Ronald Paulson, *Representations of Revolution (1789-1820)* (New Haven: Yale University Press, 1983), pp. 57-73; James T. Boulton, *The Language of Politics in the Age of Wilkes and Burke.* (London: Routledge & Kegan Paul; Toronto: University of Toronto Press, 1963).
2. Wood, p. 42.
3. [In the second chapter, "The Legal Idiom," Reid argues that Burke's judicial language, imagery, and modes of address treat justice and mercy as logically separate (like the sublime and beautiful) but equally necessary for the proper function of legal authority. —DR]
4. *Enquiry* I.vi, viii, pp. 38, 40.
5. *Enquiry* II.v, pp. 64-70.
6. William Hogarth, *The Analysis of Beauty* (London, 1753), p. 30.
7. *Enquiry* III.x, pp. 110-11.
8. *Enquiry,* III.xxvii, pp. 124-25.
9. *Enquiry* IV.xxiv, p. 157.
10. *Enquiry* II.ii, p. 57.
11. Burke *Works* (Bohn) 5:158, appr. 9% into the first of the *Letters on a Regicide Peace.* The next quotation ("the eye....") is from the same location.
12. *Enquiry* II.xiv, p. 80. For further discussion of the imagery of light in the political writings of the period, see Paulson, *Representations of Revolution*, pp. 43-47, 58-60.
13. *Enquiry* I.xiv, p. 46.
14. Paulson, p. 67.

15. P. H. Melvin offers a detailed analysis of Burke's theatrical presentation of revolutionary events. See "Burke on Theatricality and Revolution," *Journal of the History of Ideas* 36 (1975): 447-68.

16. In *Works* (Bohn) 2:353, appr. 31% into the *Reflections*.

17. In *Works* (Bohn) 2:349, appr. 30% into the *Reflections*.

18. *Correspondence* 5:369. See *Paradise Lost* 5:809-48, 877-95.

19. *Correspondence* 6:91.

20. Thomas Paine, *The Rights of Man* [1791] (Harmondsworth: Penguin, 1969), pp. 71-72.

21. *Works* (Bohn) 5:76, 77, appr. 62% and 69% into the *Letter to William Elliot*. The next sentence quotes from 5:79, appr. 81% into the *Letter*.

22. *Enquiry* III.x, p. 110.

23. *Works* (Bohn) 2:350, appr. 31% into the *Reflections*.

24. *Works* (Bohn) 2:539, appr. 52% into the *Letter to a Member*.

25. *Works* (Bohn) 5:186 appr. 44% into the first of the *Letters on a Regicide Peace*. The next phrase of Burke's ("manly, spirited...") comes from 5:198, appr. 59% into the same work.

26. *Works* (Bohn) 5:276, appr. 17% into the third of the *Letters on a Regicide Peace*.

27. *Works* (Bohn) 5:278, appr. 19% into the third of the *Letters*.

28. *Works* (Bohn) 5:407, appr. 65% into the fourth of the *Letters*.

29. *Works* (Bohn) 5:407, appr. 65% into the fourth of the *Letters*.

30. *Correspondence* 7:427.

31. *Works* (Bohn) 3:529, the final paragraph of the *Preface to and Address of M. Brissot....*

32. P. Higgonet, "The Politics of Linguistic Terrorism and Grammatical Hegemony during the French Revolution," *Social History* 5 (1980): 41-69.

33. *Works* (Bohn) 5:278, appr 19% into the third of the *Letters*. [The "universal robber" (of the world's art treasures) is Napolean. Burke prophesied that the French Revolution would end in military despotism, but he died before Napolean's coup d'état. —DR]

34. Sir Joshua Reynolds, *Discourses on Art*, ed. R. Wark (San Marino, CA: Huntington Library, 1959), pp. 151, 178. The next sentences refer to pp. 162, 109, and 51 of that work.

35. E. Waterhouse, *Reynolds* (London, 1941), pp. 9-10.

36. *LNL* at *Works* (Bohn) 5:146, appr. 88% into that work.

37. *Correspondence* 4:169.

Part Two

Burke and Revolution

GEORGE WATSON

10
Burke's Conservative Revolution

In fact and in title, eighteenth-century Britain was a revolutionary state. Its political system openly lived by the revolutionary settlement of 1689, and called it that: a triple cord of King, Lords, and Commons based on "Revolution Principles"—its continuance guaranteed by an Act of Succession in 1701 and confirmed by Jacobite defeats in 1715 and 1745-6. For many, and most eloquently for Edmund Burke, it was a settlement to be preserved through all time.

There is no great paradox about conservative revolution—the paradox is rather that revolution should ever have been thought of as distinctively radical. Many new dynasties, whether peacefully or violently instituted, claim to have restored ancestral rights; many adorn themselves with ceremonies symbolic of an heroic past. That is why there may be more to be learnt from one who, like Burke, can see the essential conservatism of the revolutionary idea than from those who mask it under a rhetoric of change. To that extent, the English Revolution of 1689 is more openly instructive than the Russian of October 1917. It demonstrates more candidly how oligarchies take power, keep it, and justify it.

Burke entered the Commons in 1765, and down to his death in 1797 his vision of human progress was contained within his conception of what 1689 meant. Near the end of his life, in a letter of December 1794, when England was as fearful of French invasion as it had been in the 1690s, he proposed to revive an association formed in 1696 to support William III and the Bill of Rights, as if little had changed over a hundred years; and he never doubted that the defence of that settlement was the first object of his political life.

The British debate of the 1790s saw itself, in any case, as in a continuous tradition from the seventeenth century. After all, it was Richard Price's address in November 1789 to the Society for Commemorating the Revolution in Great Britain that had provoked Burke's *Reflections on the Revolution in France* (1790); and Burke's bitter rejection of the French Revolution, like Price's support, are historical interpretations of the English Revolution of a hundred years before. Were the French imitating the English example, as Price had believed, or defying it? It was not the principle of revolution itself that divided the two men, but their sense of events themselves.

Burke's case for 1689 needs to be defended, so far as it can, from one easy charge of partiality. It was openly patriotic, but it was never only that. On the first day of the Warren Hastings trial, in 1788, he spoke proudly of the "general decay" of Asia and the "universal improvement" of Europe, and he never doubted that his own nation stood in the vanguard of that improvement. But to suppose that his view was nothing more than patriotic would be to risk forgetting that Burke was an Irishman, not an Englishman, and that in any case foreigners like Voltaire and Montesquieu had believed something like it too. Montesquieu had arrived in England in 1729, the very year of Burke's birth in Dublin, and the year when Voltaire ended his three-year stay. That triple coincidence has some symbolic value. At the end of *An Appeal from the New to the Old Whigs* (1791), Burke attacked the new and threatening influence of the Jacobins, fanatics whose "only claim to know is that they never doubted"; and he hailed the dead Montesquieu, their dead countryman, as a genius of "penetrating aquiline eye," erudite judgment and a "herculean robustness of mind"—a figure, as he says, like the Adam of Milton's *Paradise Lost*:

> a man capable of placing in review, after having brought together
> from the east, the west, the north and south, from the coarseness of
> the rudest barbarism to the most refined and subtle civilization, all
> the schemes of government which had ever prevailed amongst
> mankind, weighing, measuring, collating, and comparing them all,
> joining fact with theory, and calling into council, upon all this
> infinite assemblage of things, all the speculations which have
> fatigued the understandings of profound reasoners in all times.

And this man, Burke triumphantly concludes, though "tinctured with no national prejudice," had admired above all the constitutions of the world that of England. "And shall we Englishmen revoke to such a suit?" It was not just an oligarchy of Englishmen, then, in his view, that had acclaimed the settlement of 1689, but the Enlightenment of Europe. If Burke spoke for a nation, he spoke for more than that; and 1689 represented for him what all men of advanced views would enjoy, if only they could.

What was that settlement, in the imagination of the English political nation and of its foreign admirers? Burke's answer to the question was in the familiar terms of a mixed constitution compounded of monarchical, oligarchic, and popular elements, and as such it rejects the damaging charge of originality: damaging, since a notion held by one man on such a matter, or even by a handful, could have no standing beyond that of a whim. If Burke had been an original political thinker in his conclusions, he would in his own judgment, and in the judgment of others, have been so much the less a cogent one. He spoke for a people and an age. Samuel Johnson, though himself a party man and of a different party, called him "a cursed Whig, a bottomless Whig"; but he also repeatedly bestowed on him the epithet "eminent," and could see that Burke was beyond all cavil a mind above party. "If you met him for the first time in a street where you were stopped by a drove of oxen, and you and he stepped aside to take shelter but for five minutes, he'd talk to you in such a manner that, when you parted, you would say, this is an extraordinary man!"[1] It should be plain, then, that Goldsmith's famous quip in "Retaliation," written early in Burke's career in 1774, is seriously misleading: "...And to party gave up what was meant for mankind." In a parliamentary state, the choice between party and national interest is not there to be made, and Burke knew that it was not.

Burke spoke for mankind in the sense that he held the revolutionary settlement of 1689 to have been offered as a political example to all men for all time. "An act just, necessary and most honourable to this nation," he called it in a letter of November 1771, "whose liberty and prosperity it has ensured to this time—and will for ages, if its true principles be well adhered to." What marked it out was less its status as an event in history than the immutable principles it represented: principles that will survive, he went on, after "Whig and Tory, Stuart and Brunswick, and all such miserable bubbles and playthings of the hour are vanished from existence and from memory." This notion of high principles underlying events was a constant element in his thought. Principles are "stable and eternal," as he insisted in *A Letter to a Noble Lord* (1796), circumstance merely altering their application: "A particular order of things may be altered; order itself cannot lose its value."[2]

But equally, events take and hold significance only in their context. 1689 had been a revolution in Clarendon's conservative sense of a "full compassing," as Burke saw it, and not in the French: it had restored to Englishmen rights that were ancestrally theirs. Since those rights derive from no dynasty in particular, Stuart or Hanoverian, no dynasty has the right to infringe them as James II had done. That is why Burke consistently rejected both the tyrannical power of monarchy and the Jacobin notion of basing a revolutionary order on ideas "theoretic" or "systematic," as in 1789, or on notions plucked out of the air. Jacobinism was the first instance in human history of that alarming phenomenon, "a *complete* revolution"—a moral earthquake that threatened liberty itself by overturning the order on which ordered liberty must forever rest.

The unoriginality of Burke's political conclusions lies in saying better what others already believed: his originality of argument in showing why what they had long believed was true. In none of the five great causes around which his political career revolved—Parliament and the King, conciliation with America, the Irish question, India, and revolutionary France—did he merely speak for himself, or even offer to do so. His ambition was in large measure stylistic: to dignify an existent and familiar cause with superior language, to demonstrate its application and to enrich it with supporting arguments and memorable illustrations. In all this he made of himself a passage through which the Enlightenment politics of his century, dissident and extra-parliamentary as it had often been, translated itself into the parliamentary liberalism of the Victorians and after. Lord Acton, who read him in youth, saw that point at once, and loved to emphasise it. "To a Liberal," he wrote in his notes, "all the stages between Burke and Nero are little more than the phases of forgotten moons."[3] Since the *philosophes* had praised the British political system, if only fleetingly, it could be no contradiction in an Enlightenment man at Westminster to support that existing order of things; and the phrase Conservative Revolution is a coherent and intelligible one here, provided that "conservative" is seen to have nothing to do either with the eventual name of a political party or with any general opposition to reform. Reform, after all, has nothing to do with total change and a new start, since it arises out of a respect for the system that it seeks to improve. "To innovate is not to reform," Burke remarked to the Duke of Bedford severely, in *A Letter to a Noble Lord*.[4] It is precisely the reformer who has most to fear from innovation, in the "complete" style of the Jacobins or the Bolsheviks—just as the violent revolutionary has everything to fear from reforms intelligently conducted and seen to work, and everything to gain from thwarting reform till explosion-point is reached. Burke's reforming horror of complete revolution now looks surprising to some, and even original, and twentieth-century man is startled when he reads something like it in George Orwell. It is a claim that lies at the heart of *Homage to Catalonia, Animal Farm,* and *Nineteen Eighty-four.* It would have looked far less surprising in the long series of Whig parliaments that knew Robert Walpole, or Burke himself, or the young Macaulay. It is the essential dogma of Whiggism, and its chief bequest to Liberalism: "Reform that you may preserve."

To speak for a party, and yet to survive as a classic—all this demands a command of language to illustrate and enliven familiar truths. Burke's style still lacks convincing analysis, and it has driven back some notable attempts upon its secrets. The most immediate difficulty is that it lacks any evident eccentricity. Soon after his death, Maria Edgeworth planned an essay on his genius and style, but soon abandoned it; and her father Richard Lovell Edgeworth, who had known and admired Burke, felt obliged to agree with her decision. "I did not think it would be easy to write on Burke's style. Indeed his style is not peculiar, like Johnson's or Gibbon's."[5] Eighty years later, Gerard Manley Hopkins unknowingly echoed the sentiment. The beauty of good prose, he complained, cannot arise wholly out of thought, as with Burke: "Burke had no style, properly so called: his style was colourlessly to transmit his thought."[6] On his style as such, then, there seemed to be nothing to say. Or so they thought.

One hardly expects Maria Edgeworth and Hopkins to agree, still less to be wrong when they do. But in this they did and they were. Of course Burke had a style, and a formidable one. Without it, he would hardly be matter for attention at all. Largely unsuccessful as a parliamentary speaker, and profoundly unsuccessful as a public man, holding office only briefly in early career, his fame is altogether a literary one. In the end it is style or nothing.

The serious point at the heart of Maria Edgeworth's withdrawal, and Hopkins's, is that Burke's mastery of language is far easier to recognise than to characterise. Johnson and Gibbon have individual patterns of syntax: Burke does not. They also possess a manner of voice that is quickly recognised as theirs: Johnson at once weighty and witty, spicing his prose with explosive little aphorisms on the moral life; Gibbon diffusively ironic, where the irony is as delicately distributed as salt in soup. Burke does not settle so firmly into one device, or into any one set of devices. He can be as aphoristic as Johnson, in a way that shows both men to be heirs of Erasmian humanism with its love of the lively commonplace. But he less commonly attempts Johnson's acidity of tone. A clutch of Burke aphorisms always looks well:

> When bad men combine, the good must associate.
> The concessions of the weak are the concessions of fear.
> All government...is founded on compromise and barter.
> I do not know the method of drawing up an indictment against a
>   whole people.
> The people never give up their liberties but under some delusion.
> Expense may be an essential part of true economy.
> Kings will be tyrants from policy, when subjects are rebels
>   from principle.
> People will never look forward to posterity who never looked
>   backwards to their ancestors.

Such remarks would look highly unrepresentative of Johnson. They are weighty rather than witty; aphorisms, not maxims. Burke detested maxims—glib generalisations based less on any well-earned experience of affairs than on false theoretical certitudes. "Narrow wisdom and narrow morals," he called them in *Thoughts on the Cause of the Present Discontents* (1770), helped along all too easily by specious little summaries: "They are light and portable. They are as current as copper coin; and about as valuable. They serve equally the first capacities and the lowest; and they are, at least, as useful to the worst men as to the best." Knowledge has to be lived, in fact; and literature taken alone can be dangerous. As early as his notes of the 1750s, when he was still in his twenties, he was complaining that "we read too much," and above all too early: "Most books prove, affirm, demonstrate; they come with settled notions to us, and make us settle ours too early."[7] A surprising sentiment in a bookish youth. Burke could always see that literary excellence was perilous as well as tempting, though no man ever wanted it more. There is so much at stake, when one writes. And when political theorists mislead, the effects can be huge and costly, as he knew, in terms of human suffering.

Burke's style is built on the principles of his early treatise on aesthetics, *A Philosophical Enquiry into the Sublime and Beautiful* (1757), where two categories of sense are contrasted: the Beautiful all small, delicate, intricate, smooth, and bright; the Sublime big, heavy, rugged, abrupt, and gloomy.

The contrast, which in poetic terms sounds like one made between Pope and Milton, can easily be translated into the effects of his literary prose. An aphorism is beautiful, in this sense, a grand period sublime. Burke uses them both, in ingeniously contrasting and supporting ways. This is why his prose is hard to decipher, as a set of devices. Consider how he dignifies the familiar (if contentious) doctrine that a Member of Parliament is something more than a delegate—building it upwards and outwards, grandly and delicately, from its bare essentials. The point itself was at least as old as the reign of James I, in Sir Edward Coke: "And it is to be observed, though one be chosen for one particular county or borough, yet when he is returned and sits in Parliament, he serveth for the whole realm." A century later another lawyer, Sir William Blackstone, put the point again, and as flatly: "Every Member, though chosen by one particular district, when elected and returned, serves for the whole realm. For the end of his coming hither is not particular but general; not barely to advantage his constituents, but the common wealth." What Burke makes of the doctrine in his *Speech to the Electors of Bristol,* in November 1774, can now be seen more clearly for what it is:

> Parliament is not a congress of ambassadors from different and hostile interests; which interests each must maintain, as an agent and advocate, against other agents and advocates; but parliament is a deliberative assembly of one nation, with one interest, that of the whole; where not local purposes, not local prejudices ought to guide, but the general good resulting from the general reason of the whole. You choose a member indeed; but when you have chosen him, he is not a member of Bristol, but he is a member of parliament... Your faithful friend, your devoted servant, I shall be to the end of my life: a flatterer you do not wish for....[8]

Burke's rhetorical grasp here is based on a series of contrasts where big and little strikingly coexist. Not a congress but an assembly; not of ambassadors but of a nation; not of local purposes but for the general good; not of Bristol but of Parliament... The manner, too, is teasing as well as literal, the last sentence mockingly echoing polite forms of address in conversation and letters: Your faithful friend, your devoted servant... If Maria Edgeworth and her father were baffled by this range of abilities, so they might be. There is no single or dominant strand here; no eccentricity. Burke can be Johnson, or Gibbon, or neither. Gibbon's style he once called "very affected, mere frippery and tinsel," and Johnson's may have seemed to him too refined and distilled: a language for an argumentative drawing-room rather than for a deliberative assembly.[9] Burke needed the sum of them, and something more.

The place of style is crucial, since it is the mark of political civilisation, as of civilisation generally. I speak now of style in the sense of stylishness or ceremony. The other sense of that ambiguous word, as referring to what is simply distinctive, is more characteristic of the political interests of Gibbon. Burke's fascination is above all with the stylishness of politics: dress, forms of address, ceremonial procedures and the like.

That fascination can be the mark of the snob, and the charge of snobbery sticks so easily to Burke that it is worth a moment's attention to rub it off. Burke undoubtedly believed in the supreme importance of ritual in public affairs. Though he hated the improper influence of kings in parliamentary affairs, he loved courtliness and courts. The word "gentleman" echoes through his writings, and it refers to a style rather than to mere descent: one who behaves as if well-bred, whether he is that or not. Burke's severe handling of the fifth Duke of Bedford in *A Letter to a Noble Lord*, where he calls his own merits "original and personal" and Bedford's merely derivative of ancestry, strengthens his case against the charge of being a mere worshipper of birth. Birth can help; but to be a gentleman is to deport oneself, regardless of birth, in such a way as to be the carrier of the civilisation of centuries. That means above all of classical civilisation. It is to *act* civilised. "A true, natural aristocracy" is what should lead to a nation, so he argues, and not a mere aristocracy of descent. Burke's rituals and ceremonies, like the Commons he loved, are wide open to the talents.

"So to be patriots as not to forget we are gentlemen": that was the demand Burke had made in his first political treatise, the *Thoughts* of 1770. His epithet for gentleman in this elevated sense is "liberal," meaning whatever is apt to a free and civilised spirit. "It is a vile, illiberal school, this new French academy of the *sans-culottes*," he was to write a quarter of a century later of the Jacobins, in *A Letter to a Noble Lord*. "There is nothing in it that is fit for a gentleman to learn" and he urges the fifth Duke to prefer the classics that boys still learned then at Westminster, Eton, and Winchester. Style, as Burke understands it, is not an empty form, but an expression of ancient truths. What it is about is the best that mankind knows.

Seen in that light, the notorious passage acclaiming Marie Antoinette at Versailles in the *Reflections* of 1790, which has often repelled the dour spirit morning star, full of life and splendour and joy…I thought ten thousand swords must have leaped from their scabbards to avenge even a look that threatened her with insult. But the age of chivalry is gone; that of sophisters, economists, and calculators has succeeeded." "Chivalry" is a rashly chosen word here, as some might think, though Gibbon pounced upon it approvingly. "A most admirable medicine against the French disease," he called the *Reflections* in a letter of February 1791, soon after they appeared: "I admire his eloquence, I approve his politics, I adore his chivalry, and I can even forgive his superstition."[10] The word is certainly startling, and so is Burke's total argument. If the tournaments of the Middle Ages that he appeals to had style, they did not have much else. Burke profoundly believed that modern parliamentary life needs it too, but he might have guarded himself better against the charge of vulgar snobbery than he does here. All that fascination with rank, title, and protocol can easily look lickspittle, or at best feebly nostalgic: so much so, that the theoretical interest of what Burke has to say about political ceremony can be swiftly lost to view.

At all events, it would be a distortion to suppose that Burke's demand upon his nation to preserve and enhance the style of its public life was peculiar to his ageing years, when he was obsessed by a patriotic horror of a French invasion and a Jacobin rising in England. He had believed in it from the first. As a young Member, it was part of his charge against George III that the King had tried to bring Parliament into subjection by degrading its sense of its own dignity. That sense necessarily belongs to free men, as opposed to "vile, illiberal" men; and Burke could see that the demand for ritual, civility, and the civilization of manners is an inescapable aspect of private freedom. Members of Parliament, he wrote bitterly against the objectives of the King's party in the *Thoughts*, "were to be hardened into an insensibility to pride as well as to duty. Those high and haughty sentiments, which are the great support of independence, were to be let down gradually. Points of honour were no more to be regarded in parliamentary decorum than in a Turkish army…." All that puts the point about Marie Antoinette in a radically different light. If the ceremonial dignity of public life is a necessary condition of winning freedom and keeping it, then Burke's admiration for the ceremonies of the French monarchy is no idle snobbery. Misapplied as it may have been in the particular instance, it remains a political point of substantial mass and weight. A point, what is more, that the present century has had opportunities to ponder.

* * * * *

In the Germany of National Socialism, victims were robbed of their dignity and their heads close-shaven on being taken into detention; and the first act on entering Auschwitz was to be forced to strip, men and women together as newly arrived prisoners, before being put to death or to forced labour. A loss of dignity can be the first infliction a tyranny visits on its victims. When Burke speaks of the Turkish army of his day as humblingly indifferent to decorum, he means something like this. A tyrant degrades his people as part of the business of enslaving them; and the ceremonies of a free parliament—mace, processions, formal address to the Speaker by Members, and the like—are there to assert a dignity that a free legislature needs continuously to claim against any executive, whether royal or republican.

What some have seen as mere trappings and empty forms—matters, at the best, for the condescending analysis of anthropologists—Burke saw as a fortress-wall against arbitrary power. This is the first truth he has to teach the modern age, and it is one that it badly needs and often mocks. Political ceremony is something more than an empty survival from the past, to be maintained for the delight or bemusement of the unsophisticated. It is a first line of defence against tyrants.

The second truth is that ceremonies need to be old, or at least to be thought so. To survive, a free constitution demands the authority of pedigree; and the simplest evidence for that, and the most compelling, is ordinary observation: new states are more susceptible to violent overthrow than old ones. Anyone nowadays can see that an anciently established constitution like the British or the Swiss is less likely to be overturned than a newly invented state in Afro-Asia. We may debate the reasons why, but hardly the fact itself. In the same way, a new nation like the United States in the 1780s might be well advised to find itself a history quickly, if at all serious about survival—linking its forms and institutions to some age-old enactments such as Magna Charta or English common law.

The reasons why all that is true are admittedly far less clear than the fact itself; and for just that reason, the fact itself can easily be doubted. It is often tempting to suppose that what we cannot sufficiently explain is not really there, as if the limits of reality were the same as those of articulate consciousness. Hence the condescension of some modern historians towards the classic Whig doctrine of an ancestral constitution. Sir Moses Finley, in a Cambridge inaugural of 1971, has called the argument unsophisticated, whether in the mouths of ancients like the Athenians or of moderns like Burke. But that is to devalue implausibly the insignificance of credentials. Even in our dealings with individuals, we are concerned with the authority they possess, or lack, as well as with what they are in themselves. With institutions—nations and their organs of government, groups and teaching orders—such issues predominate in the mind. A court of law is always more than the individuals that compose it, if it is to count at all. A parliament is what it is because time has honoured it: not just by surviving one crisis, or several, but by conferring a longevity that suggests some inner and intrinsic strength. It is notable that we all tend to accept that view when it relates to something immediate to our own concerns, reserving easy disdain for such remoter instances as the Athenian respect for Solon, or Burke's for the revolutionary settlement of 1689. Would Professor Finley, as an academic, accept the credentials of a new and unknown university as readily as those of an established institution like his own? The very occasion for his remarks, paradoxically enough, was a Cambridge inaugural lecture—a traditional ceremony performed in due form before a university of medieval foundation where he has chosen to live and teach. No wonder if he sensed a contradiction, and his lecture ended: "Mr. Vice-Chancellor, *my* ancestral piety, at any rate, can scarcely be faulted...I have today invoked by name twenty-five Cambridge men."[11] We all believe in ancestry, when it matters—to ourselves. Like family affection, of which it is an extended instance, it is easier to mock at in others than in oneself.

Burke believed that England was a free nation because it had a tradition of freedom. Its ancestral belief in an ordered liberty had defeated the challenges of tyrants in the seventeenth century, and had enshrined itself in the settlement of 1689. That revolution was to be applauded above all because it had restored, not because it had innovated. You cannot, in that view, hope to achieve freedom by a single act claiming to come of nothing but a handful of aspirations: that was his charge against the revolution of France in 1789. Freedom, in the end, is harder than that.

What are we to say, then, to a people that has no tradition of liberty? Burke's answer can only be guessed at by extrapolating his argument. But he would surely have replied, and with justice, that if a people has no known tradition of liberty, then it cannot realistically hope to be free, or free for long. That answer is not as harsh as it may sound. What people, after all, is totally without a tradition of freedom? Germans in 1945 could look back to the ill-fated Weimar republic that had expired in 1933: they could look back to the Frankfurt parliament of 1848, and to enlightened princely states in the preceding century. Those who object that such precedents are discouragingly slight or brief may be advised to look more keenly at the achievement of the British after 1689 in making so much out of so little. For men of determined intelligence, the task of creating a political myth to live by is not an impossible one. The first requirement is to want it.

To answer in this way is altogether compatible with Burke's admiration for the British constitution—that classic instance in political history of broadening precedent—and with his sympathy for the American colonists in the 1770s, with their tradition of English constitutionalism invigorated by the independent spirit of the frontier. It explains, too, his horror of the French revolutionaries, who might after all have invoked elements in the history of their nation earlier than the 1660s, when Louis XIV declared for absolute power. That they had wilfully preferred to talk of a new order of mankind, that they had abandoned such old titles as Estates-General in favour of such new ones as National Assembly, was a matter of choice, and of wrong choice. The year 1789 could have been a French 1689, if Frenchmen themselves had chosen to make it so. They could have followed Montesquieu rather than men like Robespierre. The error exposed by Burke is not that they made a revolution, but that their revolution abandoned all sense of a national past. It denied the traditions of a people.

To demand a sense of tradition may by now sound heartless, for many oppressed peoples and for much of the Third World. It would be more useful to ask if it is wrong. Certainly human history since Burke's death in 1797 has not made it look foolish. Constitutional liberties have survived best in nations that possess long traditions of government by consent and—a possibility Burke nowhere raises—in nations like Japan and West Germany that have been conquered by those who do. Those who have leaped to liberty, by contrast, have commonly failed to hold fast to it for long. Those that have moved more deliberately, like India, though out of an ancient tradition that offered few of the supports of an ancestral constitution, have offered intermediate instances of success: faltering, rising, and faltering again. The past two centuries have not served Burke badly for instances: he was a good prophet, as prophets go. When in the *Reflections* he spoke bitterly of an "epidemical fanaticism" and of a "black and savage atrocity of mind" that revolutionary writings were spreading across France and beyond France, he was not writing hysterically, though some thought he was: in 1790 the Terror was just three years off. "Good order is the foundation of all good things." And those who, like Stalinists or Maoists, once imagined that only violent revolution in obedience to a sacred text can flourish, are by now among us the most disappointed of men.

* * * * *

The real charge against Burke is not that he was mistaken about the larger nature of what succeeds or fails in politics, but that in his own career he misconceived the way of success. Is mere "authorism," as Horace Walpole derisively called it on meeting him as a young man, or the sheer consciousness of being an author, really enough? How much can books and speeches achieve? Is politics only an art of declaring truths, and declaring them eloquently? Certainly Burke himself lived to think it was not. He died haunted by a sense of failure, personal and professional: without office, without a peerage, without any certainty of the eventual victory of British arms by sea and land. If his writings were much studied after his death, then their publishing history does little to suggest it. He is not an author often reprinted by the Victorians; and the editing of his letters, first attempted in the 1840s, was not completed untill 1977. Montalembert called him the greatest of all Englishmen, with Shakespeare; and Acton remarked that "systems of scientific thought have been built up by famous scholars on the fragments that fell from his table."[12] But then Acton had to go to Munich as a student to learn of his importance, which he found neglected at home. It is somehow not enough to be eloquent and right.

Do we want to be told the truth of politics, even if the truth is eloquently told and well? It is a reluctance in us all that has to be faced. Johnson and Gibbon have both worn better as authors than Burke: not because thay have more to say that is true and urgent, but because they are adept at taking us, as readers, so profoundly unawares. Their language knows how to startle and to shock. Even the truth needs to be at least a little surprising. Who, after all, wants to be told at length that he lives under the best constitution in the world, even if it is true—or especially if it is true; or that things would be better still if men saw more clearly how superior to all others their own system of govenment was, if they eschewed false idols and foreign intellectual deities, reformed their thoughts and used better manners? There is something irredeemably fussy about offering assertions like these, however much their eloquence is fervid and exemplary. Burke was indeed a bottomless Whig, as Johnson saw; and Whigs, like free-thinkers, love to tell you at length what they believe, and why they are right to believe it. As that arch-Tory Sir Walter Scott was soon to confide to his journal, they "will live and die in the heresy that the world is ruled by little pamphlets and speeches, and that if you can sufficiently demonstrate that a line of conduct is most consistent with men's interest, you have therefore and thereby demonstrated that they will at length after a few speeches on the subject adopt it of course."[13] There is something sadly incomplete about that view of human affairs, if only because it is easier to admire than to love. Of all the great thinkers in the revolutionary tradition, Burke is the one for whom the cold word "admirable" might most aptly have been coined. But then if his truths are by now too familiar, at least in his own nation, to be much needed there, the lasting power and effects of his witness as a parliamentarian and as a man may be among the reasons why it is so.

Notes

George Watson published "Burke's Conservative Revolution"
in *Critical Quarterley* 26 (Spring/Summer 1984)1&2: 87-99.

1. James Boswell, *Journal of a Tour to the Hebrides* (London, 1785), under 15 August 1773.
2. [Burke *Works* (Bohn) 5:126, appr. 40% into the *LNL*. In the next sentence, Watson refers to Edward Hyde, earl of Clarendon (1609-1674), whose *History of the Rebellion* [1702-04] was an important, contemporary history of the English Civil War and interregnum, well known to Burke. Burke was fond of comparing the French Revolution to the English Civil War, rather than to the Revolution of 1689, as some of his opponents did. Clarendon's *History*, in the words of the *Dictionary of National Biography*, is designed "to vindicate not so much the king as the constitutional royalists"—a purpose which Burke would have endorsed. —DR]
3. Cambridge University Library, Additional mss. 4973.
4. [*Works* (Bohn) 5:120, appr. 24% into the *LNL*. While the remark is made at the expense of the Duke of Bedford, the letter is addressed to Burke's patron, the Earl Fitzwilliam. —DR]
5. Richard Lovell Edgeworth, letter of 1805, in Marilyn Butler, *Maria Edgeworth: a Literary Biography* (Oxford, 1972), p. 239n.
6. Gerard Manley Hopkins, letter to Coventry Patmore, 20 October 1887, in his *Further Letters*, ed. C. C. Abbott (Oxford, 1956, rev.) p. 380.
7. Burke, *A Note-book*, ed. H.V.F. Somerset (Cambridge, 1957), pp. 89, 88.
8. [*Works* (Bohn)1:447-48, appr. 75% into the *Speech*. This speech, "At the Conclusion of the Poll," is usually printed together with the speech to the electors "At His Arrival At Bristol." —DR]
9. James Northcote, *The Life of Sir Joshua Reynolds* (London, 1818), 2nd ed., 2:31.
10. Gibbon, *Letters*, ed. J. E. Norton (London, 1956) 3:216. Gibbon designed the remark for his memoirs; see his *Memoirs of My Life*, edited by Georges A. Bonnard (London, 1966), p. 195, where "superstition" is characteristically exchanged for its synonym, "reverence for church establishments."
11. M. I. Finley, *The Ancestral Constitution* (Cambridge, 1971), p. 57. See also J. G. A. Pocock, *The Ancient Constitution and the Feudal Law* (Cambridge 1957); *The Invention of Tradition*, ed. Eric Hobsbawm (London, 1983).
12. Lord Acton, *Letters to Mary Gladstone* (London, 1904), pp. 56-57.
13. Sir Walter Sott, *Journal*, ed. W. E. K. Anderson (Oxford, 1972), p. 12, under 25 November 1825.

RUSSELL KIRK

11
A Revolution Not Made, but Prevented

For rightly apprehending the purpose and character of the written Constitution of the United States, one needs knowledge of that Revolution, or War of Independence, which had parted the original thirteen colonies, or states, from their old source of order and authority, as represented by the Crown in Parliament. For in essence the Constitution was drawn up to re-establish a civil social order.

Was the American War of Independence a revolution? In the view of Edmund Burke and the English Whig factions generally, it was not the sort of political and social overturn that the word "revolution" has come to signify nowadays. Rather, it paralleled that alteration of government in Britain which accompanied the accession of William and Mary to the throne, and which is styled, somewhat confusingly, "The Glorious Revolution of 1688."

Burke's learned editor E. J. Payne summarizes Burke's account of the events of 1688-89 as (in the phrase of Sir Joseph Jekyll) "in truth and in substance, a revolution not made, but prevented."[1] Let us see how that theory may be applicable to North American events nine decades later.

We need first to examine definitions of that ambiguous word "revolution." The signification of the word was altered greatly by the catastrophic events of the French Revolution, commencing only two years after the Constitutional Convention of the United States. Before the French explosion of 1789-1799, "revolution" commonly was employed to describe a round of periodic or recurrent changes or events—that is, the process of coming full cycle; or the act of rolling back or moving back, a return to a point previously occupied.

Not until the French radicals utterly overturned the old political and social order in their country did the word "revolution" acquire its present general meaning of a truly radical change in social and governmental institutions, a tremendous convulsion in society, producing huge alterations that might never be undone. Thus when the eighteenth-century Whigs praised the "Glorious Revolution" of 1688, which established their party's dom-ination, they did not mean that William and Mary, the Act of Settlement, and the Declaration of Right had produced a radically new English political and social order. On the contrary, they argued that the English Revolution had restored tried and true constitutional practices, preservative of immemorial ways. It was James II, they contended, who had been perverting the English constitution; his overthrow had been a return, a rolling-back, to the old constitutional order; the Revolution of 1688, in short, had been a healthy reaction, not a bold innovation.

The Whigs, Burke among them, here were employing that word "revolution" in its older sense. This shift in usage tends to confuse discussion today. If we employ the word "revolution" in its common signification near the end of the twentieth century, what occurred in 1688-89 was no true revolution. In the Whig interpretation of history, at least, the overturn of James II was a revolution not made, but prevented (according to the later definition of "revolution").[2]

But what of the events in North America from 1775 to 1781? Was the War of Independence no revolution?

That war, with the events immediately preceding and following it, constituted a series of movements which produced separation from Britain and the establishment of a different political order in most of British North America. Yet the republic of the United States was an order new only in some aspects, founded upon a century and a half of colonial experience and upon institutions, customs, and beliefs mainly of British origin. The American Revolution did not result promply in the creation of a new social order, nor did the leaders in that series of movements intend that the new nation should break with the conventions, the moral convictions, and the major instituions (except monarchy) out of which America had arisen. As John C. Calhoun expressed this three-quarters of a century later, "The revolution, as it is called, produced no other changes than those which were necessarily caused by the declaration of independence."

To apprehend how the leading Americans of the last quarter of the eighteenth century thought of their own revolution, it is valuable to turn to the arguments of Edmund Burke, which exercised so strong an influence in

America—an influence more telling, indeed, after the adoption of the Constitution than earlier. (Until my own generation, Burke's *Speech on Conciliation with the American Colonies* was studied closely in most American high schools.)

In his *Reflections on the Revolution in France*, as earlier, Burke strongly approves the Revolution of 1688. "The Revolution was made to preserve our *ancient* indisputable laws and liberties, and that *ancient* constitution of government which is our only security for law and liberty," Burke declares. "The very idea of the fabrication of a new government is enough to fill us with disgust and horror. We wished at the period of the Revolution, and do now wish, to derive all we possess as *an inheritance from our forefathers*. Upon that body and stock of inheritance we have taken care not to inoculate any scion alien to the nature of the original plant. All the reformations we have hitherto made, have proceeded upon the principle of reference to antiquity; and I hope, nay I am persuaded, that all those which possibly may be made hereafter, will be carefully formed upon analogical precedent, authority, and example."[3]

The Whig apology for the expulsion of James II, then—here so succinctly expressed by Burke—was that James had begun to alter for the worse the old constitution of England: James was an innovator. As Burke writes elsewhere in the *Reflections*, "To have made a revolution is a measure which, *prima fronte,* requires an apology." A very similar apology, we shall see, was made by the American leaders in their quarrel with king and parliament, and for their act of separation. The Whig magnates had prevented James II from working a revolution; the American patriots had prevented George III from working a revolution (a revolution, that is, in the twentieth-century sense of the word). If the events of 1688 and 1776 were revolutions at all, they were counter-revolutions, intended to restore the old constitutions of government. So, at any rate, runs the Whig interpretation of history.

You will perceive that already, by 1790, Burke and the Old Whigs were involved in difficulty by this troublous word "revolution." For the same word was coming to signify two very different phenomena. On the one hand, it meant a healthy return to old ways; on the other hand, it meant (with reference to what was happening in France) a violent destruction of the old order. The English Revolution and the French Revolution were contrary impulses—although for a brief while, with the summoning of the long-dormant Three Estates, it had appeared that the French movement too might be in part a turning back to old political ways.

In America, the dominant Federalists—and soon not the Federalists only—were similarly perplexed by that word. Here they stood, the victors of the American Revolution, Washington and Hamilton and Adams and Madison and Morris and all that breed; and they were aghast at the revolution running its course in France. They had fought to secure the "chartered rights of Englishmen" in America, those rights of the Bill of Rights of 1689; and now they were horrified by the consequences of the Declaration of the Rights of Man, borrowed in part from that very Declaration of Independence to which they had subscribed. The same revulsion soon spread to many of the Jeffersonian faction—to such early egalitarians as Randolph of Roanoke, Republican leader of the House of Representatives. It spread in England to the New Whigs, so that even Charles James Fox, by 1794, would declare, "I can hardly frame to myself the condition of a people, in which I would not rather desire that they should continue, than fly to arms, and seek redress through the unknown miseries of a revolution." In short, Whig revolution meant recovery of what was being lost; Jacobin revolution meant destruction of the fabric of society. The confounding of those two quite inconsonant intepretations of the word "revolution" troubles us still.

The Whig interpretation of history has been most seriously criticized, and perhaps confuted, by such recent historians as Sir Herbert Butterfield. No longer do most historians believe that James II could have worked fundamental constitutional alterations, nor that he intended to; and James was more tolerant than were his adversaries. What ruined him with the English people, indeed, was his Declaration for Liberty of Conscience, indulging Catholics and Dissenters; and what impelled William of Orange to supplant James was William's dread of a popular rising that might overthrow the monarchy altogether and establish another Commonwealth. William, too, preferred preventing a revolution to making one. For a convincing brief study of the period, I commend Maurice Ashley's book, *The Glorious Revolution of 1688*, published in 1966. Ashley doubts whether the overturn of 1688 did indeed constitute a "Glorious Revolution"; but he concludes that the event "undoubtedly contributed to the evolution of parliamentary democracy in England and of a balanced constitution in the United States of America."[4]

However that may be, Edmund Burke repeatedly and emphatically approved what had occurred in 1688 and 1689. The Whig interpretation was the creed of his party; it was the premise of his *Thoughts on the Cause of the Present Discontents* and of his American speeches. It would not do for

Burke, so eminent in Whig councils, to be found wanting in zeal for the Glorious Revolution that had dethroned a Papist. For Irish Tories had been among his ancestors; his mother, sister, and wife were Catholics (although that fact appears not to have been widely known); Burke was the agent at Westminster for the Irish Catholic interest; early in his career he had been accused by the old Duke of Newcastle of being "a Jesuit in disguise," and a caricaturist had represented him in a Jesuit soutane. "Remember, remember the fifth of November": Burke had been compelled to draw his sword to defend himself during the Gordon Riots. It was prudent for Burke to subscribe conspicuously to the Whig doctrines of 1688 and 1689.

Certainly Burke in part founded his vehement denunciation of the French Revolution upon his approbation of the English Revolution—of that "revolution" which had been a return, in Whig doctrine, to established political modes of yesteryear. Upon the same ground, Burke had attacked mordantly the American policies of George III, advocating a "salutary neglect" of the American colonies because it was to Britain's interest, as to the colonies' interest, that the old autonomy of the colonies should be preserved. It was King George, with his stubborn insistence upon taxing the Americans directly, who was the innovator, the revolutionary (in the French sense of the word), in Burke's argument; Burke, with the Rockingham Whigs, sought to achieve compromise and conciliation.

But it does not follow that Burke approved what came to be called the American Revolution. The notion that Burke rightly supported the American Revolution but inconsistently opposed the French Revolution is a vulgar error often refuted—by Woodrow Wilson, for one, in his article "Edmund Burke and the French Revolution."[5] Burke advocated redress of American grievances, or at least tacit acceptance of certain American claims of prescriptive right; he never countenanced ambitions for total separation from the authority of Crown in Parliament. Burke's stand is ably summed up by Ross Hoffman in his *Edmund Burke, New York Agent*:

> Burke had no natural sympathy for America except as a part of the British Empire, and if, when the war came, he did not wish success to British arms, neither did he desire the Americans to triumph. Peace and Anglo-American reconciliation within the empire were his objects. After Americans won their independence, he seems to have lost all interest in their country."[6]

During the decade before the shot heard round the world, Burke seemed a champion of the claims of Americans. That sympathy, nevertheless, was incidental to his championing of the rights of Englishmen. It was for English liberties that the Rockingham Whigs were earnestly concerned. If the king should succeed in dragooning Americans, might he not then turn to dragooning Englishment? It was the belief of the Whigs that George III intended to resurrect royal prerogatives of Stuart and Tudor times; that he would make himself a despot. That peril the Whigs—and Burke in particular, with fierce invective—considerably exaggerated; but it is easy to be wise by hindsight. George III was a more formidable adversary than ever James II had been. Where James had been timid and indecisive, George was courageous and tenacious; and often George was clever, if obdurate, in his aspiration to rule as a Patriot King.[7] At the end, Burke came to understand that in the heat of partisan passion he had reviled his king unjustly; and in his *Letter to a Noble Lord* (1796) he called George "a mild and benevolent sovereign."

Yet neither to the American patriots nor to Burke, in 1774 and 1775, had George III seemed either mild or benevolent. Upon the assumption that King George meant to root up the liberties of Englishmen—to trample upon the British Constitution—the dominant faction of whigs in America determined to raise armies and risk hanging. They declared that they were resisting pernicious innovations and defending ancient rights: that they were true-born Englishmen, up in arms to maintain what Burke called "the chartered rights" of their nation. They appealed to the Declaration of Rights of 1689; they offered for their violent resistance to royal authority the very apology offered by the Whigs of 1688. In the older sense of that uneasy word "revolution," they were endeavoring to prevent, rather than to make, a revolution. Or such was the case they made until a French alliance became indispensable.

II

This thesis that the patriots intended no radical break with the past—that they thought of themselves as conservators rather than as inno- vators—scarcely is peculiar to your servant. It is now dominant among leading historians of American politics. It is most succinctly stated by Daniel Boorstin in his slim volume *The Genius of American Politics* (1953).

"The most obvious peculiarity of our American Revolution is that, in the modern European sense of the word, it was hardly a revolution at all," Boorstin writes in that forthright book:

> The Daughters of the American Revolution, who have been understandably sensitive on this subject, have always insisted in their literature that the American Revolution was no revolution but merely a colonial rebellion. The more I have looked into the subject, the more convinced I have become of the wisdom of their naïveté. 'The social condition and the Constitution of the Americans are democratic,' De Tocqueville observed about a hundred years ago. 'But they have not had a democratic revolution.' This fact is surely one of the more important of our history.[8]

The attainment of America's independence, Boorstin makes clear in his writings, was not the work of what Burke called "theoretic dogma." What most moved the Americans of that time was their own colonial experience: they were defending their right to go on living in the future much as they had lived in the past; they were not marching to Zion. To quote Boorstin directly again, "The American Revolution was in a very special way conceived as both a vindication of the British past and an affirmation of an American future. The British past was contained in ancient and living institutions rather than in doctrines; and the American future was never to be contained in a theory."[9]

This point is made with equal force by Clinton Rossiter in his *Seedtime of the Republic: the Origin of the American Tradition of Political Liberty* (1953). In the course of his discussion of the thought of Richard Bland, Rossiter remarks that "[t]hroughout the colonial period and right down to the last months before the Declaration of Independence, politically conscious Americans looked upon the British Constitution rather than natural law as the bulwark of their cherished liberties. Practical thinking in eighteenth-century America was dominated by two assumptions: that the British Constitution was the best and happiest of all possible forms of government, and that the colonists, descendants of freeborn Englishmen, enjoyed the blessings of this constitution to the fullest extent consistent with a wilderness environment."[10] Men like Bland—and those, too, like Patrick Henry, more radical than Bland—regarded themselves as the defenders of a venerable constitution, not as marchers in the dawn of a Brave New World. As Rossiter continues in his chapter on the Rights of Man,[11] "Virginians made excellent practical use of this distinction. When their last royal Governor, Lord Dunmore, proclaimed them to be in rebellion, they retorted immediately in print that he was the real rebel and they the saviors of the constitution." It was the case of James II and arbitrary power all over again.

Or to turn to H. Trevor Colbourn's study, *The Lamp of Experience*:

> In insisting upon rights which their history showed were deeply embedded in antiquity, American Revolutionaries argued that their stand was essentially conservative; it was the corrupted mother country which was pursuing a radical course of action, pressing innovations and encroachments upon her long-suffering colonies. Independence was in large measure the product of the historical concepts of the men who made it, men who furnished intellectual as well as political leadership to a new nation.[12]

Here we have for authority the famous sentences of Patrick Henry, in 1775: "I have but one lamp by which my feet are guided, and that is the lamp of experience. I know of no way of judging the future but by the past." The appeal of even the more passionate leaders of the American rising against royal innovation was to precedent and old usage, not to utopian visions.

The men who made the American Revolution, in fine, had little intention of making a revolution in the French sense (so soon to follow) of a reconstitution of society. Until little choice remained to them, they were anything but enthusiasts even for separation from Britain. This is brought out in an interesting conversation between Burke and Benjamin Franklin, on the eve of Franklin's departure from London for America; Burke relates this in his *Appeal from the New to the Old Whigs:*

> In this discourse, Dr. Franklin lamented, and with apparent sincerity, the separation which he feared was inevitable between Great Britain and her colonies. He certainly spoke of it as an event which gave him the greatest concern. America, he said, would never again see such happy days as she had passed under the protection of England. He observed, that ours was the only instance of a great empire, in which the most distant parts and members had been as well governed as the metropolis and its vicinage: but that the Americans were going to lose the means which secured to them this rare and precious advantage. The question with them was not whether they were to remain as they had been before the troubles,

for better, he allowed, they could not hope to be; but whether they were to give up so happy a situation without a struggle? Mr. Burke had several other conversations with him about that time, in none of which, soured and exasperated as his mind certainly was, did he discover any other wish in favour of America than for a security to its *ancient* condition. Mr. Burke's conversation with other Americans was large indeed, and his inquiries extensive and diligent. Trusting to the result of all these means of information, but trusting much more in the public presumptive indications I have just referred to, and to the reiterated, solemn declarations of their assemblies, he always firmly believed that they were purely on the defensive in that rebellion.   He considered the Americans as standing at that time, and in that controversy, in the same relation to England, as England did to King James the Second, in 1688. He believed, that they had taken up arms from one motive only; that is, our attempting to tax them without their consent; to tax them for the purposes of maintaining civil and military establishments. If this attempt of ours could have been practically established, he thought, with them, that their assemblies would become totally useless; that, under the system of policy which was then pursued, the American could have no sort of security for their laws or liberties, or for any part of them; and that the very circumstance of *our* freedom would have augmented the weight of *their* slavery.[13]

Such were the language and the convictions of the American patriots, as Rossiter puts it, "right down to the last months before the Declaration of Independence." Then what account do we make of the highly theoretical and abstract language of the first part of the Declaration of Independence, with its appeal to "the laws of Nature and of Nature's God," to self-evident truths, to a right to abolish any form of government? Why is Parliament not even mentioned in the Declaration? What has become of the English constitution, the rights of Englishmen, the citing of English precedents, the references to James II and the Glorious Revolution?

These startling inclusions and omissions are discussed penetratingly by Carl Becker in *The Declaration of Independence: A Study in the History of Political Ideas*, first published in 1922. Indeed the language of much of the Declaration is the language of the French Enlightenment; and more immediately, the language of the Thomas Jefferson of 1776, rather than the tone and temper of the typical member of the Continental Congress.

"Not without reason was Jefferson most at home in Paris," Becker writes. "By the qualities of his mind and temperament he really belonged to the philosophical school, to the Encyclopædists, those generous souls who loved mankind by virtue of not knowing too much about men, who worshipped reason with unreasoning faith, who made a study of Nature while cultivating a studied aversion for 'enthusiasm,' and strong religious emotion. Like them, Jefferson, in his earlier years especially, impresses one as being a radical by profession. We often feel that he defends certain practices and ideas, that he denounces certain customs or institutions, not so much from independent reflection or deep-seated conviction on the particular matter in hand as because in general these are the things that a philosopher and a man of virtue ought naturally to defend or denounce. It belonged to the eighteenth-century philosopher, as a matter of course, to apostrophize Nature, to defend Liberty, to denounce Tyranny, perchance to shed tears at the thought of a virtuous action."[14]

The Francophile Jefferson, in other words, was atypical of the men, steeped in Blackstone and constitutional history, who sat in the Continental Congress. Yet the Congress accepted Jefferson's Declaration, unprotestingly. Why?

Because aid from France had become an urgent necessity for the patriot cause. The phrases of the Declaration, congenial to the *philosophes*, were calculated to wake strong sympathy in France's climate of opinion; and as Becker emphasizes, those phrases achieved with high success precisely that result. It would have been not merely pointless, but counter-productive, to appeal for French assistance on the ground of the ancient rights of Englishmen; the French did not wish Englishmen well.

Here we turn again to the quotable Daniel Boorstin (who differs somewhat with Becker). It is not to the Declaration we should look, Boorstin suggests, if we seek to understand the motives of the men who accomplished the American Revolution: not, at least, to the Declaration's first two paragraphs. "People have grasped at 'life, liberty, and the pursuit of happiness,' forgetting that it was two-thirds borrowed and, altogether, only part of a preamble," Boorstin writes. "We have repeated that 'all men are created equal,' without daring to discover what it meant and without realizing that probably to none of the men who spoke it did it mean what we would like it to mean." Really, he tells us, the Revolution was all about no taxation without representation. "It is my view that the major issue of the American Revolution was the true constitution of the British Empire, which is a pretty technical legal problem."[15]

Amen to that. Burke declared, looking upon the ghastly spectacle of the French Revolution, that it is not merely mistaken, but evil, to attempt to govern a nation by utopian designs, regardless of prudence, historical experience, convention, custom, the complexities of political compromise, and long-received principles of morality. The men who made the American Revolution were not abstract visionaries. Suffering practical grievance, they sought practical redress; not obtaining that, they settled upon separation from the Crown in Parliament, as a hard necessity. That act was meant not as a repudiation of their past, but as a means for preventing the destruction of their pattern of politics by King George's presumed intended revolution of arbitrary power, after which, in Burke's phrase, "the Americans could have no sort of security for their laws or liberties." That was not the cast of mind which is encountered among the revolutionaries of the twentieth century.

III

The careful study of history is of high value—among other reasons because it may instruct us, sometimes, concerning ways to deal with our present discontents. I do not mean simply that history repeats itself—or repeats itself with variations—although there is something in that, and particularly in the history of revolutions on the French model, which devour their own children. (Here I commend Crane Brinton's book *The Anatomy of Revolution,* and D. W. Brogan's book *The Price of Revolution.*[16]) I am suggesting, rather, that deficiency in historical perspective leads to the ruinous blunders of ideologues, whom Burckhardt calls "the terrible simplifiers"; while sound historical knowledge may diminish the force of Hegel's aphorism that "we learn from history that we learn nothing from history."

The history of this slippery word "revolution" is a case in point. Political terms have historical origins. If one is ignorant of those historical origins—if even powerful statesmen are ignorant of them—great errors become possible. It is as if one were to confound the word "law" as a term of jurisprudence with the word "law" as a term of natural science. If one assumes that the word "revolution" signifies always the same phenomenon, regardless of historical background, one may make miscalculations with grave consequences—perhaps fatal consequences.

The American Revolution, or War of Independence, was a preventive movement, intended to preserve an old constitutional structure for the most part. Its limited objectives attained, order was restored. It arose from causes intimately bound up with the colonial experience and the British constitution, and little connected with the causes of the French Revolution. In intention, at least, it was a "revolution" in the meaning of that term generally accepted during the seventeenth century and the first half of the eighteenth century.

The French Revolution was a very different phenomenon, as was its successor the Russian Revolution. These were philosophical revolutions—or, as we say nowadays with greater precision, ideological revolutions: catastrophic upheavals in the later signification of the term "revolution." Their objectives were unlimited, in the sense of being utopian; their consequences were quite the contrary of what their original authors had hoped for. To apprehend the French Revolution, we still do well to turn to the analyses by Tocqueville and by Taine; for the Bolshevik Revolution, we have the recent books by Solzhenitsyn, Shafarevich, and others. "To begin with unlimited liberty," says Dostoyevsky, "is to end with unlimited despotism." Or, as Burke put it, to be possessed, liberty must be limited.

A considerable element of the population of these United States has tended to fancy, almost from the inception of the Republic, that all revolutions everywhere somehow are emulatory of the American War of Independence, and ought to lead to similar democratic institutions. Revolutionary ideologues in many lands have played upon this American naïveté, successfully enough, from Havana to Saigon. This widespread American illusion, or confusion about the word "revolution," has led not merely to sentimentality in policy regarding virulent Marxist or nationalistic movements in their earlier stages, but also to unfounded expectations that some magic overnight, "democratic reforms"—free elections especially—can suffice to restrain what Burke called "an armed doctrine." How many Americans forget, or never knew, that in time of civil war Abraham Lincoln found it it necessary to suspend writs of habeas corpus?

Knowledge of history is no perfect safeguard against such blunders. It did not save Woodrow Wilson, who had read a great deal of history, from miscalculations about the consequences of "self-determination" in central Europe. It did not save his advisor Herbert Hoover, who knew some history, from fancying that an improbable "restoration of the Habsburg tyranny" in central Europe was a more imminent menace than live and kicking Bolshevism or the recrudescence of German ambitions. Nevertheless, knowledge of history generally, and knowledge of the historical origin of political terms, are some insurance against ideological infatuation or sentimental sloganizing.

The crying need of our age is to avert revolutions, not to multiply them. Recent revolutions have reduced half the world to servitude of body and mind, and to extreme poverty, in Ethiopia and Chad, in Cambodia and Timor, in fifty other lands. What we call the American Revolution had fortunate consequences because, in some sense, it was a revolution not made, but prevented. Folk who fancy the phrase "permanent revolution" are advocating, if unwittingly, permanent misery. The first step toward recovery from this confusion is to apprehend that the word "revolution" has a variety of meanings; that not all revolutions are cut from the same cloth; that politics cannot be divorced from history; and that "revolution," in its common twentieth-century signification, is no highroad to life, liberty, and the pursuit of happiness. The Constitution's Framers, in 1787, wanted no more revolutions; and President Washington, in 1789 and after, set his face against the French revolutionaries.

Notes

Russell Kirk's "A Revolution Not Made, But Prevented" will be published in his forthcoming book, *The Conservative Constitution.*
It first appeared, in slightly different form, in *Modern Age* 29 (Fall 1985) 4:295-303.

1. E. J. Payne, Introduction, *Burke: Select Works*, Vol. 2, *Reflections on the Revolution in France* (Oxford: Clarendon Press, 1898), pp. xiv, 304n.
2. [As Dr. Kirk says below, The Whig Interpretation of History is a concept attacked by Herbert Butterfield in his book of that name (London: G. Bell, 1931). The book is primarily a critique of the historian who "stands on the summit of the twentieth century, and organises his scheme of history from the point of view of his own day" (p. 13). In particular, Butterfield criticizes the historian who divides men and events according to whether they allegedly retard or advance the "whig" values of progress, Protestantism, and liberty. For the purposes of the present book, it is a "whig" tendency of Burke (and, much more emphatically, Macaulay) to see, in the constitutional settlements at the Revolution of 1688, the embryo of everything necessary to advance English liberty for the forseeable future. A quotation from the tenth chapter of Macaulay's *History* may serve as a good example: "The Declaration of Right, though it made nothing law which had not been law before, contained the germ of the law which gave religious freedom to the Dissenter, of the law which secured the independence of the judges,...of the law which relieved the Roman Catholics from civil disabilities, of the law which reformed the representative system...." In the last two clauses, Macaulay is interpreting the Declaration of Right from the point of view of two nineteenth-century Parliamentary reforms. It is worth noting that however quaint and self-serving the "whig interpretation of history" looked in 1931, it finds its defenders in times—such as 1939—when liberty is threatened. —DR.]
3. Burke, *Works* (Bohn) 2:304, 305, appr. 12% into the *Reflections*. In Burke's era, Whigs approved of the Revolution of 1688, and Fox's Whigs thought of the French Revolution as a Gallic equivalent of what had occurred in Britain a century earlier. But the employment of the

word "revolution" was ambiguous; Sir Joseph Jekyll, lawyer and Whig politician, early in the eighteenth century, did not use the word in its sense of coming full cycle, but thought of it as signifying radical and violent overturn; so he distinguished the triumph of William and Mary from the evil of genuine revolution. Burke found it awkward, but necessary, to make the same distinction. In short, the history of *revolution* is complex etymologically.

4. Maurice Ashley, *The Glorious Revolution of 1688* (New York: Scribner's, 1966), p. 198.

5. *Century Magazine,* September 1901.

6. Ross J. S. Hoffman, *Edmund Burke, New York Agent* (Philadelphia: American Philosophical Society, 1956), p. 191.

7. [*The Idea of a Patriot King* (1749) by Henry St. John, Viscount Bolingbroke, Tory leader and friend of Pope and Swift, argues that the monarch must protect the nation's constitution by avoiding all factions, all ambitious and interested men, and by choosing instead ministers who believe in his own principles. Principled "measures, not men," was the slogan of this movement, early in Burke's career. Burke considered this slogan hypocritical cant, and argued instead (in *Thoughts on the Cause of the Present Discontents* [1770]) for party government. See Mansfield (below) and the Introduction to volume 2 of *The Writings and Speeches of Edmund Burke* (Oxford: Clarendon, 1981), pp. 12-17. —DR]

8. D. Boorstin, *The Genius of American Politics* (Univ. of Chicago Press, 1953), pp. 68-69.

9. Boorstin, pp. 94-95.

10. Clinton Rossiter, *Seedtime of the Republic: the Origin of the American Tradition of Political Liberty* (New York: Harcourt, Brace, 1953), p. 270.

11. Rossiter, p. 395.

12. H. Trevor Colbourn, *The Lamp of Experience: Whig History and the Intellectual Origins of the American Revolution* (Chapel Hill: University of North Carolina Press, 1965), p. 190.

13. Burke, *Appeal* (Bohn) 3:30-31, appr. 26% into that work. The last interview with Franklin took place in March 1775. Burke refers to himself, in the *Appeal*, in third person.

14. Carl Becker, *The Declaration of Independence: A Study in the History of Political Ideas* (New York: Knopf, 1922), pp. 219-20.

15. Boorstin, p. 76.

16. Crane Brinton, *The Anatomy of Revolution* (New York: Prentice-Hall, 1938); D.W. Brogan, *The Price of Revolution* (London: Hamish Hamilton, 1951).

Part Three

Burke and Constitutional, Party Government

12
The British Constitution:
The Rule of Gentlemen

We have come to the tentative conclusion that in Burke's understanding, the British constitution is popular government. The difficulty with this conclusion is that popular government does not always produce good government; it is in general a problem, not the solution to all problems. Particularly, the Bolingbroke party is a problem for Britain's popular government. How does Burke meet this problem? Does his solution, the rule of gentlemen in parties, depend on statesmanship and the virtue of statesmen; or does it seek independence from statesmanship for the sake of security?

In this chapter Burke's *Thoughts [on the Cause of the Present Discontents* (1770)] will be compared with his *Reflections on the Revolution in France*, because they present different treatments of the problem of popular government. The treatments differ because both works are by intention rhetorical; for Burke recognizes the need to speak differently on different occasions. Whether they are also inconsistent on the problem of popular government will be a question for investigation, not the subject of an assumption.

In the *Thoughts*, the people, through the Middlesex constituency, show themselves to be deficient by selecting John Wilkes as their remedy for the present discontents.[1] Wilkes has made Lord Bute his enemy and has proposed, more by the implication of his outrageous provocations than by any direct insinuation, that the king discard him. But Wilkes, in so proposing, and the people, in approving of this proposal, are "fifty years, at least, behind-hand in their politics." They seek to remove the Favorite, as if the present danger of tyranny were the same as that under the Stuarts—as if it were enough to remove a favorite, without touching the system of favoritism.

In the *Reflections,* the error of the people is different. There they have been misled not by history but by philosophy; the error is more profound. Yet curiously the error is in both situations involved with the doctrine of the natural rights of man. The people in 1789 were themselves aligned with the attack on the old regime, in the name of the natural rights of man; in the 1760's they were involved in a mistaken attempt to support the old regime against a political school owing its origin to Bolingbroke's modified doctrine of the natural rights of man. In 1789 the people were in a manner for Rousseau, not for John Wilkes and against Bolingbroke's influence. Of course, in the *Reflections*, it is the French people who make this mistake; but Burke fears that the British people will follow their example, that is, that the British people are capable of doing so.

This new possibility, that the people will adopt the error they formerly opposed for the wrong reasons, does not change the problem of popular government but poses it in a different way. For Burke, it requires a defense of the old regime, of its "establishments,"[2] a defense which could be assumed in the *Thoughts,* and was concealed by the economy of its rhetoric. But the "establishments" are not wholly concealed in the *Thoughts,* for Burke's remedy for the present discontents amounts to the rule of gentlemen—"so to be patriots, as not to forget we are gentlemen." Thus, for the interpretation of the *Thoughts,* our question is: How is the rule of gentlemen consistent with popular government? But the rule of gentlemen is one of the establishments defended in the *Reflections.* Thus an inquiry into the consistency of the *Thoughts* can be aided by an inquiry into its consistency with the *Reflections,* and because of the one-sided rhetoric of the *Thoughts,* one needs such help.

The Introduction of Party

Let us review Burke's treatment of remedies for the present discontents. The remedies he discusses are five in number: first, he demands a complete restoration of the right of free election to the people; second and third, he rejects a place bill and more frequent elections; fourth, he recommends, at this conjuncture, the "interposition of the body of the people itself"; and fifth, he defends and encourages the practice of party. In the preceding chapter, the first and fourth remedies were considered under the heading of popular control; we can now discuss the fifth remedy, party.

Burke precedes his famous definition of party with an encomium upon the "great connexion of Whigs in the reign of Queen Anne":

> These wise men, for such I must call Lord Sunderland, Lord Godolphin, Lord Somers and Lord Marlborough, were too well principled in these maxims upon which the whole fabric of public strength is built, to be blown off their ground by the breath of every childish talker. They were not afraid that they should be called an ambitious Junto; or that their resolution to stand or fall together should, by placemen, be interpreted into a scuffle for places.
>
> Party is a body of men united, for promoting by their joint endeavours the national interest, upon some particular principle in which they are all agreed.[3]

But this passage is only the last term in a procession which serves to introduce the definition—a magnificent procession whose color and variety of allusion attract our love of parade and whose order of march impresses our love of logic. To lead us to the thought through the excellence of the rhetoric, we should pause to describe the members of this rhetorical train.

Heading the parade are Solon and other legislators, who go "so far as to make neutrality in party a crime against the state." They are overstraining the principle, barking for advance, as is typical of first discoverers. Next follow "the best patriots in the greatest commonwealths." who are more serene, having "always commended and promoted such connexions," led by Cicero the philosopher. They regard each other, and *idem sentiunt de republica*. Then come the practical and powerful Romans, whose spokesman is Cicero the orator, who carries the same principle a fortiori and looks upon it "with a sacred reverence." The Romans are a whole people and take some time to pass our eye, as they tramp out their devotion to private honor and public trust. Then suddenly Molière the comedian appears, shouting through his Fool, "*plus sages que les sages*," and bowing in "all the wise and good [English] men who have lived before us." Last among these are the great Whigs, who are not only wise and good, but great in success, having governed according to this principle "in one of the most fortunate periods of our history." Addison is there with his trumpet, not really to play the Whigs' tune, but to play a tune that he knows they and the people like. "The Whigs of those days" tread lightly, their sympathy reaching out to the sufferings of their friends, their imagination untempted by a desire to sacrifice their tenderest connections to the bloody idol of Milton's Moloch.[4] And so we come to "these wise men," who embody the definition of party, being so "well-principled in these maxims." The definition itself, freed from its quadruple incarnation, stands with a classic simplicity that brings quiet to the noble and venerable ceremony of its introduction.

But the definition cannot silence our surprise, after we have admired its introduction. The parade was made up of a mingled train of practitioners and praisers; but the practitioners, especially the Whigs, do not speak; and the speakers do not praise *party*. Addison, who is the test case, because "he could not applaud...for a thing which in general estimation was not highly reputable," praises desert, long-tried faith, and friendship—but not party. The four wise men, who so staunchly embodied party maxims that they safely disdained "the breath of every childish talker," kept clear of the recommendation of party which Burke makes for them. In short, we learn from this parade what was mentioned in chapter one ["The Origins of Party Government"] that there is a traditional view of party which does not mention party.

Then if Burke would follow the Whig wise men, he should not speak their praise, but repeat their deeds.   He cannot point to writings for precedent, he can only point to actions. Clearly, then, the actions are insufficient or inappropriate. In speaking praise of the Whigs, Burke is refusing to follow their example. Their example must be inapplicable: just as the tyranny they fought now wears a new guise, so the remedy they applied will not work now. As we have said before, there is a very great difference between using party and praising it; this difference marks the distance of Burke's reform. Why, then, did Burke believe it wrong or useless to follow the example of the Whig connection of the reign of Queen Anne?   One must dispose of this question before trying to understand Burke's definition of party, because his reform is less in the *content* of his definition of party than in the *giving* of it....[5]

Party Replaces Conspiracy

The subtle relation of party to necessity can be found in this passage at the end of the *Thoughts*:

> There is...a time for all things. It is not every conjuncture which calls with equal force upon the activity of honest men; but

critical exigencies now and then arise; and I am mistaken, if this be not one of them. Men will see the necessity of honest combination; but they may see it when it is too late....They may at length find themselves under the necessity of conspiring, instead of consulting. The law, for which they stand, may become a weapon in the hands of its bitterest enemies; and they will be cast, at length, into that miserable alternative, between slavery and civil confusion, which no good man can look upon without horror....Early activity may prevent late and fruitless violence. As yet we work in the light.[6]

We are now in a critical exigency, says Burke; but it still permits "early activity." Our argument suggests that Burke seriously propounds this implausibility—that there is an absolute necessity to act in the anticipation of a situation of absolute necessity. Only early activity will be successful; the moment of absolute necessity must be pushed forward, as compared to the example of the Old Whigs.

This passage decisively shows that Burke rejected the example of the Old Whigs. At the same time, it shows that party is a resort of absolute necessity or critical exigency; Burke did not claim that the practice of party was a good thing in the best circumstances, but that it was needed in bad or critical circumstances. This is the last moment when tyranny can be successfully opposed, since only "early activity may prevent *late and fruitless* violence" (emphasis added). Modern students of party sense a truth, in Burke's opinion, when they justify party as a necessary institution, rather than a good institution, which should be chosen for its own sake.

It is necessary, Burke believes, to have a regular means of anticipating cases of absolue necessity. Honest men "may find themselves under the necessity of conspiring, instead of consulting." Honest men do not conspire well; they have a distaste for dark cabal and an open trust of their rulers. At their best, they are "persons of tender and scrupulous virtue."[7] They act well only "in the light." But conspirators acting for the good have a more delicate task; they must think in private, plan public deeds in private, act out their private plans in public, and speak in public.[8] Conspiracy involves a subtle shading from private thought to public speech that is beyond the discrimination of bluff, honest men; each step must succeed in its own compass, while looking forward to the conditions of success in the following steps. Conspiracy thus requires acting well in light and in dark and in twilight; unless aided by luck, a conspirator must be able to shift the purchase of his faculties calmly and rapidly, in a manner impossible to sensitive, honest men, who often cannot refrain from showing their virtue in a display of anguish.

Only a very remarkable man, in complete command of his faculties—as distinguished from honest men with virtues less skilfully ruled—can be a successful conspirator in a good cause. But states are regularly supplied only with honest men, not with remarkable men. If a regular supply of lesser virtue is considered more important than the best virtue, infrequently seen, then states should do away with the necessity of conspiracy by good men, in times of critical exigency, since conspiracy requires remarkable men. But eliminating the necessity of conspiracy requires itself the offices of a remarkable man, like Burke—perhaps even of an especially remarkable man—since in Burke's view, it may be greater than great to obviate the need for greatness. The founder of party has to see the absolute necessity of early activity, when honest men are complacent and when even remarkable men, taught by the example and doctrine of the Old Whigs (as reported by Burke), are patiently awaiting the last tolerable provocation of tyranny.

Party regularizes the wise man's precaution, so that honest men do not have to scan the horizon for hurricane clouds. They may consult, instead of conspiring. They have an organization in being, whose business is the prevention of occasions that necessitate conspiracy: "Every good political institution must have a preventive operation as well as a remedial." Party is a preventive operation whose remedial counterpart is impeachment. But what must be done to regularize the prevention of the necessity to impeach or to resist (the king himself cannot be impeached)? Consulting instead of conspiring is the regularization of conspiracy, because "instead of" means "in anticipation of." Burke's idea is to render harmless, by rendering honest, the practice of conspiracy. The example of remarkable men plotting in a good cause will not, by doctrinal extension, give license for scoundrels, since the "plotting" will now be publicly sanctioned consultation. And since it will be so, honest men will lose their embarrassment about plotting against an established regime, while their distaste for dark cabal is left inviolate. Burke's party is a re-enactment of revolution or resistance to tyranny, but a hidden re-enactment, cautious and traditional in its presentation, rebellious only by its anticipation of the need to rebel. Burke's concealment has been successful, for he is not known as a revolutionary, though he is known for having made party respectable.

Thoughts and *Observations*

Party enables honest men to act in the light, anticipating the task of remarkable men, who act in all degrees of light and dark. Party brings clarity to the gray shadows, natural and artificial, of conspiracy, making (so far as is possible) honest men clever, and clever men honest. Since conspiracy is always a possible necessity, especially when the monarchical principle is as little valid as Burke believes, party brings clarity to politics generally. Burke's presentation of the clarity that party contributes to politics has two stages, the first in the *Observations*, the second in the *Thoughts*. We now turn to a comparison of the remedies proposed in those pamphlets, as promised earlier in the treatment of the "political school."[9]

Burke says in the *Observations* that the "canker-worm in the rose" is a "spirit of disconnexion, of distrust, and of treachery amongst public men."[10] His remedy is that ministries be established "upon the basis of some set of men, who are trusted by the public; and who can trust one another." How are such men to be recognized? Burke considers and rejects the test of trustworthiness described by the "political school" and by Bolingbroke, "under the name of *men of ability and virtue*"; this conveys no definite idea at all, and "all parties pretend to these qualities." There is a clearer test, one which "with certainty discriminates the opinions of men": "...if the disease be this distrust and disconnexion, it is easy to know who are sound and who are tainted." Men show their unshaken adherence to principle by means of their attachment to a party, for such men obviously put their private trust and faith above their interest in office, or guide their ambition by their private trust. Then the "great strong-holds of government" will be "in well-united hands," because the king will be unable to choose according to his pleasure.[11] He will be forced to choose a party composed of men who demonstrate their trustworthiness to the public by their trust in each other. In the *Observations* Burke recommends party discipline, that is, party action.

As in the *Thoughts*, Burke's desire for clarity through party action attempts to repair a defect in public men; these persons "of the first families, and the weightiest properties" are honest men.

> This body will often be reproached by their adversaries, for want of ability in their political transactions; they will be ridiculed for missing many favourable conjunctures, and not profiting of several brilliant opportunities of fortune; but they must be contented to

endure that reproach; for they cannot acquire the reputation of *that kind* of ability without losing all the other reputation they possess.[12]

Thus a reputation for constancy to the public good is incompatible with a reputation for cleverness—which we would not contest; but in addition, Burke does not wish to rely upon the ability of the truly clever man (who is also the good man) to acquire an honest reputation by concealing his art with more art.

But one must pay closer attention to Burke's rejection of the distinction proposed by Bolingbroke's school for bringing greater clarity to politics, "men of ability and virtue"; for this is Burke's most visible difference with Bolingbroke's politics. For Bolingbroke and his school, "men of ability and virtue" were understood in opposition to men of false honor and piety. The adoption of this distinction in the constitution would clarify politics, because "ability and virtue" simplified the traditional end or ends of the constitution. "Ability and virtue" mean the ability to contribute to national strength and wealth, which is a simple goal compared to the difficult and ambiguous idea of the commmon good, as discussed by Aristotle and as patronized by the aristocracy (that is, the great families). Burke does not dispute the idea of seeking a simpler substitute for virtue, but he does dispute Bolingbroke's particular substitute for virtue, because he believes that traditional honesty, which includes a certain respect for honor and piety, is more durable and reliable than Bolingbroke supposes and should not be re-educated to exclude this respect.

In order to show his objection to rule by "men of ability and virtue," Burke provides a satire on their decline from friendship to inhumanity, in a passage at the end of the *Observations.* A powerful interest, "often concealed from those whom it affects" debauches the man of ability and virtue from his legitimate connection, which would be based on mutual trust. He gets new friends with his new office. "A certain tone of the solid and practical is immediately acquired....The very idea of consistency is exploded. Then the whole ministerial cant is quickly got by heart." This person, by "frequently relinquishing one set of men and adopting another," grows into a "total indifference to human feeling, as...before to moral obligation." According to Burke, the phrase "men of ability and virtue" is, first, self-deception, then ministerial cant; it is a cover for the "interest of active men in the state"; it is a justification for simple ambition. It is so because, in hawking this phrase, the "political school" tries to make a man's public reputation depend on his cleverness, instead of his constancy.

But the curious consequence of Bolingbroke's idea is to give constancy to cleverness, and therefore to pervert cleverness. "The very idea of consistency is exploded," but not the consistent *practice* of the man who learns from a flattering phrase to prefer himself to his friends and to the public. He may begin by deserting a doltish aristocratic patron to accept a post where his talent can be exercised; yet he learns from this experience not his true worth, but the principle of desertion. His corruption shows the power of constancy, even against the renouncement of it, for the man of ability and virtue becomes as undiscriminating in his "cleverness" as the aristocratic patron who is puffed up by traditional pretensions. "Men of ability and virtue" strut as foolishly and awkwardly with their new pretensions as do "men of rank and ability" with their traditional pretensions. It does not seem possible to do away with pretensions or with the dull vanity of honesty. For this reason, honesty is in a sense more durable than Bolingbroke supposed.

Honesty is also more reliable, since those distracting aspects of honesty that Bolingbroke wishes to eliminate can be used for public purposes. The private faith of men in each other, which grows only with prolonged acquaintance and which therefore requires a stability of association found only in aristocratic status (that is, aristocracy in the usual sense), can be used to test their public trustworthiness. It is better that the great men prove their sympathy with the people than that they merely profess it. But since the interest of the people and of the great men, properly pursued, do not diverge, the great men can show their sympathy with the people by proving to be trusted friends not of the people, with whom intimacy is impossible, but of each other.

The necessary condition for this transformation of private trust into public trustworshiness is a free society where the wealth of the great men is the effect and pledge of the people's liberty. Such a free society is a commercial society—a society in which, according to the method of political economy, everybody shares in the wealth as the wealth increases by virtue of the release of private interests. In a free, commercial society, wealth gives the great men a common interest with the people, though both sides must be taught to recognize that interest. Since all share in the fruits of commerce (thought not equally), the division of the rich and poor, which so occupied the older tradition of political philosophy, has been blurred if not eradicated; and the fear of partisanship, which was rooted in a fear of the poor as well as in a fear of religious fanaticism, has been in proportion reduced. At the same time, the great men and the people are connected—not so much by the public spirit of the great men, who act for the common good, as by a hoped-for harmony of *private* interests. The respectability of party is the respectability of partial and partly private loyalties, and partial loyalties are much enhanced when private wealth-getting is encouraged. A commercial society is not by itself the sufficient condition of party government, but it helps make party government possible by making parties tolerable, in two ways: it turns men's attention from collisions of religious faith, in which only the elect are saved, to divergences of economic interest, from which all can gain; and it eases the conflict of the poor with the rich.

Since it is the task of party to anticipate conspiracy, and thus in a sense to engage in conspiracy, honesty does not quite replace cleverness, but remains in need of cleverness. Honest men may shrug off their scruples against conspiracy, if they work in the light, but they cannot supply themselves with all the cleverness they need. Clever men, in Burke's conception, will not hover around the king but around their more trustworthy aristocratic patrons; there they will be able to do less mischief. Yet, to make clever men honest, a price must be paid: "As to leaders in parties, nothing is more common than to see them blindly led. The world is governed by go-betweens. These go-betweens influence the persons with whom they carry on the intercourse, by stating their own sense to each of them as the sense of the other; and thus they reciprocally master both sides."[13]

We have seen to what extent the "political school" constituted a party and how Burke interpreted the danger of its influence. In sum, their teaching and their example permit dishonest men to act in public, "in the light." Burke's desire is to make it easier for honest men to counteract the influence of this school; the "political school" has made necessary the reform that makes party respectable. Then the suggestion that Burke's party is a hidden enactment of revolution by anticipation must be revised to say that it is a hidden *counter-revolution* against Bolingbroke's party. Bolingbroke's party is in being; Burke's praise of party is a reply to it: "When bad men combine, the good must associate...."[14]

However, as a counter to the Bolingbroke party, Burke found it insufficient to recommend party action, as he had done in the *Observations*. In that work he discussed and rejected the distinguishing principle of the "political school," the advancement of "men of ability and virtue." In the *Thoughts*, he notices another plausible maxim of Bolingbroke's political school, "Not men but measures"—a maxim of which the phrase "men of ability and virtue" is a consequence. This maxim asserts that political consistency can be discovered in measures or principles, but not in men.

Hence the statesman (especially the rising statesman) should find his support in "men of ability and virtue," who are judged by the standard of "measures" (those that state the common good more simply in terms of national strength and wealth), not in the independent great families, who consist of "men" bound together by private trust, as well as by "measures." "Not men but measures" is an anti-party slogan, if parties are made of independent aristocrats—even if their independence is derived from the people. Yet it also comes close to describing rule by party program, as opposed to rule by statesmen.

Burke denies that this maxim serves as guide to consistency in anything but subservient ambition. The attachment of men in parties, he maintains, is the best test of attachment to principle rather than interest. Thus, again for Burke, party has the purpose of bringing clarity to politics: "When people desert their connexions, the desertion is a manifest *fact*, upon which a direct simple issue lies, triable by plain men. Whether a *measure* of government be right or wrong, is *no matter of fact*, but a mere affair of opinion, on which men may, as they do, dispute and wrangle without end."[15] For the sake of "plain men," consistency in political conduct is preferred to the delicacy of statesmanship, because consistency can be made clear if men will judge it by party loyalty.

Thus "not men but measures" is the pretense of a court party or cabal, and the same is true of the slogan "men of ability and virtue," discussed in the *Observations*. The earlier pamphlet directly attacks another opposition party, now out of office like the Rockingham party. Here Burke shows that the phrase "men of ability and virtue" encourages desertion by the satire upon a place-hunter who first deserts and then is deserted—a satire which is intended to bring the lesson home to the opposition. But desertion means desertion of one's friends for power; thus there is a somewhat greater stability of association in the neighborhood of power, in the court. This is the court party, or cabal, located where all "men of ability and virtue" aim to be. The use of this phrase by the court party is an advertisement for members from the other, more aristocratic parties, which are based on private trust; such a phrase spreads the spirit of distrust, which is the cause of feeble government and consequently of popular discontents. Recruitment for the court party masquerades, and quite successfully, as hostility to all parties. In order to stop this recruitment, therefore, it is necessary to recommend not only party action, as is done in the *Observations*, but party itself, by name.[16] By this extension, Burke's attack on the court party becomes a general recommendation of party.

The *Thoughts* is more general than the *Observations*, because it concentrates upon the court cabal, that is, upon the successful rather than upon the unsuccessful deserters of party. It does not answer a particular pamphlet, but a school of pamphleteers, who are inadequately identified; and it answers with an august vagueness appropriate to constitutional pronouncements. As an inducement to action, the *Thoughts* relies on a "legend" to evoke indignation, but removes the obvious targets of indignation—Lord Bute and the King. The *Observations* contains a careful analysis of English finance and reaches a satisfied conclusion on that account; it ends with a biting indictment of the Grenville party that more evidently serves the purpose of the Rockingham party than does the *Thoughts*. The *Observations* is a first step, tentative rather than necessary, in the direction of Burke's innovation; coming so soon before the *Thoughts*, it indicates an awareness of innovation and caution in causing it.

We may summarize the meaning of the public praise of party. Party has been distinguished from cabal or faction by its disciplined independence, not by the goodness of its end. Party thus brings clarity to politics; by this added clarity, politics is made easier; it is within the capacity, not of the common man able to understand party principles, but of honest men, who Burke argues are the aristocrats (in the usual sense of the word). Party permits honest men to act publicly while they are resisting tyranny. Thus statesmen need be no more than simple, honest men—perhaps aided by go-betweens. They do not have to question the value of honesty by the occasional use of dishonest means, or of dark cabal, to thwart dishonest men and to restore the primacy of honesty in the constitution. Burke's reason for introducing party then agrees with the view of some modern students of party—that party conflict replaces violence. The advantage of party, as presented in the *Thoughts*, is that it does not demand great ability; honest men can fight tyranny openly without causing a civil war. The disadvantage may be that party conflict, even when it successfully replaces the use of violence, does not avoid all the evils of violence. As it allows the discrimination of public men to decay in a party conflict made continual by the prudent anticipation of all sides, does it not also, by frequent calls to action, encourage cynicism in rulers and inattention in the people?[17]

Such is Burke's reform of the practice of the Old Whigs. It confirms the view that party government is opposed to statesmanship, but one should observe that Burke does not suppress the alternative. There remains in the *Thoughts* and in the *Reflections* a tension between party government and statesmanship, between "these great men" (the Old Whigs) and the great families, the present Whigs whose sole rule would be "austere and insolent domination," but who supply the constitution with a fund of honest and trustworthy ministers.

A Party System

There are many kinds of party: Which kind does Burke defend? Let us return to his definition: "Party is a body of men united, for promoting by their joint endeavours, the national interest, upon some particular principle in which they are all agreed." Party is a part of the nation acting for the whole—the traditional definition of party. But there is an obvious difference between the traditional definition and this one. Burke, though himself a party member and here an advocate of party action, does not define party from the standpoint of a participant but from that of an observer. He clearly distinguishes "*the* national interest" from "*some* particular principle," whereas the party member, from his standpoint, would consider the two identical. Burke's definition, while defending party, is skeptical of its claims. The part acting for the whole *is* the whole, in a way, like the government of a country; but if the part acts only "upon some particular principle," does it not remain a simple part, only contributing to the whole? The difficulty is that Burke defines "party" in the singular, but also in the universal. The first inquiry, then, must be: Which does he mean? Is party the means of applying true principles, as for Bolingbroke, in which case only one party is legitimate; or is the legitimacy of a plurality of parties desirable, as in a modern party system?

Certain remarks of Burke strongly suggest the latter:

> If he [a statesman] does not concur in these general principles upon which the party is founded, and which necessarily draws on a concurrence to their application, he ought from the beginning to have chosen some other, more conformable to his opinions.[18]

> Preferring this connexion, I do not mean to detract in the slightest degree from others. There are some of those, whom I admire at something of a greater distance, with whom I have had the happiness also perfectly to agree, in almost all the particulars, in which I have differed with some successive administrations....[19]

It seems that several parties, which can be identified by their adherence to various principles (sometimes coinciding in application) though not to any special principles, are legitimate, if not equally desirable.

Any other conclusion would be improbable, if we remember the division into parties of British politics in Burke's day. Speaking in such general terms, Burke cannot have supposed that his praise of party would cause the Bedfords and Grenvilles to merge with the Rockinghams; on the contrary, its effect, if any, would be to encourage the maintenance of division. On October 29, 1769, Burke wrote to Lord Rockingham, contrasting their party with "the Bedfords, the Grenvilles, and other knots, who are combined for no public purpose, but only as a means of furthering with joint strength the private and individual advantage."[20] The Rockinghams are singular in fulfilling the role of a true party; other parties should follow their example, but do not have to join them.[21] Burke does not rule out "healing coalitions"; but he does not require them, and he sees great danger in spurious coalitions: "No system...can be formed, which will not leave room fully sufficient for healing coalitions: but no coalition, which, under the specious name of independency, carries in its bosom the unreconciled principles of the original discord of parties, ever was, or will be, an healing coalition."[22] Coalitions should be permited, in order to heal the wounds of the original party discord; but Burke implies that wounds do not necessarily result from such discord, and hence that coalitions need not attempt to *prevent* party discord.

On the contrary, the Whigs and the Tories, at least in the past, "by their collision and mutual resistance have preserved the variety of this constitution in its unity."[23] Burke notes that these parties, by their union, saved the country in 1688. This statement must be compared to Burke's praise of the Old Whigs, discussed earlier; for it continues the criticism of the Old Whigs implied in the refusal to follow their example. Was it the Old Whig party, acting for the common good, that saved the constitution in 1688 and protected it thereafter? Or was it a union of parties, perhaps led by the Old Whigs, who formed a healing coalition? Burke seems to say the latter. What is desirable is not the protection of the common good by a part which acts for the whole, but the assurance of variety, which was achieved by a duality of parties in the past, and at present perhaps by more than two parties. In a crisis, the parties will unite, as after a truce; no single party will step forward to act for the whole. Thus, in the present crisis, with "a division of public men among themselves," Burke proposes that public men stand together against the court cabal, each in his own party, not all in the Rockingham party.[24] Burke has a preference for a particular party over the other parties, but he prefers the existence of a variety of parties to a single party, even that of the Old Whigs, one may suppose. We may note that the Old Whigs did not have such a tolerant view of the Tories, one of whom—Dr. Sacheverell—they took pains to prosecute.

We conclude that Burke meant to defend a party system, because of its variety, that is, for the sake of liberty, rather than a single party which would apply true principles to politics. "What is right should not only be made known, but made prevalent...."[25] What is right is liberty, which must be defended against the court cabal, but not at the cost of variety, not by "some particular principle" of a single party. Hence, as noted earlier, the common good is not under the care of a single agent but results from the action of several agents, none of which is fully dependable in its own right. Burke's conception of party thus not only implies but includes in its definition the paradox of urging party action in general. He presents as the main virtue of party a result which is visible only to an observer of a party system, not to a party member; his definition does not explain, indeed it depreciates, the motive of the party member. As distinguished from Bolingbroke, Burke is the first partisan of the two-party (or multi-party) system. Of course, not every group is a true party; some are factions. The difference between a party and a faction is that a party has principles, other than common ambition, which serve to make it independent of the court. These principles, we shall see, support the "establishments" of the constitution.

Necessitudo sortis

If there should be several parties, how should they differ, and who should belong to them? According to Burke, there are two ways in which men become party members: by family and by shared experience in government. Both are in some sense natural, for party is natural—or, rather, parties are natural. Both sources of party are plural, compared to the single source of true first principles of Bolingbroke's party. Consider the first source: "Commonwealths are made of families, free commonwealths of parties also; and we may as well affirm, that our natural regards and ties of blood tend inevitably to make men bad citizens, as that the bonds of our party weaken those by which we are held to our country."[26] Here is of course an analogy between family and party, not a statement of identity or of relation; party bonds are like natural family ties. It is a peculiar analogy, since it likens two parts of the commonwealth that seem dissimilar: the family is a part that usually claims to be no more than a part, while a party is a part that claims to act for the whole.

But could party have its basis in the family tie, such that free common-wealths display the natural articulation (in families) of all commonwealths? Party is concerned with rule, which is always the subject of some claimed superiority. Parties whose basis is in the family would have their basis in the best families or in the aristocracy, for example, "the great Whig families." When Burke discusses the aristocracy in the *Thoughts*, he identifies its leading characteristic as the possession of property, not as good birth.[27] Aristocrats are not so much the well-born as they are "men of property"—which is to imply that wealth attracts rank. Families have histories; their wealth is settled wealth; hence the best families are the settled or landed wealthy who have rank. In the first instance, then, parties are family parties, when family is understood as an institution founded in property, because property as power should be permitted "its natural operation," and property as the consequence of liberty should stand as "the effect and pledge" of the people's liberty.[28] Natural familiy ties, in this sense, prevent the party conflict (as in the Wars of the Roses) which results from the claims of family honor; for family honor inspires men to claim to be more than a part of the state and tends to make men bad citizens. Family property, however, is secured by a general recognition of property rights, a recognition that is not only compatible with patriotism, but *causes* it, since the insecurity of property is a prime motive for the original contract.[29] On the other hand, we have seen that Burke mutes the claim of party to act for the whole; so, with this interpretation, his analogy of family and party holds.

Burke's view of the family as a source of party is so undynastic that one must examine the other source he gives—common experience in government. "The great Whig families" are families of substance that have descended from the men who shared the responsibility for governing or watching the government for three decades following the Revolution; these "Revolution families" were not necessarily the most ancient families. In a previous discussion, it was suggested that rule is a kind of private property because it requires many individual judgments whose line of consistency marks an individual path. Sharing in rule is thus almost always a memorable experience. The experience of governing (or of opposing) becomes the private property of a group, and the memory of it becomes the *raison d'être* of the group. Proud of its achievements and aspirations while in office, the group stays together to repeat or to vindicate its achievements and to fulfil its aspirations. Thus a party develops the "history" which constitutes its character and usually comes to dominate the souls of its members; this healthy development works to unify the party like a "healing coalition."

This source of party is like the Roman *necessitudo sortis*, which Burke explains at the end of the *Thoughts*. The Romans, he says, carried the principle of *idem sentire de republica* a long way.

> Even the holding of offices together, the disposition of which arose from chance, not selection, gave rise to a relation which continued for life. It was called *necessitudo sortis*; and it was looked upon with a sacred reverence. Breaches of any of these kinds of civil relation were considered as acts of the most distinguished turpitude.

The relation of *necessitudo sortis* was not merely of passing significance for Burke, because he used as his motto on the first page of the *Thoughts* a passage from Cicero's impeachment of Verres, in which Cicero accuses Verres of faithlessness to his fellow consul by *necessitudo sortis*: "*Hoc vero occultum, internum, domesticum malum, non modo non existit, verum etiam opprimit, antequam perspicere atque explorare potueris.*"[30] The present discontents are caused by feeble government, which is caused by distrust among public men, distrust whose operation Burke characterizes in this quotation. *Necessitudo sortis* seems to be the relationship whose proper functioning Burke wishes to restore.

But Burke does not conceive of party exactly as the Roman *necessitudo sortis*. In the British constitution, obligation arises from shared rule; rule is not given by fate, however, but awarded by selection. Burke wants rule by selected trustworthy ministers, men of property and therefore men of a certain ambition. Men of property naturally reach for political power, but their ambition is trustworthy, because they are not desperate. Is the principle of selection, then, merely to reward the ambition of an undesperate group? Does this ambition have to be associated with the common good? Burke does seem to require such an association:

> Men thinking freely, will, in particular instances, think differently. But still as the greater part of the measures which arise in the course of public business are related to, or dependent on, some great *leading general principles in government*, a man must be peculiarly unfortunate in the choice of his political company if he does not agree with them at least nine times in ten.[31]

We observe, first, that he does not specify a single general principle of government, not even the common good, but rather welcomes a plurality of principles, which would doubtless conflict with one another in practice. The *"leading general principles in government,"* here so haughtily italicized, were "a mere affair of opinion" on the previous page. It seems still that Burke insists upon "principledness," rather than upon any particular principle. Secondly, Burke distinguishes thinking freely about particular measures from choosing political company. Choosing one's political company is not inconsistent with thinking freely, because measures which arise in the course of public business are "related to, or dependent on," general principles. "Disagreement will naturally be rare" because another party "more conformable to his opinions" is available to the dissenting party member. What causes this neat division of public measures according to several leading principles which gives every man not "peculiarly unfortunate" the opportunity of 90 per cent agreement with his friends?

It is impossible that the cause is the law of nature in the traditional sense, for the operation of natural law upon men's consciences would produce a simple unanimity of opinion, if it produced any harmony. It would produce neither the harmony which results from the interplay of conflicting opinions nor the partial harmony of like-thinking men. At the same time, Burke's description of political opinion as if it were found in compartments is not consistent with our experience, or with his statement elsewhere,[32] of the difficulty and unclarity of practical judgments. It is not true that men, in the face of the circumstances of politics, come to conclusions so readily reconciled. The solution to this problem seems to be that the cohesiveness, as well as the plurality, of parties is caused by the development of party "history" through common and different experience in governing. The different party histories are the means by which public measures are related to leading general principles; when a man enters the House of Commons, his choice is easy because he is confronted with several parties, each with a consistent history developed from a certain common experience.

Yet if a man chooses a party, he must first have chosen clarity; that is, he must have decided not to try to exercise his practical wisdom in isolation. He has chosen to act in concert rather than merely to "think freely." Then he does not merely adhere to a party because of some principle but acts in pursuit of some private ambition; for if he adhered to party on principle alone, in the absence of simple, true principles like Bolingbroke's first principles, parties would not have the high cohesiveness which Burke attributes to them *in potentia*. And if such a man were not free to act on ambition, it would have to be admitted that party discipline would impose upon his freedom. According to Burke, there is a law of nature on which parties base their development and with which they have occasional correspondence. When applied, however, this law of nature yields no clear choice of political company, no obvious leading principle of government; it must somehow be reconciled to the history of parties, which is apparently based on their experience and acquired without obvious reference to such a law.

Private and Public Trust

Parties are formed for both the higher and lower reasons for which men agree—and we suggest that, in Burke's view, association for the higher reasons is made possible by the lower:

> When I see in any of these detached gentlemen of our times the angelic purity, power and beneficence, I shall admit them to be angels. In the mean time we are born only to be men. We shall do enough if we form ourselves to good ones. It is therefore our business carefully to cultivate in our minds, to rear to the most perfect vigour and maturity, every sort of generous and honest feeling that belongs to our nature. To bring the dispositions that are lovely in private life into the service and conduct of the commonwealth; so to be patriots, as not to forget we are gentlemen.[33]

Generous and honest feeling and lovely dispositions seem to be less than virtue; in the context, they are opposed to angelic virtue. They may be identified as the causes of private trust, which Burke says make up the foundation of public trust—or of adherence to leading general principles in government. But private trust among gentlemen (by whom Burke means men of property) cannot be separated from their natural inclination to secure political power which corresponds to their wealth. "The dispositions that are lovely in private life" might therefore seem to be poisonous in public life, at least in tendency, because they cause oligarchical cabals. But Burke seems to believe, on the contrary, that private trust, precisely because it establishes a certain collective selfishness in public life, makes possible adherence to principle in public life. A detached man may be virtuous, but he is weak;[34] only men acting in concert have strength. Men acting in concert who have common experience in government will achieve consistency on public measures merely by virtue of their *amour propre*. Their ambition, or concern for private property of one kind, counteracts their avarice, or concern for private property of the usual kind. Consequently, their private trust, which is mingled with avarice when they have no chance to act in government, is mellowed by ambition, when they do have the chance to act. At the same time, their avarice counteracts their ambition, because their property is settled and would be endangered by political instability.[35]

Their motive is not pure, for they are not simply acting for the common good; they are defending their past deeds, including their misdeeds. But public consistency, in men of some private standing, makes such men independent in public, which is sufficient for Burke's mixed government.[36] Burke provides for the obvious danger of mere consistency—that it may bring a consistent evil—by defending (though indirectly) a plurality of parties, that is, by defending a kind of inconsistency. Defense of the plurality of parties is a recognition that mere principledness, without reference to the common good, is insufficient. It is also a recognition of the composition of motives that gentlemen have in joining a party, as well as a security against the possible ill effects of the composition. And finally, it is a limitation upon his preference for the Rockinghams. Burke does not say directly that party permits the use of private vices or of dispositions which can become vices to turn private trust into public trust, but we believe that no other interpretation finds his meaning. He does say the following:

> It is never...wise to quarrel with the interested views of men, whilst they are combined with the public interest and promote it; it is our business to tie the knot if possible, closer. Resources that are derived from extraordinary virtues, as such virtues are rare, so they must be unproductive. It is a good thing for a monied man to pledge his property on the welfare of his country; he shows that he places his treasure where his heart is; and, revolving in this circle, we know that "wherever a man's treasure is, there his heart will be also."[37]

In some current opinion, Burke is considered to be naïvely hopeful by having held that parties can be based upon principle rather than interest. This view underestimates Burke's realism in composing principles of interests, and in substituting *any* public principle (that is, principle known to the public) for *the* common good, as the basis of party. Burke saw "not men but measures" was the excuse of unprincipled men, as well as a high-minded slogan. He proposed that men of principle be held to the standard of private trust, in order to keep unprincipled politicians from claiming the right to desert their friends. But the standard of private trust is imperfect: among men of property, it allows collective avarice; and among oligarchical politicians, it allows collective ambition. In order to prevent the dangerous effects of Bolingbrokian humbug, Burke was forced to accept the dull vices of gentlemanly privilege. His parties of principles are tinged with interest so that they may be more than a mere cover for interest.[38]

For Burke, the "program" of a party is found in its history, what it has done, not in its plans for the future. Consistency is a rationalization of past judgment of public measures, and a party sustains its history when it insists upon being "not inconsistent with our former behaviour in the last opposition," as Lord Rockingham once put it.[39] Burke never wrote a program for the Rockingham party in the sense of a modern party program—that is, a demonstration of the advantages to be gained from the enactment of particular public measures derived from an application of the party's principles. But he did write "A Short Account of a Late Short Administration," which listed the achievements of the Rockingham administration of 1765-66. The conception of the party history as a program accords with eighteenth-century practice in Britain; as another example, one may recall the stubborn attachment of the Grenville party to the wisdom of the Stamp Act. Yet this conception does not simply describe eighteenth-century practice: a majority of the House of Commons were still independents; and there was a growing number of "men of ability," with a taste for administration and a sliding attachment to the party in office. Burke castigated the former for their tendency to support every administration, and the latter for their subservience to the king's private pleasure.

When the party program is a history of party judgments and decisions, it is bound to include hostility to certain persons, as that of the Rockinghams for Pitt [the elder], which memorialized certain disagreeable incidents of the past. The modern party, seeking to apply its party principles, attacks its opponents for their principles with a hostility whose sources is less personal, whatever hatreds it looses. One of the changes made in the *Thoughts*, after Burke had circulated it to his party, was the moderation of its aspersions upon Pitt.[40] The following is an evident allusion to Pitt, perhaps a moderated aspersion:

> In a connexion, the most inconsiderable man, by adding to the weight of the whole, has his value, and his use; out of it, the greatest talents are wholly unserviceable to the public. No man, who is not inflamed by vain-glory into enthusiasm, can flatter himself that his single, unsupported, desultory, unsystematic endeavours, are of

power to defeat the subtle designs and united cabals of ambitious citizens. When bad men combine, the good must associate; else they will fall, one by one, an unpitied sacrifice in a contemptible struggle.[41]

Yet this recommendation of group action is not only an allusion to Pitt; it also upholds the basis of the modern party program by lessening the reliance upon statesmanship. A party's history begins with the statesmanship of its members; but Burke encourages what might have been deplored, that judgments made in certain circumstances become, by virtue of the vanity of party members, the standard of political wisdom in later circumstances. This concession to the vanity of a party is intended to prevent the weakness of individual vanity and to procure the strength of group action; group acts are always stronger, or always more dependably strong, than the deeds of an individual man. This does not dissolve the traditional distinction between party and faction, but it does reverse the presumption of that distinction: connections in politics, Burke says, are "essentially necessary for the full performance of our public duty, accidentally liable to degenerate into faction."[42]

Parties are necessary, rather than good; they are contingent for their good upon the evil circumstance of "ambitious citizens." But their tendency to degenerate is only accidental. This is a very important change from the traditional view of party,[43] which we must pause to record. The traditional view was that party functioned as an occasionally good instrument, whose use even by trustworthy men was subject to some, though not to all, of the evils of faction; for good men who conspired set an example of which bad men might take advantage. In this view, healthy politics excludes the recognition of the regular necessity for party, because party has the inevitable tendency to degenerate into faction. In this view, the deeds of great men, which show the virtue of statesmanship, and the deeds of individual men, which show the need for statesmanship, conform to the nature of politics, whose complexity Burke has chosen to simplify with the introduction of party. One cannot deny that this reference to Pitt, if such it be, is a fine statement of the need for and the methods of political responsibility. A wise statesman must wish to give weight to his wisdom and must be willing to sacrifice his pet ideas for his fundamental design and to shake off the irritations caused by his necessary associates. He must act in concert with others, perhaps in a party. But acting together, we have argued, does not require the respectability of party. A statesman can act without the assurance of success or ease or immunity and take the consequences of failure as a result of a poor or unlucky connection. In a free society, he might suffer no more than the taste of opprobrium. But when party is respectable, connection is regularized and almost unavoidable; a statesman loses the advantage of his judgment in choosing how and with whom to connect and learns to march and shout. In the *Thoughts*, Burke has argued from the use of connection to the imposition of it.

Yet Burke regarded party as natural; how he did so is yet unclear. We have a partial answer to this inquiry: Parties are properly composed of men of property who have, in the past, acted together in public. Party thus depends upon the "natural operation of property" and upon the natural fondness of men of property for their own past deeds. These causes produce a natural grouping of parties, such that a man entering the House of Commons can find a group with which he can agree nine times in ten. But the relation of party to the law of nature that guides a statesman's prudence remains obscure; it will be considered in the next chapter....

Notes

Harvey Mansfield's esssay comes from his book,
Statesmanship and Party Government: A Study of Burke and Bolingbroke
Chicago: University of Chicago Press, 1965, pp. 164-67, 173-90.

1. [Some knowledge of John Wilkes (1727-1797) is helpful as background to Burke's *Thoughts on the Cause of the Present Discontents* [1770] and his views of party government generally.

Burke's views of party government came into focus during the period of "the Wilkes affair" in the 1760s. Burke had aligned himself firmly with the "Rockingham Whigs," been made private secretary and first minister to the Prime Minister, and won a seat in Parliament for the pocket borough of Wendover in December 1765. The Rockingham ministry ended in June 1766.

The proclivities of Wilkes, says the *Dictionary of National Biography*, were "literary and rakish." He won a seat in Parliament in 1761, aligned himself with William Pitt the elder (who was in the opposition at the time), and in 1762 began publishing *The North Briton*, a savagely anti-administration journal. In April 1763, *The North Briton* implied that King George had approved a deliberate lie in the speech from the throne, and the court determined to prosecute Wilkes. Since the journal was anonymous and Wilkes an M.P., his case produced important legal questions. Over the next two years, he was lodged briefly in the Tower, challenged to duel (and wounded in the stomach), lionized in the salons of France, convicted of libel, and successfully courted by Boswell, with whom he ascended Vesuvius. After the fall of the

Grenville ministry (July 1765) Wilkes hoped that the new, Rockingham ministry (which had supported him during his exile) would get him a pension, a pardon, or a place in the government. The next spring, Burke assured him of the continuation of the party's subsidy, but held out hope for neither pardon nor place.

The Wilkes affair became more pressing in March 1768, when Wilkes won a huge victory in the Middlesex election. Wilkes, who had never been pardoned, surrendered himself to the law, and was imprisoned. Riots broke out, and the next February the House of Commons resolved that Wilkes was "incapable" of serving there. Now the dispute embroiled the Commons with the electors of Middlesex, with "Junius" (see p. 16n6 above) taking Wilkes's side and Samuel Johnson the Crown's.

Burke's *Thoughts* assumes a knowledge of the Wilkes affair, but it aims, more broadly, to establish the idea of party government and the Rockingham Whigs as the bearers of the true principles of Whiggism, as Mansfield's essay argues. —DR]

2. *Reflections* in *Works* (Bohn) 2:363, appr. 36% into the work. For evidence of the orderliness of this defense and of the *Reflections* as a whole, see J. T. Boulton, "The *Reflections*: Burke's Preliminary Draft and Methods of Composition," *Durham University Journal*, 14 (1953): 114-19, and John Morley, *Burke* (New York: Macmillan, 1879), p. 149.

3. *Thoughts* in *Works* (Bohn) 1:375, appr. 92% into the work.

4. *Paradise Lost* 1:392. Moloch, the proud warrior-king, sought adherents to the claims of honor with grand disregard of distracting connections, such as Burke believes to be the necessary support of honor. In his Trinity College debating club, Burke once spoke the speech of Moloch (*Paradise Lost* 2:43) and received applause, the secretary noted, "It being in character"; but for the Whigs, it seems that the example of Moloch is too stern and demanding. See Arthur P. I. Samuels, *The Early Life, Correspondence, and Writings of Burke*, p. 266.

5. [In the pages that I have omitted from his essay, Mansfield argues that the Whigs whom Burke admires in the Revolution of 1688-89 and after had to act as "conspirators" out of necessity. Because public, party activity was considered divisive, they had to form secret "cabals," where loyalty among co-conspirators was high, in order to achieve necessary, constitutional ends, especially the replacement of James II with William and Mary. —DR]

6. *Thoughts* in *Works* (Bohn) 1:379, two paragraphs from the end.

7. *Thoughts* in *Works* (Bohn) 1:373, appr. 89% into the work. Cf. *Correspondence* 2:373; 3:89-90, 381.

8. Cf. *Appeal* in *Works* (Bohn) 3:81, appr 70% into that work: "...such devious proceedings [as determining the just occasion for revolution]...must ever be on the edge of crimes."

9. [In his fifth chapter, "The Bolingbroke Party," Mansfield describes thinking of the "political school" (the phrase is Burke's) of Bolingbroke and his followers. Among Burke's responses to this school are his *Thoughts* (1770) and the earlier *Observations on a Late Publication, Intituled*, "The Present State of the Nation" (1769). The publication to which Burke's *Observations* refers was written by William Knox and George Grenville, the prime minister whose fall in 1765 opened the way for the Rockingham Whigs' year-long administration. —DR]

10. *Observations* in *Works* (Bohn) 1:293, 188, appr. 90% and 3% into the work.

11. *Observations* in *Works* (Bohn) 1:295-96, appr. 92% into the work.

12. *Observations* in *Works* (Bohn) 1:294, appr. 91% into the work.

13. *Appeal* in *Works* (Bohn) 3:97, appr. 84% into the work.

14. *Thoughts* in *Works* (Bohn) 1:372, appr. 88% into the work. [This is the most famous sentence from the *Thoughts*, and an important part of Burke's defense of party: "When bad men combine, the good must associate; else they will fall, one by one, an unpitied sacrifice in a contemptible struggle." —DR]

15. *Thoughts* in *Works* (Bohn) 1:377, appr. 95% into the work.

16. There is a hint of the necessity in the *Observations,* where Burke says that those who renounce the principle of adherence to connections advertise their treachery to their connections. *Works* (Bohn) 1:296, appr. 93% into the work.

17. Cf. *Reflections* in *Works* (Bohn) 2:336, appr. 25% into the work.

18. *Thoughts* in *Works* (Bohn) 1:378, appr. 96% into the work. Note the "general principles upon which the party is founded"—i.e., founded in particular; the difficulty is repeated.

19. "Letter to the Sheriffs of Bristol," in *Works* (Bohn) 2:38, appr. 90% into the work.

20. *Correspondence* 2:101.

21. *Correspondence* 2:377.

22. *Observations* in *Works* (Bohn) 1:295, appr. 92% into the work.

23. Appr. 33% into the third of the *Letters on a Regicide Peace* in *Works* (Bohn) 5:291.

24. *Thoughts* in *Works* (Bohn) 1:371, appr. 87% into the work.

25. *Thoughts* in *Works* (Bohn) 1:373, appr. 89% into the work.

26. *Thoughts* in *Works* (Bohn) 1:373, appr. 89% into the work.

27. *Thoughts* in *Works* (Bohn) 1:318, 323, appr. 17% and 24% into the work. Cf. *Appeal* in *Works* (Bohn) 3:85-86, appr. 74% into the work, and *Reflections* in *Works* (Bohn) 2:323, appr. 19% into the work.

28. *Thoughts* in *Works* (Bohn) 1:323, appr. 24% into the work.

29. *Reflections* in *Works* (Bohn) 2:331-33, appr. 23% into the work.

30. Cicero, *In Verrem* 2.1.15.

31. *Thoughts* in *Works* (Bohn) 1:378, appr. 96% into the work. Emphasis in the original.

32. *Appeal* in *Works* (Bohns) 3:16, appr. 14% into the work. Cf. *Correspondence* 2:372.

33. *Thoughts* in *Works* (Bohn) 1:378-79, appr. 96% into the work.

34. *Thoughts* in *Works* (Bohn) 1:376, appr. 93% into the work. This is further proof that party adherence is not caused by a natural law that is the standard of virtue, but by some principle, perhaps the natural law, which states the means of overcoming weakness.

35. Burke regards ambition as a greater menace than avarice. "Speech on the Nabob of Arcot's Debts," in *Works* (Bohn) 3:192-93, appr. 92% into the work; Sir Henry Cavendish, *Debates of the House of Commons,* 2 vols., (London, 1848) 1:312-13; Cf. "Thoughts and Details on Scarcity," *Works* (Bohn) 5:89, appr. 26% into the work, and "Speech on Hastings," in *Works* (Bohn) 7:131. [The final reference is appr. 7% into the speech on Feb. 17, 1788, the "fifth" day, identified as Feb. 18, 1788 (and called the "third day") in the Little Brown editions. —DR]

36. It is Burke's argument against a Place Bill, the third proposed remedy for the present discontents, that the aristocracy needs a tolerable outlet for ambition. *Thoughts* in *Works* (Bohn) 1: 367-68, apr. 82% into the work.

37. Appr. 58% into the third of the *Letters on a Regicide Peace,* in *Works* (Bohn) 5:315.

38. See Alfred de Grazia, *Public and Republic* (New York, 1951), pp. 40-41.

39. John Brooke, *The Chatham Administration, 1766-68* (London, 1956), pp. 85, 96-98.

40. *Correspondence* 2:109.

41. *Thoughts* in *Works* (Bohn) 1:372, appr. 88% into the work.

42. *Thoughts* in *Works* (Bohn) 1:373, appr. 89% into the work.

43. See *The Complete Works of George Savile, First Marquess of Halifax,* ed. Walter Raleigh (Oxford, 1912), pp. 157-58, 225-27.

13
Constitutional Government and Revolution

"Who now reads Bolingbroke? Who ever read him through?" asked Burke in 1790 in the *Reflections*. And who now reads Burke? Perhaps whoever—meaning no offense—compiles *Bartlett's Familiar Quotations*, although even he, more probably, just reads the previous editions of *Bartlett's*. English schoolboys no doubt hear of Burke, and maybe they are exposed to an occasional excerpt. American schoolboys scarcely know him. If they are exposed to anything, it is likely to be no more than the passage about the function and duty of a representative in the "Speech to the Electors of Bristol at the Conclusion of the Poll," and that is presented as a curiosity. No, though always brilliantly quotable, the prose is unfashionable and there is too much of it. It takes a lot of digging to get to the quotations. As for the substance, Burke speaks for the side that lost, resoundingly, quite a while ago. "When our grandchildren have made up their minds, once for all," wrote John Morley in 1888, "as to the merits of the social transformation which dawned on Europe in 1789, then Burke's *Reflections* will become a mere literary antiquity, and not before." Morley's grandchildren, if not his children, did make up their minds, and his great-great-grandchildren do not remember what the problem was that called for the making-up of minds.

But there was a problem. Enormous, in our eyes incredible, social injustices have been gradually remedied in the nearly two centuries since the French Revolution, although others remain or have newly appeared. Perhaps the good that has been achieved is a legacy of the revolution, and perhaps it is not. But this is certain. The French Revolution was the first of the totalitarian movements that have drenched the Western world in blood, particularly in our own century. This is what Burke prophetically saw and this is what he hated.

"Is it an infirmity to wish," asked Morley, that some "phrase of generous hope," such as "lighted up in the spirits" of Wordsworth, of Coleridge, and of Charles James Fox, "had escaped from Burke" on the fall of the Bastille? The large-hearted Fox exclaimed: "How much the greatest event it is that ever happened in the world, and how much the best." It was a fatuous remark, like Lincoln Steffens' when he came back from the Soviet Union thinking he had been into the future and seen it work, or like many a now charitably forgotten celebration of one or another wave of the future in the 1930s. And it is an infirmity to wish that Burke had said something of the sort. For it would have been the expression at best of a "fine illusion," as Morley himself implies, and not necessarily fine at that.

Burke saw further and deeper instantly and without illusion. He saw a "chaos of levity and ferocity." He was no more given to automatic adulation of "the people" than of kings, knowing that "liberty, when men act in bodies, is *power*," and that power is to be judged by the use that is made of it, by its distribution, and by the limits put on it. Simply the seizure of power by a great many enthusiastic people is in itself no cause for rejoicing. Burke knew that to begin by despising everything is to set up "trade without a capital," and he saw that the French revolutionaries, despising all about them, all their predecessors and all their contemporaries, must also "despise themselves until the moment in which they become truly despicable." Their liberty was not liberal, he wrote, their humanity was "savage and brutal." He was clear that moderation and reason—the very reason in whose name the revolution was made—would count for nothing in an escalation of fervor from one assembly to the next, until a soldier who could secure the obedience of the armies to himself "on his personal account" would become "the master of your Assembly, the master of your whole republic." Thus in 1790 did Burke unhesitatingly foretell the rise of Napoleon.

Then and for some years more, Burke beheld in England the spectacle of well-born, high-living swells—Fox's companions, despite all Fox's virtues and talents—and of high-minded dissenting divines, seeing only what they wanted to see and extolling the Parisian mobs ("excuse the term, it is still in use here," Burke remarked) from Brooks's or from their pulpits.[1] The French, these safely distanced people were pleased to believe, had merely and at long last acted on the principles of the English Revolution of 1688 and emulated the recent American one. Revolutionary principles were all one, all equal, all good. They had, in fact, too long been neglected in England itself. For the flaws of English government were also gross. The rhetoric of these people was ever apocalyptic. All that was wrong at the root and all remedies had to be applied at the root. "Something they must destroy," said Burke, "or they seem to themselves to exist for no purpose." Mere reform would not do.

Burke understood his radical compatriots. He did not delude himself about their steadiness of purpose. "Almost all the high-bred republicans of my time have, after a short space," he observed, "become the most decided, thorough-paced courtiers; they soon left the business of a tedious, moderate, but practical resistance to those of us whom, in the pride and intoxication of their theories, they have slighted as not much better than Tories....These professors, finding their extreme principles not applicable to cases which call only for a qualified or, as I may say, civil and legal resistance, in such cases employ no resistance at all. It is with them a war or a revolution, or it is nothing."[2]

Though not often amused, Burke could sometimes dwell on the radical chic hilarity of it all. "Is it not a singular phenomenon," he wrote in a public letter to the Duke of Bedford, after the *Reflections*, "that whilst the *sans-culotte* carcase-butchers, and the philosophers of the shambles are pricking their dotted lines upon his hide, and like the print of the poor ox we see at the shop-windows at Charing-cross, alive as he is, and thinking no harm in the world, he is divided into rumps, and sirloins, and briskets, and into all sort of pieces for roasting, boiling, and stewing, that all the while they are measuring *him*, his grace is ...fawning on those who have the knife half out of the sheath—poor innocent!"[3]

Such were the flirtations of the upper class and of assorted visionaries. One reason, not the chief reason but an interesting if marginal one, why Burke was never taken in is that he was invincibly middle class and something of an Irish upstart at that; certainly not, as Sir Philip Magnus writes, "the best of good fellows," like Fox. Burke did not gamble, he did not hunt, he cared nothing for horseflesh. He was Church of England all right—and so, later, less seriously, was Disraeli—but he not only began at a considerable remove from the upper-class establishment, he never, like Disraeli, with whatever degree of detachment, became an establishment-follower.

"I was not," Burke wrote, "like his grace of Bedford, swaddled, and rocked, and dandled into a legislator.... I possessed not one of the qualities, nor cultivated one of the arts, that recommend men to the favor and protection of the great.... At every step of my progress in life (for in every step was I traversed and opposed), and at every turnpike I met, I was obliged to show my passport, and again and again to prove my sole title to the honor of being useful to my country....Otherwise no rank, no toleration even, for me.[4]

Burke was, of course, very far from being a philistine. He was a man of letters before, after, and while he was a politician, and his circle was that of the finest spirits and intellects of the day. But this was not a time or a place in which the artistic and intellectual elite, which was Burke's class, aspired to mingle with the social aristocracy.

The greatly more significant, the decisive reason why Burke did not for a moment go along with the gilded Whig radicals was that Burke confronted events in France with a coherent set of attitudes. He had what he once noted that Shelburne, with whom he served briefly and unhappily in 1782 in the second Rockingham government, and who now as the Marquis of Lansdowne was befriending various radical divines, signally lacked. "He wants what *I* call principles," Burke said of Shelburne, "not in the vulgar sense of a deficiency of honor, or conscience—but he totally wants a uniform rule and scheme of life." Burke had principles, he had a coherent rule and scheme, which he applied to the revolution in France. These principles are of enduring interest, as is Burke's steady sense of their limits. For one of his principles was the principle that on most occasions in politics principle must not be allowed to be controlling. His mind, Christopher Hobhouse wrote, was equal to the application to every question of both tests: principle, and expediency or prudence. "It was this double approach to political thought that made Burke the colossus that he is. He strides the gulf between the reactionary and the progressive, between the empiricist and the doctrinaire."

In our own time of dogma to the left and dogma to the right, and also curious though it be, of unvarnished populism to the left and to the right, when on numerous issues, in a phrase of Burke, "rival follies" mutually wage an unrelenting war, a time when change is widely counted a self-evident virtue, an age of futurism and millenarianism—there is much to learn from Burke. Our problem is the totalitarian tendency of the democratic faith, to which we have become increasingly committed, and the apparent inconsistency and arbitrary tendency of most remedies against the totalitarian tendency of populist democracy. Our problem has been, and is most acutely now, the tyrannical tendency of ideas and the suicidal emptiness of a politics without ideas, "the opposite evils," in another phrase of Burke, "of intolerance and of indifference." These are problems Burke addresses. There is in our past a usable Burke.

His thought yields no systematic philosophy, but it proceeds from a whole view. And a number of fully developed and firmly held propositions can be readily extracted from it. The first of these is that nowhere should there be any lodgment of uncontrolled, arbitrary power, not in any person, not in any electorate, not in any institution of government. Burke fought the King's prerogative, of course. That was what the Whig Party was about, that is what the *Thoughts on the Cause of the Present Discontents*, published in 1770, was about. And that was why Burke supported the American side in the War of the Revolution. He said much later, when accused of inconsistency in opposing the French Revolution although he had held with the American, that he considered "the Americans as standing at that time, in that controversy, in the same relation to England, as England did to King James II, in 1688." He fought the exercise of arbitrary power in his native Ireland. He fought arbitrary power as exercised in the administration of Warren Hastings in India, securing Hastings's indictment by the House of Commons and pursuing Hastings through seven long years of trial.

Arbitrary power in the people was no more tolerable than in kings or colonial proconsuls. "These old fanatics of single arbitrary power," he wrote in the *Reflections*, "dogmatized as if hereditary royalty was the only lawful government in the world, just as our new fanatics of popular arbitrary power maintain that a popular election is the sole lawful source of authority." Men thirst after power, he wrote a few years later, and whether they want it "vested in the many or the few" depends chiefly on their estimate of their own chance to exercise it. What mattered was less the source of the power than whether it was arbitrary or limited. And the way to prevent power being arbitrary was to ensure that it was nowhere total. A good constitution, therefore, distributed power so that no man or institution held it all, and all who held it balanced and checked one another.

So it was in the British constitution, the Crown, the Lords and the Commons sharing power, and limiting the power of each. What had gone wrong early in the reign of George III was that Parliament had become an instrument of the Crown, joining it in exercising control over the people, rather than controlling it in behalf of the people An additional safeguard against arbitrary power was an independent judiciary, not as a sharer of power, but as a counterweight. "Whatever is supreme in a state," Burke wrote in the *Reflections*, "ought to have, as much as possible, its judicial authority so constituted as not only not to depend upon it, but in some sort to balance it. It ought to give a security to its justice against its power. It ought to make its judicature, as it were, something exterior to the state."

But it was not enough that power be distributed, in no place arbitrary, and in no single place total. The entire edifice of power, with its many interior chambers and partitions, must rest on consent. Neither the distribution of power nor its basis in consent ensure good and wise government. Power is to be limited so that the chances of its wielders doing the bad and the unwise thing may be minimized; and so that when they do it anyway, the harm they cause will be less than total. And power should seek to rest on consent so that its distribution and its exercise may be stable—stability being a prime value, both as an end and as a means; as an end, because though truth may be preferable to peace, "as we have scarcely ever the same certainty in the one that we have in the other, I would, unless the truth were evident indeed, hold fast to peace"; as a means, because stability is a source as well as a fruit of consent, making the beneficent exercise of power possible though by no means certain.

A representative, electorally responsible institution was critical, therefore, not merely as a sharer of power, but as a generator of consent. Yet it was not the sole generator of consent, nor did it need to be elected by universal suffrage, or to mirror its constituents' desires with perfect fidelity in order to be effective.

Actually a parliament that is a creature strictly of a majority of the people "told by the head" was in Burke's view a menace, because it was all too likely to regard itself as sovereign, and to seize total power, riding roughshod over other institutions.

But it is necessary here to emphasize Burke's pragmatism, and his sense of place and circumstance. "Circumstances," he says in the *Reflections*, "give in reality to every political principle its distinguishing color and discriminating effect. The circumstances are what render every civil and political scheme beneficial or noxious to mankind." Even though he saw clearly and in great detail what had gone wrong in France, he would not be drawn, in the course of controversies that raged following publication of the *Reflections*, into making affirmative recommendations for the structure and composition of French institutions. "I must see with my own eyes," he said,

> touch with my own hands, not only the fixed, but the momentary circumstances, before I would venture to suggest any political

project whatsoever. I must know the power and disposition to accept, to execute, to persevere....I must see the means of correcting the plan, where correctives would be wanted. I must see the things; I must see the men....The eastern politicians never do anything without the opinion of the astrologers on the *fortunate moment*.... Statesmen of more judicious prescience look for the fortunate moment too; but they seek it, not in the conjunctions and oppositions of the planets, but in the conjunctions and oppositions of men and things. These form their almanac.[5]

In a system like the present one in the United States, therefore, where the executive and a bicameral legislature have both evolved toward election by universal suffrage, but from different constuencies and with staggered terms, Burke would not likely have perceived the dangers that were so evident in the sovereign French Assembly, and that might have arisen in 18th-century England from a sovereign House of Commons elected by universal suffrage; although he would likely have diagnosed the same danger in a Gaullist type of presidency, little countervailed by parliamentary institutions and acting on the basis of the presumed consent to its actions of the people, "told by the head" at the last election or referendum. Even so, Burke wrote two years after the *Reflections* that the English constitution was "not made for great, general, and proscriptive exclusions [from the franchise, as of Irish Catholics]; sooner or later it will destroy them, or they will destroy the constitution."

The fundamental point was, and remains, that consent and stability are not produced simply by the existence and function of popularly elected institutions, although absolute power may be. Elections, even if they are referenda, do not establish consent, or do not establish it for long. They cannot mean that much. Masses of people do not make clear-cut, long-range decisions. They do not know enough about the issues, about themselves, their needs and wishes, or about what those needs and wishes will appear to them to be two months hence. "The will of the many and their interest must very often differ"—an echo here, in some part, of Rousseau, but Burke did not suggest that anything positive followed from this observation, such as the right of a minority, seized somehow of the Rousseauian "general will," to rule. He argued only that there was nothing natural or necessary about allowing a majority to prevail. Rule by a majority obtained where it did, he pointed out, by convention and habit, and did not obtain universally on all occasions and for all purposes even where established. And where a majority does rule unrestrained, it is capable of great and cruel oppression of minorities.

The people are something else than a majority registered on election day, although by convention and for lack of any other suitable method, we let various majorities, including electoral ones, settle various things in various contexts on various occasions. The people begin with the "little platoon we belong to in society," what today we call groups, and they are found in places to which they are attached, in divisions of the country, what we call constituencies, which "have been formed by habit, and not by a sudden jerk of authority"—not by the assembly in Paris dividing France into equal squares, or by a reapportioning federal district judge, one might add, using a computer to so divide a state. No man will ever "glory in belonging to the Chequer No. 71," and yet "public affections," meaning consent to the institutions of government, must begin "in our families...pass on to our neighborhoods and our habitual provincial connexions," and so on to the nation. No jet age can change that.

The people then form into parties, under leadership they trust and find natural. Their temper, the temper of both the greater number and weight of them or of significant groups of them, is readily determinable, and no one can long govern against it, except by suppression, which is not government, as Burke remarked when urging conciliation with America. A nation, he said, "is not governed, which is perpetually to be conquered." Widespread dissatisfaction with government does not need the ballot box to express itself—Burke was far from deprecating direct political action, including civil disobedience in cases of necessity—and it must be met and conciliated, even if not shared by a numerical majority of the population, for law cannot deal with it. "I do not know the method," goes one of his most famous sentences, "of drawing up an indictment against an whole people."[6]

Such was the people, as Burke used the term, in place, gathered, led, manifesting its temper in many ways and over a span of time as a people, or as one or another sizable community within the body of the people, not speaking merely on occasion in momentary numerical majorities. The influence of the people, so conceived, must be a dominant one because their consent is essential. That consent may be withdrawn regardless of elections; it must be preponderant, not merely majority consent, and is yielded not only and not even chiefly to the electoral verdict, but to institutions validated by time and familiarity and composed from time to time of men who are trusted because they are seen to have "a connexion with the interest...the sentiments and opinions of the people."

George III's slogan, "not men, but measures," was pernicious precisely because consent is in large part the consequence of confidence in, and identification with, men. "The laws reach but a little way. Constitute government how you please, infintely the greater part of it must depend upon the exercise of the powers which are left at large to the prudence and uprightness of ministers of state." Consent will not long be yielded to faceless officials, or to mere servants of one man, who themselves have no "connexion with the interest of the people." In opposing the cant of "not men, but measures," Burke therefore resisted rule by non-party ministers who lacked the confidence of the Commons. By the same token we may today oppose excessive White House staff-government by private men whom Congress never sees. There are substantial differences of degree in the case of an elected executive seeking to control a large, permanent civil service, but it was not for nothing that the American Constitution provided for "executive Departments" and for Senate confirmation of the appointments of great officers of state.

Safeguards against arbitrary power, resistance to total power, assurance of stable government which is responsive and capable of generating long-term consent—these are agnostic objectives. Any true believer will want total power to achieve the true ends of government, and will be a democrat or an authoritarian depending, as Burke said, on which scheme or system he thinks will bring him nearer to total power. But any thorough-going agnostic might well also be a radical democrat, believing that nothing matters and that the merest whim of the majority is as good a guide to social action as anything else; and perhaps this is simply another form of true belief; like reliance on astrology or oracles. In any case Burke was neither a true believer nor a thorough-going agnostic. He was a Christian, and if anything something of a mystic, but no ideologue.

True believers—though not Christians—theorists and ideologues made the French Revolution, and for Burke a politics of theory and ideology, of abstract, absolute ideas was an abomination, whether the idea was the right of the British Parliament to tax the American colonies or the rights of man. Such a politics cannot work as politics. It begins and ends by sacrificing peace, and it must proceed from one bloodbath to another, and from one tyranny to another. Ideas are the inventions of men and are as arbitrary as their will. The business of politics is not with theory and ideology but with accommodation.

"All government, indeed every human benefit and enjoyment," Burke said in 1775 in urging conciliation with America,[7] "every virtue, and every prudent act, is founded on compromise and barter. We balance inconveniences; we give and take; we remit some rights, that we may enjoy others; and we choose rather to be happy citizens, than subtle disputants." He would not enter into "distinctions of rights...these metaphysical distinctions; I hate the very sound of them." They were, he found later, what the French Revolution was about. These revolutionaries build their politics, he wrote in the *Appeal from the New to the Old Whigs*, a year after the *Reflections*, "not on convenience but on truth; and they profess to conduct men to a certain happiness by the assertion of their undoubted rights. With them there is no compromise....Their principles always go to the extreme."[8]

The presumption, the arrogance of these Frenchmen's assurance in their new discovery apalled Burke. Those "rights of man" were an invitation to another round of religious wars and persecutions, not likely to be any the less fanatical or bloody for the irreligiousness of the new dogma. "The foundation of government is...not in imaginary rights of men," Burke argued, "but in political convenience, and in human nature...." Government thus stops short of "some hazardous or ambiguous excellence," but it is the better for it.

Men do have rights, Burke wrote in the *Reflections,* but as civil society is made for the advantage of man, "all the advantages for which it is made become his right." The rights of man, this is to say, have no independent, theoretical existence. They do not preexist and condition civil society. They are in their totality the right to decent, wise, just, responsive, stable government in the circumstances of a given time and place. Under such a government, a partnership Burke calls it, "the restraints on men, as well as their liberties, are to be reckoned among their rights," and "all men have equal rights, but not to equal things," since a leveling egalitarianism which does not reward merit and ability is harmful to all and is unjust as well.

Civil society is a creature of its past, of "a great mysterious incorporation," and of an evolution which in improving never produces anything "wholly new," and in conserving never retains anything "wholly obsolete." It may malfunction—the English constitution did in 1688—and then drastic measures may be called for to restore it to its true self, but that true self ought never to be altered, and certainly society ought never be uprooted, never be razed to the gound and replaced with some wholly new construct. This passionately held faith and his depreciation of the rights of man form the basis of Burke's reputation as the purveyor of a conservative doctrine unfit for modern consumption, as the last apologist for an oppressive social order now long dead and unlamented, as an obscurantist reactionary, an opponent not only of humanitarian reform, but of reason itself.

The conservative reputation does not fit the Whig of the 1770s and 80s, to be sure, the advocate of consent and limited power, the friend of the American Revolution, or even the critic of the totalitarian tendencies of the French Revolution. But Burke's contemporary adversaries and his later detractors resolve the contradiction by accusing him of having abandoned his earlier convictions. He got frightened, he got old, his sympathy dried up, he went tory, perhaps he was not even altogether of sound mind. John Morley's opinion, however—and Morley was critical of much in the *Reflections*—was that Burke "changed his front, but he never changed his ground," and this opinion can be shown to be correct. The same principles, the same "uniform scheme and rule of life" that informed the earlier Whig animated the author of the *Reflections*. The latter work is, therefore, not to be so simply rejected. "Fly from the French Revolution," Burke cried in Parliament in 1791. The liberal tradition did not fly from the revolution. It fled from Burke instead, and that was a mistake.

Of course there are moments in the *Reflections* that are nothing but sterile reaction. There is the passage that Tom Paine tellingly picked up in which Burke makes love to Marie Antoinette, that "Roman matron," and laments that "the age of chivalry is gone...gone—that...chastity of honor, which felt a stain like a wound...which ennobled whatever it touched, and under which vice itself lost half its evil by losing all its grossness." With this passage, says Sir Philip Magnus, "the Romantic Movement in English literature had begun," which is certainly too bad. But even here Burke exaggerates a valid point, namely that manners, civility, certain forms and standards of behavior, what he calls the "public affections," are founded in custom and are all easily exploded by a shallow reason. They are nothing but "pleasing illusions which make power gentle and obedience liberal"; they are "the decent drapery of life." But without them society and government are brutal, conflict is naked. It is all too easy and it is fatal to keep tearing them off until not only is a king merely a man and a queen just a woman, but also "a woman is but an animal, and an animal not of the highest order."[9]

Again there is the passage where we are told that the poor must be trained to obedience and labor, "and when they find, as they commonly do, the success disproportioned to the endeavor, they must be taught their consolation in the final proportions of eternal justice." Not an edifying sentence. But Burke had a social conscience, if a perplexed one. He puzzled, with feeling, over how to rescue people doomed to "servile, degrading, unseemly, unmanly...unwholesome...pestiferous occupations," but asked, "What is the use of discussing a man's abstract right of food or medicine? The question is upon the method of procuring and administering them."[10] And yet again Burke surely treated much too lightly the abuses of the French monarchy, aristocracy, and clergy, and the misery they bred. France needed a revolution, if anything more than England in 1688 or America in 1776, though not the one it got, and Burke should have seen this. Nor, finally, was Burke without his share of anti-Semitism, though it was of a variety that barely rises to the notice of anyone who has lived through the first half of the 20th century.

But all this cannot on any fair reading be taken as central to the *Reflections*, and much will be missed by those who do so take it. First there is in the worst, as it might be viewed, of Burke's so-called conservatism a powerful realism that any political thought denies or ignores at its peril. You cannot start from scratch, he maintained, and expect to produce anything but a continual round of chaos and tyranny, until you return to the remnants of what you sought to destroy. Perfection is unlikely in human contrivances, and so the professed purpose of any scheme that attempts to start fresh will be defeated. The old vices tend to reappear in new institutions, if their causes have not been attacked, but only their outward manifestations, which were the old institutions. Meanwhile the price has been paid of teaching men to yield as little respect to new institutions as was shown for the old, and in a continual round of change, men unmoored from their past "become little better than the flies of summer."[11] Even in pursuit of the most radical reforming ends, it is, moreover, simple practical common sense "to make the most of the existing materials." A politician, Burke lectured, contemplating in sheer unbelieving wonder the destruction of the church in France and the confiscation and dismantling of productive church property, a politician, "to do great things, looks for a *power*, what our workmen call a *purchase*." Here, in the church, were revenues, here was a bureaucracy. To destroy all this and scatter it rather than use it seemed to Burke the height of stupidity—and subsequent French history proved him right. In the same spirit, reading Condorcet's dictum that the American Constitution "had not grown, but was planned," that it had taken no weight from the centuries but was put together mechanically in a few years, John Adams commented in the margin: "Fool, Fool!"

Continuity—a practical necessity, if nothing else—was for Burke the principle of reform, not of opposition to it. Even revolutionary reform, as in England in 1688 and in America a century later, might be called for by a "grave and overruling necessity," in order to conserve by correcting. But the science of government is practical and intended for practical purposes. Cause and effect are most often obscure, and it is, therefore, "with infinite caution that any man ought to venture upon pulling down an edifice which has answered in any tolerable degree for ages the common purposes of society."[12] This is conservatism, no doubt, but what is behind it is not wish, or tired old age, or romantic delusion, or moral obtuseness, or class interest, but good practical wisdom.

Burke's conservatism, however, served another purpose as well. In order to survive, be coherent and stable and answer to men's wants, a civil society had to rest on a foundation of moral values. Else it degenerated—if an oligarchy, into interest government, a government of jobbers enriching themselves and their friends, and ended in revolution; or if a full democracy, into a mindless, shameless thing, freely oppressing various minorities and ruining itself. Burke's pragmatism, strong as it is, did not go the length of taking mind out of politics. Metaphysics, yes; mind and values, no. But where are a society's values to be found? In theory? Metaphysics, abstract rights would always clash with men's needs and their natures, and with various unforeseeable contingencies.

Theories were not fit to live with, and any attempt to impose them would breed conflict, not responsive government enjoying the consent of the governed. The rights of man cannot be established by any theoretical definition; they are "in balances between differences of good, in compromises sometimes between good and evil, and sometimes between evil and evil. Political reason is a computing principle: adding, subtracting, multiplying, and dividing, morally and not metaphysically, or mathematically, true moral denominations."[13] The visions of good and evil, the denominations to be computed—these a society draws from its past and without them it dies. Burke was strong for the union of church and state, since he viewed religion as a major source of the values that held a society together. He even praised, on the same score, the ancient prejudices of the people, using the word in a somewhat different sense than we do, and warned against exchanging the people's old superstitions—"the religion of feeble minds"—for new.

For many millions of us, organized religion no longer plays the role Burke assigned to it, and we want nothing of superstition and prejudice.

Burke may have regretted the Enlightenment, but it did occur. The Age of Reason continues, if not quite as pretentiously and self-confidently as it began. Precisely for that reason, however, the problem to which Burke spoke is even more acute for us. A valueless politics and valueless institutions are shameful and shameless, and what is more, man's nature is such that he finds them, and life with and under them, insupportable. Doctrinaire theories of the rights of man, on the other hand, serve us no better than Burke thought they would. The computing principle is still all we can resort to, and we always return to it following some luxuriant outburst of theory in the Supreme Court, whether the theory is of an absolute right to contract, or to speak, or to stand mute, or to be private. We find our visions of good and evil and the denominations we compute where Burke told us to look, in the experience of the past, in our tradition, in the secular religion of the American republic. The only abiding thing, as Brandeis used to repeat, and as Burke might not have denied, is change, but the past should control it, or at least its pace. We hold to the values of the past provisionally only, in the knowledge that they will change, but we hold to them as guides.

This is not, as Holmes once remarked, a duty, it is a necessity. How else are we to know anything? What is the use of empty "rationalists," such as were discovered at many a university some years ago, who being confronted with various demands for instant change, found that they believed nothing and could not judge any change as better or worse than another? They drove the very seekers after change up the wall in frustration. Nobody wants everybody not to believe in anything. And who wants politicians who, as Burke said, "see no merit or demerit in any man, or any action, or any political principle" except in terms of a desired political end, and who "therefore take up, one day, the most violent and stretched prerogative, and another time the wildest democratic ideas of freedom, and pass from one to the other...."

Our problem, as much as Burke's, is that we cannot govern, and should not, in submission to the dictates of abstract theories, and that we cannot live, much less govern, without some "uniform rule and scheme of life," without principles, however provisionally and skeptically held. Burke's conservatism, if that is what it was, which at any rate belongs to the liberal tradition, properly understood and translated to our time, is the way.

Notes

Alexander M. Bickel's essay was published under the title
"Reconsideration: Edmund Burke," in *The New Republic*, March 17, 1973, pp. 30-5.
The notes are by the present editor.

1. Brooks's, a London club founded in the middle of the eighteenth century, was known for the literary and political figures who attended it, and for high gambling losses.
2. *Reflections* in *Works* (Bohn) 2:336, appr. 35% into the work.
3. *LNL* in *Works* (Bohn) 5:145, appr. 86% into the work. Burke is actually addressing his patron, the Earl Fitzwilliam, although his remarks are made at the expense of "his grace," the Duke of Bedford.
4. *LNL* in *Works* (Bohn) 5:124-25, appr. 36% into the work.
5. *Letter to a Member of the National Assembly* in *Works* (Bohn) 2:548, appr. 75% into the work.
6. *Speech on Conciliation with America* in *Works* (Bohn) 1:476, appr. 43% into the work.
7. *Speech on Conciliation with America* in *Works* (Bohn) 1:500, appr. 81% into the work.
8. *Works* (Bohn) 3:109, appr. 96% into the work.
9. In this paragraph, Bickel has been following Burke's argument in the *Reflections*, appr. 30% into the work.
10. The three quotations in this paragraph come from *Reflections* in *Works* (Bohn) 2: 514, 431, and 333, appr. 98%, 64%, and 24% into the work.
11. *Reflections* in *Works* (Bohn) 2:367, appr. 38% into the work.
12. *Reflections* in *Works* (Bohn) 2:334, appr. 24% into the work.
13. *Reflections* in *Works* (Bohn) 2:335, appr. 24% into the work.

Part Four

Burke and the Radical Mind

14
The Organic Society and Human Perfection

The mood of England in the Industrial Revolution is a mood of contrasts. The title, *Contrasts,* which Pugin was to make famous, epitomizes the habit of thinking of the early industrial generations. We can properly begin our own study by an essay in contrasts between lastingly influential men and ideas. My first contrast is between Edmund Burke and William Cobbett....

Edmund Burke has been called "the first modern Conservative"; William Cobbett "the first great tribune of the industrial proletariat." Yet Cobbett began his political career in England under the patronage of William Windham, an intimate friend of Burke, and one who made Burke's principles his standard in politics. It was Windham, consciously the political heir of Burke, who welcomed back from the United States, in 1800, the famous young anti-Jacobin pamphleteer, William Cobbett. It was with money raised by Windham that Cobbett started publication of his famous *Political Register,* which became, and until Cobbett's death in 1835 continued, the most influential Radical publication in the land. The fierce young anti-Jacobin died a great Radical, who had been hunted to the courtroom and prison, on charges of sedition, by others of the political heirs of Burke. But the association of Burke and Cobbett, through Windham, serves as an introduction to the more important association, which we should now make. In the convulsion of England by the struggle for political democracy and by the progress of the Industrial Revolution, many voices were raised in condemnation of the new developments, in the terms and accents of an older England. Of all these, two have survived as the most important: Burke and Cobbett. In spite of all their differences, this fact prevails. They attacked the new England from their experience of the old England, and, from their work, traditions of criticism of the new democracy and the new industrialism were powerfully begun: traditions which in the middle of the twentieth century are still active and important.

Burke's attack was upon democracy, as we now commonly understand it. The event which drew his fire was the Revolution in France, but his concern was not only with France; it was, perhaps primarily, with the running of a similar tide in England. He did not believe that this could be kept back, but his stand was none the less firm:

> You see, my dear Lord, that I do not go upon any difference concerning the best method of preventing the growth of a system which I believe we dislike in common. I cannot differ with you because I do not think *any* method can prevent it. The evil has happened; the thing is done in principle and in example; and we must wait the good pleasure of an Higher Hand than ours for the time of its perfect accomplishment in practice in this country and elsewhere. All I have done for some time past, and all I shall do hereafter, will only be to clear myself from having any hand, actively or passively, in this great change.[1]

Now that the change has happened, or is supposed to have happened, a man in such a position is evidently isolated. The confutation of Burke on the French Revolution is now a one-finger exercise in politics and history. We check the boiling by pouring in cold water. His writings on France are annotated as I have seen in the story of the Creation in a Bible in a railway waiting-room: "historically untrue." This sort of thing is indeed so easy that we may be in danger of missing a more general point, which has to do less with his condemnations than with his attachments, and less with his position than with his manner of thinking. The quality of Burke is the quality indicated by Matthew Arnold, in his comment on him in "The Function of Criticism at the Present Time": "Almost alone in England, he brings thought to bear upon politics, he saturates politics with thought."[2] Arnold himself is one of the political heirs of Burke, but again this is less important than the kind of thinking which Arnold indicates by the verb "saturates." It is not "thought" in the commmon opposition to "feeling"; it is, rather, a special immediacy of experience, which works itself out, in depth, to a particular embodiment of ideas that become, in themselves, the whole man. The correctness of these ideas is not at first in question; and their truth is not, at first, to be assessed by their usefulness in historical understanding or in political insight. Burke's writing is an articulated experience, and as such it has a validity which can survive even the demolition of its general conclusions. It is not that the eloquence survives where the cause has failed; the eloquence, if it were merely the veneer of a cause, would now be worthless. What survives is an experience, a particular kind of learning; the writing is important only to the extent that it communicates this. It is, finally, a personal experience become a landmark.

My point can be illustrated in one very simple way. In politics Burke is, above all, the great recommender of prudence as the primary virtue of civil government. We know this; we receive it as an idea. Burke's formal opponents, knowing it, think they can destroy him when they can set against the principle such a sentence as this, from the tribute of a great admirer:

> His abilities were supernatural, and a deficiency of prudence and political wisdom alone could have kept him within the rank of mortals.[3]

As we look, now, at Burke's political career, we confirm the estimate of the deficiency. Common prudence was lacking at one crisis after another, and his political wisdom, in the practical sense, was halting or negligible. Yet this does not affect his estimate of political virtue. Burke is one of that company of men who learn virtue from the margin of their errors, learn folly from their own person. It is at least arguable that this is the most important kind of learning. Burke says of the leaders of the National Assembly:

> Their purpose everywhere seems to have been to evade and slip aside from *difficulty*. This it has been the glory of the great masters in all the arts to confront and to overcome; and when they had overcome the first difficulty, to turn it into an instrument for new conquests over new difficulties; thus to enable them to extend the empire of their science; and even to push forward, beyond the reach of their original thoughts, the landmarks of the human understanding itself. Difficulty is a severe instructor, set over us by the supreme ordinance of a parental guardian and legislator, who knows us better than we know ourselves, as he loves us better too.... He that wrestles with us strengthens our nerves, and sharpens our skill. Our antagonist is our helper. This amicable conflict with difficulty obliges us to an intimate acquaintance of our object, and

compels us to consider it in all its relations. It will not suffer us to
be superificial. It is the want of nerves of understanding for such a
task, it is the degenerate fondness for tricking short-cuts, and little
fallacious facilities, that has in so many parts of the world created
governments with arbitrary powers.[4]

The truth of this can be generally attested, and the wrestling is not less
important, nor less fruitful, when under the shadow of general difficulty a
man's antagonist is in certain aspects himself. Moreover, the connexion
between the quality of this process in individuals and the quality of civil
society is major and indisputable. We do not need to share Burke's support
of the Bourbons against the Assembly to realize the authority of this:

> If circumspection and caution are a part of wisdom, when we work
> only upon inanimate matter, surely they become a part of duty too,
> when the subject of our demolition and construction is not brick and
> timber, but sentient beings, by the sudden alteration of whose state,
> condition, and habits, multitudes may be rendered miserable....The
> true lawgiver ought to have a heart full of sensibility. He ought to
> love and respect his kind, and to fear himself. It may be allowed to
> his temperament to catch his ultimate object with an intuitive
> glance; but his movements towards it ought to be deliberate.
> Political arrangement, as it is a work for social ends, is to be only
> wrought by social means. There mind must conspire with
> mind....If I might venture to appeal to what is so much out of
> fashion in Paris, I mean to experience, I should tell you that in my
> course I have known and, according to my measure, have
> cooperated with great men; and I have never yet seen any plan
> which has not been mended by the observations of those who were
> much inferior in understanding to the person who took the lead in
> the business. By a slow but well-sustained progress, the effect of
> each step is watched; the good or ill success of the first gives light
> to us in the second; and so, from light to light, we are conducted
> with safety through the whole series. We see that the parts of the
> system do not clash. The evils latent in the most promising
> contrivances are provided for as they arise. One advantage is as
> little as possible sacrificed to another. We compensate, we
> reconcile, we balance.[5]

Nothing is more foolish than to suppose, as reformers of many kinds have
done, that this is merely a recommendation of conservatism. It is equally

foolish for conservatives to suppose that such conclusions are any kind of argument against the most radical social reform. Burke is describing a process, based on a recognition of the necessary complexity and difficulty of human affairs, and formulating itself, in consequence, as an essentially social and cooperative effort in control and reform. No particular policy can dispense with such recognitions; no description of policy, by a "tricking short-cut," can arrogate them to itself.

Yet when this has been said, the direction of effort, the decision of what is necessary, remain to be discussed. Here, Burke belongs most certainly to what Arnold called an "epoch of concentration." It is not true to say that he resisted all reform, but his heaviest fire is reserved for all schemes of wholesale innovation or radical reconstruction:

> Reform is not a change in the substance or in the primary modi-
> fication of the object, but a direct application of a remedy to the
> grievance complained of.[6]

Politics is a business of practical expediency, not of theoretical ideas. His comment on the unfortunate Dr. Price can stand as a general comment on the whole philosophical and literary tradition which was promoting social change:

> Wholly unacquainted with the world in which they are so fond of
> meddling, and inexperienced in all its affairs, on which they
> pronounce with so much confidence, they have nothing of politics
> but the passions they excite.[7]

The point has been echoed by thousands of lesser men, and is now a commonplace of diatribe, yet the criticism contained in the last clause keeps its force, and might even be applied to Burke himself. Even where the value of a tradition of thought in politics is most certainly to be acclaimed, this observation is not to be forgotten as an important limiting clause.

Burke served the causes of his day, and in particular the cause of opposition to democracy. He argued that the tendency of democracy was to tyranny, and he observed, further, that

> those who are subjected to wrong under multitudes are deprived of
> all external consolation. They seem deserted by mankind, over-
> powered by a conspiracy of their whole species.[8]

This again is an observation from experience. It did not need complete democracy for its realization; it was, in the bad times, Burke's own feeling about himself, under the sway of a majority opinion that was against him. This is not to deny that the observation about democracy may be reasonable. Yet, as the argument has gone since Burke's day, his position has come to seem paradoxical. It is commonly argued, in this kind of criticism of democracy, that the individual is oppressed by the mass, and that, generally speaking, virtues are individual in origin and are threatened by mass society. Burke had no experience of anything that could be called a mass society, but he could not in any case have accepted such an argument. His position, quite unequivocally, is that man as an individual left to himself is wicked; all human virtue is the creation of society, and is in this sense not "natural" but "artificial": "art is man's nature." The embodiment and guarantee of the proper humanity of man is the historical community. The rights of man include the right to be restrained:

> Government is a contrivance of human wisdom to provide for human *wants*....Among these wants is to be reckoned the want, out of civil society, of a sufficient restraint upon their passions. Society requires not only that the passions of individuals should be subjected, but that even in the mass and body, as well as in the individuals, the inclinations of men should frequently be thwarted, their will controlled, and their passions brought into subjection. This can only be done *by a power out of themselves;* and not, in the exercise of its function, subject to that will and to those passions which it is its office to bridle and subdue. In this sense the restraints on men, as well as their liberties, are to be reckoned among their rights.[9]

In so far as democracy is a system which enables individuals to decide how they should govern themselves (this is not its only definition, but it was a common one, in association with doctrines of economic individualism, when Burke was writing), this is a substantial criticism. As Burke says, in opposition to the main tenor of eighteenth-century thinking:

> We are afraid to put men to live and trade each on his own private stock of reason; because we suspect that the stock in each man is small, and that the individuals would do better to avail themselves of the general bank and capital of nations and of ages.[10]

Seventy years later, this was to be the basis of Matthew Arnold's recommendation of Culture.

In opposition to the ideas of individualist democracy, Burke set the idea
of a People:

> In a state of *rude* nature there is no such thing as a people. A
> number of men in themselves have no collective capacity. The idea
> of a people is the idea of a corporation. It is wholly artificial; and
> made, like all other legal fictions, by common agreement. What the
> particular nature of that agreement was, is collected from the form
> into which the particular society has been cast.[11]

The whole progress of man is thus dependent, not only on the historical
community in an abstract sense, but on the nature of the particular
community into which he has been born. No man can abstract himself from
this; nor is it his alone to change:

> Society is indeed a contract. Subordinate contracts for objects of
> mere occasional interest may be dissolved at pleasure—but the state
> ought not to be considered nothing better than a partnership
> agreement in a trade of pepper and coffee, calico or tobacco, or
> some other such low concern, to be taken up for a little temporary
> interest, and to be dissolved by the fancy of the parties. It is to be
> looked on with other reverence; because it is not a partnership in
> things subservient only to the gross animal existence of a temporary
> and perishable nature.   It is a partnership in all science; a
> partnership in all art; a partnership in every virtue, and in all
> perfection. As the ends of such a partnership cannot be obtained in
> many generations, it becomes a partnership not only between those
> who are living, but between those who are living, those who are
> dead, and those who are to be born.[12]

It can now be observed that Burke shifts, in this argument, from *society* to
state, and that the essential reverence for society is not to be confused, as
Burke seems to confuse it, with that particular form of society which is the
State at any given time. The observation is important, but Burke would not
have been impresed by it.   In his view, there was nothing in any way
accidental about any particular form; the idea of society was only available
to men in the form in which they had inherited it. Moreover, the progress of

human society was "the known march of the ordinary providence of God"; the inherited form was divine in origin and guidance, the instrument of God's will that man should become perfect:

> Without...civil society man could not by any possibility arrive at the perfection of which his nature is capable, nor even make a remote and faint approach to it....He who gave our nature to be perfected by our virtue, willed also the necessary means of its perfection—He willed therefore the state—He willed its connexion with the source and original archetype of all perfection.[13]

The difficulty about this position, of course, comes when the State form changes, as it had done in France, and yet is considered, in its new form, as a destroyer of civil society. If the creation of State forms is "the known march of the ordinary providence of God," then even the great changes which Burke was resisting might be beyond human control. He recognized this himself, late in his life, although the recognition did not modify his resistance:

> They who persist in opposing this mighty current in human affairs will appear rather to resist the decrees of Providence itself, than the mere designs of men.[14]

The difficulty serves to illustrate once again Burke's period. His doctrines rest on an experience of stability, containing imperfections, but not essentially threatened. As the current of change swelled, the affirmation became a desperate defence. And even while Burke was writing, the great tide of economic change was flowing strongly, carrying with it many of the political changes against which he was concerned to argue. He speaks from the relative stability of the eighteenth century against the first signs of the flux and confusion of the nineteenth century, but he speaks also against those rising doctrines which the eighteenth century had produced, and which were to become the characteristic philosophy of the change itself. In doing so, he prepared a position in the English mind from which the march of industrialism and liberalism was to be continually attacked. He established the idea of the State as the necessary agent of human perfection, and in terms of this idea the aggressive individualism of the nineteenth century was bound to be condemned. He established, further, the idea of what has been called an "organic society," where the emphasis is on the interrelation and continuity of human activities, rather than on separation into spheres of interest, each governed by its own laws.

> A nation is not an idea only of local extent, and individual momentary aggregation; but it is an idea of continuity, which extends in time as well as in numbers and in space. And this is a choice not of one day, or one set of people, not a tumultuary and giddy choice; it is a deliberate election of the ages and of generations; it is a constitution made by what is ten thousand times better than choice, it is made by the peculiar circumstances, occasions, tempers, dispositions, and moral, civil, and social habitudes of the people, which disclose themselves only in a long space of time.[15]

Immediately after Burke, this complex which he describes was to be called "the spirit of the nation"; and by the end of the nineteenth century, it was to be called a "national culture."

Examination of the influence and development of these ideas belongs to my later chapters. It is sufficient to note here Burke's own definitions. It is in these terms that Burke has lasted, but the survival involves a separation of these ideas from the rest of Burke's statement. We see him, now, when we see him as a whole, crippled by many kinds of misunderstanding. We set his polemics against the subsequent "known march." He seems to us blind to many of the changes which, even as he wrote, were transforming England. How else, we ask, could he have written, in the middle of a sixty-year period which saw 3,209 Acts of Enclosure of traditional common land, such a sentence as this?:

> The tenant-right of a cabbage-garden, a year's interest in a hovel, the goodwill of an alehouse or a baker's shop, the very shadow of a constructive proerty, are more ceremoniously treated in our parliament, than with you the oldest and most valuable landed possession.[16]

Of all English thinkers, Burke should have recognized most clearly the common ownership, through custom and prescription, of these four million acres that Parliament diverted into private hands. The point is not one of polemic against Burke; it is, rather, an indication of the flux of history and judgment. The "organic society," with which Burke's name was to be associated, was being broken up under his eyes by new economic forces, while he protested elsewhere. The epitaph on all his polemic is this, in his own brilliant judgment:

> Wise men will apply their remedies to vice, not to names; to the causes of evil which are permanent, not to the occasional organs by which they act, and the transitory modes in which they appear. Otherwise you will be wise historically, a fool in practice. Seldom have two ages the same fashion in their pretexts and the same modes of mischief. Wickedness is a little more inventive....It walks abroad, it continues its ravages, whilst you are gibbeting the carcase, or demolishing the tomb. You are terrifying yourselves with ghosts and apparitions, whilst your house is the haunt of robbers.[17]

The vigour of the insight serves only to underline the irony, when applied to Burke himself.

* * *

Burke and Cobbett, when their thinking has been followed through, are very distinct, almost antagonistic figures. Burke did not live to give an opinion of Cobbett the Radical, but it is likely that he would have shared Coleridge's feelings in 1817:

> I entertain toward...Cobbets...and all these creatures—and to the Foxites, who have fostered the vipers—a feeling more like hatred than I ever bore to other Flesh and Blood.[18]

Cobbett, as dogmatically, has left record of a characteristically limited view of Burke:

> How amusing it is to hear the world disputing and wrangling about the motives, and principles, and opinions of *Burke*! He had no notions, no principles, no opinions of his own, when he wrote his famous work....He was a poor, needy dependant of a Borough-monger, to serve whom, and please whom, he wrote; and for no other purpose whatever....And yet, how many people read this man's writings as if they flowed from his *own mind*....[19]

Yet to put together the names of Burke and Cobbett is important, not only as contrast, but because we can only understand this tradition of criticism of the new industrial society if we recognize that it is compounded of very different and at times even directly contradictory elements. The growth of the new society was so confusing, even to the best minds, that positions were drawn up in terms of inherited categories, which then revealed unsuspected and even opposing implications. There was much overlapping, even in the opposite positions of a Cobbett and a Burke, and the continuing attack on Utilitarianism, and on the driving philosophy of the new industrialism, was to make many more strange affiliations: Marx, for instance, was to attack capitalism, in his early writings, in very much the language of Coleridge, or Burke, and—of Cobbett. Utilitarianism itself was to have unsuspected implications, and Liberalism was to divide into a confusion of meanings. It is no more than one would expect in the early stages of so great a change. The effort which men had to make, to comprehend and to affirm, was indeed enormous; and it is the effort, the learning, in experience which it is important for us to know. We can still be grateful that men of the quality of Burke and Cobbett, for all their differences, were there to try to learn and record, and so magnificently to affirm, to the last limits of their strength.

Notes

Raymond Williams's essay appeared as Chapter One, *Contrasts,* in
Culture and Society, 1780-1950 (New York: Columbia University Press;
London: Chatto & Windus, [1958] *c.*1980), pp. 3-12, 19-20.

1. Letter, 21 November 1791, to Lord Fitzwilliam. *Correspondence* 6:435.
2. In *Complete Prose Works of Matthew Arnold*, ed. R. H. Super, (Ann Arbor MI: University of Michigan Press, 1962) 3:266.
3. Lord Charlemont, 19 August 1797; cited in Philip Magnus, *Edmund Burke, A Life* (London, 1939), p. 296.
4. *Reflections* in *Works* (Bohn) 2:437, appr. 67% into the work.
5. *Reflections* in *Works* (Bohn) 2:439-40, appr. 67% into the work.
6. *LNL* in *Writings* (LB-12) 5:186, appr. 24% into the work.
7. *Reflections* in *Works* (Bohn) 2:286, appr. 4% into the work.
8. *Reflections* in *Works* (Bohn) 2:397, appr. 50% into the work.
9. *Reflections* in *Works* (Bohn) 2:333, appr. 24% into the work.
10. *Reflections* in *Works* (Bohn) 2:359, appr. 34% into the work.
11. *Appeal* in *Works* (Bohn) 3:82, appr. 71% into the work.
12. *Reflections* in *Works* (Bohn) 2:368, appr. 38% into the work.

13. *Reflections* in *Works* (Bohn) 2:370, appr. 39% into the work.

14. *Thoughts on French Affairs* [written in December 1791] in *Works* (Bohn) 3:393, the penultimate sentence.

15. "Speech on the Reform of the Representation in the House of Commons," in *Works* (Bohn) 6:146-47, appr. 30% into the work.

16. *Reflections* in *Works* (Bohn) 2:423, appr. 61% into the work.

17. *Reflections* in *Works* (Bohn) 2:412-13, appr. 56% into the work.

18. Letter to T. J. Street, 22 March 1817; Nonesuch Coleridge; pp. 668-669.

19. *Political Register*, 8 June 1816.

15

Ireland, "Circumstances,"
and Modern Anti-Communism

It is reasonable...to assume that his vision of Ireland—an oppressed and dangerous Ireland—was a permanent part of Burke's imaginative landscape. His relation to Ireland made impossible for him two of the stock responses of Englishmen to the opening stages of the Revolution: that of approval for what seemed an anti-Papist reformation and that of "It can't happen here." "Here," for Burke, was not only England but also Ireland, so that revolution for him was from the beginning a thing imaginable. This goes some way to explain the alertness and promptitude of Burke's response, the fact that he was the first man of importance in England to descry and denounce a danger which within a few years agitated the mind of every man of property. This explains Burke's sensitivity, his nose for smoke; it does not, however, explain the intensity of his counter-revolutionary passion. He was not himself by the standards of the time a man of property, although he managed to maintain a certain state; the charges that he was working for a bribe or a pension cannot, as we have seen, be sustained;[1] his attachment to the Whig oligarchs was real, but hardly passionate; Burke at the time of the composition of the *Reflections* was ageing, disappointed, and overworked, burdened with the enormous complexities of the management of the impeachment of Warren Hastings. From a man in such a situation, aware of the danger in France, one might expect a prudent word of warning, hardly more. Whence, then, comes the tremendous emotional force that animates not only the misleadingly named *Reflections* but all his writings on the Revolution, up to and including the fourth *Letter on a Regicide Peace,* left unfinished at his death?

A question of this type, whether it concerns the living or the dead, cannot be answered with certainty. I should like to offer here a conjectural answer which seems to me to be in full accord with what we know of Burke's life and writings. This is that Burke, in his counter-revolutionary writings, is partially liberating—in a permissible way—a suppressed revolutionary part of his own personality. These writings—which appear at first sight to be an integral defence of the established order—constitute in one of their aspects—and this to Burke not the least important—a heavy blow against the established order in the country of Burke's birth, and against the dominant system of ideas in England itself.

Burke's Political Passion: Its Irish Sources

The established order in Ireland was *the Protestant ascendancy,* the legalized supremacy of the Protestant minority over the Catholic majority. This supremacy rested on the revolutionary settlement of 1688, still commemorated in Belfast and environs as the glorious origins of permanent Roman Catholic subordination. Burke as a Whig necessarily adhered to the principles of the Glorious Revolution; whether or not self-interest originally guided the Irish adventurer in adhering to the Whig cause, it is clear that personal loyalties, habits, and intellectual convictions—matters that Burke was not disposed to separate too sharply—soon bound him closely to the Whigs as a body. But if Burke as a Whig cherished, at least in theory, the Glorious Revolution, Burke as an Irishman, with close emotional bonds to the conquered, detested the Protestant ascendancy which that Revolution had riveted on the people of his country. This detestation seems in some of his earlier declarations to be covered by "a politic, well-wrought veil"; it becomes open, and even violently so, in the unguarded writings of his last years. "I think I can hardly exaggerate the malignity of the principles of Protestant ascendancy as it affects Ireland.... " [2] "The word protestant is the charm, that locks up in the dungeon of servitude three millions of your people.... " [3]

Burke's view of Irish history, and his feelings about it, come to the surface in a remarkable unfinished letter to his son, Richard, written in 1792. If members of the ascendancy in Ireland were wise, he says, they would not lay stress upon the origin of their property in confiscation.

> They would not set men upon calling from the quiet sleep of death any Samuel, to ask him, by what act of arbitrary monarchs, by what inquisitions of corrupted tribunals, and tortured jurors, by what fictitious tenures, invented to dispossess whole unoffending tribes and their chieftains! [sic] They would not conjure up the

ghosts from the ruins of castles and churches, to tell for what attempt to struggle for the independence of an Irish legislature, and to raise armies of volunteers, without regular commissions from the Crown in support of that independence, the estates of the old Irish nobility and gentry had been confiscated. They would not wantonly call on those phantoms, to tell by what English acts of parliament, forced upon two reluctant kings, the lands of their country were put up to a mean and scandalous auction in every goldsmith's shop in London; or chopped in pieces, and cut into rations, to pay the mercenary soldiery of a regicide usurper. They would not be so fond of titles under Cromwell, who, if he avenged an Irish rebellion against the sovereign authority of the parliament of England, had himself rebelled against the very parliament whose sovereignty he asserted full as much as the Irish nation, which he was sent to subdue and confiscate, could rebel against that parliament, or could rebel against the king, against whom both he and the parliament, which he served, and which he betrayed, had both of them rebelled.[4]

As for the native Irish, if they had indeed committed the crime of rebellion, "they rued it in their persons and in those of their children and grandchildren even to the fifth and sixth generations."

The contrast between this passionate outburst and the references in earlier, public speeches to the untroubled harmony of Ireland's connexion with Britain, is proof of the tension that long existed between Burke's public *persona* and so important a part of his feelings as that which concerned his people and the land of his birth.[5] This tension was released by the French Revolution, and specifically by the welcome given to that Revolution by Dr. Price and his friends. For Price and his friends, by placing the French Revolution in the line of the English one, were reminding Burke of how revolutionary, how anti-Catholic, and to him how alien had been the English revolution.[6] This intruding vision had to be exorcized: much of the argument—both of the *Reflections* and the *Appeal from the New to the Old Whigs* consists of an attempt to show that the English Revolution, unlike the French one, had not been really revolutionary at all—an attempt which we can judge successful only by choosing to forget about the contributions of the contemporaries of Henry VIII and of Oliver Cromwell. But the drama of Burke's writings about the Revolution, and much of their power, comes from the collaboration in them of two personalities. It is as if the words and actions of Price and his friends had awakened, within that reasonable elderly Whig, a slumbering Jacobite.[7]

In relation to England and Europe the "Jacobite" position is of course a counter-revolutionary one.[8]   But in relation to Ireland, the Jacobite aspiration is objectively revolutionary, since it is an expression of the will of the conquered people to shake off its servitude. Thus, where Burke is at his most extravagantly counter-revolutionary, in relation to France and Europe, he is most subtly subversive in relation to the existing order in his own country. His argument, addressed to the nobility and gentry of England, seeks to persuade these classes that their interests are bound up with Catholicism in Europe, that Catholicism is a bastion of order while Protestantism in its militantly anti-Catholic forms—the Protestantism of the Dissenters and their sympathizers—is the natural seed-bed of Jacobinism. [9] This argument, if accepted, was ultimately ruinous to the prevailing caste-system in Ireland, to which the doctrine that loyalty required anti-Popery was the breath of life. And the argument was accepted in its "pro-Catholic" part, though later and more hesitantly than Burke hoped. It is known that Burke's words carried great weight with the classes to which they were addressed, and that they played a part in the evolution of British policy in the direction he desired.[10] The Catholic Relief Act of 1793—and in 1795 the foundation of Maynooth—a Catholic seminary with State support—were important steps in this direction. Under the Union, the protestant ascendancy was progressively dismantled, except in the one region, Eastern Ulster, where it had a wide popular base. From the point of view of an ordinary member of the ruling class in Ireland in Burke's day, these were revolutionary developments, initially fostered by the dissemination of an ostensibly counter-revolutionary tract. Still from the same point of view, the spectre of Jacobinism had been cunningly used to rehabilitate Popery and Papists.[11] There can be no doubt that the rehabilitation of Catholicism was part of Burke's intention; he explicitly argues in this sense, seeking to inculcate a preference for "superstition" as against atheism. That it was only a part of his intention is obvious: he detestation of Jacobinism is real and even obsessive; there is no question of its being feigned for an ulterior motive. Yet his anti-Jacobinism cannot be separated from his sense of identification with Catholics, that is to say from his Irish origins.

In a letter of 1795 he says that his "whole politics centre in anti-Jacobinism"; that "the first, last and middle object of Jacobin hostility is religion"; that the practice of Catholicism by its professor "forms as things stand, the most effectual barrier, if not the sole barrier against Jacobinism";

and "that in Ireland particularly the Roman Catholic religion should be upheld in high respect and veneration."[12]   The Burke who was revolted by the Jacobin persecution of "refractory" priests and nuns was the same Burke who had been revolted by the hanging and quartering of the "rebel" Father Sheehy in 1766.[13]   He could not then cry out in open protest; he had candidly explained to Irish friends why he could not attempt publicly to defend an accused Irish papist.[14]   But it was possible for him to champion publicly the cause of the French Catholics, in 1790-97, and in championing them, indirectly to vindicate and so raise up his family and fellow-countrymen. Is it unreasonable to see in the extraordinary flow of controlled but passionate eloquence that begins with the *Reflections*, the release of an inner indignation long pent up by prudent policy?

The significance of Burke's Irishness in relation to his writings on the French Revolution has I think been generally underestimated or misunderstood.   This tendency is encouraged by the requirements of classification: "Burke on Ireland" is a separate matter from "Burke on France" or "Burke on America." Yet—as Yeats so clearly saw—it is all the same Burke. Burke was never a man of tidy compartments, and we may be sure that the feeling and ideas—not separate compartments either—of the man who writes to Sir Hercules Langrishe about Ireland are identical with those of the man who writes to M. de Pont about France.

The tendency to miss the significance of Burke's Irishness is also encouraged by other factors. These include the general impression that Burke is Anglo-Irish and belongs in the Protestant tradition.[15]   In fact there is nothing "Anglo" at all about what we know of his family connexions and he himself—at least in the late writings with which we are here concerned—eschews the designation "Protestant." Finally, some who have been impressed by Burke's writings on the French Revolution have ignored the Irish factor, probably because of a conviction that, in comparison with the mighty issues treated in the *Reflections*, the concerns of Ireland were trivial and parochial. As a general proposition this is very defensible, yet it is misleading in relation to Burke. The Irish situation is of little importance on the scale of the great Revolution, yet it was the Irish situation that had formed Edmund Burke, and Ireland and Jacobinism constituted the alternating and overlapping preoccupations of his last, haunted years. The author of the *Reflections on the Revolution in France* wrote in the *persona* of an Englishman—which is in itself a cause of confusion—but was in fact Irish to the marrow of his bones.

* * * * *

The First Modern Propagandist

...[I]t was [James] Mackintosh, the most acute of Burke's early critics, who first defined—as early as 1791—the real character of the *Reflections*: "It is the manifesto of a counter-revolution...."

Mackintosh's observations on Burke's method, and his definition of the character of his book, represent Burke as above all a propagandist. Whatever about the "above all"—a matter to which we shall return—there can be no doubt that Burke was a conscious and deliberate propagandist. He has some claim indeed to be the first modern propagandist: the first to be conscious of a need for organized effort, adequately financed, and reinforced by "State action," to mould public opinion on questions of ideology and international policy.[16] He was the first also to give a lead in such an effort.[17] His originality of course should not be exaggerated: since the Reformation and Counter-reformation all Western Europe had rung with propaganda; the eighteenth century was the heyday of the pamphleteer. Burke's originality was not in engaging in propaganda, but in thinking seriously about its nature and its power and on how best to use it. He was acutely conscious of the part which the anti-religious and other propaganda of Voltaire and his friends had played in undermining the *ancien régime*, and of the need for an organized counter-attack. His treatment of this subject in the *Reflections*—see the passage beginning "Along with the monied interest, a new description of men had grown up...I mean the political men of letters"—[18] receives further development in the second of the *Letters on a Regicide Peace*:

> The correspondence of the monied and mercantile world, the literary intercourse of academics, but, above all, the press, of which they [the middle class] had in a manner entire possession, made a kind of electrick comunication everywhere. The press in reality has made every government, in its spirit, almost democratick. Without it the great, the first moments in this Revolution could not, perhaps, have been given.[19]

Burke was disgusted at the lack of interest among the French aristocratic refugees in propaganda. In January 1791 he wrote to one of these seeking certain information—details about the French system of land tenure—which might be "useful hereafter in any Systematick proceeding towards disposing the publick in this Country in your favour which I wish some French Gentlemen here would undertake under the direction of some judicious English."[20] Burke continued to press this idea, but was dismayed by the apparent inertia of the French nobility in this domain, compared with the activity of their opponents. "...The Emissaries of the Usurpation here are exceedingly active in propagating Stories which tend to alienate the minds of people of this Country from the suffering Cause. Not one french Refugee has intelligence or spirit enough to contradict them."[21] He urged that the French emigrés should raise money for this purpose: "If their avarice or their dissipation will afford nothing to their honour or their safety—their Case is additionally deplorable."[22]

In this, as in much else, Burke was in advance of the time which he was defending: it was left to him, singlehanded, to conduct the effective propaganda of the counter-revolution. In his own writings he is—among other things—a conscious propagandist. He uses emotional language by deliberate policy. There was nothing new, for him, in this; as a practical politician he had long been aware of the value of verbal violence. Before the outbreak of the French Revolution, and when his mind was occupied with quite different matters, he had written to a colleague in Opposition, suggesting that if the Opposition did not intend to give up altogether, they ought "to change that tone of calm reasoning which certainly does not belong to great and affecting interests...[a] style of argument, so very different from that by which Lord North was run down...."[23]

Two years later, in connexion with the impeachment of Warren Hastings, he developed his theory of verbal violence, in rebutting a suggestion from Lord Chancellor Thurlow that "the calm mode of Enquiry" would be the most rewarding approach: "The *calm mode of Enquiry* would be a very temperate method of our losing our Object; and a very certain mode of finding no calmness on the side of our adversary. Our being mobbish is our only chance for his being reasonable."[24]

He became increasingly "mobbish" as the "great and affecting interest" of the reaction to the French Revolution took hold: the *Reflections*, as compared with the later *Letters on a Regicide Peace* almost seems a model of the "calm mode of Enquiry." In relation to *Appeal from the New to the Old Whigs* (1791) he shows himself as consciously committed to that method of tactical over-statement[25] which distinguishes the true propagandist from the mere believer in a cause. Writing to his son Richard, and having noted that only about 10 per cent even of the Whigs favour the French Revolutionary principles, he goes on: "It may be asked, why I represent the whole party as tolerating, and by a toleration countenancing, these proceedings. It is to get the better of their inactivity and to stimulate them to a publick declaration.... "[26]

The fact that Burke writes as a conscious propagandist and practical politician, with an eye to the probable immediate consequences of his words, is too often left out of acount by undiscriminating admirers, who like to think of him as essentially a political philosopher. The importance of the propaganda element shoud not, however, be exaggerated either. There is no reason at all to doubt the sincerity of Burke's indignation, aroused by the discovery of the existence and character of English sympathy with the French Revolution. This indignation burns quite as brightly in his private correspondence as in his published tracts. The opinion, presented by Marx and others, that it was all feigned, that he was simply "playing the Romantic"[27] as he had "played the Liberal," cannot be seriously defended. Calculation comes in, not in pretending an emotion which is not there, but in deciding how much of a genuinely-felt emotion to release publicly; how far to let oneself go. In certain circumstances—had the Whigs been in office, for example, and he with them—Burke could hardly have "let himself go" at all. But when he does decide to let go, he inevitably releases greater forces than any calculation could determine in advance. He enters the controversy as a Whig, and ends up the idol of the Tories. He "runs down" his friend Charles James Fox, as he had once run down Lord North. It is extremely improbable that these results were calculated in advance. It is more probable that Burke had never fully realized—until the events in France provided the critical test—how profoundly he was at odds with much that was fundamental in the philosophy of Englishmen with whom he had allied himself: Englishmen who cherished the principles of the Glorious Revolution and of the Enlightenment, and felt these principles to be essentially the same, or at least to have a common root—a rational rejection of superstition.

Nor did the Tories—despite their praise of him—seem much better to him. They were lukewarm and pragmatic, prepared to sustain a limited war with France, but not dedicated to the counter-revolutionary principle. Towards the end the practical politician Burke seems to die away; the *Letters on a Regicide Peace* are certainly propaganda but it is a strange, passionately personal sort of propaganda, the prophetic outpouring—almost at times the raving—of a man isolated, inconsolably bereaved,[28] dying, yet rejoicing in his incomparable power to express his fury in words whose sheer exuberance is still astounding. The *Letters* are the deathless propaganda of a dying man in favour of "a long war"—a war which did not in fact end until nearly twenty years after his death.[29]

Burke, Modern Conservatism, and Anti-Communism

It is not surprising that in our own time the counter-revolutionary propaganda in Burke's late writings should have been used for the purposes of the cold war. The first to realize the possibilities of Burke for twentieth-century anti-communism seems to have been A. V. Dicey, who, in an article published in 1918 hit upon the simple but effective expedient of substituting "Russia" for "France" in a number of Burke's most ardent counter-revolutionary invectives.[30] It was not however until the setting in of the real cold war, in the late forties, that Burke's works began to be systematically quarried for anti-communist purposes and that Burke's stature as a systematic thinker began to be correspondingly exalted. The process began with the publication of *Burke's Politics*, an anthology with an introduction by Ross Hoffman and Paul Levack in 1949. A number of American scholars and writers, and including a strong Catholic element, set themselves to extol Burke as a great political philosopher and exponent of Natural Law, as well as of a stable order, foreshadowing the Atlantic Community.[31] Members of this school were disposed to overlook or minimize the practical, polemical, and propagandist elements in Burke's writing and to magnify the importance and consistency of his "philosophy." They attached inordinate importance to two sentences of Hoffman's and Levack's:

"Burke's politics...were grounded on recognition of the universal law of reason and justice ordained by God as the foundation of a good comunity. In this recognition the Machiavellian schism between politics and morality is closed...." [32] Mr. Peter J. Stanlis, one of the most productive writers in this group, sees 1949—the year of the Hoffman epiphany—as the beginning of a "counter-revolution on traditional grounds" in Burke scholarship. A reviewer of Mr. Peter J. Stanlis in the *Burke Newsletter*—of which Mr. Peter J. Stanlis was co-editor—averred that he could "think of no sentence in the whole range of modern scholarship that has had greater effect than this apparently simple factual statement by Messrs. Hoffman and Levack."[33]

To present Burke as a sort of semi-official spokesman for the law of nature has the effect of conferring on his writings a superhuman authority. To challenge Burke's argument is then to fly in the face of nature. And as Burke himself, in a very different connection, sardonically observed: "The nature of things is, I admit, a sturdy adversary."[34] A sturdy ally also.

Both Burke and the sturdy ally were enlisted for specific political purposes. The *Burke Newsletter*, which recorded the progress of the "counter-revolution in Burke scholarship," was originally published as part of *Modern Age*, an American right-wing periodical.[35] "Burke studies," according to Burke's American biographer, Mr. Carl B. Cone, "are a very self-conscious part of our contemporary conservative revival."[36] The specific utility of Burke for the conservative revivalists has been most clearly explained by one of their intellectual leaders, Mr. Russell Kirk:

> Burke's concept of the comity of nations and of the law of nations, and of the necessity for combining against revolutionary fanaticism apply almost unaltered to the present circumstances of this nation....Burke is little "dated"....
>
> For America plays today the role which was Britain's at the end of the eighteenth century: like the English then we Americans have become, without willing it, the defenders of civilization against the enemies of order and justice and freedom and the traditions of civility. Ours are imperial duties, requiring imperial intellects for their execution.[37]

Burke's writings, then, are to be a school for "imperial intellects," preparing them for the "imperial duties" imposed on them by the need to combat "revolutionary fanaticism." They are to furnish splendid language and respected antecedents—in the venerable penumbra of the Natural Law and of "order, justice, and freedom"—to validate the policy of American counter-revoutionary imperialism, and to train minds in the service of this policy.[38]

More astute conservative minds than Mr. Kirk's have already perceived that Burke is not an entirely reliable ally. Some reasons for this are discussed in Section II of this introduction.[39] It is clear, however, that appropriately expounded, Burke's later writings, beginning with the *Reflections*, can supply copious and precious material for counter-revolutionary indoctrination, adaptable to imperial purposes. Once we make the equation Jacobin = Communist—as we can without significantly departing from the principles of Burke's hostility to Jacobinism—we can derive from Burke's later writings a repertory of maxims and incitements in support of—and even going beyond—the foreign policy, which is associated with the name of John Foster Dulles, and which still exerts a powerful influence over United States action today.

For Burke, as for Dulles, the revolutionary doctrine is the expression of incarnate evil: "Those who have made the exhibition of the 14th day of July are capable of every evil. They do not commit crimes for their designs; but they form designs that they may commit crimes. It is not their necessity, but their nature that impels them."[40] This evil has a central and strategic habitation from which it must be dislodged: "This evil in the heart of Europe must be extirpated from that center, or no part of the circumference can be free from the mischief which radiates from it, and which will spread circle beyond circle, in spite of all the little defensive precautions which can be employed against them."[41] It is a formidable enterprise—to be opposed by armed force—for the subversion of all values:

> We now have our arms in our hands; we have the means of opposing the sense, the courage and the resources of England to the deepest, the most craftily devised, the best combined and the most extensive design that ever was carried on, since the beginning of the world against all property, all orders, all religion, all law, and all real freedom.[42]

The evil doctrine, the armed forces at the disposal of those professing the doctrine, and the sympathizers with the doctrine in other lands constitute one united threat which must be met with force.

> We are at war with a system, which, by its essence, is inimical to all other governments, and which makes peace or war, as peace and war may best contribute to their subversion. It is with an *armed doctrine* that we are at war. It has, by its essence, a faction of opinion, and of interest, and of enthusiasm, in every country. To us it is a Colossus which bestrides our channel. It has one foot on a foreign shore, the other upon the British soil. Thus advantaged, if it can at all exist, it must finally prevail.[43]

The struggle against the *armed doctrine* is a *"religious war,"*[44] a "new crusade."[45] It must be waged not merely by armed force abroad but by repression at home; the Judges "should directly censure the circulation of treasonable Books, factious federations and any communication or communion with wicked and desperate people in other Countries."[46]

The "domino" theory of President Eisenhower—which still inspires American policy in the Far East—had an early exponent in Burke: "If Spain falls, Naples will speedily follow. Prussia is quite certain....Italy is broken and divided; Switzerland is jacobinized, I am afraid, completely."[47]

The war he preaches against the armed doctrine is total, ruthless, and ideological. He foresees, very early, that such warfare will be more cruel than any past warfare and accepts the necessity for this:

> The mode of civilized war will not be practised; nor are the French who act on the present system entitled to expect it. They, whose known policy is to assassinate every citizen whom they suspect to be discontented by their tyranny, and to corrupt the soldiery of every open enemy, must look for no modified hostility. All war, which is not battle will be military execution. This will beget acts of retaliation from you; and every retaliation will beget a new revenge. The hell-hounds of war, on all sides, will be uncoupled and unmuzzled. The new school of murder and barbarism, set up in Paris, having destroyed (so far as in it lies) all the other manners and principles which have hitherto civilized Europe, will destroy also the mode of civilized war, which more than anything else, has distinguished the christian world.[48]

From the point of view of a Dulles or of a Dean Rusk, indeed, the disadvantage of Burke's counter-revolutionary writings is that they go further than prudent counter-revolutionists in our time have so far judged practicable. For Burke scornfully condemns the idea that what we now call "containment" will suffice against the doctrine; it must be destroyed at its centre:

> In France is the bank of deposit and the bank of circulation, of all the pernicious principles that are forming in every state. It will be a folly scarcely deserving of pity, and too mischievous for contempt to think of restraining it in any other country, whilst it is predominant there.[49]

If Burke's counter-revolutionary writings are literally transposed into modern terms they are appropriate not so much to the moderate Right as to the farthest reaches of American reaction. Their rhetoric contains the justification for a policy of preventive war. They could have been invoked in favour of war with the Soviet Union in the forties. They could now be used in favour of war with China.

Circumstances and America's "Imperial Duties"

Such a conclusion should in itself be a warning against facile transposition. The fact that Burke advocated counter-revolutionary war against France does not permit his authority to be legitimately invoked in support of counter-revolutionary war against Russia, China, or any other nation today. Communist principles are certainly fully as detestable, from a Burkian point of view, as Jacobin principles. But the circumstances are widely different, and Burke repeatedly refuses to recommend or endorse a course of action without knowing in detail the circumstances of the case:

> Circumstances (which with some gentlemen pass for nothing) give in reality to every political principle its distinguishing colour and discriminating effect. The circumstances are what render every civil and political scheme beneficial or noxious to mankind.[50]

And again:

> I must see with my own eyes, I must, in a manner touch with my own hands, not only the fixed but the momentary circumstances, before I could venture to suggest any political project whatsoever. I must know the power and disposition to accept, to execute, to persevere. I must see the means of correcting the plan, where correctives would be wanted. I must see the things; I must see the men.[51]

We cannot guess what Burke might advise could he see "the things" and "the men" of today. Certainly he would favour whatever course of action seemed to him, *in the circumstances*, most appropriate to prevent the spread of Communist principles and power. It is inconceivable that, in the circumstances of the thermo-nuclear balance of terror, he could support a policy of war with the Soviet Union. It is even improbable that, in the circumstances of present relations between the main branches of the human race, he would favour war with China.[52] Nor do his writings really imply support for that policy which those who most often quote him with approval are in fact pursuing: the "containment" of Communism by multiple forms of intervention in the underdeveloped world. It is not just that he explicitly rejects a similar policy in the circumstances of his own day; changed circumstances could warrant changed policy.[53] There is something more fundamental in Burke to which the realities of the "containment" policy are necessarily repugnant. Burke distinguished between revolutionary movements arising from "wantonness and fullness of bread" and those which draw their sustenance from "the bottom of human nature." Those Asian movements which the "containment" policy is pledged to crush—such as the Front of National Liberation in Vietnam—can hardly be said to arise from "wantonness and fullness of bread." Burke understood very well the feelings of a conquered people—feelings that were necessarily in his own bones—and he even reluctantly condoned that form of revolutionary action which comes first to a desperate peasantry: agrarian terrorism.[54] Burke also understood the force of those national and even tribal loyalties which are at least as important as any ideological factors in the revolutionary movements of today. The implications of "containment," that world-wide American *ascendancy*, could never be wholly attractive to him.[55] Inevitably there is in such a policy an element of hubris, of the overweening, which repelled Burke, and against which he expressly warned the England of his day:

> Among precautions against ambition, it may not be amiss to take one precaution against our *own*. I must fairly say, I dread our *own* power, and our *own* ambition; I dread our being too much dreaded. It is ridiculous to say we are not men; and that as men, we shall never wish to aggrandize ourselves in some way or other. Can we say, that even at this very hour we are not invidiously aggrandized? We are already in possession of almost all the commerce of the world. Our empire in India is an awful thing. If we should come to be in a condition not only to have all this ascendant in commerce, but to be absolutely able, without the least control, to hold the commerce of all other nations totally dependent upon our good pleasure, we may say that we shall not abuse this astonishing, and hitherto unheard-of, power. But every other nation will think we shall abuse it. It is impossible but that, sooner or later, this state of things must produce a combination against us which may end in our ruin.[56]

This passages seems to have escaped the attention of Mr. Russell Kirk when he invoked the authority of Burke, and the example of Burke's England, in support of America's "imperial duties" today. Burke was a counter-revolutionary but he cannot easily be accounted an imperialist; he showed a deep distrust for contemporary forms of imperialist psychology, not merely in relation to America, in his earlier years—an America then an object, not a source, of imperialism—but in relation to India and Ireland in his later years, and also because of the implications of such psychology for the imperial power itself. One cannot legitimately invoke Burke's authority in support of *any* specific policy to be applied in circumstances unknown to him. But particularly one cannot invoke it in support of a policy which contains strong elements about which he is known to have had profound misgivings: the extension of imperial commitments, the crushing of spontaneous peasant movements, *ascendancy*, hubris.[57]

It may well be argued that in our day the practice of counter-revolution, which Burke favoured, required what he did not favour: the extension of imperialism. Modern conditions—on this argument—put the prime nuclei of revolutionary infection out of reach. All that can be done is to prevent the infection from spreading to other lands. Some countries—notably the advanced, industrialized countries, Western Europe and Japan—are in a postion to resist the infection on their own. But in those lands which are not in such a position—many of the poor countries—the thing must be done for them, and this necessarily involves the assertion of authority over them, directly or indirectly, by the counter-revolutionary power. This assertion of authority is likely to be called "aid" rather than imperialism but it does contain the essence of imperial rule: the final say is not with a native authority but with a foreign one.

If counter-revolution required imperialism in the circumstances of today, then Burke's thought as it has come down to us from its formulation in different circumstances is inapplicable as a whole. We can, however, reasonably hold that a conservative who fears the over-extension of his country's power—as Senator Fulbright does—can claim descent from Burke with just as much validity as the practitioners of counter-revolutionary containment.

Notes

This chapter is taken from Conor Cruise O'Brien's Introduction
to Burke's *Reflections* (Harmondsworth: Penguin, 1969), pp. 33-41, 51-67.
The notes are by O'Brien, unless otherwise indicated.

1. It is doubtful, in any case, whether eloquence of the order of the *Reflections* could be mercenary. An ambassador of a certain small but diplomatically significant country once argued

his official case with the present writer [writes O'Brien]. Finding his argument unacceptable he sighed and said: "They pay me to say these thing, but why should I insist? They don't pay me all that much."

2. *Works* (Bohn) 6:58, appr. 33% into the *Second Letter to Sir Hercules Langrishe* (1795).

3. *Works* (Bohn) 6:69, appr. 45% into the *Letter to Richard Burke, Esq.* (1792).

4. *Works* (Bohn) 6:77, appr. 90% into the *Letter to Richard Burke*. Dated by Dr. J. A. Woods as before 19 February 1792.

5. Compare the highly idealized view of Irish history in the famous *Speech on Conciliation with the Colonies* (1775) in *Works* 1:484, appr. 56% into the work: "It was not English arms, but the English constitution, that conquered Ireland." In the same speech Burke uses the purity of Protestantism in some of the colonies as an argument in their favour. Both points are in sharp contrast with the tone of his last writings.

6. The trouble of Burke's mind, in relation to the impact of the Glorious Revolution in Ireland, is clear from a tortuous passage in the letter, from which I have already quoted, to Richard Burke. Burke does not "presume to defend" the Irish for their rebellion against the English parliament but thinks, first, that "palliation" and "extenuation" should be admitted; that the Irish resisted King William "on the very same principle that the English and Scotch resisted King James"; finally, that the "Irish Catholics must have been the very worst and the most truly unnatural of rebels"—had they not supported King James.

7. Obviously it is not suggested that Burke was politically a Jacobite: he was far too practical a man to be anything of the kind. The point here is that he was emotionally in sympathy with the Catholics of Ireland, whose Jacobite loyalty was at the root of the penalties still being imposed on them in Burke's time.

8. ["Jacobite" refers to support for the descendants of the deposed James II of England, particularly "the Young Pretender," "bonnie" Prince Charles Edward, whose defeat at Culloden in 1745 transferred Jacobite hopes from the realm of politics to myth. The term has no relation to "Jacobin," which refers to the most radical strand of French revolutionary thought. —DR]

9. "A man is certainly the most perfect Protestant who protests against the whole Christian religion." (*[First] Letter to Sir Hercules Langrishe*, 1792, *Works* (Bohn) 3:313, appr. 34% into the work.) See also the sarcastic references in *A Letter on the Affairs of Ireland* (1797) to "the Protestant directory of Paris...and the Protestant hero, Buonaparte...." (*Works* (Bohn) 6:87, appr. 75% into the work. In an English context, however, Burke in the *Reflections* writes in the character of a Protestant, but one who does not violently condemn the Roman system of religion, pp. 257-70 (Penguin edn., appr. 59%-63% into the work).

10. Burke had tried—with less success—to make use of the American Revolution in the same sense. The persecution of "a *nation*"—as he described the Irish Catholics—might once perhaps have been conducted with safety: "But there is a revolution in our affairs which makes it prudent to be just." ("Speech at Bristol," Works (Bohn) 2:155, appr. 66% into the work.

11. See Carl B. Cone, *Burke and the Nature of Politics: The Age of the French Revolution* (Lexington, KY: University of Kentucky Press, 1964), pp. 487-88. Burke came to be regarded as "the chief, if not the sole mover of all the measures with respect to Irish Catholics."

12. "Letter to William Smith, Esq.," 26 May 1795, in *Works* (Bohn) 6:53, appr. 62% into the work.

13. See *Correspondence* 1:248-49.

14. *Correspondence* 1:215-16. He asks his uncle—whose son had abducted a Protestant heiress, which was a capital offence—to reflect "how newly and almost as a stranger I am come about these people"—in England—and that "many industrious endeavours" had been made to ruin him. (To Patrick Nagle: 14 October 1765.)

15. Thus the late Joseph Hone in his excellent biography *W. B. Yeats (1865-1939)* (London, 1942), stated that Yeats was "haunted by the question: how to bring the aristocratic and Protestant tradition of Swift, Berkeley, and Burke into line with the modern 'Gaelic' nationalism" (p. 379). In fact Burke was as "Gaelic" as any modern nationalist and more Gaelic than some. Burke seems more aristocratic in a literary retrospect than he did to his contemporaries, who were inclined to regard him as "an Irish upstart from the Catholic underworld across the Bristol Channel" (Sir Philip Magnus, *Edmund Burke*, p. 216). Burke's relation to Protestantism is discussed in the text.

16. The principal role of the State in the matter was to be the suppression of the propaganda of the other side. See pp. 169-70.

17. A modern French writer on the counter-revolution states: "Parmi tous les théoriciens de la contre-révolution, le premier, dont les œuvres aient eu un retentissement international, a été l'Anglais Edmund Burke," Jacques Godechot (*La Contre-Révolution, 1789-1804*, Paris, 1961.)

18. *Reflections* in *Works* (Bohn) 2:382, appr. 43% into the work.

19. *Works* (Bohn) 5:259, six paragraphs from the end. Burke here seems to anticipate Marshall McLuhan.

20. *Correspondence* 6:206-8; Burke to Vicomte de Cicé, 24 January 1791. A detailed questionnaire is appended, essentially similar to what a modern counter-propagandist might put to, for example, a Tibetan refugee in order to gather material for a speech at the United Nations.

21. *Correspondence* 6:241-3; Burke to Chevalier de la Bintinaye, March 1791.

22. *Correspondence* 6:243.

23. *Correspondence* 5:436-45; Burke to Windham, c. 24 January 1789. He went on to recommend the publication of "strong manifestoes."

24. *Correspondence* 6:197; Burke to W. Adam, 4 January 1791.

25. *Under-statement* also: "Falsehood and delusion are allowed in no case whatever: but, as in the exercise of all the virtues, there is an economy of truth. It is a sort of temperance, by which a man speaks truth with measure that he may speak it the longer." Penultimate paragraph of the first of the *Letters on a Regicide Peace* in *Works* (Bohn) 5:230.)

26. *Correspondence* 6:315-20; Edmund Burke to Richard Burke, Jr., 5 August 1791. It was a shrewdly calculated blow. "There is not a single man in opposition who will not be understood to be in Burke's opinion an Enemy to the present constitution of this country, for who, will it be said, can know them so well as Mr Burke?" Portland to Lawrence, 23 August 1791. (*Sheffield Papers.*)

27. Marx did know some of Burke's writings. There is a bitter footnote about Burke in *Capital*: "The sycophant—who in the pay of the English oligarchy played the romantic *laudator temporis acti* against the French Revolution just as, in the pay of the North American colonies at the beginning of the American troubles, he had played the liberal against the English oligarchy, was an out-and-out vulgar bourgeois." (*Capital* I, Moscow, 1954, p. 760n2.) Earlier he had described Burke as the man whom both Parties in England regard as the model of a British Statesman (*N.Y. Daily Tribune*, December 1855). From a Marxian point of view there is of course no contradiction between the two descriptions.

28. [Burke's son, Richard, in whom he had exorbitant hopes, died in 1794. —DR]

29. "I speak it emphatically and with a desire that it should be marked, in a *long* war; because without such a war, no experience has yet told us that a dangerous power has ever been reduced to measure or to reason." Appr. 55% into the first of the *Letters on a Regicide Peace*, [1796] in *Works* (Bohn) 5:195.

30. "Burke on Bolshevism," in *Nineteenth Century and After*, July-December 1918. See also A. A. Baumann: *Burke the Founder of Conservatism*, London, 1929.

31. "He saw...what we Americans are groping for today as we seek to organize a stable, international order..." (*Burke's Politics*, New York, 1949, p. xxxvi.) This effort demanded a "restoration," which is not further defined. Presumably the "rolling back of the Iron Curtain" was included in it.

32. *Burke's Politics*, 1949, p. xv.

33. Warren Fleischauer in *Burke Newsletter*, Spring-Summer 1963.

34. Appr. 22% into the third of the *Letters on a Regicide Peace*.

35. This arrangement held good from 1959 to the beginning of 1961 when, as a result of changed editorial policy, *Modern Age* ceased to publish the *Burke Newsletter*. There were always some neo-conservatives who disliked the emphasis on Burke. As a student of the neo-conservative movement has pointed out, there are "manifold problems in trying to package Burke for the American Market." (E. Cain, *They'd Rather be Right*, New York, 1963.)

36. *Burke Newsletter*, Spring 1962. Mr. Cone is uneasy about elevating Burke's rhetoric into a philosophy: "I think there are reasons for doubting some of his statements when we remember that Burke was invariably pleading a cause.... " True, but then the "contemporary conservative revival" is pleading a cause too.

37. *Burke Newsletter*, Winter 1962-63. Mr. Kirk was reviewing Mr. Clinton J. Rossiter's *Conservatism in America*, which had "reservations about Burke as a guide to conservative action in our time." There is an edition of the *Reflections* with an introduction by Mr. Russell Kirk in a series called "Classics of Conservatism" (New Rochelle, NY, n.d.). In it he describes the *Reflections* as "the work which is now the foundation of modern conservatism in Britain, America, and Western countries generally."

38. "Burke," writes Professor Alfred Cobban, "has escaped from the more foolish jibes of the left in Britain only to fall a victim to the uncritical adulation of the right in America....These attempts to condemn or applaud the ideas or annex the name and reputation of Burke, like any other attempt to exploit the past to the advantage of transient political interests, are not history." *Edmund Burke and the Revolt Against the Eighteenth Century*, Preface to Second Edition (London, 1960).

39. [In that section, O'Brien notes that nineteenth-century proponents of Home Rule for Ireland, including Gladstone, found an ally in Burke, against contemporary conservatives. —DR]

40. *Letter to a Member of the National Assembly* [1791] in *Works* (Bohn) 2:534, appr. 40% into the work.

41. *Heads for Consideration on the Present State of Affairs* [written in November 1792]. *Works* (Bohn) 3:409, penultimate paragraph.

42. *Preface to M. Brissot's Address to his Constituents* [1794] in *Works* (Bohn) 3: 525-26, appr. 79% into the work.

43. Appr. 16% into the first of the *Letters on* a Regicide Peace [1796] in *Works* (Bohn) 5:164-65.

44. *Remarks on the Policy of the Allies* [begun in October 1793]; emphasis as in the text, in *Works* (Bohn) 3:442, appr. 69% into the work.

45. Appr. 13% into the second of the *Letters on a Regicide Peace* [1796] in *Works* (Bohn) 5:234.

46. Edmund Burke to Richard Burke, Sr., 24 July 1791; *Correspondence* 6:307.

47. *Remarks on the Policy of the Allies* [begun in October 1793] in *Works* (Bohn) 3:441, appr. 66% into the work.

48. *Letter to a Member of the National Assembly* [1791] in *Works* (Bohn) 2:542-43, appr. 60% into the work.

49. Fourth paragraph of the second of the *Letters on a Regicide Peace* in *Works* (Bohn) 5:232.

50. *Reflections* in *Works* (Bohn) 2:282, ten paragraphs into the work.

51. *Letter to a Member of the National Assembly* [1791] in *Works* (Bohn) 2:549, appr. 77% into the work.

52. "...You ought not, in reason, to trifle with so large a mass of the interests and feelings of the human race. You could at no time do so without guilt; and be assured you will not be able to do it long with impunity." *Speech on Conciliation with the Colonies*, [1775] in *Works* (Bohn) 1:457, appr. 13% into the work.

53. See the passage from *Letter to a Member of the National Assembly* in *Works* (Bohn) 2:542-43, quoted on p. 172.

54. "Dreadful it is; but it is now plain enough that Catholick *defenderism* is the only restraint upon Protestant *Ascendancy*." *Sheffield Papers*; Burke to Hussey, 18 January 1796. "Defenderism" was the term in use for the form of agrarian terrorism then practised in Ireland. About thirty years before some of Burke's own relatives had been implicated in the similar movement of the White Boys. *Correspondence* 1:147-48.

55. Not that the techniques of containment would always be abhorrent to him. He repudiated what he called a *"strange notion"*—"that one State has not a right to interfere according to its discretion, in the interior Affairs of another." (*Sheffield Papers*; Burke to Grenville, August 1792.) What is in question now, however, is precisely the "discretion" with which the "right" is exercised.

56. *Remarks on the Policy of the Allies* [begun in October 1795] in *Works* (Bohn) 3:448, appr. 81% into the work.

57. The argument about *prestige*, on which the justification of America's Vietnam war has been made to hinge, is one of which he once disposed effectively: "They tell you, Sir, that your dignity is tied to it. I know not how it happens, but this dignity of yours is a terrible incumbrance to you; for it has of late been ever at war with your interest, your equity, and every idea of your policy. Shew the thing you contend for to be reason; shew it to be common sense; shew it to be the means of attaining some useful end; and then I am content to allow it what dignity you please. But what dignity is derived from the perseverance in absurdity, is more than I could ever discern." (*Speech on American Taxation* [1774]) in *Works* (Bohn) 1:393, appr. 21% into the work.

Part Five

Burke and the Conservative Mind

16
Religion and Politics

Burke's political religion has its roots deep in three convictions. The first is that civil society rests on spiritual foundations, being indeed nothing less than a product of Divine will; the second, that this is a fact of significance so profound that the recognition of it is of vital moment, both for the corporate life of the State and for the lives of each and all of its members; and the third, that whilst all forms of religion within the nation may play their part in bearing witness to religion, this is peculiarly the function of an Established Church, in which the "consecration of the State" finds its appropriate symbol, expression, and support.

On the first of these convictions it would be needless to enlarge. Enough to reinforce what has been already said by a single sentence which contains the sum of the whole matter: "They"—he is speaking of both reflecting and unreflective men—"conceive that He who gave our nature to be perfected by our virtue, willed also the necessary means of its perfection. He willed therefore the State. He willed its connection with the source and original archetype of all perfection."[1] It follows that the problem how to unite the secular and the sacred in the life of the State, much as it may perplex many minds, is not one that, in its general aspect at any rate, troubles Burke. As the product of Divine will and of the "stupendous wisdom" that operates throughout the ages, the State is in itself inherently and inalienably sacred. It is not an institution, secular in its nature and then made sacred by an "alliance" with a Church. This is the very fallacy he rejects when touching incidentally on the large and thorny topic of Church and State: "An alliance between Church and State in a Christian commonwealth is, in my opinion, an idle and a fanciful speculation. An alliance is between two things that are in their nature distinct and independent, such as between two sovereign States. But in a Christian commonwealth, the Church and the State are one and the same thing, being different integral parts of the same whole."[2] And this "whole," this State in the larger and more comprehensive sense of the word, is always, in its entire constitution, and not merely in its ecclesiastical institutions, however important and august, the result of that "Divine tactic" which presides over the evolution of a nation. It is needless, however, to labour this point further. For if civil society does not rest on theistic and (we may add) on Christian foundations, if it be not vitalised through and through by the spirit of God, it must be evident by this time that Burke's political teaching is false precisely where he most passionately believed it to be true.

But if this be fact; if God, Providence, stupendous wisdom, Divine tactic, be of a verity thus operative in the growth and gradual organisation of civil society, it is not a matter to which the citizens of any State can afford to shut their eyes. On the contrary, its recognition by every citizen, small or great, is fraught with results of momentous significance. So, at least, Burke will have it. And if we grant his premises, his inference is unimpeachable. It is not credible that the citizens of any commonwealth can see the will of God in the history of their country, in the institutions under which they live, in the civic functions they discharge, in the ends to which they give their lives, without their attitude being influenced thereby. With the belief that "God willed the State," if it be indeed a real, and not a merely notional belief, there inevitably comes a reverent and dutiful, and even at times a quietistic spirit, such as can hardly be expected where the social system is regarded as begotten, sustained, and sanctioned by merely secular forces and a merely secular utility. For however true it may be—and happily there is no need to deny it—that even the most secularly minded of citizens may love his country, respect its laws, and if need be lay down his life for it, there must always be a difference in political motive between him and his genuinely religious-minded neighbour. For, of course, political motive, like all motive, reflects the nature of the object that evokes it; and, so long as this is so, it is idle to suppose that the citizen who accepts his station and its duties as prescribed by the supreme object of human worship will not be profoundly influenced thereby. As man and as citizen, he will most certainly be different; and there are no differences between man and man that go deeper than differences in constitution of motive.

But Burke goes much further than this. Not only did he believe that religion makes a difference; he was convinced that it makes a better citizen.

And the peculiar interest of his writings here lies, not in mere eloquent generalities, but in his specification of the quite definite ways in which the vitality of the religious spirit must influence the citizen's outlook on the world of politics.

The difficulty of doing full justice to him here is that the glowing sentences of his rhetoric lose so much by translation into the cold and cut-and-dried statements of abbreviated exposition. But, *per contra*, it is just because critics are apt to think eloquence is not argument, that it is important to note how definite and how forcible are the reasons which here, as in so many of Burke's pages, underlie the rhetoric. First and central is the bold assertion that it is only a religious consciousness that can appreciate in its true significance the persistence and continuity of national life. This sounds audacious. But on no point is Burke more insistent. In one passage we have the affirmation that, were the religious consciousness destroyed, "no one generation could link with another," and "men become little better than the flies of a summer"[3]; and in another the sweeping prediction that "the commonwealth itself would, in a few generations, crumble away, be disconnected into the dust and powder of individuality, and at length dispersed to all the winds of heaven." Words can no further go. If these be true, the conscious dependence of the human on the Divine, and the continuity of a nation's life stand and fall together.

Not that Burke was unaware that there are other resources by which generation may be made to link with generation. "Prescriptive constitution," "entailed inheritance," "bank and capital of the ages," "experience of the species," and other phrases of like import, are all of them conceptions suggestive of ways in which political continuity may be sustained and fostered. The point is that Burke, though himself the prolific author of such phrases, is convinced that more is needed. They may suggest that the national life is a legacy: they do not, or at any rate not sufficiently, suggest that it is a supreme trust. They bear witness to the fact that a nation has a history: they do not enough convey the still more strengthening reminder that it has an assured leading and destiny, in the light of which its traditions and achievements gain an enhanced significance. For it is never enough for Burke that social organisms should be thrust forwards to an astonishing pitch of development by the mere *vis a tergo* of natural evolutionary forces, which, so far as evolutionists can tell, may quite possibly be fortuitous and aimless. He craves for more. To illuminate the struggles of the past, to dignify and intensify the responsibilities of the present, and to guarantee the future against the decadence and defeat with which, in a world of turbulent human wills, it is constantly menaced, it seemed to him the sheet anchor of a true political faith that the whole great drama of national life should be reverently recognised as ordered by a Power to which past, present, and future are organically knit stages in one Divine plan. "There is an order that keeps things fast in their place; it is made to us, and we are made to it,"[4] so runs his creed.

Results follow. For a belief such as this transfigures at a stroke the idea of the service of the State; and it does this, he tells us, especially in the case of "persons of exalted station." There is a paradox in Plato which declares that it is in vain to expect any man to be a great statesman unless he cares for something greater than politics. And though it may seem foolhardy to apply it to Burke, to whom politics were as the breath of his nostrils, it is none the less applicable. For both thinkers see the pitfalls that all too obviously lie in wait for the mere secular politician—the absorption in affairs, the greed for power, the sinister promptings of self-interest, the spirit of faction. And both would look for remedy in the same direction—in that purification of motive that springs from the elevation of the vocation of the statesman into nothing less than a ministry of the unseen. "All persons possessing any portion of power," so run the words, "ought to be strongly and awfully impressed with an idea that they act in trust; and that they are to account for their conduct in that trust to the one great Master, Author, and Founder of society."[5] The words are in the very spirit of Plato, if we do but translate the language of a theistic faith into the reasoned terminology of Platonic metaphysics.

But it is not to "persons of exalted station" alone that this line of thought applies. In truth, it never applies with so much force and urgency as in democracies, where political power has been cut up into minute fragments and portioned out in wide franchises. For it is just the wide distribution of political power that may disastrously impair the sense of individual responsibility. Burke has some weighty sentences here. The people, he points out, are, to a far less extent than are princes and other persons of exalted station, "under responsibility to one of the greatest controlling powers on earth the sense of fame and estimation. The share of infamy that is likely to fall to the lot of each individual in public acts is small indeed; the operation of opinion being in the inverse ratio to the number of those who abuse power. Their own approbation of their own acts has to them the appearance of a public judgment in their favour. A perfect democracy is therefore the most shameless thing in the world. As it is the most shameless, it is also the most fearless. No man apprehends in his person he can be made subject to punishment. Certainly the people at large never ought: for as all punishments are for example towards the conservation of the people at large, the people at large can never become the subject of punishment by any human hand."[6]

Few will deny that in this passage Burke touches with a sure hand one of the dangers of democracy. It is so much easier for human nature to be eager to share power than to take its share of responsibility in using it. Nor would it be difficult to point the moral by reference to the capriciousness, or the levity, or the indifference that is too often found in the democratic electorates which have come into being since Burke's day. The question with many is to find the remedy. And the remedy to which Burke would have us turn is characteristic. The only adequate safeguard against these dangers of popular power is to be found in the vitality of the religious spirit in the class or classes whose will is law. For that, and that alone, can bring the citizen to realise that, in the giving of vote or the duties of office, he is fulfilling what Burke does not hesitate to call a "holy function." The words, no doubt, must sound extravagant to secular minds, to whom politics altogether is nothing more than a matter of most mundane business, and very far indeed from being "holy." But they are not the less on that account significant of the civic importance of religion as understood by one of the greatest of all its exponents. Reverently religious in his own life, convinced by his diagnosis of human nature that man is "a religious animal," and insistent always that religious institutions are an organic element in the body-politic, it was inevitable that Burke should recoil from a merely secular citizenship as unequal to the demands and burdens which the State imposes on its members. Secular minds may reject his teaching. To them it can only seem a devout imagination. But they can be in no doubt, if they have read his pages, that to leave this aspect out would make his political message a wholly different, and, in his eyes, an impoverished thing.

Nor, perhaps, is it rash to assume that the vast majority of the religious world would be in substantial sympathy with Burke's insistence on the political value of religion, so far at any rate as we have considered it. Presumably all religious organisations, including such as are frankly, and even bitterly, hostile to established Churches, unite in the aspiration that the religious spirit may permeate life, of which political life is not the least part, from end to end. Even those who protest that politics ought to be kept separate from religion, and religion from politics, must be aware, no matter how sharply they distinguish secular and religious organisations and their work, that they carry their religion with them in the constitution of their motives, as these operate in the performance of all important work done by them for the world. That any citizen should be religious, and that he should *not* be influenced thereby in motive, even in the most secular of transactions, can only mean that in certain departments of life he is not religious. Fullness of life, and of strife, may have made the Churches many, yet one must do them the justice of supposing that they all alike desire to leaven the entire social system with Christian conscience and Christian charity. And if this be so, they can hardly fail to sympathise with the spirit of Burke's teaching as a plea for the alliance of citizenship and religion.

Burke, however, as is well known, would have his readers go a step further. Neither the sanctuaries of the heart nor the sanctuaries of voluntary Churches are enough for him. For, as he found the Church of England in possession of its prescriptive inheritance, material and spiritual, he insists, with all the argument and eloquence in his resourceful treasury, that it ought to stand as a recognition of religion by the nation in its corporate capacity. Convinced, as we have seen, that civil society as an organic whole is a sacred institution, he pled for a national and visible recognition of that fact. The "corporate fealty and homage" of the State to religion was to him simply the public acknowledgment that "God willed the State." And this general principle was backed by arguments as definite as they are forcible.

One is the claim, which controversy has made familiar, that religion—and not least because of the intimacy of its connection with education— is too momentous a national interest to be left to what he calls "the unsteady and precarious contribution of individuals."

Another is the plea that the clergy of an established Church occupy a position which effectively strengthens their hands as upholders of morality and moral valuations. Not only can they bring the consolations of religion to the hapless and the heavily burdened poor; not only can they minister, no less, to "the distresses of the miserable great"; they can also, from a position of independence, such as he thinks is not enjoyed by a clergy directly dependent on popular support, instruct "presumptuous ignorance" and rebuke "insolent vice," whether in high estate or low. "The people of England," he declares, "will not suffer the insolence of wealth and titles, or any other species of proud pretension, to look down with scorn upon what they look up to with reverence; nor presume to trample on that acquired personal nobility which they intend always to be, and which often is, the fruit, not the reward (for what can be the reward?) of learning, piety, and virtue."[7] And it is but an extension of this democratic demand for an independent aristocracy of the spirit that leads him on to welcome[8] the "modest splendour and unassuming state, the mild majesty and sober pomp" of religious ceremonial, and to justify an ecclesiastical hierarchy such as may (to quote a phrase that has become familiar) "exalt its mitred front in courts and parliaments."

A third point is that it is when a clergy enjoys the recognised position, and the financial independence which the establishment of religion gives, that they are best placed to resist all temptations to yield to tyrannical pressure either from above or from below, and, by consequence, peculiarly well fitted to stand for a genuine political liberty. "The English," he says, "tremble for their liberty from the influence of a clergy dependent on the Crown; they tremble for the public tranquillity from the disorders of a factious clergy, if it were made to depend upon any other than the Crown. They therefore made their Church, like their king and their nobility, independent."[9]

Nor, finally, could he regard it as other than a good application of public money, and not least in the interests of the poorer classes, that it should be devoted to religious purposes. He puts the point with unqualified directness:

For those purposes they [i.e., those who believe that God willed the State] think some part of the wealth of of the country is as usefully employed as it can be in fomenting the luxury of individuals. It is the public ornament. It is the public consolation. It nourishes the public hope. The poorest man finds his own importance and dignity in it, whilst the wealth and pride of individuals at every moment makes the man of humble rank and fortune sensible of his inferiority, and degrades and vilifies his condition. It is for the man in humble life, and to raise his nature, and to put him in mind of a state in which the privileges of opulence will cease, when he will be equal by nature, and may be more than equal by virtue, that this portion of the general wealth of his country is employed and sanctified.[10]

Nor does it in the least shake him in this that the Church, thus supported by the general wealth, should have its own tenets and tests, and that these should exclude the conscientious nonconformist. Invoking the Lockian principle, which no one is likely to dispute, that a voluntary society can exclude any member she thinks fit on such conditions as she thinks proper, he transfers the principle, with a surprising indifference to the significance of the transition, to the Church that claims to be national.[11] It is precisely on this ground, indeed, that he argues, in 1772, against the petition, in which not only certain of the clergy of the Church, but doctors and lawyers, claimed to be relieved from subscription to the Articles. And the line he took here is all the more remarkable, because he was far from thinking that the Church was perfect. Both Articles and Liturgy, he frankly admits, are "not without the marks and characters of human frailty."[12]   This was, of course, to be lamented; but it was not enough to precipitate a change. Against a change he urges that there is no real grievance—none for the petitioning clergy, who may easily find pulpits and congregations to suit their views in one or other of the many Churches that are tolerated; and none for the taxpayer, who, if he be one of the minority who dissent from the creed of the Church, is not to be supposed to subscribe to the creed because he consents to pay his tax. Nor has he much difficulty in showing that, in suggesting subscription to Scripture as substitute, the petitioners were opening up as many difficulties as those they wished to escape. *Some* test of membership, he insists, every Church must impose; men must not expect to be paid by taxation "for teaching, as Divine truths, their own particular fancies." And this being so, he would rather have subscription to the Articles, with all their imperfections, than anything that can be put in their place.

There is much in this that will no doubt invite criticism in days when both Church establishment and Creed subscription are more burning questions than they were then. But it is not necessary to embark here on either of these highly controversial topics. Enough if what has been said makes it clear how far Burke carried his repugnance to anything that savoured of the secularisation of the State.

For it is not Burke's defence of Church establishment that is the central interest in his apologia for religion in politics; it is rather the grounds on which this rests—grounds which will appeal to many besides those who stand for established religions. Is it true that the belief that God has willed the State is fraught for citizens with these momentous issues which Burke ascribes to it? Is it a fact that the State is a sacred thing? Is it incontrovertible that the trite distinction between secular and sacred is a pernicious and false dualism? Is it the case that religion is the basis of civil society? These are questions that go deeper far than the vexed controversy about Church establishments. For it is not the adherents of established Churches alone, it is the whole religious world that finds itself nowadays in the presence of critics and assailants more numerous, more formidable, more scientific than the atheists and infidels of Burke's abhorrence and denunciation. For the nineteenth century has seen the advent, not to say—for not a few would say it—the triumph, of naturalism. And in political theory naturalism, of course, means not only that the social organism, like other organisms, comes to its maturity through the action of biological laws, but that the prolonged process of struggle and survival through which it emerges, finds all the explanation available in the operation of quite secular conditions and causes, possibly in the last resort mechanical, but at any rate such as leave no room for the agency of any final cause or providential agency whatsoever. Nor is it doubtful that any such notion as that the course of history and the evolution of nations are "the known march of the ordinary providence of God," would receive but a chilling welcome at the hands of naturalism. If so, the practical inference is obvious. Ill would it become the statesman to cherish one thought, or utter one word, about a "Divine tactic," "a stupendous wisdom," a "Divine Disposer," or what not. Let the will of evolution be done! Enough for him to be content, as the naturalistic thinkers are content, to learn from experience what the facts and forces are that are thrusting on his country he knows not whither. Enough for him to shape these facts and control these forces in the interests of the public good, or whatever other end he can find, and sufficiently believe in, to vitalise the civic will to strenuous service. Nor presumably would either theoretical or practical naturalism resent the imputation that it leads to a throroughgoing secularisation of the State.

Nor can it be denied that it would be in vain to seek for a refutation of naturalism in the pages of Burke. He does not prove, he never dreams of proving that man is a religious animal, or that the object of religious faith is real. His religion is a faith, not a philosophy; and those who wish to find these fundamentals of the faith made good by proof, must go, not to Burke but to the theologians, or to the idealistic philosophers who are not afraid to give the world a philosophy of religion. And yet Burke's teaching has its claims upon the thinker. It sugests a problem which is theoretically, as well as practically, of the first rank. For, by the passionate conviction and definiteness of statement wherewith he specifies the ways in which the vitality of the religious consciousness influences the attitude of the citizen of all ranks and grades towards his station and its duties—a matter on which he could speak with the voice of experience—he prompts the question as to what is likely to happen should religious belief suffer eclipse. Will that consciousness of imperious political obligation, which so often has had its root in theism, survive? Will the faith that men and nations have a destiny no less assured and divinely guided than their past history, still play its part in fostering that belief in ideals in which lies the nerve of political struggle? Will an unselfish devotion to the public good still persist? Hardly can it be denied that hitherto the resolute and dutiful civic spirit has thriven, not only in illustrious instances, but amongst masses of the people, in close alliance with religion. To quicken and sustain it, more has seemingly been needed than the consciousness of ties to home, to comrades, to neighbourhood, to nation, to humanity. The appeal to altar has been as potent as to hearth. "It is in the form of imagination," says a writer on political obligation, who never ventured on a statement till he felt that his foot was planted on experience,[13] "the imagination of a supreme, invisible, but all-seeing ruler that, in the case at least of all ordinary good people, the idea of an absolute duty is so brought to bear upon the soul as to yield an awe superior to any personal inclination." If this be true, how is the gap to be filled should this article of practical faith become in the eyes of "all ordinary good people," as doubtless it already is to naturalistic scrutiny, no better than an imaginative figment best relegated to the scrap-heap of past, or passing, phases of metaphysical illusion? For the strength and vitality of motives depends ultimately upon the objects to which they attach themselves, and by which they are fed and fostered. And so long as this is so, it would seem something of a venture to remove a God, a "Divine Disposer," a "Providence," a "Divine tactic," from the human horizon without finding some substitute.

This, indeed, seems to be well recognised, for naturalistic minds do not revolt against political theism without putting something in the place of the deity deposed and the "Divine tactic" superseded. Sometimes it is the Nation which, following a French lead, they set on the secular altar of civic devotion.[14] And sometimes, and not by any means only amongst avowed positivists, it is Humanity. Nor is it to be doubted that both are great and enduring objects to which the minds and hearts of men will never look in vain for incentive and support.

This, however, is not a statement that Burke of all men would have been likely to challenge. There is abundant room in his scheme of life, as we have already seen,[15] both for the nation and humanity. No writer in our language, or in any language, is less open to the charge of underestimating the strength of the patriotic motive. To this we need not return. But then it has to be remembered that it was not the nation as a merely secular institution that aroused this passion of patriotism, but the nation consecrated in his imagination as product and instrument of the Divine will. It is not worth asking whether his patriotism would have survived the destruction of his theism, because in his mind the two things are one and indivisible.

Similarly with the larger, though far less closely knit, object, humanity. Burke was not blind to it. Despite his denunciations of French fraternity, he never failed, as we have seen, to recognise that his own country, and all countries, were parts of a larger whole. But this larger whole was not the humanity of positivism or naturalism; it was "the great mysterious incorporation of the human race"; and the mystery that encompassed it was not the mystery that, to the agnostic, shuts out the faith that the fortunes of the race are shaped and controlled by spiritual forces, but the mystery which, however dark and inscrutable (the words are his own), is still compatible with the belief that the course of civilisation is "the known march of the ordinary providence of God." Certainly for the mind of Burke there could be no ultimate rest in the idea of humanity. How could there be, when it was to him of the essence of humanity, by the perennial vitality of the religious consciousness, to bear its witness to the dependence of the human on the Divine? It needs no words to prove that if man be "a religious animal," if atheism be against both human instincts and human reason, as Burke declared it was, "humanity" was ill fitted to be offered to the world as a *substitute* for God. For, though it may need few words to prove that, if humanity be severed by the sword of science from divinity, and God left out as but an ancient idol, the apotheosis of humanity is the deposition of divinity; it is not less obvious that the idea of a humanity, in every individual soul of which the belief in God is eternal and ineradicable, is the strongest of all securities against the secularisation of human life. Yet nothing less than this was the creed of Burke, to whose profoundly religious spirit the attempted secularisation of history and politics was nothing less than a conspiracy to denationalise the nation and to dehumanise the race.

Notes

"Religion and Politics" appears as Chapter Eight in
John MacCunn's *The Political Philosophy of Burke* (London: Arnold, 1913), pp. 122-43.

1. *Reflections* in *Works* (Bohn) 2:370, appr. 39% into the work.
2. "Speech on the Petition of the Unitarian Society," in *Works* (Bohn) 6:115, fourth paragraph.
3. *Reflections* in *Works* (Bohn) 2:367, appr. 38% into the work.
4. "Speech on the Reform of Representation in the House of Commons," in *Works* (Bohn) 6:151, four paragraphs from the end.
5. *Reflections* in *Works* (Bohn) 2:365, appr. 37% into the work.
6. *Reflections* in *Works* (Bohn) 2:365, appr. 37% into the work.
7. *Reflections* in *Works* (Bohn) 2:375, appr. 41% into the work.
8. *Reflections* in *Works* (Bohn) 2:370, appr. 39% into the work.
9. *Reflections* in *Works* (Bohn) 2:372, appr. 40% into the work.
10. *Reflections* in *Works* (Bohn) 2:370, appr. 39% into the work.
11. See the "Speech on the Acts of Uniformity" [1772] in *Works* (Bohn) 6:91-102.

12. "Speech on the Acts of Uniformity," in *Works* (Bohn) 6:95, appr. 42% into the work.
13. Professor T. H. Green.
14. E.g., Charles H. Pearson in *National Life and Character* [1893] (London: Macmillan, 1913).
15. [Here and in the next paragraph, MacCunn refers to pp. 23, 27 of the book from which this chapter is taken. —DR]

17
Burke and the Moral Imagination

"Everybody knows," Burke writes of the members of the French National Assembly, "that there is a great dispute amongst their leaders, which of them is the best resemblance of Rousseau. In truth, they all resemble him. His blood they transfuse into their minds and into their manners. Him they study; him they meditate; him they turn over in all the time they can spare from the laborious mischief of the day, or the debauches of the night. Rousseau is their canon of holy writ; in his life he is their canon of *Polycletus*; he is their standard figure of perfection. To this man and this writer, as a pattern to authors and to Frenchmen, the foundries of Paris are now running for statues, with the kettles of their poor and the bells of their churches."[1]

I have presented Rousseau in his essential influence as the extremist and foe of compromise.[2] In contrast to Rousseau, Burke is usually and rightly supposed to embody the spirit of moderation. Many of his utterances on the French Revolution, however (the passage I have just quoted may serve as a sample), are scarcely suggestive of moderation, and towards the end he becomes positively violent. There is at least this much to be said in justification of Burke, that in his writings on the Revolution, he is for the most part debating first principles, and when it comes to first principles, the issue raised is not one of moderation, but of truth or error. Burke was no mere partisan of the *status quo*. He was not opposed on principle to revolutions. He is perhaps open to the charge of pushing too far his admiration for the Revolution of 1688. His attitude towards the American Revolution was consistently one of compromise and in many respects of sympathy. He did not stand in any undue awe of those in authority. No one could on occasion call them to a stricter accounting or show himself a more disinterested champion of the victims of unjust power. He recognized specifically the abuses of the Old Régime in France, and was ready to admit the application to these abuses of fairly drastic remedies. If he refused, therefore, to compromise with the French Revolution, the reason is to be sought less in the field of politics than in that of general philosophy, and even of religion. He saw that the Revolution did not, like other revolutions, seek to redress certain specific grievances, but had universal pretensions. France was to become the "Christ of nations" and conduct a crusade for the political regeneration of mankind. This particular mixture of the things of God and the things of Cæsar seemed to him psychologically unsound, and in any case subversive of the existing social order of Europe. The new revoltionary evangel was the final outcome of the speculations that had been going on for generations about a state of nature, natural rights, the social contract, and abstract and unlimited sovereignty. Burke is the chief opponent of this tendency towards what one may term metaphysical politics, especially as embodied in the doctrine of the rights of man. "They are so taken up with the rights of man," he says of the members of this school, "that they have totally forgotten his nature." Under cover of getting rid of prejudice they would strip man of all the habits and concrete relationships and network of historical circumstance in which he is actually implicated and finally leave him shivering "in all the nakedness and solitude of metaphysical abstraction." They leave no limit to logic save despotism. In his attack on the enemies of prejudice, by which was meant practically everything that is traditional and prescriptive, Burke has perhaps neglected unduly certain minor though still important distinctions, especially the distinction between those who were for getting rid of prejudice in the name of reason, and those who, like Rousseau, were for getting rid of it in the name of feeling. The rationalists and the Rousseauists were actually ready to guillotine one another in the Revolution, an opposition prefigured in the feud between Rousseau and various "philosophers," notably Voltaire. Rousseau was as ready as Burke, though on different grounds, as I shall try to show presently, to protest against the "solid darkness of this enlightened age."

By the dismissal as mere prejudice of the traditional forms that are in no small measure the funded experience of any particular community, the State loses its historical continuity, its permanent self, as it were, that unites its present with its past and future. By an unprincipled facility in changing the State such as is encouraged by Rousseau's impressionistic notion of the general will, the generations of men can no more link with one another than the flies of a summer. They are disconnected into the dust and powder of individuality. In point of fact, any political philosophy, whether that of Hobbes or of Rousseau, which starts from the supposition that men are naturally isolated units, and achieve society only as the result of an artifice, is in its essence violently individualistic. For this atomistic, mechanical view of the State, Burke is usually supposed to have substituted an organic, historical conception. Much of his actual influence, in Germany and elsewhere, has certainly been along these lines. Yet this is far from being the whole truth about Burke. A one-sided devotion to the organic, historical conception is itself an outcome of the naturalistic movement. It may lead to fatalistic acquiescence in traditional forms, and discourage, not merely abstract rationalism, but a reasonable adjustment of these forms to shifting circumstance. It relates itself very readily to that side of the romantic movement that exalts the unconscious at the expense of moral choice and conscious deliberation. Once obscure this capacity in the individual, which alone raises him above phenomenal nature, and it will not be easy in the long run to preserve his autonomy; he will tend, as so often in German theory, to lose his independent will and become a mere organ of the all-powerful State. Though Taine, again, often professes to speak as a disciple of Burke in his attacks on the French Revolution, it is not easy to see a true follower in a philosopher who proclaimed that "vice and virtue are products like sugar and vitriol."

The truth is that Burke is in no sense a collectivist, and still less, if possible, a determinist. If he had been either, he would not have attained to that profound perception of true liberty in which he surpasses perhaps any other political thinker, ancient or modern. For one who believes in personal liberty in Burke's sense, the final emphasis is necessarily not on the State but on the individual. His individualism, however, is not, like that of Rousseau, naturalistic, but humanistic and religious. Only, in getting the standards by which the individual may hope to surpass his ordinary self, and achieve humanism or religion, he would have him lean heavily on prescription. Burke is anti-individualistic in that he would not set the individual to trading on his own private stock of wit. He would have him respect the general sense, the accumulated experience of the past that has become embodied in the habits and usages that the superficial rationalist would dismiss as prejudice. If the individual condemns the general sense, and trusts unduly his private self, he will have no model; and a man's first need is to look up to a sound model and imitate it. He may thus become exemplary in his turn.

The principle of homage and service to what is above one has its culmination and final justification in fealty to God, the true sovereign and supreme exemplar. Burke's conception of the State may be described as a free and flexible adaptation of genuinely Platonic and Christian elements. "We know, and what is better, we feel inwardly, that religion is the basis of civil society, and the source of all good and all comfort." "God willed the state." (Thus to conceive the highest in terms of will is Christian.) "He willed its connection with the source and original archetype of all perfection."[4] (The language is here Platonic.) Not merely religion but the actual church establishment is held by Englishmen to be essential to their State, as being indeed the very foundation of their constitution.

"Society is indeed a contract," though the basis of the contract is not mere utility. The state is not to be regarded as a partnership agreement in a trade of pepper and coffee. It is not, as a contemporary pacifist has maintained, the "pooled self-esteem" of the community, but rather its permanent ethical self. It is, therefore, a partnership in all science and art and in every virtue and perfection. "As the ends of such a partnership cannot be obtained in many generations, it becomes a partnership not only between those who are living, but between those who are living, those who are dead, and those who are to be born."[5]

Though Burke thus uses the language of contract, it is plain that he moves in a different world from all those, including Locke, for whom the idea of contract meant that man has certain rights as a free gift of nature and anterior to the performance of his duties. Talk to the child, says Rousseau, of something that will interest him—talk to him of his rights, and not of his duties.[6] To assert, as Burke does in the main, that one has only concrete historical rights, acquired as the result of the fulfilment of definite obligations, is evidently remote from Rousseau's assertion that a man enjoys certain abstract rights simply because he has taken the trouble to be born. The difference here is not merely between Burke and Rousseau, but also between Burke and Locke. The final superficiality of Locke is that he granted man abstract natural rights anterior to his duties, and then hoped that it would be possible to apply this doctrine moderately. But it has been justly said that doctrines of this kind are most effective in their extreme logical form because it is in this form that they capture the imagination. Now if the out-and-out radical is often highly imaginative in the fashion that I have attributed to Rousseau, the Whigs and the liberals who follow the Whig tradition are rather open to the suspicion of being deficient on the side of imagination. One cannot help feeling, for instance, that if Macaulay had been more imaginative, he would have shown less humanitarian complacency in his essay on Bacon. Disraeli again is said to have looked with disdain on J. S. Mill because of his failure to perceive the rôle of the imagination in human affairs, a lack that can scarcely be charged against Disraeli himself, whatever one may think of the quality of his imagination.

Now Burke is the exceptional Whig, in that he is not only splendidly imaginative, but admits the supreme rôle of the imagination rather more explicitly than is common among either Christians or Platonists with whom I have associated him. He saw how much of the wisdom of life consists in an imaginative assumption of the experience of the past in such fashion as to bring it to bear as a living force upon the present. The very model that one looks up to and imitates is an imaginative creation. A man's imagination may realize in his ancestors a standard of virtue and wisdom beyond the vulgar practice of the hour; so that he may be enabled to rise with the example to whose imitation he has aspired. The forms of the past and the persons who administer them count in Burke's eyes chiefly as imaginative symbols. In the famous passage on Marie Antoinette one almost forgets the living and suffering woman to see in her with Burke a gorgeous symbol of the age of chivalry yielding to the age of "sophisters, economists, and calculators." There is in this sense truth in the taunt of Tom Paine that Burke pities the plumage and forgets the dying bird. All the decent drapery of life, Burke complains of the new philosophy, is to be rudely torn off. "All the super-added ideas, furnished from the wardrobe of a moral imagination,...are to be exploded as a ridiculous, absurd, and antiquated fashion."[7]

The apostles of the rights of man were, according to Burke, undermining the two principles on which everything that was truly civilized in the European order had for ages depended: the spirit of religion and the spirit of a gentleman. The nobility and the clergy, who were the custodians of these principles and of the symbols that embodied them and ministered to the moral imagination, had received in turn the support of the learned. Burke warns the learned that in deserting their natural protectors for Demos, they run the risk of being "cast into the mire and trodden under the hoofs of a swinish multitude."[8]

Burke is in short a frank champion of aristocracy. It is here especially, however, that he applies flexibly his Christian-Platonic, and humanistic principles. He combines a soundly individualistic element with his cult of the traditional order. He does not wish any static hierarchy. He disapproves of any tendency to deal with men in classes and groups, a tendency that the extreme radical shares with the extreme reactionary. He would have us

estimate men, not by their hereditary rank, but by their personal achievement. "There is," he says, "no qualification for government but virtue or
wisdom, actual or presumptive. Wherever they are actually found, they have
in whatever state, condition, profession or trade, the passport of Heaven to
human place and honor." He recognizes, to be sure, that it is hard for the
manual worker to acquire such virtue and wisdom for the reason that he lacks
the necessary leisure. The ascent of rare merit from the lower to the higher
levels of society should, however, always be left open, even though this
merit be required to pass through a severe probation.

In the same fashion, Burke would admit innovations in the existing social
order only after a period of severe probation. He is no partisan of an inert
traditionalism. His true leader or natural aristocrat, as he terms him, has, in
his adjustment of the contending claims of new and old, much of the
character of the "trimmer" as Halifax has described him. "By preserving the
method of nature in the conduct of the State, in what we improve we are
never wholly new; in what we retain, we are never wholly obsolete." "The
disposition to preserve, and ability to improve, taken together, would be my
standard of a statesman." In such utterances Burke is of course simply
giving the theory of English liberty at its best, a theory almost too familiar
for restatement. In his imaginative grasp of all that is involved in the task of
mediating between the permanent and the fluctuating element in life, the
Platonic art, as one may say, of seeing the One in the Many, he has had few
equals in the field of political thinking.

Burke is, however, in one important respect highly un-Platonic, and that
is in his attitude towards the intellect. His distrust of what we should call
nowadays the intellectual may be variously explained. It is related in some
respects to one side, the weak side, one is bound to add, of Christianity. "A
certain intemperance of intellect," he writes, "is the disease of the time, and
the source of all its other diseases." He saw so clearly the dangers of this
abuse that he was led at times, as the Christian has at times been led, to look
with suspicion on intellect itself. And then he was familiar, as we are all
familiar, with persons who give no reasons at all, or the wrong reasons, for
doing the right thing, and with other persons who give the most logical and
ingenious reasons for doing the wrong thing. The basis for right conduct is
not reasoning but experience, and experience much wider than that of the
individual, the secure possession of which can result only from the early
acquisition of right habits. Then, too, there is something specifically English
in Burke's disparagement of the intellect. The Englishman, noting the
results of the proneness of a certain type of Frenchman to reason rigorously

from false or incomplete premises, comes to prefer his own piecemeal good sense and proclivity for "muddling through." As Disraeli told a foreign visitor, the country is governed not by logic but by Parliament. In much the same way Bagehot in the course of a comparison between the Englishman and the Frenchman in politics, reaches the semi-humorous conclusion that "in real sound stupidity the English are unrivalled."

The anti-intellectual side of Burke reminds one at times of the anti-intellectual side of Rousseau: when, for instance, he speaks of the "happy effect of following nature, which is wisdom without reflection and above it."[9] The resemblance is, however, only superficial. The wisdom that Rousseau proclaimed was not *above* reflection but *below* it. A distinction of this kind is rather meaningless unless supported by careful psychological analysis. Perhaps the first contrast between the superrational and the subrational is that between awe and wonder.[10] Rousseau is plainly an apostle of wonder, so much so that he is probably the chief single influence in the "renascence of wonder" that has resulted from the romantic movement. The romantic objection to intellect is that by its precise analysis and tracing of cause and effect, it diminishes wonder. Burke, on the other hand, is fearful lest an indiscreet intellectual activity may undermine awe and reverence. "We ought," he says, "to venerate where we are unable presently to understand." As the best means of securing veneration, Burke leans heavily upon habit, whereas the romantics, from Rousseau to Walter Pater, are no less clearly hostile to habit because it seems to lead to a stereotyped world, a world without vividness and surprise. To lay stress on veneration meant for Burke, at least in the secular order, to lay stress on rank and degree; whereas the outstanding trait perhaps of the state of nature projected by Rousseau's imagination, in defiance of the actual facts of primitive life so far as we know them, is that it is equalitarian. This trait is common to his no-state and his all-state, his anarchistic and his collectivistic Utopia. The world of the *Social Contract*, no less than that of the *Second Discourse*, is a world without degree and subordination; a world in which no one looks up to any one else or expects any one to look up to him; a world in which no one (and this seems to Rousseau very desirable) has either to command or to obey. In his predominant emphasis on equality,[11] Rousseau speaks, to some extent at least, not merely for himself but for France, especially the France of the last two centuries. "Liberty," says Mallet du Pan, "a thing forever unintelligible to Frenchmen."[12] Perhaps liberty has not been intelligible in its true essence to many persons anywhere. "The love, and even the very idea, of genuine liberty," Burke himself admits, "is extremely rare." If the basis of the genuine liberty is, as Burke affirms, an act of subordination, it is simply incompatible with Rousseauistic equality.

The act of subordination to any earthly authority is justified only in case this authority is looking up to something still higher; so that genuine liberty is rooted in the virtue that also underlies genuine Christianity. "True humility, the basis of the Christian system, is the low, but deep and firm foundation of all real virtue. But this, as very painful in the practice and little imposing in the appearance," he goes on to say of the French revolutionists, "they have totally discarded."[13]   They have preferred to follow Rousseau, the great "professor and founder of the philosophy of vanity." Rousseau himself said that he based his position on the "noblest pride," and pride is, even more than vanity, the significant opposite of humility. I have already spoken of Rousseau's depreciation of humility in favor of patriotic pride. The problem of pride versus humility is, of course, not primarily political at all. It is a problem of the inner life. Rousseau undermined humility in the individual by substituting the doctrine of natural goodness for the older doctrine of man's sinfulness and fallibility. The forms and traditions, religious and political, that Burke on the other hand defends, on the ground that they are not arbitrary but are convenient summings up of a vast body of past experience, give support to the imagination of the individual; the imagination, thus drawn back as it were to an ethical centre, supplies in turn a standard with reference to which the individual may set bounds to the lawless expansion of his natural self (which includes his intellect as well as his emotions). From a purely psychological point of view, Burke's emphasis on humility and on the imaginative symbols that he deems necessary to secure it, reduces itself to an emphasis on what one may term the centripetal element in liberty. Rousseau, at least the Rousseau that has influenced the world, practically denies the need of any such centripetal element in liberty, inasmuch as what will emerge spontaneously on the disappearance of the traditional controls is an expansive will to brotherhood. If one rejects like Burke this gospel of "universal benevolence," it is hard not to conceive of liberty in Burke's fashion—namely, as a nice adjustment between the taking on of inner control and the throwing off of outer control. "Society," he says, "cannot exist unless a controlling power upon will and appetite be placed somewhere, and the less of it there is within, the more there must be without."[14]   This adjustment between inner and outer control, which concerns primarily the individual, is thus seen to determine at last the degree to which any community is capable of political liberty. True statesmanship is in this sense a humanistic mediation and not an indolent oscillation between extremes. "To make a government requires no great prudence. Settle the seat of power; teach obedience: and the work is done. To give freedom is still more easy. It is not necessary to guide; it only requires to let go the rein. But to form a *free government*—that is, to temper together these opposite elements of liberty and restraint in one consistent work, requires much thought, deep reflection, a sagacious, powerful, and combining mind."

I have already said that Burke is very exceptional in that he is a splendidly imaginative Whig. As a matter of fact, most of the typical Whigs and liberals in the Whig tradition, are, like Burke, partisans of liberty in the sense of personal liberty and of moderation. They do not, however, give their personal liberty and moderation the same basis of religion and humanistic control. On the contrary, they incline to be either rationalists or emotionalists, which means practically that they found their ethics either on the principle of utility, or else on the new spirit of sympathy and service, or more commonly on some compound of these main ingredients of humanitarianism. The liberty of Burke, I have tried to show, is not only religiously grounded, but involves in its political application a genuine humanistic mediation. The Whig compromise, on the other hand, is only too often an attempt to compromise between views of life, namely, the religious-humanistic and the utilitarian-sentimental, which are in their essence incompatible. Thus the liberalism of J. S. Mill is, compared with the liberalism of Burke, open to the charge of being unimaginative. Furthermore, from a strictly modern point of view, it is open to the charge of being insufficiently critical. For the liberty Mill desires is of the kind that will result only from the traditional spiritual controls, or from some adequate substitute, and his philosophy, as I shall try to show more fully later, supplies neither.

Burke can scarcely be charged with the form of superficiality that consists in an attempt to mediate between incompatible first principles. One may, however, feel that he failed to recognize the full extent and gravity of the clash between the new principles and the old; and one may also find it hard to justify the obscurantist element that enters into his defence of his own religious and humanistic position. One might gather from Burke that England was almost entirely made up of Christian gentlemen ready to rally to the support of the majestic edifice of traditional civilization, to all the decencies of life based finally on the moral imagination, whereas the "sophisters, economists, and calculators" who were destroying this edifice by their substitution for the moral imagination of an abstract metaphysical reason were almost entirely French. He does indeed refer to the English deists, but only to dismiss them as obscure eccentrics. The English intellectuals and radical thinkers of his own time he waves aside with the utmost contempt, opposing to them not those who think more keenly, but those who do not think at all:

> Because half a dozen grasshoppers under a fern make the field ring with their importunate chink, whilst thousands of great cattle, reposed beneath the shadow of the British oak, chew the cud and are silent, pray do not imagine that those who make the noise are the only inhabitants of the field; that, of course, they are many in number; or that, after all, they are other than the little, shrivelled, meagre, hopping, though loud and troublesome, insects of the hour.[15]

In this passage we have the obscurantist Burke at his weakest. The truth is that the little, meagre, hopping insects of the hour were representatives of an international movement of a vast scope, a movement destined finally to prevail over the prejudice and prescription that Burke was defending. Moreover, this movement was largely, if not indeed primarily, of English origin. "It is from England," says Joubert, "that have issued forth, like fogs, the metaphysical and political ideas which have darkened everything." It is hard to trace the main currents of European life and thought from the Renaissance, especially the rise of humanitarianism in both its utilitarian and its sentimental aspects, and not assent in large measure to the assertion of Joubert. Burke's conception of man and of the State with its strong tinge of Platonic realism (in the older sense of the word) and its final emphaisis on humility, or submission to the will of God, has important points of contact with the mediæval conception. Now, even before Francis Bacon, men from the British Islands played an important part in breaking down this realism. Duns Scotus discredited reason in theology in favor of an arbitrary divine will, and so released reason for use in the secular order. William of Occam asserted a nominalism that looks forward to our type of realism, that is, not of the One but of the Many, and, therefore, at the opposite pole from the mediæval variety. Roger Bacon is significant for the future both by his interest in the physical order and by the experimental temper that he displays in dealing with this order.

To come to a later period, the upshot of the civil convulsions of seventeenth-century England was to diminish imaginative allegiance to the past. The main achievement of Cromwell himself was, as his admirer Marvell avowed, to "ruin the great work of Time." As loyalty to the great traditions declined, England concentrated on the utilitarian effort of which Francis Bacon is the prophet, and thus did more than any other country to prepare and carry through the industrial revolution, compared with which the French Revolution is only a melodramatic incident.

If the Christian classical England that Burke took to be truly representative has survived in a place like Oxford, utilitarian England has got itself embodied in cities like Birmingham, so that the opposition between the two Englands, an opposition that is one of first principles, has come to be written on the very face of the landscape. The Englishman, however, does not proceed by logical exclusions, and is capable of maintaining in more or less friendly juxtaposition things that are ultimately incompatible. Thus a young man receives a religious-humanistic training at Oxford as a preparation for helping to administer the British Empire in India, an empire which is, in its origins, chiefly an outcome of the utilitarian and commercially expansive England. The kind of leadership that Burke desired, the leadership of the true gentleman, still plays no small part in the affairs of England and of the world. The Englishman whom he conceives to be typical, who "fears God, looks up with awe to kings, with affection to parliaments, with duty to magistrates, with reverence to priests, and with respect to nobility," is still extant, but is considerably less typical. Above all, his psychology is not that of the great urban masses that owe their existence to the industrial revolution. What Birmingham stands for has been gaining steadily on what Oxford stands for, and that even at Oxford itself. I have said that the only effective conservatism is an imaginative conservatism. Now it has not only become increasingly difficult to enter imaginatively into certain traditional symbols, but in general the imagination has been drawn away more and more from the element of unity in things to the element of diversity. As a result of the type of progress that has been proclaimed, everything good has come to be associated with novelty and change, with the piling up of discovery on discovery. Life, thus viewed, no longer involves any reverence for some centre or oneness, but is conceived as an infinite and indefinite expansion of wonder and curiosity. As a result of all this intoxication with change, the world is moving, we are asked to believe, towards some "far-off divine event." It is at this point that the affinity appears between the utilitarian or Baconian, and the emotional or Rousseauistic side of the humanitarian movement. The far-off divine event is, no less than Rousseau's state of nature, a projection of the idyllic imagination. The felicity of the the divine event, like that of the state of nature, is a felicity that can be shown to involve no serious moral effort or self-discipline on the part of the individual. Rousseau himself put his golden age in the past, but nothing is easier than to be a Rousseauist, and at the same time, like the Baconian, put one's golden age in the future. The differences between Baconian and Rousseauist, and they are numerous, are, compared with this underlying similarity in the quality of their "vision," unimportant. I remarked at the outset that the modern political movement may be regarded in its most significant aspect as a battle between the spirit of Rousseau and that of Burke. Whatever the explanation, it is an indubitable fact that this movement has been away from Burke and towards Rousseau. "The star of Burke is manifestly fading," Lecky was able to write a number of years ago, "and a great part of the teaching of the *Contrat Social* is passing into English politics." Professor Vaughan, again, the editor of the recent standard edition of Rousseau's political writings, remarked in his introduction, apparently without awakening any special contradiction or surprise, that in the essentials of political wisdom Burke is "immeasurably inferior to the man of whom he never speaks but with scorn and loathing; to the despised theorist, the metaphysical madman of Geneva."

Burke will be cherished as long as any one survives in the world who has a perception of the nature of true liberty. It is evident, however, that if a true liberalism is to be successfully defended under present circumstances, it will not be altogether by Burke's method. The battle for prejudice and prescription and a "wisdom above reflection" has already been lost. It is no longer possible to wave aside the modernists as the mere noisy insects of an hour, or to oppose to an unsound activity of intellect mere stolidity and imperviousness to thought—the great cattle chewing their cud in the shadow of the British oak. But before coming to the question of method, we need to consider what the triumph of Rousseau has actually meant in the history of modern Europe, during and since the Great Revolution. A survey of this kind will be found to involve a consideration of the two chief political problems of the present time, the problem of democracy and the problem of imperialism both in themselves and in their relation to one another.

Notes

"Burke and the Moral Imagination" appears as Chapter Three in
Irving Babbitt, *Democracy and Leadership* (Boston: Houghton Mifflin, 1924), pp. 97-116.

1. *Letter to a Member of the National Assembly* in *Works* (Bohn) 2:535, appr. 42% into the work.
2. [Babbitt's previous chapter concerned "Rousseau and the Idyllic Imagination." —DR]
3. On Rehberg, Savigny, etc. [Burke's influence on German thinkers is the subject of a number of essays, indexed in C. Gandy and P. Stanlis, *Edmund Burke: A Bibliography of Secondary Studies to 1982* (New York and London: Garland, 1983), under "Burke: Reputation and Influence: Germany," p. 348. —DR]
4. The three preceding quotations are from *Reflections in* Works (Bohn) 2:362, 370, appr. 36% and 39% into the work.
5. *Reflections* in *Works* (Bohn) 2:368, appr. 38% into the work.
6. *Emile*, Book 2.
7. *Reflections* in *Works* (Bohn) 2:348-49, appr. 30% into the work.
8. *Reflections* in *Works* (Bohn) 2:351, appr. 31% into the work.
9. *Reflections* in *Works* (Bohn) 2:307, appr. 13% into the work.
10. See Irving Babbitt, *Rousseau and Romanticism* (1919), pp. 49ff.
11. It would not be easy to find in an English author of anything like the same intellectual distinction the equivalent of the following passage from Proudhon (*Œuvres*, 2:91): "L'enthousiasme qui nous possède, l'enthousiasme de l'égalité,...est une ivresse plus forte que le vin, plus pénétrante que l'amour: passion ou fureur divine que le délire des Léonidas, des Saint Bernard et des Michel-Ange n'égala jamais."
12. Cf. E. Faguet, *Politiques et moralistes*, 1:117: "Il est à peu près impossible à un Français d'être libéral, et le libéralisme n'est pas français." See also 3:95.
13. *Letter to a Member of the National Assembly* in *Works* (Bohn) 2:536, appr. 45% into the work.
14. *Letter to a Member of the National Assembly* in *Works* (Bohn) 2:555, appr. 93% into the work.
15. *Reflections* in *Works* (Bohn) 2:357, appr. 33% into the work.

PETER J. STANLIS

18

Burke and the Natural Law

Burke's Appeals to the Natural Law—1761-1789

To appreciate fully Burke's appeals to the Natural Law in Irish, American, domestic, and Indian affairs, it is necessary to understand the historical conditions and immediate circumstances which called forth his pleas, and to examine the manner in which Burke sought to establish the principles of Natural Law through practical political action. It is generally conceded by historians of all schools of thought that during most of the eighteenth century Ireland was to England as an abject slave to a proud master. Morley has clearly summarized the essential nature of the problem Ireland faced:

> After the suppression of the great rebellion of Tyrconnel by William of Orange, nearly the whole of the land was confiscated, the peasants were made beggars and outlaws, the Penal Laws against the Catholics were enacted and enforced, and the grand reign of Protestant Ascendancy began in all its vileness and completeness. The Protestants and landlords were supreme; the peasants and the Catholics were prostrate in despair. The Revolution brought about in Ireland just the reverse of what it effected in England. Here it delivered the body of the nation from the attempted supremacy of a small sect. There it made a small sect supreme over the body of the nation.[1]

Even in the last decade of the century, after a series of mild reforms, Burke could lament that sectarian differences kept the people of Ireland as much apart as if they were not only separate nations, but separate species. To complicate and intensify the differences in religion and the tyranny of the penal laws, Ireland, like the American colonies at a later date, was subjected to a commercial policy by which England severely restricted her industry and fettered her economic productivity to enrich Bristol and Manchester merchants. The greater part of the people of Ireland lived out their lives in extreme poverty, often without even the elemental necessities of life. This dual problem of religious and economic tyranny was further intensified in Burke's time by George III's assumption that his arbitrary will was the law of the land.

Since Ireland was much weaker than America and closer to England, the abstract "right" of the king and parliament to rule there by arbitrary will was far more successful and tyrannical, and was intensified by differences in religion. Burke observed that in his coronation oath "the king swears he will maintain...'the laws of God.' I suppose it means the natural moral laws." Burke complained, nevertheless, that under English kings Ireland had suffered "penalties, incapacities, and proscriptions from generation to generation," and was "under a deprivation of all the rights of human nature."[2] Burke summarized the "vicious perfection" of the system by which England deprived her Irish subjects of their natural rights:

> It was a complete system, full of coherence and consistency; well digested and well composed in all its parts. It was a machine of wise and elaborate contrivance; and as well fitted for the oppression, impoverishment, and degradation of a people, and the debasement in them of human nature itself, as ever proceeded from the perverted ingenuity of man.[3]

Those in Britain who wished to rule by arbitrary will found that the best means of depriving the Irish of the rights of nature was to exclude them from the protective benefits of the constitution. Burke objected strongly to this policy:

> Our constitution is not made for great, general, and proscriptive exclusions; sooner or later it will destroy them, or they will destroy the constitution....This way of proscribing men by whole nations, as it were, from all the benefits of the constitution to which they were born, I can never believe to be politic or expedient, much less necessary for the existence of any state or church in the world.[4]

The long-standing great political pretexts for exercising arbitrary power were that the Irish people were by nature turbulent, and that the authority of the English state had to be maintained. Burke denied the first charge, and said of the second: "The coercive authority of the state is limited to what is necessary for its existence."[5] This did not include the statutes of persecution against Irish liberty, property, trade, and manufactures, nor the suppression of their education, professions, and religion. "Nothing can be more absurd and dangerous," wrote Burke, "than to tamper with the natural foundations of society in hopes of keeping it up by certain contrivances," and he appealed to Britain to "restore nature to its just rights and policy to its proper order."[6] Burke agreed with Dr. Johnson in hating England's stern debilitating policy against Ireland, and would have preferred to see the authority of the English government perish rather than be maintained by such iniquity.

Burke knew that the ultimate grounds for persecuting Ireland were religious, and in appealing to the Natural Law against the arbitrary will of rulers he defended the religious rights of Ireland's Catholics on the same grounds that he defended the Protestant Dissenters' claims of conscience in the Relief Bill of 1773. At that time Burke invoked "an author who is more spoken of than read, I mean Aristotle," and he applied the Greek philosopher's distinction between power and moral right: "Yes...you have the power, but you have not the right" because "this bill is contrary to the eternal laws of right and wrong—laws that ought to bind all men, and above all men legislative assemblies."[7] Burke's attack on the English government's failure in Irish affairs to distinguish between its power and moral right, implies his belief in the Natural Law. Except in Indian affairs, Burke's belief in the Natural Law is perhaps nowhere more explicit than in the "Tract on the Popery Laws," which resulted from his two winters in Dublin, 1761-1762 and 1763-1764. The time is important, because it shows that the fundamental principles of Burke's political philosophy were fixed in his mind even before he entered British public life. In the "Tract on the Popery Laws" the distinction between political power and moral right, between Hobbes's theory of arbitrary will and Cicero's "right reason," underscores Burke's strong appeals to the Natural Law:

> It would be hard to point out any error more truly subversive of
> all the order and beauty, of all the peace and happiness, of human
> society than the position that any body of men have a right to make
> what laws they please; or that laws can derive any authority from

their institution merely and independent of the quality of the subject-matter. No arguments of policy, reason of state, or preservation of the constitution, can be pleaded in favour of such a practice. They may, indeed, impeach the frame of that constitution; but can never touch this immovable principle.   This seems to be, indeed, the principle which Hobbes broached in the last century, and which was then so frequently and so ably refuted. Cicero exclaims with the utmost indignation and contempt against such a notion; he considers it not only as unworthy of a philosopher, but of an illiterate peasant; that of all things this was the most truly absurd, to fancy that the rule of justice was to be taken from the constitutions of common-wealths, or that laws derived their authority from the statutes of the people, the edicts of princes, or the decrees of judges....Everybody is satisfied that a conservation and secure enjoyment of our natural rights is the great and ultimate purpose of civil society; and that therefore all forms whatsoever of government are only good as they are subservient to that purpose to which they are entirely subordinate.   Now, to aim at the establishment of any form of government by sacrificing what is the substance of it; to take away, or at least to suspend, the rights of nature...is preposterous in argument...and cruel in its effect.[8]

The Hobbist theory of sovereignty, that the will of the state is the ultimate measurement of law, is nowhere more false, according to Burke, than in religion:

Religion, to have any force on men's understandings, indeed to exist at all, must be supposed paramount to laws, and independent for its substance upon any human institution. Else it would be the absurdest thing in the world; an acknowledged cheat. Religion, therefore, is not believed because the laws have established it; but it is established because the leading part of the community have previously believed it to be true.[9]

In Ireland more than four-fifths of the people adhered to their inherited Catholicism: "This religion, which is so persecuted in its members, is the old religion of the country, and the once established religion of the state." Compared with a claim based on such historical prescription, wrote Burke, "An opinion at once new and persecuting is a monster." The whole of

Burke's objection to such religious persecution, based on the theory that arbitrary legislative will, rather than Natural Law, is the foundation of social justice, is summarized in one sentence in his "Tract on the Popery Laws": "They have no right to make a law prejudicial to the whole community...because it would be made against the principle of a superior law, which it is not in the power of any community, or of the whole race of man, to alter.—I mean the will of Him who gave us our nature, and in giving impressed an invariable law upon it."[10]   Nothing is more plain than that Burke's defense of religious conscience and freedom in Ireland rests on the Natural Law.

Burke applied the same Natural Law principles in attacking the economic restrictions and civil disabilities imposed upon Ireland. For Burke, the right of holding private property in Ireland, no less than that of following religious conscience, depended not upon the will of any legislators, but was secured "on the solid rock of prescription, the soundest, the most general, and the most recognized title between man and man...a title in which not arbitrary institutions, but the eternal order of things gives judgment; a title which is not the creature, but the master, of positive law; a title which...is rooted in its principle in the law of nature itself, and is, indeed, the original ground of all known property; for all property in soil will always be traced to that source, and will rest there."[11]   The Irish penal laws which "disabled three-fourths of the inhabitants from acquiring any estate of inheritance for life," which excluded Catholics from military service, the legal profession, and all public offices, which prohibited any private or public education and proscribed the clergy, were a total "deprivation of society," and Burke's arguments for their repeal are based throughout on the eternal law of reason and general justice, the Natural Law.

Had Burke's utilitarian critics read his "Tracts on the Popery Laws" with greater care, they would have found that in this early work he expressly rejected the principle that utility is the sole source, test, and ultimate foundation of thought. Although Burke had a principle of utility, he was no utilitarian. He generally gave prior consideration to equity in law, because the necessary legal means of achieving any social end had to be grounded in the moral law before Burke would consider the social consequences. The following passage proves that for Burke both equity and utility were derived from "the substance of original justice," the Natural Law:

> In reality there are two, and only two, foundations of law; and
> they are both of them conditions without which nothing can give it

any force: I mean equity and utility. With respect to the former, it grows out of the great rule of equality, which is grounded upon our common nature, and which Philo, with propriety and beauty, calls the mother of justice. All human laws are, properly speaking, only declaratory; they may alter the mode and application, but have no power over the substance of original justice. The other foundation of law, which is utility, must be understood, not of partial or limited, but of general and public utility, connected in the same manner with, and derived directly from, our rational nature; for any other utility may be the utility of a robber.[12]

To reinforce his assertion that "law is a mode of human action respecting society and must be governed by the same rules of equity which govern every private action," Burke quoted supporting passages from Cicero, Paulus, and Suarez. Throughout his argument the primacy of equity to utility, and the subordination of both to Natural Law, is clearly evident.

Burke confessed that among the first thoughts that crossed his mind on being elected to parliament in 1765 was the hope that he might achieve some measure of justice for his native land. His political career bears out his hope. The affairs of Ireland called forth Burke's powers as a practical statesman on several important occasions, and vitally influenced his own career. Throughout his life Burke maintained a correspondence with Irishmen such as Dr. Leland and Lord Kenmare, whose major interest was religious emancipation, and he wrote private and public letters to Edmund Pery, Thomas Burgh, William Smith, and Sir Hercules Langrishe, all members of the Irish parliament. Burke and Lord Nugent obtained some small commercial favors for Ireland in 1778, and further concessions were made in 1779. Burke was instrumental in drawing up the Savile Act of 1778, which eased restrictions on Catholics in England and became the model for similar legislation in Ireland. In 1779-1780 the grievous restrictions on the Irish export trade were repealed, and in 1782 additional economic and religious disabilities were slightly lifted, and greater legislative independence was achieved by the Irish parliament. Burke's part in these reforms was auxiliary to the crisis brought on by the American war, which compelled the English government to conciliate Ireland. Burke's active attempt to "fix the principles of free trade in all the parts of these islands, as founded in justice, and beneficial to the whole," cost him his Bristol constituency in 1780, but he saw his principle fulfilled in 1785 in Pitt's famous Irish propositions, based on Adam Smith's theory of free trade. The French Revolution provoked another crisis in Irish affairs. To the last month of his life Burke labored to prevent Ireland from resorting to Jacobin principles of revolution. Burke's lifelong struggle to extend the benefits of equal citizenship to Ireland under the British constitution is an important practical manifestation of his belief that Natural Law supplied the ethical norms of every just society.

In practically every discussion of Burke's part in American colonial affairs, it has been the universal opinion of positivist scholars that against George III's claim of an abstract right to tax the colonies, Burke took his stand almost completely on the principle of utilitarian expediency, and that therefore he rejected all belief in "natural right" based upon the Natural Law.[13] Burke certainly did attack the metaphysical abstract "right" of taxation assumed by Townshend, Grenville, and Lord North, and his own words reveal precisely how far "expediency" applied in his attack:

> I shall not now enquire into the right of Great Britain to tax her colonies; all that is lawful is not expedient, and I believe the inexpediency of taxing our colonies, even supposing it to be lawful, is now evident to every man.[14]

> I am resolved this day to have nothing at all to do with the question of the right of taxation....I put it totally out of the question....I do not examine, whether the giving away a man's money be a power excepted and reserved out of the general trust of government; and how far all mankind, in all forms of polity, are entitled to an exercise of that right by the charter of nature. Or whether, on the contrary, a right of taxation is necessarily involved in the general principle of legislation, and inseparable from the ordinary supreme power. These are deep questions, where great names militate against each other; where reason is perplexed; and an appeal to authorities only thickens the confusion. For high and reverend authorities lift up their heads on both sides; and there is no sure footing in the middle. The point is the "great Serbonian bog, betwixt Damiata and Mount Casius old, where armies whole have sunk." I do not intend to be overwhelmed in that bog, though in such respectable company.[15]

The first passage reveals that expediency was an important practical element in Burke's attack, while the second shows that Burke believed in the existence of rights under "the charter of nature," but that out of fear of a useless quarrel in metaphysics, he did not wish to discuss the American problem in terms of "rights." Nothing could be more false than the conclusion of Morley and the "respectable company" of critics who have followed him that these passages prove Burke made "expediency" the complete antithesis of "natural rights," that he rested his case on expediency and therefore denied all belief in Natural Law. Later we shall see that Burke's "expediency" is not the expediency of the utilitarian calculator, but a manifestation of moral prudence, which is not contrary to the Natural Law, but an essential part of its practical fulfillment.

Certainly the American colonies never considered it merely "inexpedient" to be taxed without their legislative consent. To them, as to Burke, the abstract "right" of taxation without representation was positively unjust. It was a constant threat to or actual violation of their property rights, and the attempt to enforce unjust taxation resulted in threats to their lives and liberty under the British constitution which they, like Burke, believed was founded on Natural Law:

> It is the glory of the British Prince and the happiness of all his subjects that their constitution hath its foundation in the immutable laws of nature; and as the supreme legislature, as well as the supreme executive, derives its authority from that constitution, it should seem that no laws can be made or executed which are repugnant to any essential law of nature.[16]

This memorable appeal to Natural Law was spoken by James Otis in 1768. Whereas the colonists, in their petitions of grievances, came more and more to appeal directly to the Natural Law, Burke's appeals were almost always indirect, through the British constitution, which was for him merely the practical means of guaranteeing the "rights" of Natural Law throughout the empire: "Our constitution," Burke said in parliament, "was a provident system, formed of several bodies, for securing the rights, the liberties, the persons and the properties of the people."[17] In both domestic and American affairs Burke felt that George III and his ministers, in trying to make the power of the Crown supreme, had placed their arbitrary will above the constitution and therefore had violated the sovereignty of Natural Law: "The same baneful influence," said Burke in 1770, "under which this country is governed, is extended to our fellow sufferers in America; the constitutional rights of Englishmen are invaded..."[18] and the "unalienable rights of their constituents" are defeated by "ministerial requisitions that are altogether arbitrary and unjust." In February 1772, Burke said in parliament: "When tyranny is extreme, and abuses of government intolerable, men resort to the rights of nature to shake it off."[19] Burke regretted and opposed the arbitrary principles and policies of the king, and favored the American cause not because the colonists had an abstract "right" to rebel against British rule, as Tom Paine and Dr. Price argued, but because Britain had imprudently invoked its sovereign power as an abstract "right" to tax and rule the colonists by arbitrary decrees, and above all, because the king and parliament were themselves in rebellion against rules of prudence in the Natural Law by their denial of the colonists' civil rights under the constitution.

Burke saw that constitutional liberty in England would stand or fall upon the outcome of the struggle with America, that if the British government succeeded in destroying liberty abroad, Englishmen would soon have none at home. In March 1775, he said: "In order to prove that the Americans have no right to their liberties, we are every day endeavouring to subvert the maxims which preserve the whole spirit of our own."[20] Before seeing how the king's "oppressive stretches of power" in America were paralleled in Britain, it will be useful to summarize Burke's reactions to the arbitrary decrees passed against the colonies. In March 1774, the Boston Port Bill was passed, taking away the city's trade and in effect revoking its charter. Burke promptly attacked it: "I call this bill unjust, for is it not fundamentally unjust to prevent the parties who have offended from being heard in their own defence. Justice...is not to be measured by geographical lines nor distances." Such an act, he added in private, is "the doctrine of devils"; it is "contrary to the nature of man and the nature of things." "Franchises," he continued, "are for the preservation of men's liberties, properties, and lives....It is bad to take away a charter; it is worse to take away a city." Such a "proscription of whole cities and provinces is to take away from them benefits of nature...deprive them of their civil privileges, and...strip them of their judicial rights." When the bill was extended to all New England, Burke again objected: "You sentence...to famine at least 300,000 people in two provinces, at the mere arbitrary will and pleasure of two men." In short, these acts of parliament toward America "take away the rights of men" and prove that when power becomes arbitrary, when legislative authority is placed above constitutional and Natural law, "a man may be regulated out of his liberty, his property, and his life."[21] As with British rule in Ireland, Burke charged that in her American policy Britain was "endeavouring to invert the order of nature," and that her claimed "right" to rule the colonies by arbitrary decrees was totally opposed to the British constitution and Natural Law.

Burke's practical endeavors to restrict the arbitrary powers of the king and to preserve civil liberty in America are among the best-known episodes of his political career. Almost from the moment he entered parliament in 1765 he was absorbed in American affairs, and as the intellectual guide and manager of the Rockingham Whigs he did more than any other man to make his colleagues and the British public aware of the fatal course they were following. The one measure of tax relief enjoyed by America in the decade before the Revolution was passed by the short-lived Rockingham administration of 1766, which repealed Grenville's odious Stamp Act. It was on this occasion that Burke, in his first appearance in the House of Commons, revealed his political greatness. On March 9, 1766, Dr. Johnson wrote of Burke's initial speech: "He has gained more reputation than perhaps any man at his first appearance ever gained before. He made two speeches in the House for repealing the Stamp Act, which were publicly commended by Mr. Pitt, and have filled the town with wonder. Mr. Burke is a great man by nature, and is expected soon to attain civil greatness."[22] From 1766 until the conclusion of hostilities with America Burke continued to fill the political world with wonder. In pamphlets such as his early masterpiece *Thoughts on the Cause of the Present Discontents* (1770), in parliamentary speeches such as his *Speech on Conciliation* (1775), and in public essays such as his *Letter to the Sheriffs of Bristol* (1777), Burke struggled to maintain the natural rights of Americans under English constitutional law. In 1771 Burke became the agent in parliament for the colony of New York. Through this post he acquired a complete mastery of details and knowledge of the civil temper of the colonists, which he utilized throughout his exposition of constitutional and Natural Law principles. Burke's writings on American affairs received Morley's unqualified admiration: "It is no exaggeration to say that they compose the most perfect manual in our literature, or in any literature, for one who approaches the study of public affairs, whether for knowledge or for practice."[23] Despite the eloquence and wisdom of Burke's efforts on America's behalf, he did not succeed in convincing the British public that great empires can best endure when grounded upon the solid foundation of constitutional and Natural law. The principles Burke taught were learned from the bitter lessons of history; afterwards, his words remained as a constant reminder and depository of political wisdom for those who were to rule the British Empire in the nineteenth century.

* * * * *

Burke's speeches in Indian affairs reveal his legal erudition at its best and also provide the clearest expression of the Natural Law in his political philosophy. Burke was actively concerned in the affairs of India from at least March 21, 1780, when he spoke on the renewal of the East India Company's charter, until April 23, 1795, when Hastings was acquitted. His first important appeal to the Natural Law occurred on December 1, 1783, in his speech supporting Fox's East India Bill. "This bill," Burke said, was "intended to form the Magna Charta of Hindostan," yet he noted that those who opposed it did so on the grounds "that the bill is an attack on the chartered rights of men."[24] Here, for the first of several times in Indian affairs, he made a vital distinction between what he considered the true "natural rights" derived from the classical and Scholastic Natural Law, and false or arbitrary claims to "rights." Because the word "rights" was an abstraction, and subject to various interpretations, Burke approached his problem semantically. "The phrase of 'the chartered rights of men,'" he noted, "is very unusual in the discussion of privileges conferred by charters of the present description." All previous charters, he continued, such as those of King John and Henry III, "may, without any deceitful ambiguity, be very fitly called *the chartered rights of men*," because they are merely written documents expressly recognizing the sanctity of the Natural Law, to which all public measures should conform:

> The rights of men, that is to say, the natural rights of mankind, are, indeed, sacred things; and if any public measure is proved mischievously to affect them, the objection ought to be fatal to that measure, even if no charter at all could be set up against it. If these natural rights are further affirmed and declared by express covenants, if they are clearly defined and secured against chicane, against power and authority, by written instruments and positive engagements, they are in a still better condition: They partake not only of the sanctity of the object so secured, but of that solemn public faith itself, which secures an object of such importance. Indeed, this formal recognition, by the sovereign power, of an original right in the subject, can never be subverted, but by rooting up the holding radical principles of government, and even of society itself.[25]

But, Burke remarked, "the charter of the East India Company" is "formed on principles the *very reverse* of those of the great charter." He elaborates this crucial point: "Magna Charta is a charter to restrain power, and to destroy monopoly. The East India charter is a charter to establish monopoly, and to create power. Political power and commercial monopoly are *not* the rights of men; and the rights of them derived from charters, it is fallacious and sophistical to call 'the chartered rights of men.' These chartered rights...do at least suspend the natural rights of mankind at large; and in their very frame and constitution, are liable to fall into a direct violation of them."[26]

If the East India Company had governed in India "under the controul of the sovereign imperial discretion, and with the due observance of the natural and local law," Burke would have opposed revoking its charter. But the company refused to recognize the Natural Law and the local laws of India, which guaranteed the natives' rights; it insisted that the charter granted by parliament left its officials free to govern India as they saw fit. The company, Burke concluded, had violated its "subordinate derivative trust," had "notoriously, grossly abused" its power; parliament could not stand by in total indifference to the moral law, nor make a sale of its duties, but should adopt Fox's bill and "provide a real chartered security for the *rights of men* cruelly violated under that charter."[27] For Burke the issue was of conflicting claims to sovereignty, and his choice is clear: "If I kept faith...with the Company," he said, "I must break the faith, the covenant, the solemn, original, indispensable oath, in which I am bound, by the eternal frame and constitution of things, to the whole human race." Burke's eloquent appeal to the "natural rights" of traditional Natural Law enabled him, in his first great attack on abuses in India, to transcend the commercial and national powers which sacrificed human rights to a narrow self-interest.

In February 1785, two years after Fox's bill had been rejected in the House of Lords, Burke made his famous speech exposing the hoax of the Nabob of Arcot's debts.[28] There is only one appeal to nature in this long speech, but it is an explicit defense of the enduring character of Natural Law:

> The benefits of heaven to any community ought never to be connected with political arrangements, or made to depend on the personal conduct of princes.... The means of subsistence of mankind should be as immutable as the laws of nature, let power and dominion take what course they may.[29]

In a short speech in March 1787 Burke made a general protest against those in parliament who wished to obstruct Hastings's impeachment: "I rise in support of the eternal principles of truth and justice, and those who cannot or dare not support them are endeavouring to cough them down." Hastings had a small group of powerful friends, most of whom were skilled lawyers, and they succeeded in throwing up an endless series of legal impediments to keep the impeachment from coming to an issue. "The greatest obstruction of all," Burke lamented, "proceeded from the body of the law. There was no body of men for whom he entertained a greater respect...for the profession itself he felt a degree of veneration, approaching almost to idolatry." However, when the lawyers among the opposition tried to invalidate the impeachment by dissolving parliament, Burke protested: "These gentlemen of the law, driving us from law to law, would, in the end, leave us no law at all." As Burke wrote to Dundas in December 1787, these obstructions were further complicated because "all the local knowledge of India is in the hands of the person prosecuted by the House of Commons," and Hastings had suppressed or destroyed the main sources of information. Burke secured a large body of detailed evidence on India from Philip Francis, Hastings's mortal enemy and prejudiced accuser, and also from the records of the India House. But as manager of the impeachment Burke took his stand against Hastings mainly on the Natural Law, and Hastings himself supplied Burke with material for his most severe indictments.

Burke made it clear that Hastings's defense ultimately rested on the argument that he had the right to rule India through arbitrary power. Hastings claimed this right on two accounts; first, because parliament, through the East India Company, had granted him unlimited power to rule in India, and second, as Burke summarized him, because "the whole history of Asia is nothing more than precedents to prove the invariable exercise of arbitrary power."[30] Throughout his impeachment speeches Burke frequently reminded his hearers of Hastings's claim:

> Mr. Hastings comes before you...he says, "I had arbitrary power to exercise, and I exercised it. Slaves I found the people, slaves they are; they are so by their constitution; I did not make it for them; I was unfortunately bound to exercise it, and I did exercise it...." In India, to use the words of Mr. Hastings, the power of the sovereign was everything, the rights of the people nothing. ...The prisoner...assumes to exercise a power which extended to the property, liberty, and life of the subject....He makes the corrupt practices of mankind the principle of his government; he collects together the vicious examples of all the robbers and plunderers of

Asia, forms the mass of their abuses into a code, and calls it the
duty of a British governor.[31]

As manager for the prosecution, Burke saw that he was obliged to destroy
Hastings's assumption that sovereignty rested solely in a governor's arbitrary
will, a principle which totally contradicted the ethical norms of Natural Law.

Burke's most extended and eloquent attack on Hastings's claim of
arbitrary power, made on February 16, 1788, derives wholly from his ardent
faith in Natural Law:

> Will you ever hear the rights of mankind made subservient to the
> practice of government? It will be your lordships' duty and joy—it
> will be your pride and triumph, to teach men, that they are to
> conform their practice to principles, and not to derive their
> principles from the wicked, corrupt, and abominable practices of
> any man whatsoever. Where is the man that ever before dared to
> mention the practice of all the villains, of all the notorious
> depredators, as his justification? To gather up, and put it all into
> one code, and call it the duty of a British governor? I believe so
> audacious a thing was never before attempted by man. "He had
> arbitrary power!" My lords, the East India Company have not
> arbitrary power to give him. The king has no arbitrary power to
> give. Neither your lordships, nor the Commons, nor the whole
> legislature, have arbitrary power to give. Arbitrary power is a thing
> which no man can give. My lords, no man can govern himself by
> his own will; much less can he be governed by the will of others.
> We are all born—high as well as low—governors as well as
> governed—in subjection to one great, immutable, pre-existing law,
> a law prior to all our devices and all our conspiracies, paramount to
> our feelings, by which we are connected in the eternal frame of the
> universe, and out of which we cannot stir. This great law does not
> arise from our combinations and compacts; on the contrary, it gives
> to them all the sanction they can have. Every good and perfect gift
> is of God: all power is of God; and He who has given the power,
> and from whom alone it originates, will never suffer it to be
> corrupted. Therefore, my lords, if this be true—if this great gift of
> government be the greatest and best that was ever given by God to
> mankind, will he suffer it to be the plaything of man, who would
> place his own feeble and ridiculous will on the throne of divine

justice? It is not to be overturned by conquest; for by conquest, which is the more immediate designation of the hand of God, the conqueror succeeds to that alone which belonged to the sovereign before him. He cannot have absolute power by succession; he cannot have it by compact; for the people cannot covenant themselves out of their duty to their rights....[32]

The whole of Burke's argument against Hastings's theory of sovereignty is contained in a few aphorisms infused with the Natural Law: "Law and arbitrary power are at eternal hostility....We should be brought back to our original situation; we should be made to know ourselves as men born under law. He that would substitute will in the place of law is a public enemy to the world...against law, no power can be set up." "There never was a man who thought he had no law but his own will, who did not also find that he had no ends but his own profit."[33] To Burke, who maintained that since the introduction of the Roman law into Britain "the law of nature and nations (always a part of the law of England) came to be cultivated," nothing could be more destructive of the ethical norm necessary for a just society than Hastings's theory of sovereignty based upon arbitrary will.

Hastings's claim that arbitrary power was the normal mode of rule in Asia implied that there was no univeral law of just conduct on essential principles, as taught by the Natural Law. Burke emphatically rejected such a contention:

> This gentleman has formed a geographical morality, by which the duties of men in public and private stations are not to be governed by their relation to the great Governor of the universe, and by their relation to one another, but by climates. After you have crossed the equinoxial line, all the virtues die....Against this geographical morality I do protest, and declare therefore, that Mr. Hastings shall not screen himself under it, because...the laws of morality are the same everywhere; and actions that are stamped with the character of peculation, extortion, oppression, and barbarity in England, are so in Asia, and the world over.[34]

Burke's great sympathy for the people of India was only exceeded by his fear that Hastings's friends, in defending him, would introduce his "Eastern" principles into England: "The doctrine that in the East there are no laws, no rights, no liberties, is a doctrine which has not only been stated by the prisoner at the bar, but has been disseminated with a wicked activity throughout this country." Burke valued his public services in Indian affairs above anything else in his career, because in addition to his primary aim of bringing Hastings to justice and reclaiming national honor, Burke wished to destroy the corrupting influence against the constitution which the England nabobs had come to exercise in parliament. Although Hastings was acquitted and later came to be held in high honor, Burke purified Parliament of Hastings's Eastern morality and raised the moral level of British colonial policy abroad. These larger derivative consequences of Hastings's trial were enormously important in preserving Britain's constitutional liberty and colonial supremacy.

To disprove Hastings's contention that morality varied in time and place, Burke read widely in Oriental jurisprudence. He read the *Koran*, the *Shasta,* and the *Heyada;* he quoted Tamerlane's *Institutes*, recently translated by Major Davy, Hastings's former secretary; he used Joseph White's translations of the *Institutes of Timour* (Oxford, 1783), and Jean Baptiste Tavernier's *Travels into Persia and the East Indies* (1677). Burke placed the results of his reading before the House of Lords: "The morality of the East, my lords, as far as respects governors, is as pure as our own....Mr. Hastings finds no authority for his practice, either in the Koran or in the Gentoo law....The same laws, the same sacredness of principle, however they may be disobeyed, both in Europe and in Asia, are held and strictly maintained." Burke finally concluded:

> Mr. Hastings has no refuge—let him run from law to law; let him fly from common law, and the sacred institutions of the country in which he was born; let him fly from acts of parliament...still the Mohammedan law condemns him...let him fly where he will—from law to law—law, thank God, meets him everywhere—arbitrary power cannot secure him against law; and I would as soon have him tried on the Koran or any other eastern code of laws as on the common law of this kingdom.[35]

Against Hastings's theory of geographical morality and arbitrary power, Burke set the traditional conception of Natural Law, and like all of his predecessors back to Aristotle he insisted that its imperative ethical norms are universally valid.

Since Hastings's acts were, in Burke's words, "crimes...against those eternal laws of justice which you [the judges] are assembled here to assert," it was necessary for his prosecutors to follow "rules drawn from the fountain of justice," and to condemn him in terms of the eternal Natural Law. "I impeach him," said Burke, "in the name and by the virtue of those eternal laws of justice, which ought equally to pervade every age, condition, rank, and situation in the world." Burke believed that the function of courts of law was to reflect through human institutions the spirit of the divine Natural Law: "Courts of justice were links of that great chain of which the first and great link was Divine Justice." Despite the fact that many parts of Burke's speeches were reported in the third person, and give only an approximate idea of his principles and argument, nothing is clearer than that the appeal to Natural Law is at the heart of his impeachment of Hastings.

Mr. Burke next entered into a disquisition upon the nature of government, of which we lament our inability to give an adequate idea; but we will endeavour...to give the general scope of his reasoning. He first laid it down as a general principle, that all law and all sovereignty were derived from Heaven; for if the laws of every nation, from the most simple and social of the most barbarous people, up to the wisest and most salutary laws of the most refined and enlightened societies, from the Divine laws handed down to us in Holy Writ, down to the meanest forms of earthly institution, were attentively examined, they would be found to breathe but one spirit, one principle, equal distributive justice between man and man, and the protection of one individual from the encroachments of the rest. The universality of this principle proved its origin. Out of this principle laws arose, for the execution of which sovereignty was established; and all, viz. that principle, those laws, and that sovereignty, were thus evidently derived from God....If, then, laws and sovereignty were sacred, as being the gift of God for the benefit of the people; and if the laws and sovereignty of India were, as he contended them to be, founded upon the same principle of universal justice, then Mr. Hastings, as a British governor, sent, not to conquer or extirpate, but to preserve and cherish, was bound to protect the people of that country in the use of those laws, and shield that sovereignty from encroachment or usurpation.[36]

Since the East India Company was a state in the disguise of a merchant, Burke's strictures on Hastings's violations of Natural Law principles and sovereignty were doubly significant, because he believed that above all other men legislators stood in the place of God and were accountable to Him in the practical uses of political power, and were therefore most bound by the moral dictates of the Natural Law. To understand the deepest implications to Burke's political philosophy in his lifelong devotion to the Natural Law, one must examine his reaction to the French Revolution.

Burke and the Natural Law in French Affairs—1789-1797

In 1769, exactly two decades before the French Revolution, Burke had predicted in his *Observations on "The Present State of the Nation"* that the chronically desperate financial condition of France would culminate in "some extraordinary convulsion" that would shake the whole system of government and would have a tremendous effect on all Europe. In 1789 Burke was the first public man in Britain to realize that the revolution was far more than an alteration in the government of France. Burke wrote to his son in November 1792 that the revolution was "an event which has nothing to match it, or in the least to resemble it, in history." He felt that the revolution violated "the whole system of policy on which the general state of Europe has hitherto stood," that the revolutionists tried to make themselves "paramount to every known principle of public law in Europe," and that they sought to establish "principles subversive of the whole political, civil, and religious system of Europe." In 1796 Burke summarized his impressions of the strange and powerful effect the revolution had produced on men's imaginations; he found it "a vast, tremendous, unformed spectre" which "subdued the fortitude of man," and went "straight forward to its end, unappaled by peril, unchecked by remorse, despising all common maxims and all common means." For Burke 1789 was "a revolution in dogma"; it was a "total departure...from every one of the ideas and usages, religious, legal, moral or social, of this civilized world."[37] So catastrophic was the French Revolution, that it compelled Burke against his will and temperament, to become a political theorist in defense of the traditional principles of civilized society, among which the Natural Law held a pre-eminent position.

Throughout Burke's writings on French revolutionary affairs, more often than not his belief in the Natural Law was implicitly assumed, and supplied the spirit that permeates all of his references to God and discussions of religion, society, Church, and State, the nature of the social contract, political sovereignty, and the security of private and corporate liberty and property. It is too frequently forgotten that Burke's initial response to the French

Revolution, revealed in October 1789 in his "Letter to M. Dupont on the French Revolution," was warm-hearted, cautious, and friendly.[38]   In this letter Burke expressed his unwillingness to form a positive opinion upon matters with which he was imperfectly acquainted. He agreed with his young friend's hope that the French deserved liberty, and stated that if, under the new order of things, law is made paramount to will, if prescriptive rights to life, liberty, and property are maintained, if civil liberty is regarded as man's birthright rather than the reward of merit or industry, as something inherent in man rather than a favor granted from the state, or a subject for endless metaphysical speculations about political power and social systems, he would look with favor upon the revolution.[39]

True liberty, Burke cautioned, is "not solitary, unconnected, individual, selfish liberty, as if every man was to regulate the whole of his conduct by his own will." Such "liberty" was but another name for arbitrary power, such as George III had claimed over the colonies or Hastings over India, and Burke knew it could not be reconciled to civil liberty under Natural Law. Like Aristotle, Burke believed man was by nature a political animal, so that true liberty must be "social freedom," a condition which required restriction on raw will and prevented anyone from exercising arbitrary power. Such liberty, said Burke to his young friend, was but another name for justice, and was consonant with the supremacy of Natural Law, of right reason over the "dangerous dominion of will." If in France he found that "the citizen…is in a perfect state of legal security with regard to his life, to his property, to the uncontrolled disposal of his person," he would share the general joy in such a revolution.

Burke's hope for France lasted less that four months. By the beginning of 1790 Jacobin doctrinaire radicalism had begun its attacks on religion, private property, and traditional political institutions. Events across the Channel gradually convinced Burke that the revolutionists had no respect for the classical and Scholastic tradition of Natural Law, which was the whole foundation of civil society in all Europe. In place of Natural Law legal principles, such as that prescription formed the best claim to property, the revolutionists invoked egalitarian speculations centered in the abstract "rights of man" to sanction the arbitrary seizure of corporate and private property. When Englishmen professed to admire these French methods of reform, Burke assumed the offensive against the revolution. An occasion presented itself on February 9, 1790, during the debates on estimates for the army, for Burke to attack the violations of property in France:

> They…laid the ax to the root of all property, and consequently
> of all national prosperity, by the principles they established, and the
> example they have set.…They made and recorded a sort of *institute*
> and *digest* of anarchy, called the rights of man, in such a pedantic
> abuse of elementary principles as would have disgraced boys at
> school.[40]

As Burke's great object was to warn his countrymen against the principles
and example of the French, his speech on the army estimates revealed in
miniature the essential argument he was to follow in his struggle to maintain
the principles of traditional Natural Law against the revolutionary "natural
rights" of France. Although many scholars have failed to grasp this
fundamental distinction between traditional Natural Law and revolutionary
"natural rights," Burke understood the distinction perfectly and left no doubt
that the basis of his attacks on the revolutionists was that they violated the
Natural Law: "They are naturally pointed out, not by having outraged
political and civil laws, nor by their having rebelled against the state, as a
state, but by their having rebelled against the law of nature, and outraged
man as man."[41] Burke wrote this sentence in October 1793, and it may be
taken as the touchstone in all that he wrote of French affairs, from February
1790 through his posthumous *Fourth Letter on a Regicide Peace* (1797).

Although Natural Law is most explicitly stated in Burke's writings on
Irish and Indian affairs, its tacit assumption and intense moral spirit is clearly
evident throughout his most famous work, the *Reflections on the Revolution
in France*, which appeared in November 1790. Before considering Burke's
subtle appeals to the Natural Law in the *Reflections*, the historical
importance of this great work should be understood. Alfred Cobban did not
exaggerate in calling the *Reflections* "the greatest and most influential
political pamphlet ever written." If we consider only Burke's immediate
practical intention, to warn his countrymen and Europe against French
revolutionary principles and to exalt a Christian and Natural Law conception
of civil society, the *Reflections* was the most successful book of the
eighteenth century "Enlightenment," and it was almost totally opposed to the
prevailing spirit of the age.

* * * * *

Burke's appeals to the Natural Law in Indian affairs demonstrated his belief that all men are born "in subjection to one great, immutable, pre-existing law, a law...paramount to our feelings, by which we are connected in the eternal frame of the universe...." The rest of this passage revealed that implicit in man's connection with this immutable law is a conception of divine contract. "This great law does not arise from our combinations and compacts," Burke wrote, but on the contrary, it gives to them all the sanction they can have." In effect he said that God contracted with Himself never to be unjust to man. Thus, the Natural Law was the moral standard in all human contracts. This conception of a divine contract and of the ethical norm of Natural Law underscored Burke's statement in Indian affairs that the greatest and best gift of God to man was government, for the state was the necessary means by which man could live according to the Natural Law. In Burke's *Reflections* all of these ideas are to be found more fully developed in his conception of the social contract.

To Burke man's relationship to civil society is a moral necessity; it cannot be voluntaristic, for that would exalt will above right reason; nothing could be more false and wicked than the Lockian theory of a voluntary and revocable social contract based upon a hypothetical state of nature. The moral primacy and binding necessity of the Natural Law, as the true basis of the social contract, has never been more eloquently expressed, even by Cicero, than in the *Reflections*:

> Society is indeed a contract. Subordinate contracts for objects of mere occasional interest may be dissolved at pleasure—but the state ought not to be considered as nothing better than a partnership agreement in a trade of pepper and coffee, calico or tobacco...to be taken up for a little temporary interest, and to be dissolved by the fancy of the parties. It is to be looked on with other reverence; because it is not a partnership in things subservient only to to gross animal existence of a temporary and perishable nature. It is a partnership in all science; a partnership in all art; a partnership in every virtue, and in all perfection. As the ends of such a partnership cannot be obtained in many generations, it becomes a partnership not only between those who are living, but between those who are living, those who are dead, and those who are to be born. Each contract of each particular state is but a clause in the great primæval contract of eternal society, linking the lower with the higher natures, connecting the visible and invisible world, according to a fixed

compact sanctioned by the inviolable oath which holds all physical
and all moral natures, each in their appointed place. This law is not
subject to the will of those who by an obligation above them, and
infinitely superior, are bound to submit their will to that law. The
municipal corporations of that universal kingdom are not morally at
liberty at their pleasure, and on their speculation of a contingent
improvement, wholly to separate and tear asunder the bands of their
subordinate community, and to dissolve it into an unsocial, uncivil,
unconnected chaos of elementary principles. It is the first and
supreme necessity only, a necessity that is not chosen, but chooses,
a necessity paramount to deliberation, that admits no discussion,
and demands no evidence, which alone can justify a resort to
anarchy. This necessity is no exception to the rule; because this
necessity itself is a part of that moral and physical disposition of
things, to which man must be obedient by consent or force: but if
that which is only submission to necessity should be made the
object of choice, the law is broken, nature is disobeyed, and the
rebellious are outlawed, cast forth, and exiled, from this world of
reason, and order, and peace, and virtue, and fruitful penitence, into
the antagonist world of madness, discord, vice, confusion, and
unavailing sorrow.[42]

This vital passage contains in essence all that Burke said about the social
contract throughout many parts of his *Reflections*. It reveals his belief in a
transcendent moral duty beyond all will or power, a duty imposed by the
"primæval contract" of God's "inviolable oath," binding man through the
Natural Law to his civil obligations. "The great ruling principle of the moral
and natural world," said Burke, is not "a mere invention to keep the vulgar in
obedience." He clearly agreed with Pufendorf's principle that "by the
observance of *Natural Law*, it must be supposed that God laid an obligation
on man to obey this *law*, as a *means* not arising from Human invention or
changeable at Human pleasure."[43] Burke regarded the Natural Law as a
divinely ordained imperative ethical norm which, without consulting man,
fixed forever his moral duties in civil society.

Throughout the *Reflections* the spirit of the Natural Law and Burke's
conception of the divine contract which binds all men appears in various
forms—in his discussions of the English constitution, in his principle of
political sovereignty, in his idea that civil liberty is an inheritance and private
property is secured by prescription, and above all, in his conception of the

divine and social functions of Church and State. He states that Britain's "constitutional policy" works "after the pattern of nature" and that her "political system is placed in a just correspondence and symmetry with the order of the world" and is held together "by the disposition of a stupendous wisdom, moulding together the great mysterious incorporation of the human race.... " By "preserving the method of nature in the conduct of the state," deliberation is made "a matter not of choice, but of necessity," and political justice is thus secured.[44] Even more explicitly than in Indian affairs Burke insists in the *Reflections* on the divine origin of the state: "He who gave our nature to be perfected by our virtue, willed also the necessary means of its perfection.—He willed therefore the state.—He willed its connection with the source and original archetype of all perfection."[45] Indeed, Church and State are for Burke but two aspects of the same thing—God-given instruments to bring man to his highest spiritual and social perfection, through which man becomes united to the Godhead: "Every sort of moral, every sort of civil, every sort of politic institution, aiding the rational and natural ties that connect the human understanding and affections to the divine, are not more necessary, in order to build up that wonderful structure, Man." Through the Church, Burke continues, the state is consecrated, "that all who administer in the government of men, in which they stand in the person of God himself, should have high and worthy notions of their function and destination." Clearly, his conception of the divine contract in human affairs implies that all power is a divine trust: "All persons possessing any portion of power ought to be strongly and awfully impressed with an idea that they act in trust: and that they are to account for their conduct in that trust to the one great Master, Author, and Founder of society....Power...to be legitimate must be according to that eternal, immutable law, in which will and reason are the same."[46] The belief that power is a divine trust is evident in Burke's conception of the function of Church and State; it reappears throughout his extensive discussions of political sovereignty, which I shall examine in another chapter.

In Burke's discussions of Irish affairs, he regarded prescription in property rights as one of the great derived principles of Natural Law. In 1772 he had said in parliament: "If the principle of prescription be not a constitution of positive law, but a principle of natural equity, then to hold it out against any man is not doing him injustice."[47] In the *Reflections* he repeated this principle: "By the laws of nature, the occupant and subduer of the soil is the true proprietor; there is no prescription against nature."[48] But the revolutionists in the National Assembly, through their false conception of "natural rights," declared that all property was usurped which was not held on terms consistent with man's "original" nature. Their contention overturned prescription as the basis of ownership:

> With the National Assembly of France, possession is nothing, law and usage are nothing. I see the National Assembly open reprobate the doctrine of prescription, which one of the greatest of their own lawyers [Domat] tells us, with great truth, is a part of the law of nature. He tells us, that the positive ascertainment of its limits, and its security from invasion, were among the causes for which civil society itself has been instituted. If prescription be once shaken, no species of property is secure, when it once becomes an object large enough to tempt the cupidity of indigent power. I see a practice perfectly correspondent to their contempt of this great fundamental part of natural law.[49]

The National Assembly, said Burke, left nothing but their own arbitrary pleasure to determine what property was to be protected and what subverted. He admitted that he saw no reason why landed estates could not be held otherwise than by inheritance. In opposing the wholesale confiscations of Church lands in France, Burke warned his countrymen against the example established by the National Assembly in its violation of the Natural Law:

> I hope we shall never be so totally lost to all sense of the duties imposed upon us by the law of social union, as, upon any pretext of public service, to confiscate the goods of a single unoffending citizen. Who but a tyrant...could think of seizing on the property of men, unaccused, unheard, untried, by whole descriptions, by hundreds and thousands together?[50]

To Burke one of the great means of fulfilling the Natural Law was through prescription, which maintained the law of social union by protecting the private property of men and institutions.

* * * * *

The most serious error in the interpretation of Burke's political philosophy and practical career in parliament has been the general failure to perceive his full and lifelong acceptance of the classical and Scholastic conception of the Natural Law. Utilitarian and positivist critics, who made no distinction between the ethical norms of traditional Natural Law and the revolutionary eighteenth-century "rights of man" doctrines derived from a supposed "state of nature," accepted Burke's attacks on abstract "rights" as a rejection of the Natural Law, and claimed him as a conservative utilitarian. Yet Burke had an encyclopedic knowledge of the tradition of Natural Law in Western thought, and of the common law in England, which is saturated with the spirit of Natural Law. In every important political problem he ever faced, in Irish, American, constitutional, economic, Indian, and French affairs, Burke *always* appealed to the Natural Law. What is more, by Natural Law Burke always meant essentially the same thing, and he applied it as the ultimate test of justice and liberty in all human affairs. As a practical statesman he feared abstractions and was reluctant to take his mind from concrete political problems. But to Burke no *moral* problem was ever an *abstract* question; he therefore conceived of statecraft as the practical application in concrete human affairs of primary moral principles, clearly evident to man's right reason. It is in this vital sense that the Natural Law is implicitly affirmed in all of Burke's great parliamentary concerns. Generally, Burke was content to fulfill the Natural Law indirectly, through the concrete constitutional, legal, and political instruments of the state. But when the state itself was corrupted from its true function, and became the instrument of arbitrary tyranny and injustice, as in the penal code against Ireland, the rule of Hastings, in India, and of the revolutionists in France, Burke's appeals to the Natural Law became explicit. In its relative simplicity as a code of ethical principles, and in its enormous complexity in practical application, the Natural Law absorbed Burke's whole intellectual and emotional nature. It was so deeply rooted in him, so refined through his sensitive temperament, that even when it was not explicitly mentioned it appeared as his basic instinct and conviction. The Natural Law was his moral anchor, securing him to the most vital and enduring religious and political traditions of Europe.

Burke's faith in the Natural Law supplied the religious spirit which infuses his entire political philosophy. He was the foremost modern Christian humanist in politics because he saw the world and the nature of man through the revelations of Christianity and the right reason of Natural Law. His world of right reason and Nature was the Stoical world of Aristotle and Cicero and the Christian world of St. Thomas Aquinas and Hooker, and not the rationalistic world of eighteenth-century "nature," based upon mathematical science and empirical philosophy and systematized into an optimistic deism or pantheism. Burke's vision of reality was not centered in the natural sciences, in the cosmos or in the visible world of physical things, but in the divinely created and humanly developed world of man, the transfigured and complex world of civil institutions, with its laws and customs, its art and corporate wisdom, its invisible tissue of loyalties and prejudices, all of which gave cohesion and concreteness to the divine contract, which connected man in the eternal frame of the universe. Man was essentially a religious and political being, born in subjection to one great, immutable pre-existent law; his primary duty as citizen and statesman was to determine, obey, and promote in civil society the divine law ordained by God for his spiritual and temporal benefit. Only by accepting the supernatural or natural laws of God, and the divinely given instruments of civil society, could man flourish and bring himself to that degree of perfection which gave him an exalted yet subordinate place in the creation.

Notes

This essay is taken from Chapter Three in
Peter J. Stanlis, *Edmund Burke and the Natural Law*
(Ann Arbor: University of Michigan Press, 1958), pp. 40-51, 58-69, 71-75, 83-84.

Citations from Burke's *Works* (volume numbers given in arabic numerals) refer to the Bohn edition unless otherwise noted. Citations from Burke's *Speeches* (volume numbers given in Roman numerals) refer to the four-volume edition of his speeches, assembled by John Wright and published in 1816.

1. John Morley, *Burke* (London: Macmillan, 1879), pp. 22-23. See also pp. 24-27.
2. See Burke, "A Letter to Sir Hercules Langrishe," 3:311, 315, appr. 30% and 38% into the work. Hereinafter this will be cited as "Letter to Langrishe." See also Burke, "On the Penal Laws Against Irish Catholics," 3:289, appr. 50% into the work. Hereinafter this will be cited as "Laws Against Irish Catholics."
3. "Letter to Langrishe" 3:343, final paragraph. For a detailed account of this English system of persecution, see Morley, *Edmund Burke: A Historical Study* (London: Macmillan, 1867), pp. 180-186 and 191-193.
4. "Letter to Langrishe" 3:305, 317, appr. 17% and 43% into the work. See also pp. 303-307, 319, 331-338. See also Burke "Tract on the Popery Laws" 6:24, appr. 45% into the work. Hereinafter this will be cited as "Popery Laws."
5. "Popery Laws," 6:34, appr. 68% into the work.
6. "Popery Laws," 6:48 (final sentence of the work), 45, appr. 93% into the work.
7. *Speeches* I:151 (7 Dec 1772, "East India Restraining Bill," final paragraph). See also *Speeches* I:328. Yet as in American affairs, Burke rested the practical side of his case for

Ireland on moral prudence rather than on abstract right: "I do not put the thing on a question of right" ("Letter to Langrishe," 3:334, appr. 79% into the work).

8. "Popery Laws," 6:21-22, 29-30, appr. 39% and 57% into the work. To enforce this appeal to Natural Law Burke quoted Cicero's *De Legibus.*

9. "Popery Laws," 6:32-33, appr. 64% into the work.

10. "Popery Laws," 6:21, appr. 39% into the work..

11. "Letter to Richard Burke," 6:80, final paragraph of the work. See also "Letter to Langrishe," 3:324, appr. 57% into the work.

12. "Popery Laws," 6:22, appr. 40% into the work.

13. For example, see Morley, *Edmund Burke: A Historical Study* (1867), pp. 135-152.

14. *Speeches* I:20 (9 January 1770). This idea recurs frequently in Burke's speeches on American affairs.

15. *Speeches* I:303-304 (*Speech on Conciliation with America*, appr. 45% into the work; corresponds to Bohn 1:479).

16. House of Representatives of Massachusetts to Conway, Feb. 13, 1768, Almon, *Prior Documents*, pp. 181-182.

17. *Speeches* IV:136 ("Traiterous Correspondence Bill," 9 April 1793). See also I:214, 237 (*Speech on American Taxation*, appr. 58% into the work and eight paragraphs from the end; corresponds to *Writings* (Oxford) 2:439-40, 459-60. See also *Speeches* I:257.

18. *Speeches* I:16-17 ("Address on the King's Speech," 9 Jan. 1770). See also I:327 (*Speech on Conciliation with America*, appr. 79% into the work; corresponds to Bohn 1:479). The king had so corrupted the House of Commons, Burke lamented, that "the ground and pillar of freedom is...held up only by the treacherous underpinning and clumsy buttresses of arbitrary power." (*Speeches* I:195, appr. 27% into the *Speech on American Taxation*; corresponds to *Writings* (Oxford) 2:422.)

19. *Speeches* I:110. See also 111 ("Speech on the Acts of Uniformity," appr. 75% into that work; corresponds to *Works* (Bohn) 6:99-100).

20. *Speeches* I:295. (*Speech on Conciliation with America*, appr. 34% into the work; corresponds to Bohn 1:471). See also *Speeches* I:298 (corresponds to Bohn 1:474) and I:20.

21. For these passages see respectively *Speeches* I:176 ("Speech on the Boston Port Bill, 25 March 1774), 233; *Correspondence* (1844) IV, Appendix 493, 474, 476-77, 488-89, 490-93; *Speeches* I:270; and *Correspondence* (1844) IV, Appendix 495.

22. James Boswell, *Life of Samuel Johnson* (New York: E.P. Dutton, 1949) I:320.

23. Morley, *Burke* (1879), p. 81.

24. *Speeches* II:413, 409, appr. 9% and 5% into the "Speech on Fox's East India Bill; corresponds to *Writings* (Oxford) 5:386, 384. The following two footnotes refer to the same speech.

25. *Speeches* II:410; corresponds to *Writings* (Oxford) 5:383-84.

26. *Speeches* II:410; corresponds to *Writings* (Oxford) 5:384. A fragment on monopoly found among Burke's papers is worth noting here: "'Monopoly' is contrary to 'Natural Right.' Monopoly is the power...of exclusive dealing in a commodity...which others might supply if not prevented by that power. No monopoly can, therefore, be prescribed in; because contrary to common right....The State, representing all its individuals, may contract for them; and therefore may grant a monopoly" (*Correspondence* (1844) IV, Appendix, 459; see also pp. 460-462; *Speeches* IV: 310.

27. *Speeches* II:412-413 ("Speech on Fox's East India Bill," appr. 8% into the work; corresponds to *Writings* (Oxford) 5:386.) See also the following portions of the same work, in *Speeches* II: 428 (27%), 476 (83%), 478, 486-87, and 490 (final sentences of the speech).

28. For a good account of this fraud, see Morley, *Edmund Burke: A Historical Study* (1867), pp. 205-207.

29. *Speeches* III:162 (Appr. 79% into the "Speech on the Nabob of Arcot's Debts"; corresponds to *Writings*(Oxford) 5:537). See also III:163. This passage may be interpreted as a reference to *physical* rather than *moral* laws of nature, in which case the reference is merely an analogy.

30. *Speeches* IV:356 ("Speeches in the Impeachment of Warren Hastings," Fourth Day, 16 Feb. 1788; corresponds to *Works* (Bohn) 7:96, appr. 58% into the speech.) See also *Speeches* IV:357; II:446-447 ("Speech on Fox's East India Bill," appr. 48% into the speech; corresponds to *Writings* (Oxford) 5:415-16); *Speeches* III:66.

31. *Speeches* IV:354 ("Speeches in Impeachment," 16 Feb. 1788; 54% into the speech), 472, 479, 367. In securing absolute rule, Burke noted that Hastings acted on a principle of sovereignty centered in power alone: "He declares that in a division between him and the Nabob 'the strongest must decide'" (*Speeches* II:434). The same applied in divisions with England: "Here Mr. Burke read from parts of the defence of Mr. Hastings, passages, stating, that whenever he thought the laws of England militated against the interests of the Company, he was at liberty to violate them" (*Speeches* IV:476-77). [Stanlis's references to *Speeches* IV: 472ff. come from Burke's "Speeches in Reply" on May 28 and 30, 1794. The texts do not correspond exactly with the Bohn edition. —DR]

32. *Speeches* IV:357-58 ("Speeches in Impeachment," Fourth Day, 16 Feb. 1788, appr. 62% into the speech; corresponds to *Works* 7:99).

33. *Speeches* IV:374-75 ("Speeches in Impeachment," Fifth Day, 18 Feb. 1788, seventh paragraph; corresponds to *Works* 7:129. For other examples in Indian affairs of Burke's attacks on the theory of sovereignty based upon arbitrary power, see *Speeches* II:429, 431-32, 434, 446-47, 460, 473, 475-76; III:57, 68, 74, 86, 99, 175-76, 223-25, 266, 280; IV:307, 313, 328, 354-63, 368, 374-75, 475-76, 478-79, 489-91, 499.

34. *Speeches* IV:354 ("Speeches in Impeachment," Fourth Day, 16 Feb. 1788, appr. 54% into the speech; corresponds to *Works* 7:94).

35. *Speeches* IV:366-67 ("Speeches in Impeachment," Fourth Day, 16 Feb. 1788, appr. 89% into the speech; corresponds to *Works* 7:118). See also *Speeches* IV:481.

36. *Speeches* IV:477.

37. See *Correspondence* (1844) 4:24, Appendix 519, 544, 547. See also *Letters on a Regicide Peace* in *Works* 5:155, 215, appr. 5% and 80% into the first of the *Letters*.

38. For the various theories concerning M. Dupont's identity, see Thomas Copeland, *Our Eminent Friend Edmund Burke* (New Haven: Yale University Press, 1949), pp. 190-245. Professor Copeland's own theory is doubtful. [The correspondent was Charles-François Depont See *Correspondence* 6:31-32, 39-50. —DR]

39. *Correspondence* 6:39-50.

40. "Speech on the Army Estimates," in *Works* 3:275, appr. 54% into the speech. See also pp. 276-78. The italics are Burke's.

41. "Remarks on the Policy of the Allies," in *Works* 3:453, ten paragraphs from the end of the work.

42. *Reflections* in *Works* 2:368-69, appr. 38% into the work. See also p. 370. Charles E. Vaughan dismissed this passage as "a mere metaphor," and F. J. C. Hearnshaw condemned it as "resounding nonsense." H. V. S. Ogden stated that "Burke was imbued with the importance of the differences between peoples, and for him the contract is an *ex post facto* abstraction of particular validity, not an initiating act of universal application." Ogden concluded by agreeing with Vaughan: "A contract between the dead, the living and the unborn is only a contract by metaphor." John A. Lester called this passage "the work of Burke's moral idealism," a criticism too abstract to be meaningful. He too failed to mention the Natural Law. It is ironical that the

positivist Morley, who also never mentioned the Natural Law in Burke, recognized in a general way, and apart from any consideration of contract, that the ultimate basis of Burke's politics lay in a "mysticism" that transcended a naturalistic explanation of life: "At the bottom of all his thoughts about communities and governments there lay a certain mysticism. It was no irony, no literary trope, when he talked of our having taught the American husbandman 'piously to believe in the mysterious virtue of wax and parchment.' He was using no idle epithet, when he described the disposition of a stupendous wisdom, 'moulding together the great mysterious incorporation of the human race.' To him there actually was an element of mystery in the cohesion of men in societies, in political obedience, in the sanctity of contract; in all that fabric of law and charter and obligation, whether written or unwritten, which is the sheltering bulwark between civilization and barbarism. When reason and history had contributed all that they could to the explanation, it seemed to him as if the vital force, the secret of organization, the binding framework, must still come from the impenetrable regions beyond reasoning and beyond history" (*Burke* (1879), p. 165). This was the closest Morley ever came to recognizing the sovereignty of Natural Law in Burke's political philosophy.

43. Pufendorf, *Of the Law of Nature and Nations* (Oxford, 1703), p. 117. Pufendorf's italics.

44. *Reflections* in *Works* 2:307-309, appr. 13% into the work.

45. *Reflections* in *Works* 2:370, appr. 38% into the work.

46. *Reflections* in *Works* 2:364-66, appr. 36% into the work.

47. *Speeches* I:114 ("Speech on the Church Nullum Tempus Bill," 17 Feb. 1772; corresponds to *Writings* (Oxford) 2:366. See also *Annual Register* (1767), pp. 290, 293-94.

48. *Reflections* in *Works* 2:493, appr. 89% into the work. See also 492. *Letter to Richard Burke* in *Works*: 6:80 (final paragraph).

49. *Reflections* in *Works* 2:422, appr. 60% into the work. See also 423.

50. *Reflections* in *Works* 2:377, appr. 42% into the work. See also pp. 378-79.

GERALD W. CHAPMAN

19
The Organic Premise

Burke means many things to many men. His prelacy in conservatism is commonly recognized; yet, as Harold Laski says, Burke also gives "deep comfort to men of liberal temper."[1] He is neoclassic, but also romantic; he is a nationalistic citizen of the world and a Tory Whig, a throwback to the seventeenth century and a seminal thinker for the nineteenth, an Irishman who reveals much that is best in the English mind, a busy-buzzing M.P. whom at least three respectable judges–Hazlitt, Arnold, and Leslie Stephen–have called the greatest prose writer in English literature. He is one of those great amphibious Englishmen, not quite liberal, not quite conservative, poetically open in his thinking, broadly practical in his poetry, whose diffuse and many-mansioned thought seems always implicit with a coherent and synthetic system which, however, is never achieved. Laski, after a cautious sizing-up from an opposing camp, pronounced Burke the greatest figure in the history of English politics, and sensed in his writings the latent but obscure presence of "a system which, even in its unfinished implications, is hardly less gigantic than that of Hobbes or Bentham."[2] Observing that Burke's emphasis on expediency is not, to his mind, a real "release from metaphysical inquiry," Laski went on to suggest "that what was needed in Burke's philosophy was the clear avowal of the metaphysic it implied."[3] One might like to agree, and to announce that at last, after a century and a half of mellowing, the metaphysical system is ready to be avowed, that one can drag it out of obscurity into the limelight and the applause of the world. But no. Pin Burke down at one point, and he dances away at another, in what Hazlitt called admiringly, his "circumgyrations."

His thought is a master-solvent of antinomies–metaphysics and common sense, poetry and practicality, liberalism and conservatism, neoclassicism and romanticism, Christianity and pragmatism, to name but a few. Every digging after "Burke's system" to date has come up with something bleached of the full meaning and value of the context—"Burke's sense." One is reminded of nothing so much as the affectionate frustration of a modern interpreter of Hooker:

> He is both a Humanist and a Protestant, both a Thomist and an Augustinian, both a rationalist and a traditionalist; he believed both in authority and freedom, both in consent and obligation, both in law and sovereignty, both in uniformity and toleration, both in Church and State, both in human nature and in the Fall.[4]

Something there seems to be about the characteristically English mind which is a living paradox. Possibly, somewhere in the depths of Burke's "experienced benignity" may have lain, or may lie, a system. To ignore a latent coherency and rational dependence in his *ad hoc* propositions is surely to miss a principal feature in his thought and a source of his quality. But the possibility of abstracting a system is small. One may suspect that dying in 1897, or 1997, Burke would have bequeathed the same character of splendidly unfinished thought, and that for future as for present readers he will remain a living paradox.

More than any other single figure, he typifies the union, in his own thinking, of what are perhaps the two greatest achievements of English culture to date–its literary imagination and its success in practical politics.

Certain specific drifts of his thought are, of course, evident. Burke is a key—if not the first great—exemplar of the *geschichtlichen Sinn* in one of its forms—a mode of imaginative sensibility to the past, and to the present as continuous with the past, which has added a new dimension to human experience. It has not gone unappreciated. Coleridge perceived, and learned from Burke's historical sense. The strange and passionate Novalis remarked of the *Reflections:* "Burke has written a revolutionary book against the Revolution."[5] Later in the century Lord Acton, then only twenty-four, perceived the amazing subtlety and novelty of Burke's penetration of history even in the youthful *Essay Towards an Abridgement of English History,* which Burke turned off at twenty-eight. As there is little doubt, he said, that "Burke was our greatest statesman," so if he had persisted, he "would have been the first of our historians." Acton admired Burke's freedom from pedantry, capacity for scholarship, vigor of experience–and his intelligent appreciation of the medieval:

> Several generations of men were still to follow, who were to derive their knowledge of the Middle Ages from the Introduction to Robertson's *Charles V,* to study ecclesiastical history in the pages of Gibbon, and to admire Hume as the prince of historians. At the age of thirty [*sic*], Burke proved himself superior to that system of prejudice and ignorance which was then universal, and which is not yet completely dissipated.[6]

Burke had the imagination to seize a contemplative order of history which was imperfectly conscious, obscurely felt, in the cultural life of his period, and which the life of his period sorely required. Clinging to his theory that romanticism and the recovery of medieval sympathies among Protestants were intimately related, Acton concluded, in a note near the end of his life: "History issues from the Romantic School. Piecing together what the Rev[olution] snapped. It hails from Burke, as Education from Helvetius, or Emancipation from the Quakers."[7] Accepting Acton's view, Herbert Butterfield could state as late as 1955 that Burke—instead of Sir Walter Scott—"exerted the presiding influence over the historical movement of the nineteenth century."[8] Certainly one cannot turn to Burke from the cunning succinctness of Hume, or the erudite analyses and massive ironic portraiture of Gibbon, without sensing that one is present somehow in a new world—superficially familiar, yet at bottom strangely altered and intense.

Burke is hardly a romantic medievalist, however, To understand his thought with reference to political developments in early nineteenth-century Germany, where his influence was enormous, is almost inevitably to short-change its neo-classic, eighteenth-century, practical, and characteristically English, spirit. Conservative followers in Germany—his friend Brandes, Rehburg, and Möser—admired Burke's sense of living in history, and what appeared to them his aristocratic responsibility and attack upon natural law; romantic organicists—Novalis, Adam Müller, and Stein—abstracted from him an idealization of the medieval state to accommodate their own admiration of the ancient Holy Roman Empire. The common denominator of all, as of the publicist Gentz, was that they used Burke's name, example, and ideas to express their hatred of the French Revolution. Much of the dust raised by these men has settled upon Burke's reputation and obscured his full quality. As Reinhold Aris justly remarks: "When Burke praised the age of chivalry he was using a historic flourish to strengthen his position, but he would have been horrified at the idea that someone would use his arguments to revive feudalism."[9] In spirit, Burke is really more comparable with the half-romanticist, half-classicist Goethe, who called himself a "moderate liberal"—one who

> tries, with the means at his command, to do as much good as ever he can, but is cautious of wishing to destroy immediately by fire and sword faults which are often inevitable. He endeavours by intelligent progress gradually to suppress public wrongs, without simultaneously spoiling just as much that is good by taking violent measures. He contents himself, in this always imperfect world, with what is good, until time and circumstance favour the attainment of something better.[10]

Burke approaches politics in a hardheaded and present-minded fashion, as well as with that quality of imagnation which might be called romantic and historical; he turns upon hard fact, wherever it is to be met, a contemplative subtlety and concrete appreciativeness. He is committed to a *practical* approach to politics, and those features in his thought which link with the romantic and the medieval rise, as it were, as by-products of other and, one may think, equally significant features—his old-fashioned love of liberty, his classical discipline; his humanitarianism; his prosaic duties as an M.P.; his lawyer's respect for process, negotiation, and specific reason; his confidence that the natural law persists; his play of satire and concern for decorum; his confidence in common sense. As G. M. Young observes, classical criticism of every kind is "a form of public service," whose interest is not "to expatiate on the result, but to show how it was brought about, because by studying that you may be able to produce something like the same result yourself."[11] It asks "how to do it." Confronted with a novel occasion, Burke searches its texture of necessities, its correlation of component factors, for the course of action latently most effective, and for the "principles" or fruitful generalities which may be applied in future occasions to produce, or avoid, like effects, or which at least increase one's inntelligence of probabilities. Hence his emphasis upon "common sense." Unwilling to jump with each fashionable evolution of opinion, Burke suspends commitment until the rear dimensions of experience and old partiality, various, multiform, and intricate, are brought up to be compared critically, and, if possible, reconciled. He applies new knowledge wherever it throws a clear light, but would apply it in moderation—that is, intelligently—with due regard to its ascertained limits within the context of the familiar and the past. He tries not to be one of those whose accurate and logical reasonings bring them up against an impasse, or who, being too exquisite in their conjectures of the future, can only bring to the gross emergences of actuality an immense surprise. Common sense, restrained by the actual, is often blind to hypothetical goods and obstinate within the familiar, but it is also capable of great delicacy of adjustment to novel occasions. Unburdened with the vanity of hypostatized systems, it is more natively responsive to main events. It is the particular stage of intelligence in which the relation of imagined probabilities to a factual situation is clearly descried. There is much truth in Laski's conclusion that Burke "is destined doubtless to live rather as the author of some maxims that few statesmen will dare to forget than as the creator of a system";[12] he will live by the example of his moral elevation and by the perpetual relevance of his thought "in that middle ground between the facts and speculation [where] his supremacy is unapproached."[13] A man in politics, Burke said, must seek "the exactest detail of circumstances, guided by the surest general principles that are necessary to direct experiment and inquiry, in order again from those details to elicit principles, firm and luminous general principles, to direct a practical legislative proceeding."[14]

Even at those moments when, one feels, the vast seething stability of the organic commonwealth looms hauntingly in his imagination, Burke is less interested in painting his fancy of it, or in spinning a theory about it, than in deciding how, in all common sense, one had best behave, and in keeping his generalizations "useful" or "expedient." He is intent upon abstracting *axioms of practical method*, whose spirit W. E. H. Lecky has caught in so brilliant an epitome that one can do no better than to quote him at length:

> Government is obliged to discharge the most various functions, to aim at many distinct and sometimes inconsistent ends. It is the trustee and the guardian of the multifarious, complicated, fluctuating, and often conflicting interests of a highly composite and artificial society. The principle that tends towards one set of advantages impairs another. The remedies which apply to one set of dangers would, if not partially counteracted, produce another. The institutions which are admirably adapted to protect one class of interests, may be detrimental to another. It is only by constant

adjustments, by checks and counterchecks, by various contrivances adapted to various needs, by compromises between competing interests, by continual modifications applied to changing circumstances, that a system is slowly formed which corresponds to the requirements and conditions of the country, discharges the greatest number of useful functions, and favours in their due proportion and degree the greatest number of distinct and often diverging interests. The comparative prominence of different interests, tendencies, and dangers, must continually occupy the legislator, and he will often have to provide limitations and obstacles to the very tendency which he wishes to make the strongest in his legislation.[15]

Furthermore, though in his attacks upon "metapoliticans," upon natural rights, *raison,* and conventional contract theory, Burke seems, at times, as German romanticists thought, to desert natural law for a philosophy of organic process, yet the fact remains that every effort to draw his implicit assumptions into an organic focus sooner or later, after every partial success, will confront the obstinate and opaque presence of Nature.[16] View it from what perspective you will, Nature will not yield, will not takes its place in the system. At point after point, Burke's magnificent intellect pushes beyond and shatters that Nature which had become a platitude of the salon, and that Nature which only named a comfortable emotion and was idolized either as a set of propositions or as a mythic image. One thinks of his grasp of American character and growth; his awareness of the mutual relatedness and interpenetrative correspondence of elements in the empire, in the constitution, in the "commonwealth" of Europe; his reaching out into the uniqueness of Indian life; his watching, horrified, the "unfolding of the Germ of Jacobinism."[17] Time after time, guided as it were by some intuitive navigation, his thinking breaks upon the mystery of organic process. Yet only to retract on other occasions. When all is said, an older idea of nature remains essential in his thought, a clear and distinct concept of "law" acccessible to reason, including that "eternal, immutable law, in which will and reason are the same."[18] His search for practical principles, for example, implies belief in a human nature more or less recurrent within actual political occasions, no matter how cautious he is about predicting the limits of its possibilities.

The whole tradition of English empiricism (not to mention Christian humanism) lies behind him; and in many ways, what was happening to

English empiricism, generally speaking, explains the status of Nature in his thought.

Bacon, to take a representative figure, is an example of English empiricism in a dramatic early stage. His imagination is still active about first principles, still charged with grateful vision and jealous of its purity. He is busied with originating new strategy to solve the age-old conflicts of permanence and change. Bacon is dedicated to changing the world by learning the "causes," the limitations of possibility, of change in nature. His metaphysics pushes him constantly into the realm of hard fact and practical suggestion, but always in behalf of the larger aim—the "interpretation" of nature. The Nature that emerges in his thinking is significant of things to come in the way that the child is father of the man. A vision of things melts into subtle crevices of the mind and silently motivates thinking. Visions are causes in history. The Nature which Bacon isolates for thought, however exquisitely subtle and beautiful its movements, amounts in the end to a uniform texture of causes, fixed in a static eternity of relation. True, "in nature nothing really exists beside individual bodies," but within the *acts and changes* of individual bodies there is a "latent process" which is "perfectly continuous" though invisible in its causal texture, and this causal texture "embraces the unity of nature in substances the most unlike."[19] Thus, the causal texture (rational unity) of concrete change is the true object of philosophy, and hence the name "rational empiricism." Rational empiricism is the faith that all concrete particulars are generated by interlocking principles which, though very intricate and obscure, can nevertheless be inferred from their "effects." The empiricist always watches concrete "effects," discriminates abstract relations or connections among them, in hopes thereafter to direct his knowledge to the discovery, generation, or control of new "effects." This is true, for example, of Newton, who in the *Opticks* fatefully labels the up-and-down method "analysis" and "synthesis":

> By this way of analysis we may proceed from compounds to ingredients, and from motions to the forces producing them; and in general, from effects to their causes, and from particular causes to more general ones, till the argument end in the most general. This is the method of analysis: and the synthesis consists in assuming the causes discovered, and established as principles, and by them explaining the phenomena proceeding from them.[20]

But later empiricists, turning their thought to politics, art, morals, history, and psychology, wade into unsuspected deeps of metaphysical darkness, from which, generally speaking, English empiricism only begins to emerge, in its theoretical foundations, in the twentieth century (for example, in the works of Whitehead and Russell). For it is the paradox of rational empiricism, fully illustrated in Bacon's own arguments, that in shuttling back and forth between fact and law, selecting facts to form laws and forming laws to explain facts, it tends to complete itself in systems of greater and greater abstraction from the very "experience" it pronounces solely real. Later inheritors of empiricism, like Burke, faced the obstinate paradox that the more empirical they became the less rational, and the more rational the less empirical. They came to experience more than they could rationally account for. Thus they wrestled with insistent dualisms of permanence and change, unity and multeity, generality and particularity, abstraction and circumstance, ideality and fact. Facts had penumbras and fringe areas of meaning that defied classification and experimental rule, and unfolded vistas of startling complexity and nuance. One thinks of Montesquieu's idea of "spirit"; of Burke's response to the "great contexture of the mysterious whole"; of Sir Joshua Reynolds' trying to decide what "Idea" was; of Lord Kames's being haunted by "relations":

> Cause and effect, contiguity in time or in place, high and low, prior and posterior, resemblance, contrast, and a thousand other relations connect things together without end. Not a single thing appears solitary and altogether devoid of connection: the only difference is, that some are intimately connected, some more slightly, some near, some at a distance.[21]

One may also remember that Kames goes on puzzling until he describes a work of art as like an "organic system" in which it is required that "its parts be orderly arranged and mutually connected, bearing each of them a relation to the whole, some more intimate, some less, according to their destination."[22]

Partly from this love quarrel of the rational and empirical faculties, whose marriage Bacon sang with such hope, something indeed like "organicism" is born. The texture of enduring causes too subtle for sense and *a priori* reason is a haunting certainty which must somehow be reconciled with fleeting fact and value. The practical empiricist, like Burke, discovers his need for a self-legislated restraint of reason in order to continue "empirical." He resists the threat of mental inflation; he stops the dangerous spiral of his thinking, so as not to break his moorings in experience and perish in the thin air of conceptual abstraction. Thus, though he may not escape believing in a universal order of causes, he shies from it with reverent caution. He is committed to the theory of a strict, overarching rational order, but also to an exploration of actual existence for its latent and emergent circumstances. Nature yields something to History, and the chain of causes is submerged in the chain of events. He may grow resentful of other empiricists, trenchant intellects who cling fast to rational systems, to "metaphysics," without staying open to the nuances of actuality and practice which have a vital bearing on the case at hand. He becomes suspicious of their "reason," though he may learn from it, and cultivates in himself an imaginative sagacity which, turning outwards upon current or past events, and being nourished by his general power of experiencing, searches for "practical" principles—which, "feeling the effect" (a constant motif in Burke), then grasps discrete circumstances into a unity expressive of latent particular relations.

In this reaction from the Nature of mechanico-materialism and its "philosophy of death,"[23] as Coleridge called it, Burke indeed approximated thinking of an "organic" character. A host of conditioning ideas like *continuity, the virtual, permanence* and *change, spirit, coalescence, interrelation,* and *vital character* threw open vistas of perception in his experience and suggested to him frequently that reality is like *this* and not like *that*. For example, it occurred to him as early as 1774, in the quiet of his notes, that the "real character" of the English parliament derived from its reconciliation of permanence and change, past and present: from the perpetuity of its actualization within novelties of the historical process.

> Nothing is more beautiful in the theory of parliaments than that principle of renovation, and union of permanence and change, that are happily mixed in their constitutions:—that in all our changes we are never either wholly old or wholly new:—that there are enough of the old to preserve unbroken the traditionary chain of the maxims and policy of our ancestors, and the law and custom of parliament; and enough of the new to invigorate us and bring us to our true character, by being taken fresh from the mass of the people; and the whole, though mostly composed of the old members, have, notwithstanding, a new character, and may have the advantage of change without the imputation of inconstancy.[24]

The idea of *the organic* is implicit insofar as the term implies a recognition that reality presents itself as a fabric of actualizing possibilities requiring the human mind to make endless reconciliations of possession and emergence, each emergent as it is assimilated, modifying the whole tenor of the possessed, by an endless feeling attention to incursions of novelty, like showers of meteoric light within the atmosphere of the familiar. No example could seem clearer. Yet this reconciliation of permanence and change in English institutions Burke called "the pattern of nature."[25] The importance of this perpetual confrontation of tradition, law, or custom, with change, was that the more changes it withstood or negotiated, without loss of its essentials (principles, fundamentals), the more likely that its principles correspond with Nature, to which an empirical appeal is always open. Burke's organicism, therefore, is not thoroughgoing or exclusive; natural law is still a regulative notion; one has to do with an "organicism," so to speak, evolved and sustained on strictly empirical premises; one confronts another antinomy reconciled in practice when it might appear irreconcilable to logic.

Wherever one turns, the story is the same. There seems hardly a trend of Burke's thinking for which there is no countertrend almost equally essential, locked up in the mystery of his quality and not to be shaken out. Patterns of meaning break toward system, then stop, or fall away; ideas familiar enough at one point appear elsewhere suffused with uniqueness, in flickering degrees of intensity and in fresh relations; what is dark or tentative at one point is clarified at another, but rarely completed. Burke's organicism is a premise for experience, not a systematic philosophy of the kind which soared into fashion during the nineteenth century, after his death; it has affinities with Hooker instead of with Hegel, with Wordsworth instead of with Novalis, or in this century with Whitehead instead of, say, with Heidegger. It is practical and imaginatively open, and must be experienced many-sidedly as a spirit of his thought within *ad hoc* occasions.

One must search his particular judgments, then, not for a system, but for a characteristic activity, of which they are *ad hoc* expressions. The unity in Burke's thought would seem to lie in the character of his intelligence as it operates upon the life of his time. It is a mode of imaginative practicality which has appeared in English culture within many very different and often cross theoretical positions—a peculiar fusion of poetic conception and literary brilliance, ethical awareness and religious reverence, preference for concrete inquiry and compromise, common sense and sense of duty, and what Fox called a "reverse of selfishness." Burke was at once, for his time, its exemplar, and in some measure, by rendering it conscious, its creator.

Notes

The essay by Gerald Chapman comes from his book, *Edmund Burke: The Practical Imagination* (Cambridge, MA: Harvard University Press, 1967), pp. 1-12.

1. Harold Laski, *Political Thought in England from Locke to Bentham* (London, 1944),p. 172.
2. Laski, pp. 213-214.
3. Laski, pp. 206-207.
4. Christopher Morris, *Political Thought in England: Tyndale to Hooker* (London, 1953), p. 197.
5. Reinhold Aris, *History of Political Thought in Germany from 1789 to 1815* (London, 1936), p. 270.
6. *The Rambler,* April 1858, quoted in *Essays on Church and State,* ed. Douglas Woodruff (London, 1952), pp. 455-456. Acton probably valued the many passages which suggest an organic grasp of history. For one example among many, it occurred to Burke as early as 1757 that Roman *municipia,* provinces, and colonies in early Britain, though "dissimilar parts," were however, "far from being discordant": "[They] united to make a firm and compact body, the motion of any member of which could only serve to confirm and establish the whole; and when time was given to this structure to coalesce and settle, it was found impossible to break any part of it from the empire.

By degrees the several parts blended and softened into one another" (Burke, *Works* (Bohn) 6:220, appr. 15% into the *Abridgement of English History.*)
7. Add. 5437, Acton Papers, Cambridge Univ. Library, quoted in Herbert Butterfield, *Man on His Past: the Study of the History of Historical Scholarship,* Wiles Lecture (Cambridge, England, 1955), p. 70. Cf. Alfred Cobban, *Edmund Burke and the Revolt Against the Eighteenth Century: A Study of the Political and Social Thinking of Burke, Wordsworth, Coleridge, and Southey* (London, 1929), pp. 258-268.

Chapman adds a long explanatory footnote to establish the thoroughly English, Elizabethan, and Jacobean roots of Burke's organicism, as opposed to theories of organic growth that originated with Leibnitz or elsewhere on the continent.

Whatever the hap of ideas derived from it, Chapman concludes, a historical sense has continued a lively part of English culture *mutatis mutandis* from early times down to the present moment—for example in the criticism of T. S. Eliot—and it very much interested Burke to clarify it and keep it alive for his own day. Not before Burke, however, did the historical sense rise to such brilliantly self-conscious expression as specifically part of the national character; perhaps Acton's remark has a virtual truth.
8. Butterfield, *Man on His Past,* p. 18. The list of great or near-great historians whose thought was shaped by Burke is astonishingly long—for example, Macaulay, Savigny, Guizot, Niebuhr, De Tocqueville, Lecky, Stephen.
9. Aris, *Thought in Germany,* p. 309.
10. Aris, p. 187.
11. *Last Essays* (London, 1950), pp. 107-108.
12. Laski, *Locke to Bentham,* p. 213.
13. Laski, *Locke to Bentham,* p. 174.

14. Thoughts and Details on Scarcity, *Works* (Bohn) 5:87, appr. 19% into the work.

15. W. E. H. Lecky, *A History of England in the Eighteenth Century* (New York, 1882), 3:228.

16. The number of critics who associate Burke with "the organic" is legion; but very few try to expain what they mean by it. Understandably. "The organic," as it circulates in free usage, is a house of many mansions, a dark house with dark rooms, each with obscure passageways into all the others: one can walk from room to room, straining to see, and never know precisely where one is–except that one is inside a house. C. E. Vaughan is an exception: "Burke," *Studies in the History of Political Philosophy Before and After Rousseau,* ed. A. G. Little (Manchester, 1925), 2:26 ff. [Chapman at this point adds a long bibliographical note of other treatments of "the organic" in Burke.—DR]

17. Burke to Windham, Oct. 24, 1793 in *Correspondence* 7:462.

18. *Reflections* in *Works* (Bohn) 2:366, appr. 37% into the work.

19. Bacon, *Novum Organum,* Bk. 2, aphorisms ii-vi.

20. Qtd. in E. A. Burtt, *The Metaphysical Foundations of Modern Physical Science* (New York, 1932), p. 221.

21. Henry Home (Lord Kames), *Elements of Criticism,* ed. and rev. J. R. Boyd (New York, 1866), p. 31.

22. Kames, *Elements of Criticism,* p. 35. Burke apparently looked upon Kames's work as continuous with his own. When [Edmond] Malone, in 1789, suggested that Burke revise and enlarge *The Sublime and the Beautiful,* in the light of thirty years' experience, Burke answered that the train of his thinking had moved away from aesthetics–"such speculations"–and that, though the subject was new when he wrote, Lord Kames and others had "gone over the same ground" more recently. See James Prior, *Life of the Right Honourable Edmund Burke,* 5th edn. (London, 1854), p. 47;   and Donald Cross Bryant, *Edmund Burke and His Literary Friends,* Washington University Studies, New Series, Language and Literature, No. 9 (December 1939), p. 234. Kames's using the phrase "organic system" is notable. Most English thinkers at different periods who have been attracted to the organic premise, or interested in it—for example, Hobbes, Coleridge, Whitehead—are unable to accept all the implications that can be made to flow from it without qualification The "mechanical" is made to persist alongside. Whitehead, for example, described the metaphysical doctrine in *Science and the Modern World* (New York, 1925) as "the theory of organic mechanism" (ch. 5). Similarly, the "artificial animal" of the *Leviathan* is hardly more than emblematic; such hints of organicism as are present are rendered thoroughly mechanical by Hobbes's view of nature and man. Coleridge, though he hates anything smacking of the "mechanical," is not really an exception. His lifelong ambition to reconcile Plato and Aristotle in an indigenously English system amounts to little more, in one light, than his inability to rest in the notions taken in from contemporary German thought (Platonic, organic), his brilliantly felt and obscurely achieved ambition to make them jibe with the commonsensical, practical, and traditionary (Anglican, Aristotelian, and "mechanical-empirical").

23. Qtd. in Basil Willey, "Thought," *The Character of England,* ed. Ernest Barker (Oxford, 1947), p. 335.

24. Notes for Speech on Amendment on the Address, Nov. 30, 1774, *Correspondence of the Right Honourable Edmund Burke,* ed., Charles William, Earl Fitzwilliam, and Sir Richard Bourke [1844], Rivington edn. (London, 1852), 2:415-416.

25. *Reflections* in *Works* (Bohn) 2:307, appr. 13% into the work. On the persistence of Nature in his thought, see Willey, *The Eighteenth Century Background: Studies on the Idea of Nature in the Thought of the Period* (London, 1940), pp. 240-252, esp. 243-245.

FRANCIS CANAVAN

20
Prescription of Government

In relating the political order of civil society to the created order of the world, Burke's theory of prescription of government plays an important role. He says explicitly that "the doctrine of prescription...is a part of the law of nature."[1] But as the variety of scholarly interpretations of his doctrine of prescription testifies, what he meant by it and in what sense it is part of the law of nature, is by no means clear, certainly not to all who read Burke.

Paul Lucas has described Burke's theory of prescription as his "idea about the way in which an adverse possession of property and authority may be legitimated by virtue of use and enjoyment during a long passage of time."[2] The description is accurate so far as it goes. Burke certainly held that if one had held uncontested possession as the owner of a piece of property for a sufficiently long period of time, no earlier title to the property, however valid, could be revived and made to prevail against the occupant's title. Through the passage of time the occupant had acquired a title by prescription, and this in Burke's eyes was "the soundest, the most general, and the most recognized title...a title, which...is rooted in its principle, in the law of nature itself"[3] He applied the same principle, by analogy, to the possession of political authority.

Lucas goes on to say that Burke "revolutionized the meaning of prescription"[4] and that "it was through his conception of prescription that Burke attacked the natural and common laws."[5] This writer disagrees with Lucas's propositions that Burke attacked the natural law, that he "believed that prescription possessed an immanent justification,"[6] and that in his mind "time alone became the material and efficient cause of prescription."[7] This chapter, however, is not a rebuttal of Lucas's contention that Burke's "key and characteristic doctrine of prescription is not to be found in the old writings on the natural law," or in the Roman civil law, the Roman Catholic canon law, the English common law, or the many expositions of the various French "civil" or feudal laws.[8]   All that is intended here is to set forth Burke's doctrine and his reasons for it, whether it is to be found in previous writings or not.

Burke's doctrine of prescription of government, as Fennessy remarks, "is by no means an anti-rational defence of existing institutions, based on feelings of reverence for antiquity. It is a theoretical answer to a problem of political theory."[9] Burke was not speculating in a vacuum when he spoke of a prescription of government; he was arguing against what he regarded as a false and dangerous theory of the origin and nature of political authority. Burke's defense of authority as prescriptive, therefore, must be understood in the light of the theory to which it was a reply. To try to understand the Burkean doctrine of prescription in itself, without reference to the opposing doctrine, is to run the risk of missing its point.

For the present purpose, what is important is not so much what Burke's opponents really meant as what they thought they meant. There is, in fact, no reason to believe that he seriously misunderstood them, even though for polemic reasons he did reduce their arguments to their simplest and most radical form. It would be hard to oversimplify Thomas Paine's thesis in *The Rights of Man*, but it was doubtless unfair of Burke to take Paine as the exponent of the view of all the English sympathizers with the French Revolution. Nonetheless, to understand what Burke meant by prescription, we must first understand the position against which he directed the doctrine of prescription, and we must understand it as he did.

He had summarized that position several years before the French Revolution in his "Speech on the Reform of the Representation of the Commons in Parliament." Since that speech will be the subject of the following chapter, we may leave full discussion of it until then, and note only that Burke said in it that most of those seeking reform claimed the right to vote for members of Parliament as one of "the supposed rights of man as man."[10] Such an argument, as Burke pointed out, led logically not only to reform of the representation in one house of Parliament, but to popular sovereignty clear across the constitutional board. By the time Burke came to write his *Reflections on the Revolution in France* in 1790, the argument, as he understood it, had in fact taken that form. "They have 'the rights of men,'" he said, and continued:

Against these there can be no prescription; against these no argument is binding: these admit no temperament, and no compromise: any thing withheld from their full demand is so much of fraud and injustice. Against these their rights of men let no government look for security in the length of its continuance, or in the justice and lenity of its administration. The objections of these speculatists, if its form do not quadrate with their theories, are as valid against such an old and beneficent government as against the most violent tyranny, or the greenest usurpation. They are always at issue with governments, not on a question of abuse, but a question of competency, and a question of title.[11]

The point at issue between Burke, on the one hand, and the revolutionists and the whole "natural rights" school of political thought, on the other, was not a question of what made a constitution good or when authority was abused. It was "a question of title." They held that there was one and only one legitimate title to political authority: "the rights of men." Burke's counter-argument was that "*prescription*...gives right and title."[12] In the passage in which he used that phrase, he was speaking of the title to real estate, but he explained in another place: "Prescription is the most solid of all titles, not only to property, but, which is to secure that property, to Government."[13] Prescription, according to Burke, gave "right and title" not only to real property but to inherited liberties, religion, and political authority. We therefore do not understand the dispute between Burke and his "rights of men" opponents unless we see that the point at issue was precisely one of the *title* to political authority.

In the context of this dispute, the "rights of men" were reducible to one: the sovereign right of every individual in the state of nature to govern himself. From this natural right of the individual it followed that society, or at least *civil* society endowed with the authority to govern, was formed and legitimately could only be formed by a voluntary compact among individuals. The compact brought into being a sovereign people which, being composed of originally sovereign and politically equal individuals, was of necessity governed by majority rule. The people, acting by majority, were the authors and always remained the masters of the society's constitution and government.

Burke explained this doctrine of his opponents in the following terms in the sequel to the *Reflections*, which he published in 1791 under the title *An Appeal From the New to the Old Whigs*:

These new whigs hold, that the sovereignty, whether exercised by one or many, did not only originate *from* the people (a position not denied, nor worth denying or assenting to) but that, in the people the same sovereignty constantly and unalienably resides; that the people may lawfully depose kings, not only for misconduct, but without any misconduct at all; that they may set up any new fashion of government for themselves, or continue without any government at their pleasure; that the people are essentially their own rule, and their will the measure of their conduct; that the tenure of magistracy is not a proper subject of contract; because magistrates have duties, but no rights; and that if a contract *de facto* is made with them in one age, allowing that it binds at all, it only binds those who are immediately concerned in it, but does not pass to posterity.[14]

This theory, according to Burke, rested on two false principles which he restated later in the same work. The first was "that the *people*, in forming their commonwealth, have by no means parted with their power over it."[15] The other was the "principle of the right to change a fixed and tolerable constitution of things at pleasure."[16] The words to be underscored in this phrase are, once again, *at pleasure*. The object of Burke's attack was the idea that the will of a majority of the people, told by the head, was its own supreme rule.

Against this notion Burke expounded a theory of political authority derived from an Aristotelian theory of the state set in the framework of the Christian doctrine of creation. "His conception of 'nature' and the 'natural' is in its essence Greek to the core," says John MacCunn. "It is the Aristotelian conception of the organized 'natural' municipal State read into the life of the modern nation."[17] Between the Greek *polis* and the eighteenth-century national state there is, as the French say, a certain distance, and Burke did not take over Aristotle's *Politics* in its entirety. Yet he did base his notion of the state on a teleological conception of nature, as the following passage with its Aristotelian echoes reveals:

The state of civil society...is a state of nature; and much more truly so than a savage and incoherent mode of life. For man is by nature reasonable; and he is never perfectly in his natural state, but when he is placed where reason may be best cultivated, and most predominates. Art is man's nature. We are as much, at least, in a state of nature in formed manhood, as in immature and helpless infancy.[18]

Hence, while society is indeed a contract, as Burke said in the *Reflections*, it is no ordinary contract. It is "a partnership in every virtue, and in all perfection."[19] Society has a natural end or purpose, from which its fundamental law is derived, and that end is the full intellectual and moral development of human nature.

Aristotle has said as much. But Burke also saw man as a creature of God "who gave us our nature, and in giving impressed an invariable law upon it."[20] God, as the Creator of human nature, is also the ultimate author of the state. Even though the state might be founded by a voluntary compact among men—"which in many cases it undoubtedly was," Burke was willing to admit[21]—the binding force of the compact nevertheless came from God because "if no supreme ruler exists, wise to form, and potent to enforce, the moral law, there is no sanction to any contract, virtual or even actual, against the will of prevalent power."[22]

Therefore, as Fennessy has put it, "the natural foundation of society is, for Burke, the given moral relation between men, imposed and sanctioned by the act of creation."[23] Burke's ideological opponents also acknowledged Nature and Nature's God. "Both he and they," in MacCunn's words, "believe that, behind the struggles and the flux of politics, there is an objective order which (to revert once more to Burke's words) holds all things fast in their place, and that to this objective order men and nations are bound to adapt themselves."[24] But for Burke's opponents the objective moral order was the foundation of the natural and imprescriptible rights of men and therefore of the untrammeled sovereignty of the people. Burke's task was to show that, on the contrary, the moral order was the source of political obligations that bound even the people.

To this task he addressed himself with his most closely reasoned argument in *An Appeal From the New to the Old Whigs*. The objective, divinely-founded moral order, he there argues, is the source of duties as well as of rights, and duties are not subject to the will of those who are bound by them. Some duties are assumed voluntarily, but the most basic ones are not; and even voluntarily assumed duties do not for that reason fail to be obligations.[25]

"We have obligations to mankind at large," says Burke,[26] "which are not in consequence of any special voluntary pact. They arise from the relation of man to man, and the relation of man to God, which relations are not matter of choice." They are consequences of God having created men as human beings whose very nature entails morally binding relationships. Why is a man bound to act morally in his relationships with other men? Because, Burke argues, he is a man—a free, rational, and social being—and his nature as a man obliges him to act according to the relationships inherent in that nature. But why must he respect what is inherent in his nature? Because his nature is created by God who has written His will into it as its constitutive law.

The most basic moral obligations thus rest upon the metaphysics of a created universe and are the source of all subsequent and subordinate obligations: "the force of all the pacts which we enter into with any particular person or number of persons amongst mankind, depends upon those prior obligations." The pacts to which Burke refers are relations among persons established by consent. But other derived and subordinate relations are involuntary, yet nonetheless give rise to "compulsive" duties:

> When we marry, the choice is voluntary, but the duties are not matters of choice. They are dictated by the nature of the situation....Parents may not be consenting to their moral relation [to their children]; but consenting or not, they are bound to a long train of burthensome duties towards those with whom they have never made a convention of any sort. Children are not consenting to their relation [to their parents], but their relation, without their actual consent, binds them to its duties; or rather it implies their consent, because the presumed consent of every rational creature is in unison with the predisposed order of things.[27]

Two fundamental principles are laid down in this passage. First, that a relationship may be established by consent, as marriage is, yet once established it creates obligations that are independent of and superior to consent. Second, that a relationship established without consent, like that of a child (who did not ask to be conceived) toward his parents, nevertheless creates obligations. What is more, the obligations not only bind the child without his prior consent, they command his consent because "the presumed consent of every rational creature is in unison with the predisposed order of things." The child is obliged by his nature as a rational creature to consent to his obligations to his parents and to other duties that flow from his initial obligation. The consent, of course, cannot become actual until he reaches the age of reason, but in the meantime it is legitimately presumed because it is obligatory and cannot morally be refused.

In Burke's moral universe, therefore, obligation is antecedent to consent and compels consent. We *must* consent, rationally and freely, to the morally obligatory relationships that are knit into "the predisposed order of things." This order of things is, in its most fundamental meaning, the frame of the world, and, specifically, of the human world as created by God. Derivatively, it is the contingent part of that human world into which a man is born.

To illustrate this last point, one may remark that there is nothing in the nature of man as man that requires that a particular family should exist at a given time and place and in a given social situation. The particular family, therefore, is a contingent reality. Nonetheless, children are born, not to man as man, but to some particular parents who, normally at least, are the founders of a particular family. It is through them that their children get their place in sociey, with its duties as well as its rights. "Men come...into a community with the social state of their parents, endowed with all the benefits, loaded with all the duties of their situation."[28] This situation is, to be sure, contingent inasmuch as it need not have existed. But it does exist, and by existing, it creates obligations for its participants, to which their consent is mandatory.

The root of the obligations is "that the awful author of our being is the author of our place in the order of existence; and that having disposed and marshalled us by a divine tactick, not according to our will, but according to his, he has, in and by that dispostion, virtually subjected us to act the part which belongs to the place assigned us."[29] The divine act of creation extends itself in history through the providence by which God governs the world and establishes particular as well as universal obligations.

If, in this manner, we are "loaded with all the duties" of our family's situation, "so without any stipulation on our own part, are we bound by that relation called our country." For "our country is not a thing of mere physical locality. It consists, in a great measure, in the antient order into which we are born." An order is a relation or, more accurately, a network of relations and, like other human relations, it creates obligations. "The place that determines our duty to our country is a social, civil relation."[30]

It is immaterial, therefore, that "civil society might be at first a voluntary act." Even if it was, what counts is that "its continuance is under a permanent standing covenant, co-existing with the society; and it attaches upon every individual of that society, without any formal act of his own."[31]

The generation that voluntarily founded a civil society are bound by that to which they consented, as are partners in marriage. Later generations are born into the society, not only physically, but morally: they are born to the covenant or constitution and its legal political obligations. As Fennessy says, for Burke "it was not consent that made the social bond, but a created social bond that demanded the consent of free and rational creatures."[32]

These obligations may be conceived, as the men of the eighteenth century commonly did conceive them, as contractual in nature. Even so, Burke argued, a social contract is a moral engagement and does not leave certain members of the society free to change the contract merely because they are the majority:

> Neither the few nor the many have a right to act merely by their will, in any matter connected with duty, trust, engagement, or obligation. The constitution of a country being once settled upon some compact, tacit or expressed, there is no power existing of force to alter it, without the breach of the covenant, or the consent of all the parties. Such is the nature of a contract. And the votes of a majority of the people, whatever their infamous flatterers may teach in order to corrupt their minds, cannot alter the moral any more than they can alter the physical essence of things.[33]

This was a rather narrowly legalistic argument, however, and leaves the impression that the people are obliged to maintain the social contract merely because contracts are morally binding. Burke's argument rested, however, on the wider and deeper premise that man is by nature rational and, because rational, social. In saying that the Creator willed the state as the necessary means to human nature's full development and perfection, Burke meant that God willed the historically-evolved social order.

The particular form that the state took depended on "the circumstances and habits of every country."[34] But once the state, with its particular and historically conditioned form, had come into existence, its constitution became a contingent part of the moral order and was endowed with the binding force of the universal, divinely-willed moral law.

One may feel here that Burke is engaging in intellectual sleight of hand. What justifies this slide from the universal moral order, in all its majesty and perfection, to the constitution of a particular state, with its all too human imperfections, as if they were morally both of one piece? The answer, in Burke's view, is that they are of one piece.

Universal moral imperatives are, as such, abstractions and become actual only in the concrete and particular. As was said above, children are born, not to man as man, but to particular parents in a particular family. They have natural obligations, not, however, to parenthood or to parents in general, but to *their* parents. So, too, while marriage is a natural relationship and carries with it natural obligations, marriage as such exists nowhere. In the real world, Man does not marry Woman. All that happens or can happen is that John marries Mary. They thereby contract marital obligations that are rooted in the complementary natures of the two sexes. But the obligations are not to the opposite sex as such, but to each other as individual persons.

Similarly, while it is meaningful to say that God wills the state because man's rational nature requires civil society, civil society cannot exist in the abstract and simply as such. If civil society implies moral obligations, those obligations can take concrete form and become actually binding only in a particular state under a particular constitution. "Constitutions," as Burke once put it, "furnish the civil means of getting at the natural."[35] Or, as he said in praise of the British constitution, "The foundation of government is there laid, not in imaginary rights of men,...but in political convenience, and in human nature; either as that nature is universal, or as it is modified by local habits and social aptitudes."[36] In the created universe, the necessary is realized in the contingent, the universal in the particular, the natural in the conventional. The distinctions among these are valid, but in actual existence they are all of one piece. The universal moral order is the order of a real, historically-existing world.

Burke thus speaks the language of the social contract theory, but with a difference. He begins his most oft-quoted passages on the roots of political obligation with the words, "Society is indeed a contract."[37] Yet, as C. E. Vaughan points out, with some exaggeration, in Burke's hands the implications of the contract undergo a profound change:

The mere act of consent, which to Locke was all in all, has ceased to be of any importance. It has, in fact, come to stand for something very different; an obligation which is binding upon all men, whether they choose to recognise it or no. It is no longer the consent itself, but the thing to which consent has been given—no longer the contract, but the particular obligation contracted—that counts. Under these circumstances, the consent, the contract, is manifestly no true consent, no contract at all. The consent, so far from being actually given, is tacitly assumed. The contract, so far from being matter of choice, is imposed by the necessities of man's nature.[38]

The derivation of the bond of civil society from the necessities of man's nature shifts the emphasis, not only from consent to obligation, but also from rights to purposes. With Burke, the inquiry into the source of political obligation no longer begins with men's pre-political rights in a state of nature, but with the purposes of civil society. The *"real* rights of men," says Burke, are not the abstract original rights of men, but the benefits that civil society can and should confer on them. They are the goals or purposes of civil society, rooted ultimately in the nature of man and in the creative act of God. These goals are not only men's rights but, as Burke explained in *An Appeal*, are also the source of their obligations in civil society:

> Men without their choice derive benefits from that association; without their choice they are subjected to duties in consequence of these benefits; and without their choice they enter into a virtual obligation as binding as any that is actual. Look through the whole of life and the whole system of duties. Much the strongest moral obligations are such as were never the results of our option.[39]

To say this is not to deny that men have rights, nor even that these rights are in a valid sense natural. But it is to deny that the authority of civil society derives from the consent of men who were by nature independent of any civil bond and who therefore retain the natural right to make and unmake the civil bond at pleasure. The structure of authority and the form of government are framed, not in the light of the original independence and equality of men in the state of nature, but with a view to the benefits which civil society exists to confer upon them. "Government is not made in virtue of natural rights, which may and do exist in total independence of it....Government is a contrivance of human wisdom to provide for human *wants*. Men have a right that these wants should be provided for by this wisdom."[40]

The constitution of civil society is determined by human needs, not by original rights. Consequently, "the whole organization of government becomes a consideration of convenience,"[41] i.e., of aptitude for satisfying those needs, and "the true statesman...thinks of the place in which political power is to be lodged, with no other attention, than as it may render the more or the less practicable, its salutary restraint, and its prudent direction."[42] A properly made constitution is one that places power in the hands of those who have the requisite wisdom and virtue to direct society in such a way as to provide for men's genuine needs.

But the needs which civil society exists to satisfy are many and varied, and so its constitution cannot be framed for any single or narrow purpose. "The nature of man is intricate; the objects of society are of the greatest possible complexity; and therefore no simple disposition or direction of power can be suitable either to man's nature, or to the quality of his affairs."[43]   It is the ends of civil society, not its origins, that shape its constitution, but those ends are complex and so, too, should the constitution be.

But, however complex the ends of civil society, they may be subsumed under one general goal: the good of the people. This goal is the only one that government may legitimately intend: "all political power which is set over men,...being wholly artificial, and for so much a derogation from the natural equality of mankind at large, ought to be some way or other exercised ultimately for their benefit."[44]   End or purpose, however, is a coin the obverse side of which is result or effect. Political power is not justified by the ends it merely intends, but by those it actually achieves. The good of its members is the purpose of civil society but the purpose is morally inadequate unless it becomes an accomplished result.

"The practical consequences of any political tenet go a great way in deciding upon its value," Burke said. "...What in the result is likely to produce evil, is politically false: that which is productive of good, politically true."[45]   It was on this basis that he passed judgment on the French Revolution. "I cannot think that what is done in France is beneficial to the human race," he said. But, he admitted, "if it were, the English constitution ought no more to stand against it than the antient constitution of the kingdom in which the new system prevails."[46]   He used the same criterion for old institutions, but all the more easily because their results were already visible. "Old establishments are tried by their effects. If the people are happy, united, wealthy, and powerful, we presume the rest. We conclude that to be good from whence good is derived."[47]

To summarize, in his critique of the natural rights-social contract theory Burke shifted the basis of political authority from original rights, individual consent, and the sovereignty of the popular majority to the purposes and achieved results of civil society. Civil society, though in itself an artificial and conventional human construct, has a natural claim on men's obedience because it has a natural and God-given purpose: to serve the needs of human nature. Political obligation is therefore in principle antecedent to political consent. Since, however, civil society as such is an abstraction and has real existence only in concrete and historically-conditioned forms, men are obliged to accept and respect the particular constitution to which they are born. But the obligation, in the concrete, is not absolute and unqualified. That constitution has a claim on men's obedience which in fact has served them well or at least, in the exceptional case of a justified revolution, gives solid promise of doing so.

It is in this intellectual framework, which Burke went to great pains to establish, that we must set his thesis that prescription is a title to political authority. There have been those who found the framework, like the doctrine of prescription itself, mystifying. For example, G. P. Gooch says that "despite his passionate denunciation of metaphysical politics, Burke's own philosophy is suffused with mysticism. His profoundly religious temper led him to regard the moral relations and duties of man and the order of society as of divine institution."[48] Such language can be used, however, only by those who cannot tell the difference between metaphysics and mysticism. There is nothing particularly mystical about Burke's metaphysics. As Russell Kirk says, his "view of the cosmos may be true, or it may be delusory; but it is not obscure, let alone incomprehensible."[49] But without it, his doctrine of prescription is indeed incomprehensible

Burke did not mean by prescription of government—despite what he seemed to say—that government gained authority merely by lasting a long time or that men's rights and obligations in civil society were independent of natural law. He did not mean this even in his "Speech on the Reform of the Representation of the Commons in Parliament," where he said that the sole authority of the British constitution was that it had existed time out of mind.[50]

What he was getting at may be gleaned from a speech he wrote for delivery in the Commons in 1792:

> The foundations, on which obedience to government is founded, are not to be constantly discussed. That we are here, supposes the discussion already made and the dispute settled. We must assume the rights of what represents the Publick to control the individual, to make his will and his acts to submit to their will, until some intolerable grievance shall make us know that it does not answer its end, and will submit neither to reformation nor restraint.[51]

The centuries-old existence of the British constitution was sufficient proof that the nation had already decided where political authority was to be lodged. That decision was not to be reopened with every new generation, but must be taken as right and binding until some intolerable and irremediable grievance showed that government was not answering its end and was refusing to achieve the purpose for which it was instituted.

But the established constitution, however long it has endured, cannot be its own self-sufficient norm of goodness. Burke's position on this point is indicated by his answer to Warren Hastings during the latter's impeachment as the East India Company's Governor-General in India. Hastings had argued that when the Company acquired sovereignty over Indian states, it had accepted despotic and arbitrary power which he, Hastings, exercised in its name. For such was the traditional constitution of Asia and such, given the conditions of Asiatic society, was the only way in which Asiatics could be ruled.

If a prescriptive constitution were established by mere passage of time, Hastings's argument would be conclusive, at least for Burke. But Burke replied that neither the Company nor the British government could have acquired or given arbitrary power, "because arbitrary power is a thing, which neither any man can hold nor any man can give." All power is from God and

is bound by the eternal laws of Him, that gave it, with which no human authority can dispense;...The title of conquest makes no difference at all. No conquest can give such a right; for conquest, that is force, cannot convert its own injustice into a just title, by which it may rule others at its pleasure.[52]

We notice once again that the unforgivable sin is to claim the right to rule at pleasure. It matters not whether the government be constitutionally democratic or despotic:

Despotism if it means any thing, that is at all defensible, means a mode of government, bound by no written rules, and coerced by no controlling magistracies, or well settled orders in the state. But if it has no written law, it neither does, nor can, cancel the primeval, indefeasible, unalterable law of nature, and of nations; and if no magistracies control its exertions, those exertions must derive their limitation and direction either from the equity and moderation of the ruler, or from downright revolt on the part of the subject by rebellion, divested of all its criminal qualities.[53]

"There is a sacred veil to be drawn over the beginnings of all governments," according to Burke, and he was willing to contend that "prudence and discretion make it necessary to throw something of the same drapery over more recent foundations" such as British rule in India.[54] Nonetheless, in accepting governmental powers from the Mogul Empire, the East India Company accepted the responsibility "to observe the laws, rights, usages, and customs of the natives; and to pursue their benefit in all things. For this duty was inherent in the nature, institution, and purpose of the office which they received."[55]

The authority of government thus turns out once more to depend on its fulfillment of its natural purposes, and no prescription derived from mere duration will suffice to justify a government that frustrates these purposes. The prescriptive constitution is the constitution that has proved itself not only by long but by good performance, and the good performance is more decisive than the long. As Gerald W. Chapman says, prescription "makes the point that in all the depth of existence, past and present, there is no ground and sanction for any constitution or state except as by a prescriptive use it is found to be good."[56]

The same point is made by Burke's assertion that prescription can be anticipated. Speaking of the French Revolution, he said:

> If they had set up this new experimental government, as a necessary substitute for an expelled tyranny, mankind would anticipate the time of prescription, which, through long usage, mellows into legality governments that were violent in their commencement. All those who have affections which lead them to the conservation of civil order would recognise, even in its cradle, the child as legitimate, which has been produced from those principles of cogent expediency to which all just governments owe their birth, and on which they justify their continuance.[57]

Burke, of course, did not admit that the traditional French monarchy was a tyranny or that the revolutionary substitute for it was necessary. On the contrary, he said of the Revolution, "It is a recent wrong, and can plead no prescription."[58] But he did say that a revolution could be justified by "those principles of cogent expediency to which all just governments owe their birth, and on which they justify their continuance." "Then what is the standard of expedience?" he asked in another context. "Expedience is that, which is good for the community, and good for every individual in it."[59]

Now, if all just governments are founded on cogent expediency, among them must be even those governments that were violent and unjust in their commencement, but which prescription, through long usage, has mellowed into legality. Unjust in their beginnings, they have become just and have acquired a prescriptive title by their service to the people whom they govern. This is why prescription can be anticipated: the principles of cogent expediency may be operative from the beginning in a violent but necessary change of government.

Prescription of government, therefore, does not depend upon the possession of authority in good faith from the beginning. It does not answer the question whether the predecessors of those who now hold authority acquired it rightfully or whether the existing constitution was originally conceived in justice. Prescription rules out these questions as irrelevant to the only point that is now at issue: is the existing constitution legitimate and does government established under it have the right to rule? The doctrine of prescription answers that question with a qualified affirmative: yes, if it governs for the welfare of the community.

Prescription does not mean that old institutions must be preserved merely because they are old, as if, in Lucas's words, "time alone became the material and efficient cause of prescription." Burleigh Wilkins has pointed out that "Burke's opposition to slavery and the slave trade...shows that the historicity of an institution or a practice is not always in his opinion a fact of moral significance in favour of the institution or practice in question let alone a sufficient condition of its moral worth."[60]

Burke himself explicitly says: "'Monopoly' is contrary to 'Natural Right.'...No monopoly can, therefore, be prescribed in; because contrary to common right." He allows that the state "may grant a monopoly" because, "representing all its individuals," it "may contract for them." But nothing follows from this except that persons may by their own consent or that of their agents surrender the exercise of at least some of their natural rights. Burke adds that the state "ought not to grant this monopoly on arbitrary principles, but for the good of the whole."[61] The basic principle remains that prescription cannot maintain a monopoly contrary to the claims of natural or common right.

Nor is age alone a sufficient reason for preserving institutions of government, as Burke explained in his "Speech on Economical Reform" in

1780. When the reason for having them is gone, he said, "it is absurd to preserve nothing but the burden of them."[62] It is not only absurd, but dangerous, for "there is a time, when men will not suffer bad things because their ancestors have suffered worse. There is a time, when the hoary head of inveterate abuse will neither draw reverence, nor obtain protection."[63]

On the other hand, age counts for a great deal in judging the value of institutions, and it is therefore wise to recognize it. As Burke said in the same speech, "People will bear an old establishment when its excess is corrected, who will revolt at a new one."[64] There is a still deeper reason for respecting and conserving what is old. All government, Burke was convinced, "stands upon opinion,"[65] because "the only firm seat of all authority is in the minds, affections, and interests of the people."[66] But, "if we must resort to prepossessions for the ground of opinion, it is in the nature of man rather to defer to the wisdom of times passed, whose weakness is not before his eyes, than to the present, of whose imbecility he has daily experience. Veneration of antiquity is congenial to the human mind."[67]

It is to be noticed in this and the numerous other passages where Burke praises veneration of antiquity, that he presents it, not as being in itself the prescriptive title to authority, but as an explanation of why people are willing to accept authority. The statesman, therefore, is not obliged to preserve what is old merely because it is old. But it is wisdom on his part to recognize the advantage offered him by what is old, to preserve it insofar as he can, and to modify it when he must rather than abolish it. Reform, per se, is preferable to revolution.

Prescription, then, is no bar to reform. During the crisis between Great Britain and her American colonies, Burke never questions Britain's prescriptive right to legislate for the Americans, though he urged great moderation in its use. In 1777, for example, he wrote to the Sheriffs of Bristol, whose representative in Parliament he then was:

> When I first came into a publick trust, I found your parliament in possession of an unlimited legislative power over the colonies. I could not open the statute book without seeing the actual exercise of it, more or less, in all cases whatsoever. This possession passed with me for a title. It does so in all human affairs. No man examines into the defects of his title to his paternal estate, or to his established government.[68]

But Burke could contemplate a change in the prescriptive constitution, as is shown by the following passage from an *Address to the British Colonists in North America,* which he drafted as a last-minute attempt at reconciliation, probably in 1777:

> This Constitution has...admitted innumerable improvements, either for the correction of the original scheme, or for removing corruptions, or for bringing its principles better to suit those changes, which have successively happened in the circumstances of the nation, or in the manners of the people
> We feel that the growth of the Colonies is such a change of circumstances; and that our present dispute is an exigency as pressing as any, which ever demanded a revision of our Government. Publick troubles have often called upon this Country to look into its Constitution. It has ever been bettered by such a revision. If our happy and luxuriant increase of dominion, and our diffused population, have outgrown the limits of a Constitution made for a contracted object, we ought to bless God, who has furnished us with this noble occasion for displaying our skill and beneficence in enlarging the scale of rational happiness, and of making the politick generosity of this Kingdom as extensive as its fortune.[69]

Even the French Revolution, while it certainly strengthened Burke's devotion to the traditional order of things, did not lead him to make any fundamental change in the above conception of the constitution. The British constitution, he said in *An Appeal,* "is the result of the thoughts of many minds, and in many ages."[70] Let us, then, he urged,

> follow our ancestors, men not without a rational, though without an exclusive confidence in themselves; who, by respecting the reason of others, who, by looking backward as well as forward, by the modesty as well as by the energy of their minds, went on, insensibly drawing this constitution nearer and nearer to its perfection by never departing from its fundamental principles, nor introducing any amendment which had not a subsisting root in the laws, constitution, and usages of the kingdom.[71]

The prescriptive constitution does not rule out change; indeed, its development and even its survival depend on change. But it does rule out radical change, the kind of change that either is or pretends to be a clean break with the past. For it is continuity with the past that makes the constitution a predisposed order of things to which men are born and which has an antecedent claim on their obedience and consent. There is no predictable limit to the changes that a prescriptive constitution may undergo, provided that the direction of change continues to be set by the controlling end, the good of the people. But the changes must be gradual and evolutionary, "insensibly drawing [the] constitution nearer and nearer to its perfection by never departing from its fundamental principles."

Finally, prescription does not mean that authority cannot be lost by abuse. Burke urged taking political power in India away from the East India Company on a general principle that would apply against any government, however ancient, that had become inimical to the purposes of all just governments:

> that this body, being totally perverted from the purposes of its institution, is utterly incorrigible; and because they are incorrigible, both in conduct and constitution, power ought to be taken out of their hands; just on the same principles on which have been made all the just changes and revolutions of government that have taken place since the beginning of the world.[72]

What the doctrine of prescription really means, therefore, is that the abuse of political authority is the only moral ground on which it can be lost. Power is rightly taken from a government which has become "totally perverted from the purposes of its institution." But that the constitution of a state originated in wrong, or that it contains no mechanism for registering the formal consent of a majority of the present generation, is irrelevant. These are "speculative," not "real" grievances in Burke's eyes, and they do not suffice to justify the refusal of political obedience.

Yet to assert that prescriptive authority can be lost only by abuse is not to deny that all just governments depend on the consent of the governed. Burke, at any rate, thought that the two propositions were reconcilable. In his early treatise, "A Tract Relative to the Laws against Popery in Ireland," he expounded a thesis which is consistent with and throws light upon his later political theory in this respect.

Having described how the penal laws against Catholics, who were the bulk of the Irish population, deprived them of their elementary human rights, Burke remarked: "A Law against the majority of the people is in substance a Law against the people itself: its extent determines its invalidity."[73] In other words, "a Law directed against the mass of the Nation" simply lacks the authority of the law. The reason that Burke gives for this principle is significant:

> In all forms of Government the people is the true Legislator; and whether the immediate and instrumental cause of the Law be a single person, or many, the remote and efficient cause is the consent of the people, either actual or implied; and such consent is absolutely essential to its validity.[74]

This conception of the people as the ultimate authors of all law is as compatible with monarchy or aristocracy as with democracy. Burke's point here is that, under any form of government, the people, whose actual or implied consent is necessary, cannot be understood to consent to a law that excludes them "not from favours, privileges and trusts, but from the common advantages of society."[75] When the people subject themselves to government, "it is their judgment they give up, not their right."

It is their judgment they give up....Burke explains:

> The people, indeed, are presumed to consent to whatever the Legislature ordains for their benefit; and they are to acquiesce in it, though they do not clearly see into the propriety of the means, by which they are conducted to that desirable end. This they owe as an act of homage and just deference to a reason, which the necessity of Government has made superiour to their own.[76]

The necessity of government (founded in the nature of man and the will of God) requires the people to submit their judgment to the superior reason of those who govern. The consent of the governed is a rational consent, not an arbitrary one which the people may give or withhold at pleasure. Yet neither the government nor the people themselves have a "right to make a Law prejudicial to the whole community...because it would be made against the principle of a superior Law, which it is not in the power of any community, or of the whole race of man, to alter—I mean the will of Him, who gave us our nature, and in giving impressed an invariable Law upon it."[77]

The consent of the people, in short, is given by implication, and is therefore legitimately presumed, to whatever is done for their benefit. But what is clearly not done for their benefit cannot have their consent, and so is invalid. This theory of the relationship between political obligation and consent harmonizes with Burke's later statements and is not an early position that he later abandoned.

It is consistent with his later contention that the fact that "a nation has long existed and flourished under" a "settled scheme of government...is a better presumption even of the *choice* of a nation, far better than any sudden and temporary arrangement by actual election."[78] It is consistent with his statement in the *Reflections*: "There is no qualification for government but virtue and wisdom, actual or presumptive."[79] And it leads into his argument, in *An Appeal*, that the upper classes enjoy a legitimate presumption in favor of their wisdom and virtue. He there maintains that the state of civil society, which is man's truly natural state, necessarily generates a class structure which in turn generally produces a natural aristocracy of the wise and good. The members of this aristocracy "form in nature, as she operates in the common modification of society, the leading, guiding, and governing part." To deprive them of authority, in the name of the political equality of all citizens, is "a horrible usurpation."[80]

All government, for Burke, is a trust to be exercised for the benefit of the people by those who are qualified for the task by wisdom and virtue. That a nation has long existed and flourished under a constitution is an indication that the trust has been and is being fulfilled. It is also an indication that the people consent to the trustees and their government. But if, for the moment, a majority of them do not consent, it is no matter. Their consent is legitimately presumed because the natural law requires their consent to a good government. Prescription of government is a part of the law of nature.

Burke's conception of the natural aristocracy is obviously anti-democratic and has been criticized, reasonably enough, on the ground that it too facilely identifies the wise and the good with the well-born and the well-to-do. His defense of the unreformed representative system in Great Britain is simply out of date today. So, too, is his interpretation of the British constitution as a contract to which King, Lords, and Commons are parties. But his doctrine of prescription, though used to justify those governmental arrangements, has a significance that transcends them and is still relevant to political theory.

It is a continuing theoretical problem why men should be morally obliged to obey other men in civil society. The myth of the state of nature and the social contract has almost wholly disappeared from formal political thought by now. Yet the assumptions of liberal individualism which that myth embodied remain as the premises of much of contemporary political discourse, as Alexander Bickel pointed out. To those who find individualism an inadequate basis for explaining either the facts or the obligations of political life, Burke's doctrine of prescription offers an alternative that could be developed in a contemporary political theory. Without attempting such a development here, one may suggest that its central theme would be the priority of purpose to consent as the source of political obligation.

Notes

"Prescription of Government" appears as Chapter Five in
Francis Canavan, *Edmund Burke: Prescription and Providence* (Durham, NC:
Carolina Academic Press, 1987, pp. 113-35.
The essay was published under the title "Burke on Prescription of Government" in
Review of Politics 35 (1973).

1. *Reflections* in *Works* (Rivington) 5:276, appr. 61% into the work.

2. "On Edmund Burke's Doctrine of Prescription," *Historical Journal* 11 (1968), p. 36.

3. *Letter to Richard Burke* in *Works* (Rivington) 9:449, last paragraph of the work.

4. Lucas, p. 36.

5. Lucas, p. 35.

6. Lucas, pp. 40-41.

7. Lucas, p. 62.

8. Lucas, p. 36. Burke is in flat disagreement with Warburton, who holds that "the Law of Prescription directly contradicts the Law of Nature and Nations." *Alliance of Church and State* [1736] p. 127. [William Warburton, 1678-1779, was Bishop of Gloucester and collaborator with Alexander Pope, particularly on the *Dunciad*. Burke owned the 1748 edition of his book on church and state, which argues for an alliance between the two institutions on Lockean grounds. —DR]

9. R. R. Fennessy, *Burke, Paine and the Rights of Man: A Difference of Opinions* (The Hague: Martinus Nijhoff, 1963), pp. 131-32.

10. "Speech on the Reform of Representation in Commons" (1782) in *Works* (Rivington) 10:93, third paragraph.

11. *Reflections* in *Works* (Rivington) 5:119-120, appr. 23% into the work.

12. *Correspondence* 6:95.

13. "Speech on the Reform of Representation in Commons," in *Works* (Rivington) 10:96, appr. 29% into the work.

14. *Appeal* in *Works* (Rivington) 6:147, appr. 38% into the work. Cf. *Thoughts on French Affairs* in *Works* (Rivington) 7:18, appr. 13% into the work. In this chapter, subsequent references to the *Reflections on the Revolution in France* and the *Appeal* will be given by short title, page number, and approximate location. They come from vols. 5 and 6, respectively, of the Rivington edition of Burke's *Works*.

15. *Appeal*, p. 200, appr. 66% into the work.

16. *Appeal*, p. 230, appr. 81% into the work.

17. *Political Philosophy of Burke* (London: Arnold, 1913), p. 54.

18. *Appeal*, p. 218, appr. 75% into the work.

19. *Reflections*, p. 184, appr. 38% into the work.

20. "Tract on the Popery Laws," in *Works* (Rivington) 9:349-50, appr. 34% into the work.

21. *Appeal*, p. 205, appr. 68% into the work.

22. *Appeal,* p. 205, appr. 68% into the work.

23. Fennessy, p. 110.

24. MacCunn, p. 144.

25. *Appeal,* pp. 204-207, appr. 68% into the work.

26. *Appeal,* p. 206, appr. 69% into the work.

27. *Appeal,* pp. 206-207, appr. 69% into the work.

28. *Appeal,* p. 207, appr. 69% into the work.

29. *Appeal,* p. 206, appr. 69% into the work.

30. *Appeal,* p. 207, appr. 69% into the work.

31. *Appeal,* p. 205, appr. 68% into the work.

32. Fennessy, p. 114.

33. *Appeal,* pp. 201-202, appr. 66% into the work. Cf. *Reflections,* pp. 57-58, appr. 8% into the work.

34. *Appeal,* p. 133, appr. 31% into the work.

35. *Works* (Rivington) 9:112, appr. 89% into the fourth of the *Letters on a Regicide Peace.*

36. *Appeal,* p. 257, appr. 95% into the work.

37. *Reflections,* p. 183, appr. 38% into the work.

38. *Studies in the History of Political Philosophy before and after Rousseau,* ed. A. G. Little, 2 vols. (Manchester: University of Manchester Press, 1925), 2:53.

39. *Appeal,* p. 205, appr. 68% into the work.

40. *Reflections,* pp. 122-123, appr. 23% into the work.

41. *Reflections,* p. 123, appr. 23% into the work.

42. *Appeal,* p. 203, appr. 67% into the work.

43. *Reflections,* p. 125, appr. 24% into the work.

44. "Speech on Fox's East India Bill," in *Works* (Rivington) 4:11, appr. 7% into the work.

45. *Appeal,* p. 210, appr. 71% into the work.

46. "Heads for Consideration on the Present State of Affairs," *Works* (Rivington) 7:114-115, last paragraph.

47. *Reflections,* p. 310, appr. 69% into the work.

48. "Europe and the French Revolution," *Cambridge Modern History,* 13 vols. (New York: Macmillan, 1907-1911), 8:757.

49. "Burke and the Philosophy of Prescription," *Journal of the History of Ideas* 14 (1953): 368.

50. *Works* (Rivington) 10:96, appr. 29% into the speech.

51. "On the Petition of the Unitarian Society," in *Works* (Rivington) 10:51, appr. 50% into the work.

52. "Speeches in the Impeachment of Warren Hastings," Fourth Day, Feb. 16, 1788, in *Works* (Rivington) 13:166-167, appr. 62% into the speech. [Note: some editions designate Feb. 16, 1788 as the "second day."]

53. "Speeches in Impeachment," Fourth Day, in *Works* (Rivington) 13:169-170, appr. 65% into the speech.

54. "Speeches in Impeachment," Fourth Day, Feb. 16, 1788, in *Works* (Rivington) 13:95-96, appr. 6% into the speech.

55. "Speeches in Impeachment," Third Day, Feb. 15, 1788, in *Works* (Rivington) 13:24, appr. 29% into the speech.

56. *Edmund Burke: the Practical Imagination* (Cambridge, MA: Harvard University Press, 1967), p. 166.

57. *Reflections,* p. 298, appr. 66% into the work.

58. *Works* (Rivington) 8:189-191, appr. 85% into the first of the *Letters on a Regicide Peace.*

59. "Speech on the Reform of Representation in Commons," in *Works* (Rivington) 10:100, appr. 53% into the work.

60. *The Problem of Burke's Political Philosophy* (Oxford: Clarendon Press, 1967), p. 237. Cf. "Letter to Henry Dundas on the Negro Code" in *Works* (Rivington) 9:276-315.

61. "Notes on Copy-Right Bill and Monopolies Generally," *Correspondence* (1844) 4:459-60.

62. "Speech on Economical Reform" in *Works* (Rivington) 3:278, appr. 39% into the speech.

63. "Speech on Economical Reform," in *Works* (Rivington) 3:246-247, appr. 14% into the speech.

64. "Speech on Economical Reform," in *Works* (Rivington) 3:313, appr. 68% into the speech.

65. "Speech on the Reform of Representation in Commons," in *Works* (Rivington) 10:93, opening paragraph.

66. *Works* (Rivington) 9:178, appr. 23% into the *Address to the King* [written by 1777].

67. *Works* (Rivington) 9:370, appr. 62% into the "Tract on Popery Laws."

68. "Letter to the Sheriffs of Bristol," in *Works* (Rivington) 3:177, appr. 60% into the work.

69. *Works* (Rivington) 9:212, appr. 82% into the work.

70. *Appeal*, p. 261, appr. 97% into the work.

71. *Appeal*, pp. 265-66, three paragraphs from the end.

72. "Speech on Fox's East India Bill" in *Works* (Rivington) 4:111, appr. 84% into the work.

73. "Tract on Popery Laws," in *Works* (Rivington) 9:347-48, appr. 31% into the work.

74. "Tract on Popery Laws" in *Works* (Rivington) 9:348, appr. 31% into the work.

75. "Tract on Popery Laws" in *Works* (Rivington) 9:349, appr. 33% into the work.

76. "Tract on Popery Laws" in *Works* (Rivington) 9:348-349, appr. 32% into the work.

77. "Tract on Popery Laws" in *Works* (Rivington) 9:349-350, appr. 33% into the work.

78. "Speech on the Reform of Representation in Commons" in *Works* (Rivington) 10:96, appr. 29% into the speech.

79. *Reflections*, p. 106, appr. 19% into the work.

80. *Appeal*, pp., 217-219, appr. 74% into the work.

ROBERT NISBET

21
Sources of Conservatism

Conservatism did not become a part of political speech until about 1830 in England. But its philosophical substance was brought into being in 1790 by Edmund Burke in his *Reflections on the Revolution in France*. Rarely in the history of thought has a body of ideas been as closely dependent upon a single man as modern conservatism is upon Edmund Burke and his fiery reaction to the French Revolution. In remarkable degree, the central themes of conservatism over the last two centuries are but widenings of themes enunciated by Burke with specific reference to revolutionary France.

He himself was clearly aware that the French Revolution was at bottom a European revolution, but that truth had to await the writings of such ardent traditionalists as Bonald, de Maistre, and Tocqueville for its detailed statement. In Burke and in them we find the outlines of a philosophy of history that was the diametric opposite of the Whig or progressive philosophy; and we find too a perspicuous statement of the importance of feudalism and of other historically grown structures such as patriarchal family, local community, church, guild and region which, under the centralizing, individualizing influence of natural law philosophy, had almost disappeared from European political thought in the seventeenth and eighteenth centuries.[1] In the writings of Hobbes, Locke, and Rousseau, traditional society and its historically evolved groups and its traditions was recognized dimly at best, almost always with hostility. What alone was central was the hard reality of the individual; institutions were penumbral.

Burke, above any other single thinker, changed this whole individualistic perspective. His *Reflections*, by its denunciations of both Revolutionaries and the line of natural rights theorists leading up to the Revolutionaries, played a key role in the momentous change of perspectives involved in the passage from eighteenth-century to nineteenth-century Europe. Within a generation after the publication of *Reflections* a whole *Aufklärung* blazed up in the West, at its core nothing more than an anti-Enlightenment. Such voices as Bonald, de Maistre, and Chateaubriand in France, Coleridge and Southey in England, Haller, Savigny, and Hegel in Germanic thought, and Donoso y Cortes and Balmes in Spain were resonating throughout the West. In America, John Adams, Alexander Hamilton, and Randolph of Roanoke issued their own warnings and proposals. And all voices, European and American, were rich in respect to Edmund Burke as prophet.

To understand an effect upon the Western mind as immediate as Burke's *Reflections'* was, we must take careful note of the substantial vein of a traditionalism of principle as well as emotion that had been growing up in Western Europe throughout the eighteenth century. Given our normal predilection for the more exciting Enlightenment mentality of the Voltaires, Diderots, and d'Holbachs, it is easy to miss, in the histories, this counterforce to the high rationalism and individualism of the Enlightenment. But it is there all the same, a product at one and the same time of the *Church* and its still considerable numbers of philosophers and theologians committed to orthodoxy instead of the ideas of natural religion and natural ethics which had sprung out of the natural law movement of the seventeenth century. The more that the *philosophes* declared the enlightenment of their doctrines of natural rights, the more the philosophers and historians in the universities—all religiously oriented, of course—appealed to the traditions which had sustained Europe for more than a thousand years.

In addition to the church, there were the historic towns and guilds throughout Western Europe which turned increasingly, as the cosmopolitanism of the Enlightenment spread, to their own native histories, traditions, saints, heroes, governments, and crafts. There were poets, composers, performers, artists, artisans, annalists, and chroniclers quite content to work with the materials of their own communities instead of going off to Europe's capitals for possible fortune and fame. Search for native dialects, folk literature, long-ignored creators in the arts, military heroes of the distant past, and others comparable to these, was in full swing in many parts of Germany by the middle of the eighteenth century. The fascination with the Middle Ages that would grip so many minds in England and France in the nineteenth century was widely evident in Germany and Eastern Europe throughout the eighteenth century. There was no single city in Germany that could exert intellectual power over a whole nation of the sort that both Paris and London did in their countries. Traditionalism was almost inevitable in the spirit of localism that gripped Germany and also, not to be ignored, in parts of England and France.

Long before the Revolution in France, Burke, in his *Annual Register*—book reviews which he wrote himself—and speeches had made clear his distaste for the typical rationalist mind of the French Enlightenment, and for none more than Rousseau whose talent Burke recognized but whose morals and politics he found repugnant in the extreme.[2] He detested the Grub Street mentality in London, Paris, and every place else, including New York and Boston, where it was found. From the beginning of his career in England Burke was on the side of what he saw as Britain's "Great Tradition" in political history.

There was thus background, in Burke himself, and in England and in all Western Europe, for the kind of philosophy he set forth forthrightly in his *Reflections*. Few if any in Europe could equal Burke's eloquence of assault upon the Jacobins and their legislation in France, but by 1789 there was a considerable number of Europeans whose essential conservatism of mind was deeply ravaged by the Revolution. The words *conservative* and *conservatism* applied to politics did not appear in the West until about 1830, but the substance long preceded the words.

So far as English conservative thought is concerned, there is no doubt something which Burke, a devoted Whig, owed to the Tory Party, which was older and favored by the monarchy and much of the aristocracy. And Burke was a friend of that quintessential Tory, Dr. Johnson. But what Burke wrote in a letter to Boswell perhaps clarifies his relation to Tory principles: "I dined with your friend Dr. Johnson on Saturday at Sir Joshua's. We had a very good day, as we had not a sentence, word, syllable, letter, comma, or tittle of any of the elements that make politics."[3] In the general melee of post-revolutionary politics in Britain it is probable that Tories and Whigs found themselves together often on particular issues and that by the time the new Conservative Party took shape under Peel, there was mixture too of Tory and Whig tenets. But nineteenth-century British conservatism is much more the issue of Burke and his works than of any Tories. Use of "Tory" by modern British Conservatives has been somewhat more affectation than anything really substantive.

Burke paid a heavy price at home for his call to traditionalists throughout Europe to rally themselves against the French Revolution. He was widely charged, abroad as well as at home, with inconsistency bordering on faithlessness of principle in taking the position he did on the Revolution in France. How, it was asked repeatedly, could he have supported the colonists in America and other tyrannized peoples of the world as he had and now turn on the French seeking emancipation from monarchical despotism? Whigs in England, including his long time friend and ally Charles Fox, broke with him on the Revolution. However, this is not the place to try to settle accounts; all we can do here is summarize briefly the case Burke made for himself. He was upholding in France the same basic principles which had actuated his defenses of the Americans, Indians, and Irish against the "arbitrary power" of the British government. In each of these defenses he had made his case on behalf of the native, historical tradition of a people under assault by an alien power. There could be no rational talk about liberty for the Americans—after all, they were fundamentally an English people abroad, living under the same prescriptions and conventions which governed the British—without the premise of a sufficient autonomy for natural development of American potentialities. The same held for Ireland and India, in each case an indigenous morality under attack by a foreign one.

In France, the assault upon traditional government and morality came from a small group of Frenchmen, the Jacobins, but, Burke argued, the essential principles of the matter were no different from those obtaining in his defense of the American colonists. The issue was freedom then and it was the same now; the violation of freedom was no less due to the fact that the minority governing was of French blood. From Burke's point of view the Jacobins were as much aggressors upon French history and tradition as the British East India Company had been upon Indian culture. France under the Jacobins was "exactly like a country of conquest." Moreover, "acting as conquerors" the Jacobins used force on the French people precisely as would an "invading army."

In Burke's eyes the work of the Jacobins across the Channel was the very opposite of the work done by the American colonists: the work of freedom from "arbitrary power." Rather it was leveling in the name of equality, nihilism in the name of liberty, and power, absolute and total, in the name of the people. The American Revolution had sought freedom for actual, living human beings and their customs and habits. But the French Revolution was far less interested in the actual and the living—the peasants, bourgeoisie, clergy, nobility, etc.—than in the kind of human beings the Revolutionary leaders believed they could manufacture through education, persuasion, and when necessary force and terror. Not since Reformation insurrections in the name of God, Burke thought, had a revoluution occurred in Europe so monolithically consecrated to the salvation of man and to his complete spiritual remaking. Precisely as Anabaptists had been willing to lay waste to all that interfered with their creation of the New Christian Man, so the Jacobins, Burke perceived, were willing to destroy all institutions that interfered with the making of Revolutionary Man. Burke wrote: "All circumstances taken together, the French Revolution is the most astonishing that has hitherto happened in the world."[4]

Tocqueville stressed this uniqueness of the French Revolution, also specifically disavowing a significant relationship between it and the American Revolution. That revolution had been the work of men with a clear stake in society, but not the French. On this point Tocqueville agreed completely with Burke—as he did on more than a few points. The dependence of Tocquevillian analysis—in the measured language of scholarly objectivity and with no overriding suggestion of hostility—upon Burkean polemic has not yet been sufficiently appreciated, it seems to me. In theme after theme Tocqueville dilated on Burke

Echoing Burke, Tocqueville wrote that "In all the annals of recorded history, we find no mention of any political revolution that took this form," that is the form of the French Revolution. Tocqueville too looked to religious outbursts of the past for nearest precedent to the French Revolution. And Tocqueville featured the activist role of political intellectuals in the French Revolution—in striking contrast to the American Revolution. "Men of Letters," Burke had called them; Tocqueville used the same phrase. "Never," wrote Tocqueville, his very irony drawn from Burke's words, "had the entire political education [of the French people] been the work of its men of letters."

In another important respect Tocqueville was Burke's heir; that was the trans-Gallic, the whole European implication of the French Revolution. Burke wrote in his *Reflections*: "Many parts of Europe are in disorder. In many others there is a hollow murmuring under ground; a confused movement is felt that threatens a general earthquake in the political world." Tocqueville specifically designated his *Old Regime and the French Revolution* as but the first in what he planned to be series of volumes on "the European Revolution."

Tocqueville devoted a chapter to the essentially religious nature of the French Revolution, seeing it, as Burke specifically had, more nearly in sequence with the religious uprisings, devastations, and terroristic slaughters of the late Reformation than with any political revolutions, such as the English in 1688 and the American in 1776. In somewhat the same key,

Tocqueville echoes Burke's repeated charges that the French Revolutionists were men of neither experience or interest in political history or, in the true sense, political reform. "Our revolutionaries," Tocqueville wrote in the very phrasing of Burke,

> had [a] fondness for broad generalizations, cut-and-dried legislative systems, and a pedantic symmetry; the same contempt for hard facts; the same taste for reshaping institutions on novel, ingenious, original lines; the same desire to reconstruct the entire constitution according to the rules of logic and a preconceived system instead of trying to rectify its faulty parts. The result was nothing short of disastrous; for what is a merit in the writer may well be a vice in the statesman, and the very qualities which go to make great literature can lead to catastrophic revolutions.

Even the Jacobins' language, Tocqueville continued, "was borrowed largely from the books they read; it was cluttered up with abstract words, gaudy flowers of speech, sonorous cliches and literary turns of phrase." Tocqueville concludes dryly: "All they needed, in fact, to become literary men in a small way was a better knowledge of spelling."

It must be emphasized that throughout his *Reflections* Burke was addressing himself quite as much, if not more, to English as to French and other European sympathizers with the Jacobins. Richard Price and Tom Paine spoke for most of the sympathizers in declaring the French Revolution basically a copy of the American Revolution, primarily actuated by struggle for freedom from an oppressive power. But Burke (who would be joined here also by Tocqueville) saw the French Revolution as much more a struggle for absolute power than for freedom, the work primarily of political intellectuals who did not have, as did the leading American revolutionists, a "stake in society," and were in fact society's enemies.

There is some humor in the reflection that the aims Burke ascribed to the Jacobins in 1790, aims of the reconstruction of all society, of a remaking of individual consciousness, and of the installation of a totally new religion in the place of Christianity, would have seemed much more adequate and relevant to Robespierre and Saint-Just in 1793 than would have the modest, liberal aims Richard Price had given the French Revolution in the speech at Old Jewry which triggered Burke's *Reflections.*

Burke was of course right in seeing the French Revolution as unique and also as endowed with a mystique that would reach out to all Europe, even

Asia and Africa in due time, and would be perhaps the single most obsessive subject in the serious thought of the whole nineteenth century in the West. Not until the Bolshevik Revolution of 1917 would the French Revolution be at last replaced as the chief preoccupation of revolutionists everywhere and also of traditionalists and conservatives everywhere. The French Revolution is, though, the more original in its language and symbolism. In its declarations, manifestoes, and preambles to law, in its great rolling strophes and sharp, evocative images, printed by the Jacobins to reach and fit every public square in France, the French Revolution inaugurated a kind of revolution of the Word, something previously found only in evangelical, proselytizing religions. As the history of nineteenth-century Europe reveals in almost every quarter, the Jacobin Good News, suitably translated and tactically adapted, could be the equal in force of the Christian. Marxian rhetoric, and the rhetoric of Lenin and Trotsky in 1917, was secondary, in considerable measure derivative indeed.

Burke declared Rousseau to be the chief author of the French Revolution. Tocqueville, more diffident, exonerated Rousseau, by placing responsibility upon the "men of letters" who had, in the decade or so leading up to the Revolution, driven into the minds of the people, irresistible fantasies of freedom, equality, and absolute justice. But there can be no question of Tocqueville's full awareness of Rousseau's significance. Who else, after all, had argued with such passion and eloquence the case for the people, the divinely constituted people once their chains were struck off, the iniquity of all historically formed institutions, and the absolute necessity of a "Legislator" who would in the name of the people strike deeply and widely into human consciousness? Burke was blunt: "I am certain that the writings of Rousseau lead directly to this kind of shameful evil." What we know for a fact is that such Jacobins as Robespierre and Saint-Just, at the height of the Revolution, read Rousseau devotedly and regularly. Their zeal was shared, we learn from a contemporary, by a considerable number of French citizens who could be seen standing in knots at street corners reading aloud and discussing passages from the *Social Contract*, until now the least read of Rousseau's books.

Traditional groups—guilds, monasteries, corporations of all kinds—had been condemned by Rousseau, in the interest of achieving a pure general will and also the individual's own autonomy. They therefore required obliteration or substantial subordination to the nation. Aristocracy was of course marked early for extinction. But this was only the beginning. In 1791 all guilds were abolished—a goal, it is amusing to recall, that had escaped all efforts by divine-right, "absolute" monarchies of modern France. "There is no longer any corporation within the state," the Law Le Chapelier read; "there is but the particular interest of each individual and the general interest."

Inevitably the patriarchal family felt the power of the Revolution. The general belief of *philosophes* had been that the traditional kinship structure was "against nature and contrary to reason." Clearly, many Jacobin governors agreed. In 1792 marriage was declared a civil contract, and a number of grounds for divorce were made available (in 1794 the number of divorces exceeded the number of marriages). Strict limitations were placed upon the paternal authority, among them the disappearance of this authority when the sons reached their legal majority. The traditional laws of primogeniture and entail were set aside forever, with implication to property as well as family.

Property was made a special object of legislative action. The overriding aim was destruction of all linkage between property claim and the corporate organizations such as family, church, guild, and monastery which had been so long the real repositories of a very large amount of property in France—and indeed in most of Europe. With this aim went the objective of individualizing as far as possible the rights of ownership, a part of the larger aim of individualizing all of traditional society. Moreover, the mission of exterminating the aristocracy for its parasitism involved necessarily the appropriation or the atomization of the great landed estates of the aristocracy. More fluid, mobile, and moneyed types of property flourished as one of the by products of the Revolution, elevating to economic power a whole new class. Few things would be more vividly repugnant to the conservative tradition than the Revolution's relationship to property.

There is no space here for anything approaching full recital of the varied impacts of the Revolutionary government upon traditional French society. In general, the efforts of the National Assembly, the National Convention, and the Committee on Public Safety were bent toward, at one and the same time, the *individualization* of society and the *rationalization* of everything from coinage and weights and measures, to property, education, religion, and all aspects of government. Religion has perhaps claim here as one final instance of revolutionary thoroughness. At different times the government terminated all monastic and other religious vows, nationalized the Church, put all clerics on state salaries, with the binding condition that an oath of allegiance to the Revolution be taken, and then in 1793 the thrilling plan to de-Christianize France completely, piously filling the vacuum with a new religion dedicated to reason and virtue. In the interest of the new religion and also of the minds of men, elaborate rituals were written, liturgies were developed for use in meetings of the new religion, and a totally new calendar was introduced for the remaking of these minds. Control of time, of the past and its images, is vital, as Orwell emphasized in *Nineteen Eighty-Four*. The French Revolutionists were ahead of him, and the proposed new calendar would have adorned a new history of the past, repudiating and destroying the mythic or tyrannical personages long celebrated and replacing them with heroes of the Jacobins' liking. The Committee on Public Safety expressed it perfectly: "You must entirely refashion a people whom you wish to make free, to destroy its prejudices, alter its habits, limit its necessities, root up its vices, purify its desires." Robert Palmer has written: "In 1792 the Revolution became a thing in itself, an uncontrollable force that might eventually spend itself but which no one could direct and guide." And Robespierre, quoted by Palmer: "If the basis of popular government in time of peace is virtue, the basis of popular government in time of revolution is virtue and terror: virtue without terror is powerless; terror without virtue is murder."

It was the terror that shocked Europe most about the Revolution. But Burke was one of those who without diminishing the terror saw it as less insidious than a great deal of the legislation passed by Revolutionary assemblies. The true total and boundless character of the Revolution was best observed, Burke thought, in laws designed to obliterate or seriously cripple the traditional social order and at the same time to fill whatever vacuum might be left with new arms of the state.

Even more deadly, Burke argued, was the manifest wish of the Jacobin leaders to extend the work of the Revolution to all Europe, eventually to the world. Hence Burke's ardent and repeated plea for a "counter-revolution" to be launched by the European powers immediately. He wrote: "If I conceive rightly, it is not a war with France but with Jacobinism. We are at war with a principle...there is no shutting out by fortresses."

This was precisely the attitude that conservatives would take in 1917 when the Bolsheviks overthrew the Czarist government in Russia. Leninism replaced Jacobinism....

Notes

Robert Nisbet's essay comes from *Conservatism: Dream and Reality* (Minneapolis: University of Minnesota Press, 1986), pp. 1-11.

1. By "natural law," Nisbet has in mind the writers he mentions next—Hobbes, Locke, and Rousseau. Peter Stanlis's essay, by contrast, reserves the term "natural law" to refer to

Aristotle, Cicero, Aquinas, Hooker, and other writers, who, like Burke, dissented from Enlightenment rationalism. Occasionally, Burke scholars, will associate the term "natural right" with Locke, Hobbes, and Rousseau in order to clarify their difference with Burke. In *Natural Right and History* (1953), by contrast, Leo Strauss distinguishes Burke from contemporary Enlightenment thinkers—but uses the term "natural right" with reference to all of them (pp. 1-8, 294-323). —DR

2.   Burke's reviews of Rousseau's *Letter to M. d'Alembert* [1759] and *Emile* [1762] are reprinted (with minor abridgement) in Peter Stanlis, ed., *Edmund Burke: Selected Writings and Speeches* (Garden City, NY: Doubleday, 1963; reissued by Regnery—Gateway, 1984) pp. 89, 94. —DR

3.   *Correspondence* 4:47 (1 March 1779).

4.   *Reflections* in *Works* (Bohn) 2:284, appr. 3% into the work.

Bibliography

Bibliographies

Todd, William B. *A Bibliography of Edmund Burke*. London: Rupert Hart-Davis, 1964. Bibliography of primary sources.

Gandy, Clara I. and Peter J. Stanlis. *Edmund Burke: A Bibliography of Secondary Studies to 1982*. New York and London: Garland, 1983. Bibliography of writings about Burke.

Editions and Anthologies of Burke's Works

The standard edition of Burke's works is being published by Oxford (Clarendon) under the general editorship of Paul Langford. To date, two volumes have appeared. Editions of Burke's works appear on the Short Titles page. In addition to these, the following works deserve note:

Boulton, James T., ed. *A Philosophical Enquiry into the Origin of Our Ideas of the Sublime and Beautiful*. London: Routledge & Kegan Paul, 1958. Rpt. by University of Notre Dame Press, 1968. The standard edition.

Bredvold, Louis I., and Ralph G. Ross, eds. *The Philosophy of Edmund Burke: A Selection from his Speeches and Writings*. Ann Arbor: University of Michigan Press, 1960. Arranged by subject.

Copeland, Thomas W., et al, eds., *The Correspondence of Edmund Burke*. 10 vols. Chicago and Cambridge: Cambridge and Chicago University Presses, 1958-78.

Hoffman, Ross J.S. and Paul Levack, eds., *Burke's Politics: Selected Writings and Speeches of Edmund Burke on Reform, Revolution, and War*. New York: Knopf, 1949. Like the Bredvold and Ross volume, this book arranges selections from Burke according to subject.

O'Brien, Conor Cruise, ed. *Reflections on the Revolution in France*. Harmondsworth: Penguin, 1969. The text is a reprint of the standard edition, prepared by William B. Todd and published by Holt, Rinehart & Winston (New York, 1959).

Payne, Edward J. *Burke: Select Works*. 3 vols. Oxford: Clarendon Press, 1874-78. Very heavily—and usefully—annotated edition of Burke's American speeches, *Reflections*, and *Letters on a Regicide Peace*.

Stanlis, Peter J. *Edmund Burke: Selected Writings and Speeches*. Garden City, NY: Doubleday, 1963. Rpt. by Regnery—Gateway, 1984. An extremely useful anthology, containing many of the lesser known works and speeches.

Writings About Burke

Blakemore, Steven. *Burke and the Fall of Language: The French Revolution as Linguistic Event*. Hanover and London: University Press of New England, 1988.

Boulton, James T. *The Language of Politics in the Age of Wilkes and Burke*. London: Routledge & Kegan Paul; Toronto: University of Toronto Press, 1963. Excellent rhetorical criticism.

Canavan, Francis, "Edmund Burke," *History of Political Philosophy*. Leo Strauss and Josephy Cropsey, eds. Chicago: Rand McNally, 1963.

—. *Edmund Burke: Prescription and Providence*. Durham, NC: Carolina Academic Press and The Claremont Institute for the Study of Statesmanship and Political Philosophy, 1987.

—. *The Political Reason of Edmund Burke*. Durham, NC: Duke University Press, 1960.

Chapman, Gerald W. *Edmund Burke: The Practical Imagination*. Cambridge, MA: Harvard University Press, 1967.

Christie, Ian. "Myth and Reality in Late Eighteenth-Century British Politics," in *Myth and Reality in Late Eighteenth-Century British Politics and Other Papers*. London: Macmillan; Berkeley: University of California Press, 1970. Incorporates the insights of recent historiography associated with the school of Sir Lewis Namier, without the hostility of Sir Lewis.

Cone, Carl B. *Burke and the Nature of Politics*. 2 vols. Lexington KY: University of Kentucky Press, 1957, 1964. A political biography that makes use of the Burke papers, not available for public study until 1949.

Copeland, Thomas W. *Our Eminent Friend: Edmund Burke*. New Haven: Yale University Press, 1949. Not a full-scale biography, but a series of excellent insights into Burke's character. Contains a well written account of Burke's break with Fox.

Kirk, Russell. *Edmund Burke: A Genius Reconsidered*. New Rochelle, NY: Arlington House, 1967.

—. "Burke and the Politics of Prescription." *The Conservative Mind*. Chicago: Regnery, 1953.

Kramnick, Isaac. *The Rage of Edmund Burke: Portrait of an Ambivalent Conservative*. New York: Basic, 1977. A psycho-biography.

Lipking, Lawrence. "Analyzing Burke." *Eighteenth Century: Theory and Interpretation*. 20 (1979): 65-81. Review-essay of Kramnick.

Lucas, Paul. "On Edmund Burke's Doctrine of Prescription," *Historical Journal* 11 (1968):35-63. Denies the distinction between a "natural right" and a "natural law" tradition, with which conservative interpreters, such as Stanlis, associate Burke.

MacCunn, John. *The Political Philosophy of Burke*. London: Arnold, 1913; rpt. by Russell & Russell (New York, 1965).

Mansfield, Harvey, *Statesmanship and Party Government: A Study of Burke and Bolingbroke*. Chicago: University of Chicago Press, 1965.

Parkin, Charles. *The Moral Basis of Burke's Political Thought*. Cambridge: Cambridge University Press, 1956.

Paulson, Ronald. "Burke's Sublime and the Representation of Revolution." *Culture and Politics from Puritanism to the Enlightenment*. Perez Zagorin, ed. Berkeley: University of California Press, 1980, pp. 241-69.

Pocock, J. G. A. "Burke and the Ancient Constitution." *Politics, Language, and Time*. London: Methuen; New York: Atheneum, 1971, pp. 202-32.

Reid, Christopher, *Edmund Burke and the Practice of Political Writing*. Dublin: Gill and Macmillan; New York: St. Martin's Press, 1985.

Stanlis, Peter. *Edmund Burke and the Natural Law*. Ann Arbor: University of Michigan Press, 1958; rpt. by Huntington House (Lafayette, LA, 1986).

Strauss, Leo. *Natural Right and History*. Chicago: University of Chicago Press, 1953. Like many conservative interpreters, Strauss distinguishes Burke from contemporary Enlightenment theorists. However, he sees the final paragraph of Burke's *Thoughts on French Affairs* as "a preparation for Hegel" and historicism (pp. 318-20). Many of Strauss's students and intellectual descendants have, to some degree, accepted this judgment.

Weston, John C. "Edmund Burke's View of History." *Review of Politics* 23 (1961): 203-29. Explains how Providence, free will, constitutional development, and custom cooperate.

White, James Boyd "Making a Public World: The Constitution of Language and Community in Burke's *Reflections*." *When Words Lose Their Meaning*. Chicago: University of Chicago Press, 1984.

Wilkins, Burleigh Taylor. *The Problem of Burke's Political Philosophy*. Oxford: Clarendon Press, 1967.

Index

Constitution, *See* America: Constitution of the United States. *See* Burke, Edmund: *Opinions:* Constitution (British)

Copeland, Thomas W., 285, 286

Dannhauser, Werner, xix, xx
Declaration of Independence, 90, 98
Declaration of Right, 37, 38, 90
Deconstruction. *See* essay by Blakemore, Steven, 35–56
Depont, Charles-Jean-François, 227, 236
DeQuincey, Thomas, 17–20, 24
Derrida, Jacques, xvi
Dicey, A. V., 169
Disraeli, Benjamin, 26, 133, 199, 201
Dulles, John Foster, 170–71

Eden, William, 1st Baron Auckland, 68
Edgeworth, Maria, 79, 81
Edgeworth, Richard Lovell, 79
Eisenhower, Dwight, 171
Elliott, Sir Gilbert and Lady Anna, 63–64
Enlightenment, 233–34, 275–77
Experience. *See* Burke, Edmund: *Opinions:* Abstract Principle vs. Experience

Fennessy, R. R., 252, 255, 258
Finley, Sir Moses, 84–85
Fitzwilliam, William, 4th Earl Fitzwilliam, 29
Fox, Charles James, xxiii, 6, 29, 132, 133, 168, 219–20, 248, 278
Francis, Philip, ix, 11, 16, 54, 64, 128, 221
Franklin, Benjamin, 96–97
Fulbright, J. William, 175

George III, 24, 27, 83, 91, 93–94, 139
George IV, 24
Germany, 86, 197, 207, 241
—National Socialism, 84
—Weimar Republic, 85
Gibbon, Edward, 81–83, 87, 241
Goethe, Johann Wolfgang von, 242
Goldsmith, Oliver, 4, 6, 28, 29, 77
Gooch, G. P., 262
Gorbachev, Mikhail, xvii
Gray, Thomas, 14
Greene, Donald, 55
Grenville, George, xxii, 24, 118, 125, 128, 215, 218

Halifax, Marquis of. *See* Savile, George
Hart, Jeffrey, 55
Hastings, Warren, ix, x, xix, xxiii–xxiv, 21–23, 24, 31, 76, 135, 167, 219–26, 263
Hazlitt, William, xvi, 7–16, 25
Henry, Patrick, 95, 96
Higgonet, P., 69
Hobbes, Thomas, xix, 46, 197, 211, 212, 250
Hobhouse, Christopher, 134
Hoffman, Ross J. S., 93, 169, 285
Hogarth, William, 58–59
Holmes, Oliver Wendell, 144
Home, Henry, Lord Kames, 246, 250
Hooker, Richard, 240, 248
Hopkins, Gerard Manley, 79
Hume, David, 6
Hyde, Edward, 1st Earl of Clarendon, 78, 88

Impey, Sir Elijah, 24, 63
India. *See* Burke, Edmund: *India*
Ireland. *See* Burke, Edmund: *Ireland*

Jacobinism, x, xviii, xix, 5, 92, 164–65, 170, 279–80, 282
Jacobitism, 164, 176
James II, xvii, 90–91, 97
Jefferson, Thomas, 92, 97–98
Jekyll, Sir Joseph, 89, 101
Johnson, Samuel, xxiii, 5, 6, 10, 19, 24, 49, 77, 81, 87, 128, 211, 218, 277
Joubert, Joseph, 204
Junius. *See* Francis, Philip

Kames, Lord. *See* Home, Henry
Keppel, Admiral Augustus, 70
King, Walker, 20
Kirk, Russell, ix–xi, xvii, 89–102, 170, 174, 178, 262, 286
Kramnick, Isaac, 55, 286

Langrishe, Sir Hercules, 165
Language. *See* Burke, Edmund: *Imagination. See also* Revolution: and language
Laski, Harold, 239, 243
Laurence, French, 18, 20
Lecky, W. E. H., 206, 243–44
Lenin, Vladimir Ilyich, xvii, 281, 283